America's TEILHARD

Susan Kassman Sack

America's TEILHARD

Christ and Hope in the 1960s

The Catholic University of America Press *Washington, D.C.*

The paper used in this publication meets the minimum requirements
of American National Standards for Information Science—Permanence of
Paper for Printed Library Materials, ANSI Z39.48–1984.
∞
Cataloging-in-Publication Data available from the Library of Congress
ISBN 978-0-8132-3165-5

Dedicated with love to my husband, Larry Sack,

without whom this book simply would never have happened;

and to my wonderful sons, Dan, Joe, Tim, and Andy,

who put up with so much in the completion

CONTENTS

Acknowledgments ix

Introduction 1

A Short Biography of Teilhard 3
Teilhard's Christological Vision 18
The Following Chapters 23

THE THRESHOLD OF CHANGE: 1955–1960

1. The Move across the Atlantic 29

Publications in Europe 30
The Cultural Milieu of the Late 1950s 31
The American Reception of Teilhard: 1955–1960 44
Final Thoughts 55

THE EARLY YEARS: 1961–1964

2. Correspondence and Controversy 61

Early Teilhardian Interest 62
Increasing Controversy and Repercussions 77
The Teilhard Controversy in Europe 79
Controversy concerning an American Teilhard Organization 85
The Monitum and Its Interpretation 88
Final Thoughts 95

3. American Ties and Recovery 97

The Social Context of the United States in the Early 1960s 98
Concerning Americanism 101
The Cultural Situation in the United States 105
Reconciliation and the Recovery of Teilhard 114
Literary Responses to Teilhard 125
Final Thoughts 132

THE YEARS OF HOPE: 1965–1967

4. The Social Context 137

Teilhard's Influence on Vatican II 138
A Reflection on U.S. Historical Events 1965 through 1967 149
The Formation of the American Teilhard Association 162
Final Thoughts 165

5. The "Death of God" 168

Teilhard, the "Death of God," and the Secular City 169
Conferences and Symposia 176
Publications by and about Teilhard 179
Final Thoughts 198

THE BITTER YEARS: 1968–1970

6. The Social Context 203

Politics and Culture 205
Religious Issues 222
The American Teilhard Association 235
Final Thoughts 245

7. Publications 246

Significant Publications 248
Publications concerning Teilhard's Christological Vision 248
Teilhard and Henri de Lubac 258
Works in Interdisciplinary Journals 264
Publications concerning the Utilization of Teilhard's Spirituality 276
Publications of a Secular Nature 282
Final Thoughts 287

Conclusion 291

Appendix: Teilhard Publications Worldwide per Year, 1956–1971 299

Bibliography 301

Index 319

ACKNOWLEDGMENTS

Lifelong thanks to my parents, Jerry and Georgi Poniske Kassman, who always wanted a doctor of some kind in the family, and who knew that someday I'd write some kind of book! I'm so appreciative of your example of those long decades of faith, love, and service to your family and community.

My unending appreciation also goes to Bill Portier and Dennis Doyle, both of the University of Dayton, who read these chapters numerous times over the writing. Your friendship, encouragement, and compassion, especially through some very tough times, mean so very much. I also am grateful to Ursula King, who first encouraged me in this work and sent numerous references my way, and to Kathy Duffy, SSJ, who stepped in late in the process, yet offered amazing editorial suggestions. You were both wonderful! Also, great appreciation for the suggestions of colleagues Tony Smith, Daniel Martin, and Cecilia Moore, whose comments encouraged me to believe this was possible.

Thanks also go to the good people of the Lauinger Library Archives at Georgetown University, who provided assistance to an archive "newbie," as well as to Father Leon Hooper, SJ, former director of the Woodstock Theological Library Archives at Georgetown, who, knowing my time was limited, permitted me to make use of the archives very late one Fourth of July weekend, and to Dr. Vince Miller and family, who offered me a place to stay in the Georgetown area.

I also offer gratitude to Dr. Patricia Ellis, who offered her house to me as a writing sanctuary too many times to recall. The memory of those very long days spent staring at a laptop, as well as the innumerable phone calls of encouragement, will always epitomize friendship for me. What a tremendous gift you are!

Dr. Trevor Lipscombe at the Catholic University of America Press made my year when he first inquired about publishing this book. He has been a joy to work with ever since. Thank you for taking a chance on this work. Much gratitude also to copy editor Aldene Fredenburg, who fixed all those commas and an endless number of citations and patiently responded to numerous questions in a timely manner!

Finally, my unending appreciation to all the many good people of the Northwest Catholic Communities of Dayton, Ohio, my former fellow chaplains at Good Samaritan Hospital, and the numerous others who with great patience continue to teach me so much about compassion, humility, and living in the moment. May the fire of his love always reside in your heart.

America's TEILHARD

INTRODUCTION

PIERRE TEILHARD DE CHARDIN—visionary priest, paleontologist, and writer—represents one of several important religious and cultural landmarks in the French Catholicism of the mid-twentieth century and beyond. Especially from 1950 onward, however, when he moved to New York City to live, Teilhard also significantly impacted the Catholicism of the United States. This book focuses on the U.S. reception of Teilhard's work between 1960 and 1972. This period—also the decade of the counterculture, the Second Vatican Council, and the dissolution of the immigrant subculture of the church in the United States—was the crucial age during which his writing and thought were first available in North America. These were, therefore, the years in which the first American scholars responded to his theology and so set the foundation for later interpretations. In fact, over five hundred primary and secondary works were published regarding Teilhard in the United States during these years.

The intensity with which this phenomenon occurred happened as it did at this particular point in history because of the confluence of the then developing social and political milieu, the opening of the global Roman Catholic Church to the world through Vatican II, and unique developments within the U.S. Catholic Church. A study of the U.S. reception of Pierre Teilhard de Chardin in this early period contributes to an appreciation of the thought of this important figure and the impact of his work. It also further develops an understanding of U.S. Catholicism in its religious and cultural dimensions during these years. Additionally, as these social and historical events unfolded within U.S. culture during these dozen years, the manner in which Teilhard was read and the aspects of his thought that were especially deemed of value changed. At various points his work became a carrier for an almost Americanist emphasis upon progress, energy, and hope; at other times his teleological understanding of the value of suffering and exile moved to center stage. Most importantly, Teilhard wrote concerning humanity's desire for the divine and strove to place that desire for unity within the context of both religion and science. His ability to leap the interstice between the secular and the sacred and to do so within his unique, hopeful, Christological vision remains of value today, continuing to have impact upon U.S. Catholic theology.

The thought of Pierre Teilhard de Chardin is in many ways linked with the metanarrative of modernity. Like that worldview, it emphasizes universal truths, including a belief in progress and science. Yet Teilhard's thought ventures beyond this to a unique romantic, organic, and mystical cosmic vision. This vision recognizes the sacral aspects of the everyday as based in and resulting from a union with God and hence a historical consciousness originating in God yet extending far beyond biblical history. Most importantly, it includes a teleology that again culminates in God. This position places him in the role of bridge between modern and postmodern forms of thought and life. The paradigm shift between these two occurred in the 1960s in the United States; these years are, therefore, crucial to understanding just why Teilhard was received as he was in this country.

Teilhard's thought takes on far more meaning within the context of his own life story and is useful, for example, in understanding his writings about the secular world and suffering. We begin, therefore, with a short biographical sketch of Teilhard that will provide an understanding of the source of his own work and the interest it spurred. Following this is an explication of what is considered here the heart of his theological and evolutionary vision, his Christology.

A SHORT BIOGRAPHY OF TEILHARD

Pierre Teilhard de Chardin was born May 1, 1881, in Sarcenat, the Auvergne, France, one of eleven siblings.[1] His father, an amateur naturalist, frequently roamed the ancient hills of his homeland collecting samples; his mother was a pious Catholic, particularly fond of the Sacred Heart devotion. Teilhard grew older with these twin loves: that of "matter," particularly durable geologic matter such as iron and stone that had withstood the ages of time, and that of Christ, the truly durable "Dieu de fer."[2] In 1899 he entered the Jesuit novitiate at Aix-en-Provence after attending the local Jesuit school with several of his brothers. In a letter to his parents about this decision, he used a significant phrase in talking of it: "I believe God is inviting me to *leave the world*."[3] Already a tension existed between what might on the surface appear to be two dichotomous attractions—the earth and God, the natural and the supernatural. To resolve this conflict, his decision at the time was that he would simply dedicate himself and his life to God. In the end however, as we shall see, Teilhard's Jesuit training offered him the thoughtful stimulation by which to

1. Numerous biographies on Pierre Teilhard de Chardin are available. Much of what is summarized in this work is found in Amir Aczel, *The Jesuit and the Skull: Teilhard de Chardin, Evolution, and the Search for Peking Man* (New York: Riverhead, 2007); and Mary Lukas and Ellen Lukas, *Teilhard: A Biography* (New York: McGraw-Hill, 1977). Another, shorter biography is available in John J. Delaney, ed., *Saints Are Now: Eight Portraits of Modern Sanctity* (Garden City, N.Y.: Doubleday, 1981). An early biography originally published in France is that by Claude Cuénot, *Teilhard de Chardin: A Biographical Study*, ed. René Hague, trans. Vince Colimar (Baltimore: Helicon, 1965). One of several written by Henri de Lubac is *Teilhard de Chardin: The Man and His Meaning* (New York: New American Library, 1965).

2. Teilhard's fascination with the material world and this search for durability began at the age of five, when—sitting by the fire and having his hair clipped—he watched the snippets burning in the coals. He says he realized then, traumatized, that he, too, would one day disappear; he was perishable, and so must somehow find some personal security. "Dieu de fer," or "God of iron," was the name Teilhard subsequently assigned to the collection of small pieces of durables, keys, empty shell casings from the shooting range, the metal top of a banister, pieces of iron, all of which would survive fire, which he hid in a safe place and would ritualistically take out in a childish form of "adoration"; from Lukas and Lukas, *Teilhard*, 23–24.

3. Thomas A. King, SJ, *Teilhard de Chardin in The Way of the Christian Mystics* (Wilmington, Del.: Michael Glazier, 1988), 6:23.

continue his devotion simultaneously both to scientific investigation and to the cultivation of a life of prayer and spirituality.

It was also at Aix-en-Provence that several formative friendships began, particularly that with Auguste Valensin, who had studied philosophy with Maurice Blondel. Teilhard was quite taken with Blondel's theory of *l'action.*[4] In 1901, due to yet another anticlerical movement within the French Republic, the Jesuits—along with other religious orders—were expelled from France. Teilhard's novitiate moved first to Paris, then to the English Isle of Jersey. In the interim, in 1902, he took his first vows as a Jesuit. During this time, death began to haunt his family. First, his younger sister Marguerite-Marie became chronically ill, and then his oldest brother, Alberic, died; within a few years this was followed by the death of his youngest sister, Louise. These losses definitely affected the young man. For a while in the novitiate, Teilhard lost heart, turning away from science and the things of the world toward theology instead. If not for the influence of his former novice master Paul Trossard, his biography might look quite different.

On Jersey, however, his theological, scientific, and philosophical training became more intense; it then continued in Egypt and in Sussex, England, before he began, in 1912, an advanced course of study in paleontology at the Museum of Natural History in Paris. This was the same year he was ordained a Jesuit priest. Consequently, he became one of the first of the scientist-priests; certainly, he was one of the first to deal with the looming question of evolution.

Teilhard was apparently unaware of the controversies over Darwin or of the whole subject of evolution until his time at the Jesuit

4. Teilhard and Maurice Blondel would later in 1919 exchange letters over some essays Teilhard sent to Blondel for comment. Blondel warned Teilhard about the dangers of "immanentism" he found present in these but read them quite closely and was impressed with the thoughts therein. These letters have been collected and edited by Henri de Lubac, SJ, in *Blondel et Teilhard de Chardin: Correspondance* (Paris: Beauchesne, 1965; the English translation is *Pierre Teilhard de Chardin–Maurice Blondel Correspondence*, trans. William Whitman, ed. Henri de Lubac (New York: Herder and Herder, 1967). The distinguished Blondel scholar J. M. Somerville has said, "Together Blondel and Teilhard created the atmosphere that made Vatican II possible, and they seem destined to carry on and justify its best achievements for many decades to come."

training college at Ore, Sussex. Indeed, in his writings up to this point he remained a believer in the Catholic traditions of creation. In part, this situation can be explained by the fact that little contact existed between French and English philosophy at this time, especially in regard to this particular subject. Or perhaps, one might add, at least no contact existed that a candidate for priesthood was likely to breach, much less study. For Teilhard, Henri Bergson was the first writer to bridge this gap.

Especially for one whom Claude Cuénot, his first and still primary biographer, stated possessed "an incredibly synthetic mind," it is difficult to unravel the threads of influence, but Bergson made at least as much of an impact as Blondel. In reading *L'Évolution Créatrice* (The Creative Evolution) by Henri Bergson, Teilhard met a thinker who dissolved the Aristotelian dualism of matter and spirit in favor of a movement of a universe evolving through the ages.[5] For the first time, Teilhard encountered the word "evolution" with all its possible implications. Within it, he found scientific justification for the mystical unity he felt he shared with all of creation. He connected even the very sound of the word "with the extraordinary density and intensity with which the English landscape then appeared to me—especially at sunset—when the Sussex woods seemed to be laden with all the fossil life that I was exploring, from one quarry to another, in the soil of the World."[6]

It was at this point that Teilhard decidedly committed his life to the pursuit of two distinct, parallel tracks: science and religion. He began more explicitly to search for the progress he thought evident everywhere in creation—the development of matter into living organisms and the advancement of these organisms into ever more complex life forms—a process that he later termed "complexification." For Bergson, evolution was continually expanding, "a 'Tide

5. The American Teilhard Association, http://teilharddechardin.org/biography.html, accessed January 12, 2011, hereafter *ATA*; Louis Bergson, *L'Evolution créatrice* (Paris: F. Alcan, 1907; the English translation was *Creative Evolution*, trans. Arthur Mitchell (Lanham, Md.: University Press of America, 1911).

6. Teilhard de Chardin, *The Heart of Matter*, in *The Life of Teilhard de Chardin*, by Robert Speaight (New York: Harper and Row, 1967), 45.

of Life' undirected by an ultimate purpose."[7] In Teilhard's view, however, the progression of life was teleological, toward a specific destination, and was an integral component of his Christology. This destination he later named the "Omega Point" and identified it with Jesus Christ and the process of Christification.

In 1903, while Pierre was in Egypt, Pius X succeeded Leo XIII as pope. The somewhat forward-looking momentum of Leo was abandoned in favor of retrenchment and attacks on a wide variety of ideas labeled "modernism." Among the many new works eventually placed on the Vatican's *Index of Forbidden Works* was Henri Bergson's *Creative Evolution.* Teilhard was completing his novitiate and early philosophical training in England just as the Modernist crisis reached its peak, and conversations about condemned publications must have taken place among the Jesuit students.[8] It was in this ecclesiastical milieu that Teilhard attempted to articulate his emerging vision of the spiritual quality of the universe.

In the midst of this time of intellectual growth, in 1911 his oldest sister, Françoise, a Little Sister of the Poor and the only other religious in the family, died in Shanghai, China. All too soon afterward, France became involved in the First World War, and in November 1914 word came that his younger brother Gonzague had been killed in battle. Before he reached the age of thirty, five of his siblings had met death. These losses deeply affected Teilhard throughout his remaining life.

Within the month following his brother's death, Teilhard received orders to report for duty in a newly forming regiment from Auvergne. After visiting his parents and invalid sister Guiguite at home, he began his work as a stretcher bearer with the North African Zouaves, the Moroccan Light Infantry, in January 1915.

The experience of war strongly marks his later writings, as against the almost daily battle fires he struggled to make sense of the purpose of violence in the world. Indeed, he began writing extensively at this point, developing his early theories on creation and evolution,

7. *ATA.*

8. In particular, Teilhard would have been influenced by the condemnation of Alfred Loisy's books in 1903 and the issuance of *Pascendi Dominici gregis* by Pope Pius X.

as well as of matter itself. Constantly at the boundary of life and death, he sensed an urgency of leaving his intellectual testament—that of something new that he wanted to pass on to others.

From the very first, Teilhard wanted to communicate the fire of his vision. He developed his reflections in his diaries and in letters to his cousin, Marguerite Teillard-Chambon, who later edited them into a book: *Genèse d'une pensée* (Genesis of a Thought).[9] He confessed later, "The war was a meeting ... with the Absolute."[10] In 1916, he wrote his first essay, *La Vie Cosmique* (Cosmic Life), in which his developing scientific and philosophical thought was revealed, just as was his mystical life. The essay was full of images of the universe, God's involvement in the world, humanity's communion with the earth, and, of course, evolution.[11]

Although Teilhard received permission to take final vows as a Jesuit in May 1918, his Jesuit superiors were puzzled by his writings from the battlefield. They especially were concerned about his exploration of such topics as evolution and original sin.[12] Teilhard, though, was impatient to publish and to disseminate his ideas. Over time he began to realize that the greatest need of teachers in the church was "to present dogma in a more real, more universal, way—a more 'cosmogonic' way."[13] He feared that without the possibility of publication, his ideas could be disseminated only "by conversation, or as manuscripts passed under a coat."[14] All too often, Teilhard had the sense of "being reckoned with the orthodox and yet feeling for the heterodox."[15] Throughout his life, he had faith that if he had truly seen something worthwhile, then an explanation of that seeing

9. Teilhard de Chardin, *Genèse d'une pensée: Lettres 1914–1919* (Paris: Grasset, 1961).

10. Teilhard de Chardin, *The Heart of Matter* (New York: Harcourt, Brace Jovanovich, 1978), 66.

11. Teilhard de Chardin, *La Vie Cosmique*, in *Writings in Time of War* (New York: Harper and Row, 1968).

12. Aczel, *Jesuit and the Skull*, 78–79.

13. Teilhard de Chardin, *The Making of a Mind: Letters from a Soldier Priest 1914–1919* (New York: Harper and Row, 1965), 267–68.

14. Aczel, *Jesuit and the Skull*, 78. From a letter between Teilhard and his cousin, Marguerite Teilhard-Chambon, ca. 1919.

15. Teilhard de Chardin, *Making of a Mind*, 267–68.

would shine forth and be understood despite obstacles. As he says in a letter of 1919, "It's not nearly so much ideas that I want to propagate as a spirit: and a spirit can animate all external presentations."[16]

In that spirit, following the war and back in Paris, he continued to write on these topics even as he reentered studies for his doctorate at the Sorbonne. He advanced the idea of an evolving, dynamic earth, propelled by God toward himself and the fulfillment of divine destiny. By the fall of 1920, Teilhard had been appointed Chair of Geology at the L'Institut Catholique and was teaching students who excitedly knew him as an active proponent of evolutionary thought. In March of 1921, at the age of forty, he defended his dissertation for the doctorate of science from the Sorbonne.

With the degree came numerous invitations to lecture. One was from a theological institute in Belgium, where in 1922 Teilhard presented his ideas on the evolution of mammals and elucidated his view of original sin, expressing his view that the story of the biblical Adam and Eve could not be read literally. After his return to Paris, he worked more on his arguments, building a theological framework that would discard the traditional Christian concept of original sin.

The war against the Modernists initiated by Pius X had somewhat abated at his death in 1914. But the new pope, Benedict XV, renewed the attack on evolution, on "new theology," and on any number of perceived errors the Vatican Curia considered threatening. Although Teilhard understood that everything he said in public, as well as everything he wrote for publication, would be monitored by Jesuit authorities in France and in Rome, as his work advanced he increasingly was fascinated with the concept of evolution. Concurrently his superiors became ever more concerned over the direction his thought was proceeding and encouraged Teilhard to consider some field work experience. While he was absent, they hoped, the hubbub would dissipate. However, Teilhard wasn't interested, but eventually he began to understand that it might be best for both his

16. Ibid., 281. The entire quote is, "What makes me easier in my mind at this juncture, is that the rather hazardous schematic points in my teaching are in fact of only secondary importance to me. It's not nearly so much ideas that I want to propagate as a spirit: and a spirit can animate all external presentations."

academic and his ecclesiastical career if he were out of Europe for a while. Perhaps with distance the controversy over his teaching would quiet itself. The opportunity for fieldwork in China had existed since 1919, with an open invitation from the Jesuit scientist Émile Licent, who was involved in paleontological work around Tientsin. Consequently, on April 1, 1923, Teilhard sailed from Marseille on his way to China. Never again would he live long-term in his beloved home country of France.

During these early years in China, Teilhard's major interest was in the natural terrain. Although he greatly interacted with numerous ethnic groups during his travels, he rarely showed an interest in exploring their culture beyond the minimum necessary. In the beginning, he considered the Chinese a wretched people, without hope or idealism.[17] An ironic aspect of his career is that the Confucian tradition, with its concern for the "realization of the cosmic identity of heaven, earth and men," remained outside of Teilhard's concerns, at least for a vast portion of his life.[18] In a similar fashion, tribal peoples with their "earth-centered spirituality" were initially considered by Teilhard simply to be at an earlier stage in development.

It was during this trip to China, on his first paleontological expedition with Licent, that one of his most beloved works, *Mass on the World*, was written. He found himself in the Ordos desert on the feast of the Transfiguration, without either wine or wafer and therefore unable to say Mass. Teilhard instead offers up the world as the Eucharistic sacrifice in this prayer, combining religion, science, and nature in a personal mysticism. From this same desert, he shortly afterward wrote to his friend Abbé Breuil, "Mysticism remains the great science and the great art, the only power capable of synthesizing the riches accumulated by other forms of human activity."[19]

Teilhard returned briefly to France in October 1924. He resumed his teaching to wildly enthusiastic students and expanded his thinking and writing on evolution. During this time, he began

17. Aczel, *Jesuit and the Skull*, 90.

18. *ATA*. By Teilhard's return to Europe late in the 1940s this attitude toward the Chinese, as well as other cultures and religions, had greatly changed.

19. Aczel, *Jesuit and the Skull*, 93.

to use the term of Edward Suess, "biosphere," or "earth-layer of living things," in his geological schema. Teilhard also expanded this idea to include the layer of thinking beings that encompassed the earth, that layer comprised of the intelligence and thought of all creation, which he called the "noosphere" from the Greek word *nous*, meaning "mind."[20] Many who interacted with him believed he was the type of Catholic priest who could move the church forward, one who understood how to synthesize the scientific and the religious, the world and the spirit. Additionally, he was now recognized as one of Europe's first-rate scientists.

His thoughts so greatly disturbed some of the conservative French bishops, however, that they again reported him to the Vatican; this in turn put pressure on the local Jesuit superiors to silence him. Also, while he had been working in China, his theological reflection concerning original sin somehow made its way from his desk drawer to Rome, where horrified Curia officials sensed heresy. As a result, only a month after his return from China, Teilhard was called into his provincial superior to repudiate his ideas on original sin.

This demand provoked a serious crisis for Teilhard. His lifelong dilemma was now clearly delineated: how did one reconcile the creative and open mind of a scientist and philosopher with the obedience and traditional stance of the Catholic Church and the Jesuit order? Numerous friends counseled him to leave the Jesuits, but as was true throughout his life, he was reluctant to do so. While he pondered the choices to be made, he continued to travel and teach. The Jesuits, however, even after Teilhard eventually signed papers repudiating his stance on original sin, continued to press him to work in a province further out of the limelight. He was, after all, a famous Catholic Jesuit scientist who held views that the church did not espouse. He was not to be trusted. In the end, Teilhard was required to give up his home and his work at the Catholic Institute in Paris to continue his geological research in China. This he resignedly accepted and returned to China in 1926 at the age of forty-five, recognizing that most likely he would remain in exile much of the rest of his life.

20. *ATA*.

Indeed, he remained in China for most of the following eleven years, working with Licent, Davidson Black, and Johan Andersson on geological and paleontological projects. Concurrently, however, he never stopped developing his own theological and philosophical thought regarding the evolution of the universe.

Rupturing his contentment at this time was the news that the Jesuit authorities in Rome had revoked his position at L'Institut Catholique in Paris. Partly in an attempt to appease his superiors and show his orthodoxy, he began writing a book that he called *Le Milieu Divin.* He often described this work as "a little book of piety"; it contains his early suggestions as to how all human activity might be used for the evolution of the world in a positive direction.[21] What is necessary for this to occur, he wrote, is that we learn how to "see" God in the world that surrounds us. Only in seeing God in this way will we truly love God, and only through loving God will the universe evolve as it could or should.[22] This mystical way of knowing and worshipping God is the underlying foundation for all of Teilhard's spiritual and scientific propositions. It serves as the source of integrity binding together what might appear to be the natural dualism inherent between science and religion, the material world and the sacred, a joyful optimism with the sometimes-difficult realities of life on this earth.

Teilhard was permitted to return to France, the first of five times during this period of exile, in August 1927. He pushed the Jesuit censors of Rome hard, trying to get *Le Milieu Divin* published. His "geocentric approach," in which he attempted to reconcile the love of God with love for the planet, was considered irreligious, perhaps even pagan. The church was suspicious.[23] In June 1928, the assistant to the Jesuit superior general arrived while Teilhard was still in Paris to inform him that all his theological work must end or he would be banished to a location even more remote than China. He was to confine himself to scientific work only. Disappointed, Teilhard returned

21. Aczel, *Jesuit and the Skull,* 127.

22. Teilhard de Chardin, *The Divine Milieu: An Essay on the Interior Life* (New York: Harper and Row, 1960).

23. Aczel, *Jesuit and the Skull,* 128.

to China, but only after writing the first several pages of an essay, "Le Phénomène Humain," which would later evolve into what is perhaps his most important book.

Teilhard continued his work in China throughout World War II, while contributing to the creation of an international network of research in human paleontology. These years were also very rich in geological expeditions. In 1929, he traveled in Somaliland and Ethiopia for research before returning again to China. He played a major role in the excavation and interpretation of "Peking Man" at Chou-kou-tien in 1929–30. In 1930, he was a key member of Ray Chapman Andrew's Central Mongolian Expedition at the invitation of the American Museum of Natural History. The following year he journeyed across America. That voyage later inspired him to write *L'Espirit de la Terre.*[24] From May 1931 to February 1932, he explored Central Asia with the famous Yellow Expedition, which was sponsored by the Citroën automobile company.

In 1937, while presenting at a conference in Philadelphia, he was awarded the Gregor Mendel medal for his scientific accomplishments. During his lectures, he explained his evolutionary theory, including his hypotheses concerning the particular point in human development at which hominids became rational human beings. Unfortunately, an article about the symposium that appeared in the *New York Times* on March 20 misinterpreted his thoughts and stated that they concerned the common ancestry of humans and apes.[25] For American Catholics, sensitive about the whole topic of evolution, Teilhard trod too heavily on sacred ground.

He had been scheduled to receive an honorary degree from Boston College, a Jesuit school, immediately after the symposium. The then archbishop of Boston, William Henry Cardinal O'Connell, was,

24. Teilhard de Chardin, "L'Espirit de la Terre," mimeograph (in French), dated "Pacifique," March 9, 1931 Marie Therese Dubalen–Nancy Corson Carter Collection, Box 1 Folder 7, Lauinger Library Archives, Georgetown University.

25. William Laurence, "China Cave a Lead to 'Missing Link,'" *New York Times*, March 20, 1937, 9. While on this same trip, reporters from *Newsweek* questioned him as to how a Jesuit could reconcile the religious and scientific beliefs he held. Teilhard said in response, "The lack of understanding that exists in some quarters on the evolution of man can be classified solely as a lack of understanding"; "Portrait," *Newsweek*, March 27, 1939, 31.

however, offended by the reported remarks in the newspaper and refused to appear if Teilhard was honored. At the last minute, the school authorities changed their minds and cancelled the ceremony. Upon his return to Paris, he was again chastised by his superiors for the uproar, and after a stint in the hospital for exhaustion and malaria, he returned to China.

As a result of this wide-ranging field work, however, Teilhard became one of the world's most important geologists. This fame, in addition to his original theories on human evolution, made him valuable to the French government. His professional undertakings during this time period are even more impressive when one realizes the profound personal tragedies that he underwent. Between 1932 and 1936 his father, mother, younger brother Victor, and his beloved sister Guiguite all died during his absence.

It was also during this era in China that Teilhard met many of those who would remain close friends throughout the rest of his life. His warmth and ongoing optimistic belief in life seemed to attract many to him, women included. Few knew him as well as Lucile Swan, an American artist, who found herself in the Peking area in 1929 after her divorce from her husband. The friendship between Lucile and Teilhard grew much stronger in the years to come; for a long period of time they were in almost daily contact when both were in the area, and a correspondence of more than twenty years resulted from the friendship. From Lucile as well as from his cousin Marguerite Teilhard-Chambon, Léontine Zanta, Ida Treat, Rhoda de Terra, and others, Teilhard developed a true appreciation for *l'éternal féminin* and an understanding of love that certainly surpassed that of most Jesuit priests.[26]

Teilhard's final years of exile in China, 1939 to 1946, correspond fairly well to the years of World War II and the loss of Chinese Republican control. The most momentous achievement of this era for Teilhard, however, was the completion of *The Phenomenon of Man*

26. Consider, for example, the chapter "Lucile Swan," in *Spirit of Fire: The Life and Vision of Teilhard de Chardin*, by Ursula King (Maryknoll, N.Y.: Orbis, 1996), 144–54; see also in the same book pages 77–81 concerning Teilhard's relationship with his cousin Marguerite.

in May of 1940. Of all of Teilhard's great syntheses between 1938 and 1955, *Le Phénomène Humain* was perhaps the most highly developed.[27] The fundamental themes contained therein had been gestating for a long time, so when Teilhard consciously began work on it in October 1937, it progressed fairly quickly. In May 1938, he presented the preliminary sketches, and by August the first chapter was completed. The rest advanced slowly, but surely. By this time, he "saw" Christianity as the "spearhead of evolution and Christ as the only term for a universe struggling towards unity."[28]

In this book, Teilhard writes of the unfolding of the material cosmos, from creation through the development of the noosphere in contemporary times, toward his vision of the Omega Point in the future.[29] As already noted, he was a leading proponent of orthogenesis, the idea that evolution occurs in a particular, directional, or goal-driven way. To Teilhard, evolution was the cumulative process of the development of the universe, from cell to organism to planet to solar system and whole universe, culminating in communion with Christ. There is no doubt that *The Phenomenon of Man* represents Teilhard's attempt at reconciling his religious faith with his scientific interests as a paleontologist.[30] One particularly poignant observation in Teilhard's book expresses the notion that evolution is becoming an increasingly intentional process. Teilhard points to the societal problems of isolation and marginalization as significant inhibitors of evolution, especially since, in his thought, evolution requires a uni-

27. Aczel, *Jesuit and the Skull*, 188.

28. Cuénot, *Teilhard de Chardin*, 209.

29. The noosphere might be considered the skin, the film, or cloud of knowledge that surrounds the planet. It is the "thinking skin" of the universe. More than once parallels have been drawn between contemporary global communications, particularly the Internet, and Teilhard's noosphere of fifty years previous; see, for example, Philip J. Cunningham, CSP, "Teilhard de Chardin and the Noosphere," *CMC* (Computer Mediated Communication) *Magazine*, March 1997, http://www.december.com/cmc/mag/1997/mar/cunning.html, accessed March, 2012, or the groundbreaking essay concerning this, I. H. Shafer, "From Noosophere to Theosphere: Cyclotrons, Cyberspace and Teilhard's Vision of Cosmic Love," *Zygon: Journal of Religion and Science* 37 (December 2002): 825–52.

30. See in particular the foreword by Brian Swimme, Added in *The Human Phenomenon*, by Teilhard de Chardin, trans. Sarah Appleton-Weber (Brighton and Portland: Sussex, 1999), xiii–xvi.

fication of consciousness. He states, "No evolutionary future awaits anyone except in association with everyone else."[31] This statement can effectively be seen as Teilhard's demand for unity as he believes the future of the human condition necessitates it. He also asserts, "Evolution is an ascent toward consciousness," and therefore signifies a continuous upsurge or progressive movement toward the Omega Point, the teleological end of this universe. This process he referred to as "Christogenesis."

Teilhard constantly revised the book, however, because he knew that his request to publish it would face strong opposition in Rome. He was searching for a formula that would permit him to say what he needed to say and yet at the same time would ease the path through approval by the authorities. The most important contribution of his work is the way in which it places the emergence of humanity as the pivotal point of earth's evolutionary process. *The Human Phenomenon* uses a fourfold sequence of evolution: galactic evolution, earth evolution, life evolution, and consciousness evolution, to create what "might almost be considered a new literary genre."[32]

By 1941, Teilhard had a complete version of his book; one copy was sent to Father Edmund Walsh at Georgetown University. A second went to the Jesuit headquarters in Rome, with a letter requesting permission to publish. As Teilhard truly did not expect to receive this permission in a timely manner, the long delay before he received any sort of response was only to be expected.

Finally, in March 1944, one of the Jesuits reviewing Teilhard's manuscript wrote a report detailing scores of objections to the work.[33] The report was sent to the Jesuit superior with a suggestion for denial, yet Teilhard heard nothing about the status of the process until he was finally permitted to return to France in 1946 after

31. Teilhard de Chardin, *The Phenomenon of Man*, trans. Bernard Wall, with introduction by Sir Julian Huxley (New York: Harper, 1959), 35.

32. *ATA.*

33. Aczel notes that this report was written in longhand and in Latin and is still kept secret today. When the document was accidentally given to him to peruse for a few moments before it was rapidly taken away, the result was extreme consternation on the part of the Jesuit librarians. Even today, he notes, it appears that for many Jesuits Teilhard de Chardin is a sensitive topic; Aczel, *Jesuit and the Skull*, 200.

the war. In January 1947, Teilhard met outside Toulouse with those assigned the task of deciding whether the manuscript should be published. After two days of meetings and listening to myriad criticisms concerning the basic elements of his book, it was obvious that permission would be denied. Although he was supposedly permitted to publish what he wished about science, the Jesuits claimed this book went far beyond science.

In another attempt to gain approval, that September Teilhard met in the French Pyrenees with his longtime friends Monsignor Bruno de Solages and Henri de Lubac at a chateau owned by the monsignor's cousin. Over a week's time, the three pored over the manuscript in an effort to counter the objections raised in Rome.[34] Ultimately, however, they were unable to persuade the authorities to change their minds.

During this time, Teilhard was nominated as a candidate for the chair in Prehistory at the Sorbonne, soon to be vacated by his friend the abbé Henri Breuil. By May of 1947, Teilhard was exhausted from attempting to strengthen his position and from dealing with expectations. He suffered a heart attack at the beginning of June, perhaps as a result of these strains. He was therefore unable to join an expedition to Africa sponsored by the Viking Fund of the Wenner-Green Foundation in New York. He had looked forward to the trip as a pleasant interlude before the tumult began again with Rome over *The Phenomenon* and before the position began at the Sorbonne. While recovering from this setback, however, he was honored by the French Ministry of Foreign Affairs for his scientific and intellectual achievements and was made an officer in the Legion of Honor.

He recuperated enough that a year later he did travel to the United States. He was invited to give a series of lectures at Columbia University; however, the local Jesuit superior would not give his approval. A trip to Rome in 1949 to pursue the subject of the publication of

34. Ibid., 204. Monsignor Bruno de Solages and Teilhard met early in Teilhard's career. The abbé was impressed with how Teilhard was able to integrate Christianity and evolution. De Solages understood Teilhard's ideas, saw nothing heretical or subversive in them, and became one of his strongest and most powerful supporters; Aczel, *Jesuit and the Skull*, 191 and 203.

The Phenomenon personally resulted in no further progress. Teilhard came to realize that he would never be permitted to publish during his lifetime. In addition, the position at the Sorbonne was now denied him. The only bright spot was that his works were not placed on the *Index*. He returned dejectedly to Paris.

After traveling extensively for the next two years, Teilhard accepted a research position with the Wenner-Green Foundation in New York in December of 1951. For the following three years, he lived with the Jesuit priests at St. Ignatius Church on Park Avenue and walked to his office at Wenner-Green, as well as to the apartment of his secretary and friend Rhoda de Terra. Even during these last years, his correspondence with yet another friend in France, Father Pierre Leroy, displayed the lack of bitterness and continuing sense of hope that so characterized his life.[35]

In 1951, since he had already suffered one heart attack, his friends suggested that he bequeath his papers to his then official secretary in Paris, Jeanne Mortier. The concern was that rather than being published, if the papers fell into the possession of the Jesuits they would be destroyed or buried in a filing cabinet. Hoping to spend his final years in his native country, Teilhard applied once more to his superiors for permission to return permanently to France. He was politely refused and encouraged to return to America. He died Easter Sunday, April 10, 1955, in New York City. His funeral, on a rainy Easter Monday, was attended by only a few friends. Father Leroy and the ministering priest from St. Ignatius accompanied his body some sixty miles upstate from New York City, where he was buried at St. Andrews-on-Hudson, then the Jesuit novitiate.

Time Magazine published this obituary the week of his death: "Died. The Rev. Pierre Teilhard de Chardin, S.J., 74, world-renowned, French-born paleontologist, co-discoverer (in 1924) of the Peking man, the first actual remains of Paleolithic man found in Asia; of a heart attack; in Manhattan.... 'The significant fact about man,' he said, 'is the coming of thought with and through him.'"[36]

35. These were later published as Father Pierre Leroy, *Letters From My Friend, Teilhard de Chardin, 1948–1955* (New York: Paulist Press, 1980).

36. Obituary, *Time*, April 25, 1955, 104. Also included in that obituary was this

TEILHARD'S CHRISTOLOGICAL VISION

During his last years, Teilhard lived far from his beloved Paris amid the New York City Jesuit community. At the time of his death in 1955, he was known to the public primarily as the "missing link" priest, the aristocratic French paleontologist who helped to unearth and analyze the Peking Man bones found in China in the late 1930s. But another Teilhard also existed, the Jesuit writer and mystic who integrated his scientific and spiritual zeal into an unconventional understanding of the evolutionary progress of the cosmos. His spiritual writings continued to be circulated and discussed, not publicly or officially, but via mimeographed copies that circulated privately among theologians, scientists, and scholars for discussion and criticism. Following his death—through the efforts of his former secretary Jeanne Mortier and what came to be known as "The Teilhard de Chardin Foundation"—the primary sources themselves were posthumously published and translated into several languages. Henri de Lubac, his fellow French Jesuit and friend, wrote numerous treatises explicating Teilhard's work, and eventually an immense body of secondary work sprang up around his writings. As one commentator put it, "Teilhard virtually became a cult."[37]

The reasons behind that cultic devotion, primarily during the 1960s, are what this book explores. However, as will become clear, a reductive understanding of Teilhard's thought and spirituality was what often drove the fascination with and use of his writing. Not often understood was that from an early age devotion to Christ, especially to his Sacred Heart and Passion, was central to Teilhard's spirituality. The Jesuits taught him to see God at work in the world even in the midst of pain and suffering. Although he had no easy explanations for the often apparently meaningless turmoil intrinsic to human existence, he wrote often about how this is transfigured by

---

comment: "Father Teilhard regarded the Peking man as an important link between the anthropoids and modern man, saw no contradiction between Roman Catholic doctrine and scientific evidence of man's animal origin."

37. Robert Ellwood, *The Sixties Spiritual Awakening: American Religion Moving from Modern to Postmodern* (New Brunswick, N.J.: Rutgers University Press, 1994), 90.

God and provides a means by which God may enter into the heart of humankind. God, he wrote, "must, in some way or other, make room for himself, hollowing us out and emptying us, if he is finally to penetrate into us."[38]

This kenotic spirituality plays a crucial role in Teilhard's Christocentric vision, which numerous scholars consider at the heart of his life's work, and which are key in understanding his reception in the United States during these years. Indeed, at one point he wrote to a friend, "Exalting Christ over everything: this is all I can be accused of."[39] Or again,

> Throughout my life, *by means of* my life, the world has little by little caught fire in my sight until, aflame all around me, it has become almost completely luminous from within.... Such has been my experience in contact with the earth—the diaphany of the Divine at the heart of the universe on fire ... Christ; his heart; a fire; capable of penetrating everywhere and, gradually, spreading everywhere.[40]

As an appreciation of this all-encompassing vision is essential for understanding the remainder of my argument, it seems expedient to present it here briefly. First, one must realize Teilhard's Christocentric cosmology was not his own theological invention. He is, arguably, the only modern Catholic thinker who takes seriously the Cosmic Christ of St. Paul and St. John, as well as that of some of the Greek fathers, and makes this thematic in his thought.[41] It is especially in the New Testament writings where his teleological anthropocentricism appears to originate.[42]

38. Teilhard de Chardin, *Divine Milieu*, 89.

39. Francisco Bravo, *Christ in the Thought of Teilhard de Chardin* (Notre Dame, Ind.: University of Notre Dame Press, 1967), 84. Although Bravo does not provide a reference for this quote, Teilhard wrote in the same vein in 1916 to his cousin Marguerite: "I want to love Christ with all my strength in the very act of loving the universe. Can this be absurdity, blasphemy?"; Letter to Marguerite Teilhard-Chambon, March 15, 1916, Box7, Folder 20, Teilhard-Schmitz-Moormann Collection, Woodstock Theological Center.

40. Teilhard de Chardin, *Divine Milieu*, 9n.

41. These would include Rom 8:19–23, Eph 1:9–10,1 Cor 15:28, Rv 22;12–13, and finally Jn 1:1–4.

42. It is this same teleology and anthropocentrism that Stephen J. Gould later denounced and ridiculed as a "vision with a vengeance"; "Vision with a Vengeance," *Natural History* 89 (September 1980): 16–20.

As a result, the Incarnation takes on a new hue and importance for him. In Teilhard's interpretation, Christ the divine and human not only are genuinely blended into one entity, but Christ is by necessity at the center of the universe. Only Christ can give the world a transcendent outlook; because of his Incarnation, natural creation is reformed and further directed toward a higher unity. As a result, Teilhard finds the duality of the natural/supernatural divide false in many ways and discerns that matter and spirit are complementary.[43] Likewise, if one refuses to acknowledge the presence of a divine power in Christ, one refuses to believe in the Incarnation. In the Incarnation of Jesus, Teilhard finds not just the organizing synthesis of spirit and matter— as well as the subsequent unfolding of events leading to the birth, work, and passion of Christ—but that which continues beyond these into a new evolutionary theology. Teilhard therefore understood humanity and the whole of nature as combining incarnationally in a historical progression guided by and drawn forth by the Pauline Cosmic Christ. For Teilhard, "To create, to fulfill, to purify the world is for God to unify it by uniting it organically with himself. How does he unify it? By immersing himself in things, by becoming 'element' and then from this vantage in the heart of matter, assuming the control and leadership of what we now call evolution."[44] Teilhard saw Christ as giving guidance to the cosmos via evolution.

The metaphysics of Aquinas and the ancient Greek fathers suggested to him that evolution was not simply random mutations and struggles for survival. Instead, it transcended Darwinism in that it consisted of a convergent progression of life toward an even greater unity in Christ. Teilhard suggested that Christianity, from its beginning, has adopted the notion that in the one who came to earth as Jesus, the whole reason for creation, both its material as well as its

43. Consider, for example, the quote "I saw that the dualism in which I had hitherto been enclosed was disappearing like the mist before the rising sun. Matter and Spirit: these were no longer two things, but two states or two aspects of one and the same cosmic Stuff"; Teilhard de Chardin, *Heart of Matter* (San Diego: Harcourt Brace, 1966) 26. Copyright 1976 from Édition de Seuil, English translation copyright 1979 Harcourt Brace Javonovich.

44. Teilhard de Chardin, *Phenomenon of Man*, 149.

spiritual purpose, is to be found. As he put it, "The answer to the riddle of the universe is: Christ Jesus."[45]

Additionally, Teilhard's cosmology is quite Eucharistic in nature. He was, for most of his life, an ordained priest who while a young man wrote a thesis on the Eucharist and who received the sacrament daily. In the Mass, the consecrated bread and wine represented for him the whole of earthly matter formed and transformed by human activity through the direction of God. Matter, then, becomes something more than just formless "stuff." Christ's presence in the stuff of the Eucharist exemplifies Christ's presence in all the created matter of the earth. It is Christ who sustains this and constitutes it into something more.

So Jesus the man, son of Mary, serves as the historical medium by which humanity's united efforts can be drawn to Christ, the evolutive force, through both the natural and supernatural dimensions. The Incarnation means the supernatural being of God has assumed a natural form to enter our universe; Christ both inspires and claims for himself the natural desires of people. As Teilhard wrote, "There is only *one single center* of the universe; it is at once natural and supernatural; it impels the whole of creation along one and the same line, first towards the fullest development of consciousness, and later towards the highest degree of holiness: in other words towards Christ Jesus, personal and cosmic both."[46] The Christogenesis described here—in which God first Christifies himself through the Incarnation and through which Christ the "all in all" is then fully formed by drawing into a mystical consummation the entirety of life—is the heart of both Teilhard's theology and his evolutionary theory.

By contrast, much nineteenth-century theology tended to emphasize Christ's human nature at the expense of his divine nature. This had been taken to an extreme in various Modernist writings that portrayed Christ as only a human man no different from anyone else. Additionally, despite the writings of St. Paul and the Eastern fathers, Christ's power over creation has otherwise primarily been con-

45. Thomas Corbishley, *The Spirituality of Teilhard de Chardin* (New York: Paulist Press, 1971), 71.

46. Teilhard de Chardin, "Forma Christi," in *Writings in Time of War*, 253.

sidered in its juridical aspects. In other words, Christ is king because God the Father proclaimed him king. In this thought, the organic, physical side of the Incarnation is relegated to the background, so that the idea of the physical control of the cosmos by the person of the Cosmic Christ became quite inconceivable.[47]

In this cosmology, Teilhard believed Christ becomes far too removed, individualistic, dissociated from the universe. Instead, he asked, "How then, may we conceive Christ to be constituted as the cosmic center of creation? Simply as a magnification, a transformation, realized in the humanity of Christ, of that which surrounds every human monad."[48]

Teilhard claims therefore that just as each person is in a continual process of growth, of gradually further becoming himself or herself, so too is the whole cosmos a growing and developing whole. It is the same with Christ. In his human nature, he is an individual advancing in wisdom and knowledge as he learns from his mother, teachers, and friends. Through the Incarnation, there is consequently something of Christ in every creature. It is the responsibility and the privilege of each to develop the Christ-element within, so as to add to the fullness that Christ the divine being already is.

This transformative activity requires human cooperation with God's own creative action. In his spiritual classic *The Divine Milieu,* Teilhard wrote that in action, "I adhere to the creative power of God; I coincide with it; I become not only its instrument but its living extension. And as there is nothing more personal in beings than their will, I merge myself, in a sense, through my heart, with the very heart of God." He saw these words as applicable to all created beings.

For Teilhard, all the activities of our lives help to complete Christ's achievement and move the cosmos toward Christogenesis. Nor is this a solitary, individual achievement, but that of a community, a body united in a spiritualized love that is the primary unifying force.[49] As he wrote, "God who is as immense and all-embracing as

47. Teilhard de Chardin, *Science and Christ* (New York: Harper and Row, 1968), 165–66.

48. Teilhard de Chardin, "Forma Christi," 253.

49. Teilhard de Chardin, "Cosmic Life," in *Writings in Time of War,* 48.

matter, and at the same time as warm and intimate as a soul, is the center who spreads through all things ... souls are irresistibly drawn ... towards a common center of beatitude ... the multitude is bound together into one solid whole ... the Communion of Saints is held together in the hallowed unity of a physically organized whole; and this whole ... is the body of Christ."

In Teilhard's spirituality, the perfection of the Christian occurs due to the following of Christ, but here it means more than simply attempting to reproduce in one's own life the various features of Christ's own mission. The role of the church is as an agent of Christogenesis: nurturing and furthering the crucial phylum of love, building the mystical body of Christ, and assisting Christians in learning how to "see" the divine milieu, as well as becoming aware of Christ's presence in the world.

Finally, Teilhard's Christology is also exceedingly eschatological. His is an eschatology of hope, of love caught fire through the Christification of all creation. It is focused upon the Parousia, or Second Coming of Christ at the end of time, when Christogenesis is complete. As he writes in conclusion in the epilogue of *The Divine Milieu:*

> Let us believe in Revelation, once again our faithful support on our most human forebodings ... tension will gradually accumulate ... then will come the end ... the presence of Christ, which has been silently accruing in things, will suddenly be revealed—like a flash of light from pole to pole.... Like lightening, like a conflagration, like a flood, the attraction exerted by the Son of Man will lay hold of all the whirling elements in the universe so as to reunite them or subject them to His body.... Such will be the consummation of the divine milieu.[50]

THE FOLLOWING CHAPTERS

This book places the reception of Teilhard de Chardin's work in the United States within the social, historical, and theological context of the period between 1960 and 1972. The work proceeds chronologically, and each chapter contextualizes the reception of

50. Teilhard de Chardin, *Divine Milieu,* 134.

Teilhard within the cultural events and pertinent written material of the designated time period. Note that the primary task here is to discuss Teilhard's reception rather than to give an exposition of his work. Although the former does require some of the latter, that is not the principal focus.

Throughout the dozen years discussed here, the manner in which Teilhard's work was read and the groups of people who utilized it changed. Yet, in the end it was those who grasped his attempts through an integrated Christological vision to bridge the gap between nature and grace, between religion and science, and his embrace of the everyday material world who were best able to carry his thought beyond the difficult days at the end of this time period. As a result of their efforts and understanding, his thought continues to have impact upon the contemporary U.S. Catholic Church.

Chapter 1 gives a cursory examination of Teilhard's work as it was published posthumously before 1960 in France and England. It includes an overview of his reception in these countries, as publication of anything on Teilhard in the United States in this time period was almost nonexistent. This chapter briefly examines the social and religious milieu in the United States in the late 1950s. Following this will be the means and the reasons by which interest developed in Teilhard in the United States after his death, with an emphasis upon the initial attention shown by Robert Francoeur and those surrounding him who several years later formed the American Teilhard Association.

Chapters 2 and 3, focusing on the years 1961–64, reiterate that the oft-misunderstood figure of Teilhard de Chardin had immeasurable impact upon the intellectual history of twentieth-century Catholicism. Even so, many found his thought a challenge to traditional understandings of the teleology of humankind and the cosmos. When publication of his previously suppressed works began in this time period, the Catholic Church was just entering a new period of freedom stirred by the Second Vatican Council. Teilhard became a theological sensation. His emphasis on evolutionary advancement certainly matched the optimistic, progressive mood of the age. This was particularly true in the United States, where a delight in the material world and an unwavering belief in unending, hopeful progress dictated by God had already been a dominant feature of Americanist Catholicism for a century.

Many claim that Teilhard had an impact upon Vatican II itself. Certainly, as chapter 4 shows, the introduction to *Gaudium et spes* is full of Teilhardian flavor. Its Christological passages contain his favorite citations concerning Christ as the pattern of the new creation. It rings with Teilhardian optimism: "Expectation of a new earth must not weaken but rather stimulate our concern for cultivating this one."[51] The introduction reaches out to the secular world by stressing the value of the secular and the wonders of technology and science. It sees scientists working "with a humble and steady mind," as led by God, and Christ as Omega, "the goal of human history."[52] All these statements point to Teilhardian themes repeatedly found within this book, all of which had a tremendous impact on American culture during this era.

During the years of 1965 through 1967, especially, restlessness increased in the United States, at least among a certain population. This was the era exemplified by Jack and Bobby Kennedy, Martin Luther King Jr., the Freedom Riders, the beginning of the counterculture and hippiedom. This was perhaps the moment for which Teilhard—with his unique brand of hopeful Catholicism, his understanding of the value of everyday effort, the drive for unification, and his humanistic and yet spiritual kind of science—was an ideal match. As Robert Ellwood contends, "He opened a lot of windows ... and was among the first ... and perhaps the best ... of the chanticleers of the Sixties spiritual awakening."[53] It is perhaps then no surprise that these were the years, as chapters 4 and 5 explicate, that interest in Teilhard's thought was at its height.

Around 1968, a dark year politically and socially, the pace and the direction of his reception within the United States altered. Other forms of theological discourse rose to prominence. Chapters 6 and 7 explore the question of why this occurred at this particular time. It

51. *Gaudium et spes*, 3:39.
52. King, "A Holy Man and Lover of the World," *America*, March 28, 2005, 7–10.
53. Ellwood, *Sixties Spiritual Awakening*, 91.

is extremely difficult to separate the political and social upheavals in the United States (in much of the Western world, in fact) from the evolving Roman Catholic ecclesiology of the 1960s. By 1968, certain progressive movements within the country—including within the post–Vatican II Catholic Church—had begun to fracture and disintegrate. This is especially true of the "counterculture," for example, particularly those efforts linked to racial equality and the student and antiwar movements. The sense of optimistic, cohesive progress that had carried them thus far gradually dissipated, as did interest in Teilhard's vision.

One could claim that as the reception of Vatican II or other progressive moments within this country have evolved and unfolded along complex paths, in many ways so, too, has the reception of Teilhard's thought. What this book attempts to elucidate, however, is that those who caught and held onto his Christ-centered hope were able to successfully carry his thought and vision beyond the Teilhard phenomenon of the 1960s.

THE THRESHOLD OF CHANGE

1955–1960

1 THE MOVE ACROSS THE ATLANTIC

THIS CHAPTER provides a background for the introduction of Teilhard's thought to the American population. As we shall see, the initial availability of Teilhard's work in the United States in 1959 intersects with an American society that is poised on the threshold of tremendous political, social, cultural, and religious change. Why was Teilhard's thought so overwhelmingly embraced by so many from almost the very first date of publication? I suggest that this occurred for two primary reasons. First, his teleological, optimistic worldview points to a positive future, one that will ultimately prove to be beneficial for all involved despite the necessary changes required. This is consistent with the "manifest destiny" syndrome already existing in much of American society—or at least that portion of U.S. society that had previously had the most chance for agency. Second, the culture of the United States from the earliest days of European settlement had been focused on the practical, material world of daily life and the potential impact of the individual upon his or her immediate surroundings and ability to control the future. It was, without a doubt, a tremendously "modern" culture in every meaning of that word. The introduction to this work suggested that Teilhard's thought is the product of the metanarrative of modernity, particularly its emphasis upon universal truths, and a belief in progress and science. At least on the surface, therefore, it would appear that

Teilhard's thought intermeshed quite readily with these aspects of life in the United States. What particularizes Teilhard, however, is his romantic, organic, and mystical cosmic vision that allows (1) room for the sacralization of the secular; (2) a synthesis of science and religion; and (3) a new, deep, historical consciousness as exemplified by his fascination with cosmic evolution. These additional aspects of his work will prove quite important during these first years.

This characterization of Teilhard's work places him in the role of bridge between modern and postmodern forms of thought and life. The paradigm shift between these two occurred in the early 1960s in the United States, lending plausibility to the claim that his work was received as it was during these years primarily as a result of its appearance at this particular time and place.

PUBLICATIONS IN EUROPE

Because Teilhard had bequeathed his manuscripts to his former secretary in Paris, Jeanne Mortier, at his death the Jesuits could no longer prevent their publication. Mme. Mortier had already brought together an international team of scientists and scholars, named Les Amis de Teilhard de Chardin, under the patronage of the Belgian queen Marie-José, to oversee in Paris in 1955 the publication of *The Phenomenon of Man* by Éditions du Seuil. The initial five hundred copies rapidly disappeared, and the book went through several reprints, until within six years' time over ninety thousand copies had been sold.[1] *Letters from a Traveler* followed in 1956, *Le Milieu Divin* in 1957, and *The Future of Man* in 1959. Between 1955 and 1976 all thirteen volumes of the original books and essays written by Teilhard were published in the original French; other than *The Phenomenon* and *The Divine Milieu,* the essays of the collected works were arranged thematically rather than chronologically. In addition, before 1961 over five hundred essays and thirty additional books about Teilhard and his thought had been published in France alone.

1. Winifred McCulloch, *A Short History of the American Teilhard Association* (Chambersburg, Pa.: American Teilhard Association for the Future of Man, 1979), 1 (hereafter *ATA*).

Other than a few sparse pieces about his scientific work, one of the first American periodicals to take a serious look at Teilhard's theology of evolution was *CrossCurrents*, with a 1951 essay (translated from the French) by his friend Msgr. Bruno De Solages.[2] Worldwide, the number of publications grew from eighteen books in 1956 to 399 published in 1967, the apex of publication.[3]

The English version of Teilhard's primary opus was published as *The Phenomenon of Man* by Harper Collins in 1959. It included an introduction by Teilhard's former friend and fellow scientist Julian Huxley. In the United States, over fifty thousand copies of this translation sold in less than thirty months.[4] Numerous other editions followed this one, including a wildly popular paperback edition in 1961 that sold almost one hundred thousand copies in less than five years.

THE CULTURAL MILIEU OF THE LATE 1950S

The question remains, however, why so many were so very quickly attracted to this man's thought when he had died a virtual unknown (at least to most of the Christian world) a scant five years earlier. The primary answer probably lies in the synchronicity of the publication of these first books in the years that a massive change was beginning in the United States. It was, one might say, a "perfect storm" of coincidence. In particular, during these years through 1960 we can observe change in five areas, each of which contributed to the shift away from modernity already mentioned. I will briefly discuss these from a historical perspective before placing them within the context of the reception of Teilhard's work: (1) the end of the postwar consensus; (2) the dissolution of the Catholic subculture; (3) the rapid expansion of educational opportunities for all Americans, especially

2. Bruno de Solages, "Christianity and Evolution: An Introduction to the Thought of Père Teilhard," *CrossCurrents*, no. 4 (Summer 1951): 26–37.

3. Data from Alessandro Dall'Olio, SJ, "Teilhard de Chardin: Thinker Wedded to Wisdom," in *The Jesuits 1972–1977*, 82 (pamphlet, Georgetown University libarary). See the appendix for a chart of the number of worldwide Teilhard publications between 1956 and 1971.

4. *ATA*, 3.

in science; (4) a renewed sense of optimism, especially surrounding the election of John F. Kennedy; and (5) the papacy of John XXIII and his call for an ecumenical council.

The End of the Postwar Consensus

The United States dominated global affairs in the years immediately after World War II. For most of the fifteen years following 1945, there was a broad political consensus concerning the Cold War and anti-communism. Victorious in the great global struggle, its nation intact, the people of the United States were confident of their country's mission at home and abroad. U.S. leaders desired to maintain the democratic ideology they had defended at an enormous cost and to share the benefits of prosperity as much as possible. For them, as for publisher Henry Luce of *Time* magazine, this was indeed the "American Century."[5]

Still, within two years of the end of World War II, new challenges had arisen to erode at least some of that confidence. By 1948, a new form of international strain had emerged—the Cold War—between the United States and its allies on one hand and the Soviet Union and its allies on the other. In the next two decades, the Cold War generated many tensions abroad. Additionally, fears of communist subversion gripped domestic politics at home. As a result, most Americans accepted the need for a strong stance against the Soviet Union and any suspected communists. They sanctioned the growth of governmental authority, encouraged consensus in all forms of political and social life, and enjoyed the postwar prosperity that produced new levels of widespread wealth in the United States.

The Cold War demanded conformity of belief and lifestyle on behalf of the struggle for freedom. For almost fifteen years, most

5. This term, coined by *Time* publisher Henry Luce, was used to claim the historical role of the United States during the twentieth century. The son of a missionary himself, in a February 17, 1941, *Life* magazine editorial, Luce urged the United States to forsake isolationism for the missionary's role. The nation was to act as the world's Good Samaritan, spread democracy, and enter World War II to defend the highest democratic values. In terms of the "Americanism" described later in this chapter, one can positively affirm that Luce was indeed an Americanist.

Americans remained sure of this confident approach. Big government and corporations demanded "organization man" behaviors and values and rewarded them.

Socially, the nuclear but not the extended family seemed to embody the American dream. The ideal was articulated by the word "togetherness." The family was to be a political functioning unit, with the husband out in the work world bringing home the bread and the wife maintaining the home front. She was to support her partner, through her unpaid labor and emotionally through her appreciation, in every way she could.

Throughout the nation, a push existed toward a smooth organizational life in all things that mimicked that ideal of conventional family togetherness. Consensus was the expected norm. A survey of 1950s college students by Philip E. Jacob found that overwhelmingly they conformed to the value of the day as defined by David Riesman's *Lonely Crowd*.[6] They were "gloriously contented" with things as they are and "unabashedly selfish" as they "cheerfully expect to conform to the economic status quo."[7] "Social harmony" and "adjustment"—in other words, conformity—were of great importance, more so than honesty or courage. Jacob found that the students expressed a "need for religion" yet expected their real-life decisions to be "socially determined" rather than religiously guided. The ultimate source of meaning for this generation was the group, and the ultimate good religion or social milieu was that which promoted those goods.[8]

Yet a booming population, migration around the country, intense suburbanization, and educational acceleration fueled primarily by the G.I. Bill also meant the postwar world of the United States would not be simply traditional. A new way to prioritize values was necessary, and religion was the obvious means of choice. Although

6. David Riesman, Nathan Glazer, and Reuel Denney, *The Lonely Crowd: A Study of the Changing American Character* (New Haven, Conn.: Yale University Press, 1950).

7. Philip E. Jacob, *Changing Values in College* (New York: Harper and Brothers, 1957), quoted in *Revolt on the Campus*, by M. Stanton Evans (Chicago: Henry Regnery, 1961), 26.

8. Robert S. Ellwood, *The Sixties Spiritual Awakening* (New Brunswick, N.J.: Rutgers University Press, 1994), 190.

previously religion itself was synonymous with nationalism, that would shift tremendously in the decade ahead.[9] The religious messages of the time were also communal and consensual in nature and attempted to adapt to the needs of a rapidly growing and changing society. Still, religious leaders did not generally speak to society in a prophetic or activist manner but used a therapeutic approach in responding to the individual trying to cope with rapid change. In many cases, this took place by denying that change was occurring.[10]

In the end, it was the most visible results of the postwar years, including the new postwar affluence, a young and rapidly growing population, the typical postwar exultation of breeding and family togetherness, and the migration to the suburbs that helped to bring about the end of the Cold War consensus.[11] Not all Americans participated equally in these expanding life opportunities and in the growing economic prosperity. The image and reality of overall economic prosperity—and the upward mobility it provided for many white Americans—was not lost on those who had largely been excluded from the full meaning of the American Dream, both before and after the war.

Gradually these and other Americans began to question the current, dominant assumptions about American life. Challenges on a variety of fronts shattered the consensus. As a consequence, by the mid- to late 1960s such groups as African Americans, Hispanic Americans, and American women became more aggressive in trying to win their full freedoms and civil rights as guaranteed by the Declaration of Independence and the U.S. Constitution. In the 1950s, African

9. Ibid., 18.

10. Ibid., 16. See also Garry Wills, *Bare Ruined Choirs: Doubt, Prophecy and Radical Religion* (Doubleday: New York, 1972), in which Wills contends that this era was in many ways a time of "deliberate blindness," of pretending not to see the things one should not see, of "doubts that were hidden for the sake of the children" (8). Additionally, in the first chapter of this book, "Memories of a Catholic Boyhood," Wills argues that a "protective skin" was woven around Catholics that kept the church living "outside of time," "stranded in America, out of place." Indeed, the church belonged to no age, but was above them all, for it had a "special dispensation" from history, which was something it "did not have to undergo" (i8).

11. See, for example, Hugh McLeod, "The Early 1960s," in *The Religious Crisis of the 1960s* (Oxford: Oxford University Press, 2007), 60–82.

Americans launched a crusade, joined later by these other minority groups, for a larger share of the American dream.[12] Additionally, a growing anxiety fatigue existed concerning Cold War threats. The constant threat of nuclear Armageddon had become wearisome, and already by 1954 extreme anti-communism was questioned on moral and spiritual, as well as factual, grounds.

The social and religious underground that existed even in this time of consensus began to speak louder and to be heard by more.[13] "Where," they asked, "does good togetherness end and the evils of collectivism begin? Simply at the limits of the nuclear family?"[14]

The Dissolution of the Catholic Subculture

This decade of the 1950s saw a shift in the way most people understood the religious identity of their own society. In the 1940s–50s the majority tended to believe Americans still lived in a "Christian country." From 1945 to 1960 in fact, numerous scholars would claim evidence of a religious revival.[15] More churches were built for more worshippers. During the "Age of Anxiety" and the fear of nuclear annihilation by the communists, one might even claim that religion, as it became more therapeutic in nature, helped to produce a healthy, more balanced society.[16] The Christian heritage of the country was yet more explicitly proclaimed. Consider, for example, the adoption of the slogan "one nation under God," in the Pledge of Allegiance in 1954. This was the age of the religious intellectuals and public figures, such as Thomas Merton, Karl Barth, Reinhold Niebuhr, Paul Tillich, Billy Graham, Norman Vincent Peale, and Fulton Sheen. According to Gallup, the highest historical level of church attendance

12. Consider, for example, the school integration case of *Brown vs. the Board of Education* of Topeka, Kansas, in 1954.

13. Ellwood, *Sixties*, 6.

14. Ibid., 15.

15. See, for example, Mark Silk, *Spiritual Politics: Religion and America since World War II* (New York: Simon and Schuster, 1988); Robert Ellwood, *The 50s Spiritual Marketplace: American Religion in a Decade of Conflict* (New Brunswick, N.J.: Rutgers University Press, 1997) (hereafter Ellwood, *Fifties*); and Patrick Carey, *Catholics in America: A History* (Westport, Conn.: Praeger, 2004).

16. Silk, *Spiritual Politics*, 31.

was reached between 1955 and 1958 with 47 percent of the population attending church services weekly. The highest rate of church construction occurred in 1959.[17] The influence of religion on people's thoughts was considered to be increasing. Polls said that 99 percent of Americans believed in God. Seminaries, monasteries, and confidence were bursting at the seams.

But the religion boom coexisted with tensions between Catholics and Protestants and between highbrow theology and lowbrow popular faith. There was also a spiritual underground, represented by the Beats and many others.[18] As the 1960s went on, many people increasingly declared Western society as post-Christian, secular, or "pluralist."[19]

Accompanying this trend toward a pluralist society was a weakening of the process by which children were socialized into membership in Christian society and given confessional identity and basic knowledge of beliefs. This movement toward secularism crossed all religious boundaries and certainly was exhibited in American Catholic society.

Over the previous century, the immigrant Catholics to the United States had built a sophisticated subculture originally centered in the urban U.S. Northeast but extending across the nation. The resulting network of Catholic institutions, including parishes, schools, hospitals, and charitable agencies acted as a "buffer" between most Catholics and the other American religious traditions. Although it may have been geographically diverse, this subculture provided a most "distinctive spiritual and intellectual topography" to American Catholic life.[20] Catholics in America learned over the years consensual forms of worship, discipleship, and ways of being in the world that further set them apart in the culture. The Catholic subculture saw to it that the appropriate lines between clergy and laity were drawn, that criticism of priests was muted, and that any hint of scandal was hushed.

17. Ellwood, *Fifties*, 1.

18. Ibid., 6.

19. McLeod, "Early 1960s," 3.

20. William L. Portier, "Here Come the Evangelical Catholics," *Communio* 31, no. 1 (Spring 2004): 35–66.

As Mark Massa writes, most Catholics prior to 1960 "lived in a hermetically sealed universe when it came to their faith and religious practices."[21] Intellectuals and theologians generally held to some internally consistent system of thought in which everything fell into place. For Catholics following Pius X's *Pascendi,* this was neo-Scholasticism.[22]

Concurrently, as the decades passed, the subculture Catholics moved up the economic and educational ladder. This was especially true in the post–World War II boom years. The growth of labor unions, higher wages, and an expanding economy all changed the financial standing of the Catholic population, so that by 1964 Catholics outranked most Protestant groups economically.[23] In conjunction with these opportunities for upward mobility, however, many began to consider their constructed subculture as restrictive, rather than comforting. By mid-century, Catholic elites would refer to their cultural habitat as a "ghetto."[24]

In the postwar years, following the example of their fellow Americans, significant numbers of Catholics had moved to the suburbs. Ties to the customs and priorities of immigrant ancestors were diminished or completely severed, as a more than century-old Catholic consensus began to disappear. Soon, any "demographic difference between Catholics and other Americans became statistically negligible."[25]

21. Mark Massa, *The American Catholic Revolution: How the Sixties Changed the Church Forever* (New York: Oxford University Press, 2010.), xv.

22. Leo XIII, *Aeterni Patris* (August 4, 1879). This encyclical set in place the groundwork and structure of neo-Scholasticism. Pope Pius X's *Pascendi Dominici gregis* promulgated the teaching that all Catholic theology was to be consistent with that found in neo-Thomism. In *Doctoris Angelici,* 1914, Pope Pius X cautioned that the teachings of the church cannot be understood scientifically without the basic philosophical underpinnings of Thomas's major theses.

23. William Leahy, SJ, "Catholics and Educational Expansion after 1945," in *Contemporary Higher Education: Catholic Education at the Turn of a New Century,* ed. Joseph M. O'Keefe (New York and London: Garland, 1997), 48.

24. Lamenting their "spirit of separatism from fellow citizens of other religious faiths," John Tracy Ellis described Catholics as having "suffered from the timidity that characterizes minority groups, from the effects of a ghetto they have themselves fostered"; Ellis, "American Catholics and the Intellectual Life," *Thought* 30, no. 116 (Spring 1955): 388.

25. Portier, "Here Come the Evangelical Catholics," 46.

The Rapid Expansion of Educational Opportunities for All Americans

Building on the economic base left after the war, American society became more affluent in the postwar years than most Americans could have imagined in their wildest dreams before or during the war. Public policy, like the so-called G.I. Bill of Rights passed in 1944, provided money for veterans to attend college, to purchase homes, and to buy farms. The overall impact of such public policies was almost incalculable, but it certainly permitted returning veterans to better themselves and to begin forming families and caring for their children in unprecedented numbers. Additionally, World War II increased contact between Protestants and Catholics; this in turn reduced barriers and fostered mutual understanding and acceptance. This persuaded yet more Catholic families to ensure the education of their children at Catholic schools. The number of Catholics attending college in the 17–25-year age group increased from 19 percent in the 1930s to 45 percent in the 1960s, 2 percent above the national average.[26]

On top of mounting social pressures, institutions of higher learning in these years were in danger of drowning in their own success. For example, the student population attending Boston College increased from 2,000 in 1945 to over 11,000 less than twenty-five years later.[27] Similarly, in 1953, Jesuit administrators of higher education from the midwestern United States admitted that unless they were able to admit more freshmen, their institutions faced a mounting public relations problem. Additionally, these officials warned, "It is a fact that when the public makes demands, we must try to meet the demands, or be in danger of going out of existence."[28]

The rate of increase for graduate programs was much higher yet. To meet the demands, post-secondary institutions expanded, es-

26. Leahy, "Catholics and Educational Expansion after 1945," 51.

27. Ibid..

28. Ibid., 52. Due to the population crunch at Catholic institutions and the lack of certain curricular and professional programs, Catholic students constituted 25 percent of Columbia's undergraduate population in 1964 and 18 percent of the freshman class at Princeton in 1970.

pecially in regions where they were previously lacking. In addition, graduate programs were added, particularly in the fields of history, psychology, social work, and the natural sciences. Among Catholic institutions the rate was even higher than in the secular schools. The thought was that graduate work in these disciplines at non-Catholic places seriously endangered the faith of students, so Catholic programs had best be made available.[29] This type of educational growth also offered the possibility of the expansion of Catholic thought to a wider audience, thus extending Catholic influence in society. Fostering a social, political, and intellectual environment guided by Catholic teachings had always been a fundamental part of the Catholic educational commitment. But such an evangelical focus became a higher priority after World War II, as secularism spread in Western civilization. The deepening of "the ideological conflict between democracy and communism" also contributed to this sharpened focus.[30]

Then, on October 4, 1957, Sputnik was launched by the Russians. A disastrous counter-attempt by the United States to launch a satellite followed in December of that year. The rest of the world gloated at the humiliation of a country all too ready to brag of prowess and righteousness, while the nation seethed.[31] That fear and rage originated in the hatred of the Russian communists as cultivated over the previous decade. The search for scapegoats and a resurgence of the old Cold War fear of sudden annihilation commenced. The hysteria grew, everyone saying to everyone else, "Do something!"[32]

In an interesting twist, the Christmas 1957 *Newsweek* holiday essay was titled, "And the angel said unto them, Fear not. . . ."[33] It spoke of this "particularly troubled time," in which many are "beset with feelings of fear and anxiety ... perplexed and unsettled by sudden shifts of world power" and by "domestic uncertainties" all of which "threaten to blight the bright optimism of American life." The essay offered consolations from various theologians to the effect that the

29. Ibid., 53.

30. Ibid., 54.

31. *Fifties*, 185.

32. "Sputnik's Wake," *America*, October 26, 1957, 94.

33. "And the angel said unto them, Fear not . . . ," *Newsweek*, December 23, 1957, 52–53.

antidote to fear is trust in God, as it hinted that "peace of mind" therapeutic religion was not enough. One must delve deeper. Similarly, immediately following the launch of Sputnik the journal *Living Church* had offered the thought that material well-being does not necessarily demonstrate moral superiority.[34]

Instead, what was necessary was a better education for all, in addition to general social progress and money for education, science, and military budgets. As Ellwood stated, "Fresh emphasis on education, properly an open-ended enterprise, was actually the dawning of the new optimism that would characterize the Kennedy Camelot and the Great Society years of the first half of the next decade."[35] This new emphasis was fostered by the perfect storm generated by the Sputnik imperative, the baby-boom population bulge—which made for an extreme increase in the college population and a new youth culture—and the emergence of Galbraith's "affluent society" to pay for it all.[36] "In the end," commented Ellwood, "the change was spiritual."[37]

This change was also furthered by the renaissance of a new liberalism in the United States in the late 1950s as exemplified by the drive for racial justice and school integration. The Sputnik debacle reinforced this with its indirect insistence that science and education, rather than McCarthyism and restrictive consensus, were the straightest routes to a Cold War victory.[38]

A Renewed Sense of Optimism

One result of the "world-come-of-age" secular theology of the 1950s—which grew out of neo-orthodoxy or Pian Catholicism—was an increased sense of optimism. Those of faith, rather than looking

34. "Man's Moon," *Living Church*, October 20, 1957, 14. This response to the fear of change was addressed by Wills on page 22 in *Bare Ruined Choirs*: "Perfect faith and trust would quiet the soul in a peaceful attitude of rest. After all, if one possess the truth already, any change is liable to be a departure from that truth."

35. Ellwood, *Fifties*, 187.

36. John Kenneth Galbraith, *The Affluent Society* (Boston: Houghton Mifflin, 1958).

37. Ellwood, *Fifties*, 188.

38. Ibid., 175.

toward the supernatural for signs of reassurance, took hope in their capable care for the world on their own, prospering now as they never before had done.[39] The late 1950s therefore were spiritually optimistic years. Although some were concerned about the "priests of science" and the increasing emphasis upon technology, most believed the worse was past; the large, new generation moving through the burgeoning high schools were getting ready to come into their own in a new world. America was once again moving upward and onward.

Some would consider the fifties as the last "modern" decade, particularly if one defines modernity as that which, in the spirit of Jean-Francois Lyotard, includes the metanarrative of the emancipation of humanity through progress and universal truths.[40] Robert Ellwood, for example, writes that since the time of the Enlightenment the educated have believed themselves capable of freeing humanity from its shackles through better knowledge and the application of that knowledge. This knowledge is primarily found in the generalized, abstract, rational ways of thinking found in science. Within the metanarrative of modernity the particular is subordinated to the abstract, the old is inferior to the new, and the local submits to the universal.[41] The modern world especially placed power in the hands of knowledge-holding elites like professionals, teachers, civil servants, and religious leaders.

It is important to remember, however, that as widespread as this metanarrative of optimism may have been, large groups of people in the United States remained on the outskirts of it. A real boom in the economy and in the growth of knowledge did indeed exist in the United States in the 1950s and early 1960s. It might seem that almost everyone benefited from this. But there were significant segments of people—in particular the masses of those impoverished and even middle-class people of color—who were largely and essen-

39. Ibid., 188.

40. Jean-Francois Lyotard, *The Postmodern Condition: A Report on Knowledge*, trans. Geoff Bennington and Brian Massumi (Minneapolis: University of Minnesota Press, 1984), ix.

41. Ellwood, *Fifties*, 228.

tially locked out of that; this constituted one of the major and most explosive social contradictions of that time. This contradiction was one among several that would eventually help to crumble not only the postwar American consensus but also the metanarrative of Americanist progress.

The Election of Pope John XXIII

The last year of Pope Pius XII's pontificate, 1957, signified the end of an age of Roman Catholicism reaching back to the Counter-Reformation. Until this point, the church stood unflinching and unchanging, ready to do battle with atheism and modernity, but never to change colors. This was the age of Catholic confidence and Catholic triumphalism.[42]

The intellectual indemnity of universal truth was interconnected with surety about leadership, one that extended beyond papal or episcopal guidance. As a result, the fifties are seen by Jay Dolan as the culminating decade of the "golden age of American Catholic priesthood."[43] What the church had locked away as its most well-guarded secret, though, was change. Now in the late 1950s not only was the historical consciousness of the church slowly awakening, with the realization that actually the church of the apostles did look a little different from the contemporary Vatican, it was also soon to be shaken by an unexpected ecumenical council that would plunge it into an uncertain life.[44]

Within days of the election of Pope John XXIII, all of Rome and the world were astounded that the church had not only a new pope but also a new kind of pope, a prelate as cheerful and visionary as it

42. Ibid., 202.

43. James P. Wind and James W. Lewis, eds., *American Congregations*, vol 2, *New Perspectives in the Study of Congregations* (Chicago: University of Chicago Press, 1994, 248, quoted in Ellwood, *Fifties*, 203.

44. For more on this idea of the historical awakening of the church, see especially Wills, *Bare Ruined Choirs*, 21. Wills also writes, "The church's secret, hidden away in official teaching, minimized when it could not be ignored, was *change*. Other things came and went, captive to history. But the gate of hell would not prevail against this church, and the gates of hell often looked like history, or the latest products of history: 'modernism,' science, rationalism" (20).

appeared his predecessor had been dour and inflexible. His mental agility and kindness captured the imagination of all who encountered him. His January 1959 call for a new ecumenical council laid out his vision for the future in his statement that "we ... open our heart and arms to all those who are separated from this Apostolic See."[45] The council would look at the whole life of the church, including theology, canon law, discipline, worship, and perhaps most importantly of all, the role of the laity.

In so doing this council would address the reigning question of just what the church really was about. During the consensus years of the mid-1950s, Cardinal Spellman could insist that Catholicism, more than any other religion, upheld American democracy. The Catholic public believed therefore that Catholicism was the most American of religions and America the most Christian of nations. Less than five years later, however, cracks were appearing in the consensus society, including among the Catholics.[46] As has already been noted, as they rode the escalator out of the immigrant ghetto into middle-class America, the boundaries that demarcated their identity were dissolving. The world of the parochial school, Catholic labor unions, and Forty Hours devotions would soon no longer exist in a way that sufficiently defined U.S. Catholics as Catholic. A new way of being Catholic would soon be imperative; the desire for something more grew almost palpable, and the willingness to pursue a new way, at least on the part of some progressively more vocal splinter groups, increasingly evident. The sixties were getting closer, and the hope of at least some American Catholics was that the upcoming council would fulfill that desire.

45. Monsignor Albert Giovannetti, *A Portrait of His Holiness: John XXIII*, trans. John Chapin (Westminster, Md.: Newman Press, 1959), 35; retrieved from http://archive.org/stream/wehaveapopeaporto13181mbp/wehaveapopeaporto13181mbp_djvu.txt on April 11, 2013. The quote is from the new pope's first address to the world, given on October 29, 1958, at Vatican Square.

46. See, for example, David J. O'Brien, *Public Catholicism* (Maryknoll, N.Y.: Orbis, 1996), 195–229; Carey, *Catholics in America*, 93–113; Mark Massa, *Catholics and American Culture: Fulton Sheen, Dorothy Day, and the Notre Dame Football Team* (New York: Crossroad, 1999), 49–56.

THE AMERICAN RECEPTION OF TEILHARD: 1955–1960

The U.S. reception of Teilhard's work was deeply impacted by this social context and cultural matrix, particularly the ferment that was the late 1950s. Perhaps the best way to explain this impact is to first place it within the context of one man's story.

Robert T. Francoeur was born in the early 1930s in Detroit, Michigan, and at the time of his introduction to Teilhard was a seminary student from the Diocese of Steubenville, Ohio, pursuing a master's degree in theology at St. Vincent's College in Latrobe, Pennsylvania. He was, as he later wrote, one who after eight years of Catholic elementary school was part of the "bulge" of young men who entered the seminary during the religious heyday of the 1950s.[47] His thesis advisor had just criticized his master's thesis on Lecomte du Noüy as far too subjective when Francoeur found a copy of *CrossCurrents,* probably purposely left sitting by an anonymous Benedictine monk, on the library table where he usually worked. In this publication was the aforementioned essay on Teilhard de Chardin's theory of evolution by Msgr. Bruno de Solages. This happened to be the first essay on Teilhard's work published in English (although translated from the French) in an American journal.[48] Francoeur not only recognized the kinship between Lecomte du Noüy and Teilhard, but, because of his background in biology and interest in both religion and evolution, he became quite entranced with the work of the latter.

With the encouragement of his mentor, Demetrius Dunn, OSB, Robert Francoeur wrote to de Solages in Toulouse, and a long-term correspondence ensued. Eventually this circle grew to include Claude Tresmontant, a lay philosopher-theologian living in Paris who had

47. Robert Francoeur, in an email to author, June 24, 2008. Francoeur (1931–2012) was born in Detroit, Michigan. He was for a time a priest in the Diocese of Steubenville, Ohio. He was laicized in the mid-1960s and thereafter married. After obtaining a Ph.D. in experimental embryology at the University of Delaware in 1967 and an A.C.S. in sexology at the Institute of the Advanced Study of Human Sexuality in 1979, he taught for many years at Fairleigh Dickinson University in New Jersey. He was the author of twenty-two books and the author of or contributor to over one hundred other publications.

48. De Solages, "Christianity and Evolution," 26–37.

recently written a book on Teilhard.[49] Just for his own knowledge, Francoeur translated Tresmontant's book into English.

As he was in the process of so doing, Francoeur also initiated a correspondence with the Jesuit priest Walter Ong, who had lived across the hall from Teilhard in Paris while Ong was doing research for his own dissertation.[50] A correspondence between the two dated November 19, 1957, and addressed to "Mr. Francoeur" talks about Francoeur's plans to translate Tresmontant's book. Ong suggests contacting Macmillan Publishing, since one of the editors at Macmillan was then interested in "building up their publications in the 'Catholic intellectual field.'" Absolutely no doubt exists in the minds of the two that Tresmontant's book deserves translation and immediate publication, as it was far better than others being put out and far more appropriate for an American audience.[51] Ong continues on to warn Francoeur, "There is also this factor: Père Teilhard's thought is particularly fecund once you have begun to share it. Like any thinking worthy of the name, it grows in being transmitted, so that it is often difficult if not impossible to separate one's own interpretation or maturing of something suggested by Père Teilhard from his own thought."[52]

Still, Ong writes, "I pray ... that this interest of yours continues and matures. Unless we can lay hold of contemporary knowledge

49. Claude Tresmontant, *Introduction a la pensée de Pierre Teilhard de Chardin* (Paris: Editions du Seuil, 1956).

50. Father Walter Jackson Ong, SJ (1912–2003), was a professor of English literature, an American cultural and religious historian, and a philosopher. He lived with Teilhard at Études, 15 rue Monsieur, Paris (VIIe) in 1950–51, while Teilhard was briefly in residence in Paris.

51. Walter Ong to Robert Francoeur, November 19, 1957, Robert Francoeur papers, Box 1, Folder 8, Lauinger Library Archives, Georgetown University (hereafter LLA).

52. Ibid. Ong also writes in this letter, "The relationship between Bergson's, Lecomte de Noüy's and Teilhard's thought will be something you will have to puzzle through. You are quite right, I believe, in your view that the three are operating with similar insights, made possible by our own place in time, which have to do with similar phenomena but that the influence of one on the other is not to be accepted until proved." Also, "The history of cosmological or evolutionary thought which you propose as the first part of your outline will prove to be a nightmare. I should suggest rather a correlation between Pere Teilhard and Father Mersch's work on the Mystical Body, or Monsignor Guardini as a more feasible project than the larger one you propose."

and thinking in a more positive and creative way than we have done, Christ's kingdom will suffer horribly once again from our own maladroitness and smugness. But you have filled out for yourself a very large order."

Following the receipt of this letter, Francoeur happened to see an advertisement for a forthcoming edition of the same book by another translator, put out by Helicon Press of Baltimore. He convinced the editor that the proposed book would lack a glossary and bibliography but needed one, and so was hired to supply these items as well as to review the translation. The resulting book, *Pierre Teilhard de Chardin: His Thought*, was published in 1959. It was the first English-language book on Teilhard in the United States.[53]

Demetrius Dunn and Walter Ong both also put Francoeur in touch with Madame Dorothy Poulain, an American woman married to a French journalist; she was then living in Paris. Dorothy Poulain was already very active in Les Amis de Teilhard in France and was eager for a similar organization to be formed in her home country. By late 1957, she was writing to Francoeur and encouraging him to do this, in order that he would be able to publish the results of the various conferences concerning Teilhard taking place around Europe.[54]

The correspondence between Francoeur and Poulain continued for almost the next ten years, through many changes in Francoeur's life. A letter from Poulain to Francoeur in September of 1959, however, is most telling and typical of those supporting the spread of Teilhard's thought during this period: "I am so happy to see the interest beginning to be shown in Teilhard's work and thought in the U.S. My little article in the *Commonweal* brought me letters from quite a number of people, avid to know more about Teilhard and so grateful to learn that such a thought was to be found in Catholic circles—something most of them had despaired of. The desire for such as he offers is so strong, and growing daily."[55]

53. Tresmontant, *Pierre Teilhard de Chardin: His Thought*, trans. Salvator Attanasio, preface by Gustave Weigel (Baltimore: Helicon, 1959).

54. Dorothy Poulain to Robert Francoeur, October 27, 1957, Robert Francoeur papers, Box 1, Folder 7, LLA.

55. Poulain to Francoeur, September 10, 1959, Robert Francoeur papers, Box 1, Folder 7, LLA.

The 1959 article in *Commonweal* to which Poulain refers concerned a conference held in 1958 on "La Pensée de Pierre Teilhard de Chardin" at the Chateau de Cerisy at the Abbaye de Pontigny. As Poulain notes, for the first time since 1955 a group of scientists, philosophers, and theologians met to discuss the thought of Teilhard; the group included people from the Ivory Coast, Algeria, Belgium, Germany, Italy, and Spain.[56] The intention of the dialogues that took place was to show how Teilhard's work responded "to the anguish of the modern world and to a humanism closed in on itself" such as that found in Marxism and existentialism. The fact was mentioned that Teilhard abandoned the scholastic vocabulary to make his work more accessible to the world of today; also noted was that it was in part this that disturbed his critics in the classical tradition.

Henri de Lubac, Teilhard's fellow Jesuit and friend, closed the conference with a seminar on *The Divine Milieu*. De Lubac commented that "with the universe expanding before eyes, it is more than time for Christians to pay some attention to the universality of Christ, and the hopes resulting from this. The primary question is—where are we heading?" Yet, as he further wrote, misinterpretation of Teilhard's work occurs not only because of concern over his treatment of evil and suffering, but because of "the fatal hostility of those who, unable to perceive what is the essential question at any given moment of the world's history, see no reason why the question should be posed."[57] Those who are unable to see the world as Teilhard does

56. Poulain, "Christ and the Universe," *Commonweal*, January 30, 1959, 460–64. Those attending this conference included Jacques Madaule, who wrote one of the first theses on Teilhard for the Institute Catholique; Paul Chauchard, neurophysiologist and assistant director of the École des Hautes Études, as well as author of *La Création Evolutive*; Père François Russo, commenting on Teilhard's unpublished texts; Mlle. Teilhard-Chambon, Père Teilhard's cousin, speaking on their childhood and family; Père Wildiers, a Franciscan from Antwerp and friend of Teilhard; and Père Henri de Lubac.

57. Henri de Lubac, in Poulain, "Christ and the Universe," 462. De Lubac commented further that Teilhard's work demands a frame of reference in terms of time vaster than previously ever considered. The primary difficulty is how to deal with Christ the human. "Here Teilhard finds the astonishing and liberating harmony between a religion of the Christic-type and an Evolution that is convergent. Were the world a static-cosmos, relations of a conceptual or juridical order could be invoked to establish the primacy of Christ over Creation—because He has been so declared." But, he continues, as Teilhard discovers, that is simply not the case. This is an early

see no reason to ask the questions he does. What is especially important to note in this comment is de Lubac's reference not only to "seeing," a common Teilhardian theme, but to hope, and especially to hope within the context of Christ's universality. These latter two points will occur frequently throughout this work and prove quite significant in regard to Teilhard's later reception.

One of the first to "see" what Teilhard was about was the scientist Julian Huxley. As noted earlier, Huxley wrote the introduction to the 1959 edition of Teilhard's *The Phenomenon of Man*. At the November 1959 Centennial Darwin Conference in Chicago, Huxley predicted a new, evolutionary kind of religion that appeared to have its foundation in Teilhard's thought. This new religion would be synthetic in nature, narrowing the divide between the sacred and the secular, the material world and the spiritual. One of the first *Time* magazine articles published about Teilhard in December of that year noted that an American foundation was being formed for the study of his works and their translation into other languages.[58] Scientists, it states, for the most part welcome Teilhard's daring attempts at synthesis—though few go as far as Omega. Some Catholic theologians, on the other hand, were having difficulty with many of his theses.

Indeed, the *Time* article notes that in the previous spring of 1959, the Pontifical Roman Theological Academy devoted an entire issue of its quarterly *Divinitas* to deliberations on Teilhard de Chardin's ideas, calling them "a maximum of seduction coinciding with a max-

---

mention by de Lubac of Teilhard's Christology that, as has already been discussed, will within another decade be a decisive factor in the reception of his work.

58. "Religion: Toward Omega," *Time*, December 14, 1959, accessed June 22, 2011, from http://www.time.com/time/magazine/article/0,9171,894362,00.html#ixzz1QKk1rHWJ. The complete notation in the article from Huxley's introduction to *The Phenomenon* is: "A very remarkable work by a very remarkable human being." Also, "His influence on the world's thinking is bound to be important.... He has forced theologians to view their ideas in the new perspective of evolution, and scientists to see the spiritual implications of their knowledge.... The religiously minded can no longer turn their backs upon the natural world ... nor can the materialistically minded deny importance to spiritual experience and religious feeling." The article states that many Catholic theologians take a dim view of what they believe to be Teilhard's neglect of the Creator aspect of God, his virtual omission of any idea of original sin and Christ's redeeming sacrifice, and his sidestepping of the doctrine of monogenism, which states that all mankind descended from a single couple.

imum of aberration."[59] But, said the Latin foreword to the issue, "We will not apply the mark of heresy, which he perhaps does not deserve subjectively because of his good faith."

Huxley's comments and the resulting *Time* article are the first in a large collection of articles that suggest that much of U.S. society, at least, was eager to hear the thought of a scientific visionary. In particular, they awaited a visionary who looked at the world through spiritual eyes, eyes that considered it possible to bridge the gap between God and material existence.

Another article along these lines was one also published in *Jubilee* magazine in December 1959 by Wilfrid Sheed. Titled, "The Christian Phenomenon: Père Teilhard's View of Evolution," it questioned what he termed the current "panic over evolution."[60] The subtitle was "A Jesuit paleontologist presents a unique statement about man's place on the evolutionary scale."

Sheed's article asks what has happened in the years since *Humani generis,* which as a "high water mark ... discusses evolution as a so far unverified hypothesis calling neither for glib condemnation nor too great a trust." Will Catholics now only accept evolution "with bad grace?"[61] Sheed notes that in *Humani generis* Pope Pius XII was also sounding a challenge, asking Catholics to take this hypothesis into "fullest consideration" without arrogance or fear. Yet, so far, the only one who has attempted to meet the challenge to do so is Teilhard de Chardin. He created of himself an "exposed outpost in the no man's land between the conventional boundaries of science and religion." In so doing, Teilhard has come under fire as much "from scientific rigorists as from religious ones."[62] Sheed asserts that it is the overall vision of *The Phenomenon* that is most important, in large part because it "plays throughout on the reader's capacity to wonder." He argues that *The Phenomenon* is not recommended for readers "who are incorrigibly uneasy in the world of speculation. Evolution is a hy-

59. "Toward Omega," *Time,* 62.

60. Wilfrid Sheed, "Pere Teilhard's View of Evolution," *Jubilee* 7, no. 8 (1959): 42–49.

61. Ibid., 42.

62. Ibid., 48.

pothesis: Teilhard answers it with another, richer one. His opinions are not definitive."[63] In an ever-expanding age of science and technology, he notes, many question the direction of the future as well as the truth about the past. Perhaps Teilhard's work provides an answer.

Additionally, Sheed observes another important point; the book was published at a most opportune moment as talk in the church grew about a true revival of Catholic intellectualism. If Catholics were serious about this, then reaction to *The Phenomenon* would indicate as much. As Sheed remarks, "It will also indicate whether we have mastered our squeamishness about science, religion and evolution."[64]

About this same time, Harper and Row was attempting to publish the first English translation of *Le Milieu Divin*. A January 18, 1960, letter to Robert Francoeur makes it clear that this was not an easy task.[65] The hope at that time was that the book should appear in the autumn of 1960, to be followed soon after by *Lettres de Voyage* and *Le Group Zoologie*, with nine months to a year separating each. This plan was subject to approval from Madame Mortier and the French committee of Les Amis de Teilhard de Chardin.

Hugh Van Dusen also mentions that the American edition of *The Phenomenon* was in its third printing of five thousand copies, at this point, and selling more each day. He remarks on how unusual this

63. Ibid., 49. Sheed also writes in this paragraph that it is incidentally a compliment to love and a tribute to Teilhard's poetic force that he can make exciting such an apparently arid definition as this—"love is the highest form of radial energy." "For those comfortable with speculation, and/or troubled by the evidence of evolution, Teilhard offers not only an interesting hypothesis but a point of vantage from which God and evolution can be seen in the same picture ... he had put together that rarest of compounds, a synthesis of scientific knowledge and religious experience which outrages neither and which is completely free of quackery." This is yet another statement concerning the synthesis that was Teilhard's thought and the understanding of many that the gap between religion and science must be breached.

64. Ibid., 49.

65. Hugh Van Dusen to Francoeur, January 18, 1960, Robert Francoeur papers, Box 1, Folder 6, LLA. The original English title was to be *The Realm of the Divine*. The title was of course later changed. This translation was not, however, approved by Jeanne Mortier and the Paris Committee, and the lack of approval was delaying publication. Van Dusen also notes in this letter that the Marlboro book club named *The Phenomenon* Book of the Month.

is for this kind of book; at the same time, however, "it is not easy to classify, so perhaps that is part of the appeal."

Another letter from Van Dusen in April 1960 assures Francoeur that the English translation of *Le Milieu Divin* is now complete and approved, and Harper and Row hopes to publish it that October.[66] He asks for advice from Francoeur as to "the importance of this book in relation to other works of Father Teilhard." Some, he comments, who are familiar with the French edition, believe it "the spiritual counterpart to *THE PHENOMENON OF MAN*, others deny this and find it more important." He asks Francoeur as to how the book should be presented, as they find it beyond their competency to judge. Van Dusen also comments that *The Phenomenon* has just gone into a fifth printing and that something over 16,000 copies had already been sold. The interest in the book has remained steady.

This is clarified by a press release two days later from Van Dusen at "Harper & Brothers" to the "Friends of Father Teilhard." It states that *The Phenomenon* is in its fifth printing, for a total number of copies of 25,000 with about 17,000 sold.[67] In less than six months, sales figures had increased tenfold from some 500 copies to over 5,000 sold per month. His letter adds that "the way in which the book does better with each succeeding month is most heartening to all of us, and quite the reverse of the usual pattern with a new book, especially of this type. The sales numbers are really quite amazing."

The press release also remarks that *THE REALM OF THE DIVINE* is definitely to be published in October. The translation of this is by Alexander Dru and is approved by the French committee. The hopes are that it will do even better than the *PHENOMENON*. Additionally, a biography of Teilhard by Claude Cuenot is to be published by Helicon Press, Baltimore, in the fall of 1960. An English translation of Nicolas Corté's *Teilhard de Chardin: His Life and Spirit* is announced in Britain for spring publication. No American edition is planned yet. An English translation of Oliver Rabut's *Dialogue with Teilhard* will be published by Sheed and Ward, perhaps also in the fall of 1960.

66. Van Dusen to Francoeur, April 5, 1960, Robert Francoeur Collection, Box 1, Folder 6, LLA. The capitalization of the book title is Van Dusen's own.

67. Ibid.

Finally, the Tresmontant book by Helicon Press will be published in Britain with a new translation. These further publications are mentioned here so that note is taken of what must have been increasing demand for further secondary source publications on Teilhard and his thought.

Later that fall, Francoeur received yet another letter from Van Dusen, apparently in response to some earlier, ongoing correspondence regarding Harper and Brothers' further publications.[68] Van Dusen wrote that "I'm delighted that you found the translation of *The Divine Milieu* smooth reading. Unfortunately, quite serious criticism has come from other sources but, as you know, Teilhard is unusually difficult to anglicize."

It was apparently the news of the publication of these other works as well as his correspondence with many in the "Teilhardian circle" that encouraged Francoeur in his own writing and editing efforts. In early to mid-1960 he began to contact several others regarding what would become *The World of Teilhard*, a collection of essays edited by himself.[69]

What is perhaps most interesting in this initial collection, however, is that Francoeur, as well as John LaFarge, who wrote the preface for the book, explicitly note the organic nature of Teilhard's work and the desire to replicate that in this initial American book of essays. Therefore, the hope is that each essay, coming from across various disciplines, should approach its own discipline in the manner of Teilhard's unique methodology.[70] As Francoeur remarks, "This is

68. Van Dusen to "Bob" Francoeur, November 7, 1960, Robert Francoeur papers, Box 1, Folder 6, LLA.

69. Francoeur, ed., *The World of Teilhard* (Baltimore: Helicon, 1961); hereafter *World*. The book includes a preface by John LaFarge. The letter just previously mentioned, from Hugh Van Dusen to Francoeur (November 7, 1960) comments on this editorial effort of Francoeur with a note in regard to publishing anything Teilhardian: "I am afraid you will find the French committee a very difficult nut to crack, but the way may be eased for you if you assure them that you have the cooperation of such men as Father Ewing and perhaps Father Ong. They recognize Father Ong as a Teilhard specialist but I don't believe they are as familiar with Father Ewing's work as they ought to be." This comment is today rather ironic, in light of the later, far more numerous works of J. Franklin Ewing than Ong on Teilhard and Ewing's various involvements in his cause.

70. "Granted that specialization is unavoidable, we must avoid the prime danger

so because it is not what we should ordinarily call 'science' and yet it does not fall into the category of metaphysics or theology. Sometimes poetic to an extreme, it is more than mere fantasy and different from mystical ecstasy." Francoeur remarks that Teilhard calls it a "phenomenology," yet actually, none of the commonly known categories of human knowledge fits this work. It is, perhaps, closest to the thought of the ancient Greeks, in which the divisions between the "various branches of knowledge" are not so definite as we might make them today, but far more organic and unified. Classifying Teilhard's thought in airtight boxes is not possible, "for his synthesis is not a 'system' nor a closed syllogistic discipline of one branch of knowledge." It is instead "fecund, open, free, and all-inclusive." Yet, at the same time, it is a synthesis that moves quite purposefully in a particular direction. With those thoughts in mind, Francoeur concludes, readers who attempt to approach Teilhardian thought from other than this direction, those who have no desire or who refuse to "see" in this way, will most likely be sorely disappointed and confused.

The essays included in this book, therefore, are interpretations that attempt to portray and develop the thought of Teilhard "while always remaining faithful to his spirit." Perhaps, Francoeur admits, time will show that some of these reflections are not really in keeping with Teilhard's mind; with so little of his writings yet published, this is inevitable. But, if the essays encourage and awaken minds to the expanding dimensions of time, if they bring hope and optimism and enable more to see the possibility of a bridge connecting diverse disciplines, then the work has served its purpose. To this end, the book contains fifteen essays from several of Teilhard's closest friends, intellectual compatriots, and U.S. intellectuals, each of which attempts,

---

that threatens any specialist: the loss of balance and perspective, and the inability to assimilate and co-ordinate the findings of other fields"; *World,* 186. Concerning the preface written by John LaFarge, SJ, in a letter dated September 23, 1960, from "Edgar" [Bruns] to "Bob" Francoeur, Bruns writes, "Did you give any thought to my suggestion regarding Fr. LaFarge? Upon re-reading Teilhard's correspondence I noted that they had indeed known one another and Teilhard refers to LaFarge as his 'protector,' as well as one of his closest friends here in N.Y."; J. Edgar Bruns to Robert Francoeur, 9/23/1960, Robert Francoeur Collection, Box 1, Folder 4, LLA. The Jesuit John LaFarge was a long-time editor and writer for *America* magazine. He died in 1963, just a few months after participating in the Civil Rights March in Washington, D.C.

from the author's own standpoint, to build bridges between the disciplines of theology, science, philosophy, and the social sciences.[71]

An example of such bridge building is the essay by J. Edgar Bruns titled, "Theology and the 'Ultraphysics.'" In an early letter to "Father Francoeur" detailing a draft outline of this essay, Bruns makes note of Teilhard's synthesis of basic Christian doctrines and the similarity of his theology, including his "Omega Point," to that of the Greek fathers, especially Gregory of Nyssa, and their conceptions of the *parousia* and evolution.[72] Bruns ends his letter by reemphasizing the necessity of Teilhard's thought in redirecting Catholic theology in the contemporary world. This early essay of Bruns therefore, was one of the first to point to Teilhard's Christology as foundational in understanding his evolutionary worldview.

Walter Ong contributed the opening endorsement for the frontispiece of Francoeur's *The World,* and it speaks volumes concerning how Teilhard's work was already perceived, particularly in the United States: "Father Teilhard's thought has for a large and growing number of individuals been the most fecundating they have ever encountered within our present world. His thought is mankind's: persons on the most diverse fronts of activity find it giving life to their own intellectual and spiritual endeavors. The present collection bears direct witness to what his thinking has meant to a wide range of intellectual leaders. It is more than a critique of Father Teilhard's thinking: it is its continuation."[73]

This edited collection, therefore, is of significance as it was the first attempt in the Catholic United States to use Teilhard's own or-

71. These include George B. Barbour, the geologist who worked extensively with Teilhard in China (and wrote his own book *In the Field with Teilhard de Chardin* [New York: Herder and Herder, 1965] a few years later about exactly this), the aforementioned priest/writer John LaFarge, SJ, the ecclesiologist Gustave Weigel, and the French cultural studies expert Arthur Knodel. Others included are the theologian J. Edgar Bruns, philosophers John V. Walsh and James Reilly Jr., and numerous American scientists including psychiatrists, chemists, biologists, and medical doctors.

72. J. Edgar Bruns to "Father Francoeur," June 15, 1960, Robert Francoeur collection, Box 1, Folder 4, LLA. The letter was addressed to Francoeur at Saints Cyril and Methodius Church, Deer Park, N.Y.

73. Walter Ong to "Father Francoeur," August 23, 1961, Robert Francoeur collection, Box 1, Folder 8, LLA.

ganic conception of knowledge to create a unique, forward-thinking, teleological and paradigmatic vision of culture and church for a rapidly changing population. The next eight years would see this vision expand yet more, and Teilhard's work would be in the thick of it all.

FINAL THOUGHTS

The early and unexpected sales figures for *The Phenomenon* point to its tremendous popularity, first in Europe, then after 1959 in the United States. As we shall see, that trajectory will continue with the remainder of the primary and secondary sources about Teilhard. Additionally, a look at the political and social history of the era shows us that after the end of the Cold War–era in the 1950s, the political, religious, and social consensus of the United States will continue to crack due to a number of factors. Inklings of the change that would dominate the 1960s were already in the air; almost tangibly, the question already was, "Where are we headed?" Included were numerous concerns over the trajectory of science, particularly in light of the nuclear bomb and the space race. Also, Pope John XXIII's actions were already not just shaking the unchanging Catholic Church but drawing the attention of the entire world. The paradigm was shifting, but in what direction? How?

Teilhard's optimistic teleology held an answer many willingly embraced. We are indeed moving in a positive direction, it stated; we are progressing, evolution is occurring, and all this is good.

Still, the need existed to integrate and synthesize these changes into the American and Catholic worldview. How does one incorporate the new sciences, particularly evolutionary science? Is it possible to create a synthetic fabric of knowledge from the new data that expands on a daily basis? In answering these questions Teilhard's integrated, organic view of the world served as an exemplar for many.

In addition, as U.S. society became increasingly middle class and prosperous, increasingly secular and materialist, as the immigrant Catholic "ghettoes" dissolved into suburbia, questions over how to live a spiritual life abounded. The American public would increasingly attempt to determine how the spiritual could inform the secular and the material world the sacred. At a time when the emphasis was still on the nuclear family, the means by which an ordinary suburban family life could "find God" without leaving their comfortable life needed to be determined. In response to these issues, Teilhard the mystical scientist who "loved the world" exemplified a contemplative form of life that saw God in all aspects of the everyday. Even in these early years, his spiritual thought attracted many who understood that "we are spiritual beings living an earthly existence." With this in mind, it does not seem unfeasible to argue that his work was received as it was during these years primarily as a result of its fortuitous appearance at this particular conjecture of time and place.

The first essays published about Teilhard in U.S. journals point to several themes that continually reappear in discussions of his work even down to this day. The first might be the inability to adequately classify Teilhard's thought. It does not neatly fit into any one category, whether philosophy, theology, or science. Those who insist that it must meet the expected standards of one or the other and are unwilling to embrace its boundary-transcending aspects tend to be among Teilhard's strongest adversaries.

In regard to Teilhard's theses concerning evolution and spirituality, as Sheed wrote in his essay in *Jubilee*, those who do not deal well with speculation and hypothesis will be uneasy with what Teilhard is attempting. There is very little of the clearly defined, black-and-white, or walking the expected party line in Teilhard. Those who are not comfortable with shades of gray will struggle.

Finally, the inability to classify Teilhard's work will cause his thought not only to be misinterpreted but misrepresented in the future. One might say that his work itself is an evolutionary step beyond modernity, yet not necessarily in the direction of postmodernity, for its synthetic, tradition-rooted nature belies that trajectory. Although it is a sublime vision of the future, it was formed amidst the ancient volcanoes of France's Massif Central of his homeland in Auvergne, in a childhood devotion to the Sacred Heart and the Eucharist, the practice of the *Spiritual Exercises*, and in the Jesuit tradition of loyalty to church and pope. Its mystical Christological nature transcends scientific modernity and, as with all aspects of the mystical life, is not easily captured in word or picture. This is a crucial reason for Teilhard's continual use of syllogism and diagram.

It is perhaps most of all this inability to wrap one's hands around an easy, prosaic summation of Teilhard's work that both fascinates and exasperates those who read it and that repeatedly attracts those willing to encounter it with an open mind. Certainly, as chapter 2 will show, this was the source of fascination and exasperation for those, like Robert Francoeur, who appointed themselves guardians of its heritage and who tried to ensure that its own evolution and unfolding were true to Teilhard's thought.

THE EARLY YEARS

1961–1964

2 ~ CORRESPONDENCE AND CONTROVERSY

DURING THESE EARLY YEARS of the 1960s, Teilhard de Chardin's thought spread further throughout the United States, spurred onward by a rising American Catholic optimism fueled by both global and national events as well as a new generation of young Catholics. This chapter will discuss in detail several of the first publications in the United States that further disseminated Teilhard de Chardin's work as found in the popular, ecclesial, and scholarly press, including the early editions of Teilhard's own manuscripts. In addition, a further look will be given to the early controversy over Teilhard's work and how publication of various books and book reviews, including Francoeur's, were delayed by concerns; in a similar fashion, so too was formation of a formal Teilhard organization. This chapter will address the struggle to create the first of the United States Teilhard Associations at Fordham with Francoeur and several of his collaborators.

One primary focus of the church at this time was the Ecumenical Council called by Pope John XXIII. This chapter and the next will consider how the time leading up to the Second Vatican Council and its outcome were interpreted by scholars and Catholics in the United States, particularly in regard to Teilhard's influence upon it. Some of those who were hoping for definitive change in the church as a result of the Council would be among those most interested in Teilhard's thought. Many hoped that the Council would bring a new manner of the church's presence in the world, something more than "the dead inertia of merely conventional Christianity" against which Teilhard and others protested.[1]

EARLY TEILHARDIAN INTEREST

What follows is a sampling of some of the earliest and most important commentaries on *The Divine Milieu* and *The Phenomenon* that reiterate several common themes regarding these works and their early reception in the United States. Reviewers regarded Teilhard's writing as poetic or mystical, scientific or philosophical in nature, depending upon their own proclivities or worldview. Transcending how they interpreted this work, almost universally they recognized its revolutionary synthetic quality, for here was a scientist who wrote from and about a cosmology that although obviously not premodern in nature, managed to integrate the material world with the spiritual within a context amenable to contemporary society.

Additionally, that Teilhard specifically wrote to those who "love the world" gave him greater access to and agency with those skeptical about Christianity and the spiritual life. His work and his life exemplified how it might be possible to find rapprochement between a deeply lived Christianity and life in the contemporary world.

As an example, one of the best-known Catholic authors of the mid-twentieth century, Thomas Merton, wrote a review of Teilhard's *Divine Milieu* in the fall of 1960. When the review was completed, Merton as usual sent it on for perusal to the monastery censors, who, given the controversy surrounding Teilhard, passed it on to the abbot general. In response the abbot demanded that Merton read a critical attack on Teilhard, one penned, in Merton's words, "by a rather second rate theologian."[2] Merton would neither read the other book nor alter his own review, and as a result, Merton's work was published only posthumously in 1979.[3] In light of this,

1. Thomas Merton, "Teilhard's Gamble," in *Love and Living*, ed. Naomi Burton Stone and Patrick Hart (New York: Farrar, Straus and Giroux, 1979), 185.

2. Merton, *The Road to Joy: Letters to New and Old Friends*, ed. Robert E. Daggy (New York: Farrar, Straus and Giroux, 1989), 237.

3. Additionally, Merton later wrote a review of Henri de Lubac's *The Religion of*

quite appropriately, the author's note later added at the beginning of his book review states, "The following is an attempt at a positive and sympathetic appreciation of a much discussed writer who is certainly not without confusions and limitations. This particular essay is concerned with the spiritual implications of his scientific-religious mystique."[4]

Even though it was published later than the years this chapter will discuss, this review is highly significant to a historiography of Teilhard at the beginning of the 1960s. That Merton, living in a monastery hermitage hidden deep in the American Midwest, had Teilhard's *Divine Milieu* suggested to him as a "good read," and that he was so taken with the author and the book's content to write a positive review, was one thing. That Merton's publication was delayed speaks to the ongoing controversy at the time regarding all things Teilhard. Finally, in his essay Merton proficiently delineates and explores not only Teilhard's primary theological themes, but also the attraction that so many people in the United States were experiencing for his work at this time.

Merton notes in his essay that Teilhard was probably the first Catholic who successfully integrated a modern scientific worldview into an "authentically Christian" and mystical form of life. From his viewpoint Teilhard was "too profound a thinker" to concern himself with any superficial reconciliation of science and religion.[5] Instead, Merton expounded, if a conflict between the two had ever existed in Teilhard's own mind, it had been resolved in a "higher contemplative vision" that far superseded any other "absurd compromises."

In his essay, Merton reviews Teilhard's *Divine Milieu,* which he sees as far less controversial than *The Phenomenon.* He does admit though that it is still "independent in its thought" and so might "trouble minds" who fear any vestige of originality and see such a thing as "somehow dangerous." "But I do not think any responsi-

---

Teilhard de Chardin, a review that was first copyrighted in 1967 and then included as "Teilhard's Gamble" in *Love and Living,* 185–91. This essay will be further explored later in this chapter.

4. Merton, "The Universe as Epiphany," in *Love and Living,* 171.

5. Ibid., 171.

ble theologian who takes the trouble to interpret the author's true meaning will find in it anything he can possibly condemn."[6]

Within the very first section of his essay on Teilhard's *Divine Milieu* Merton notes that Teilhard begins his book by confronting the accusation that Christianity is an "entirely negative religion which seems to prescribe a complete alienation from life, from human values and from the world."[7] In that worldview, the Christian is to live a life of passivity and indifference, dismissing challenges and blindly submitting to the will of God. God, therefore, exerts nothing more than an inexorable, "authoritarian pressure." For this sort of Christian all material things are dangerous, temptations that might lead one away from union with God. However, Merton notes that Teilhard agrees that this belief system is not actually Christian at all; it is a disembodied Christianity that belies the Incarnation, the central dogma underlying it. For Teilhard, humanity exists for Christ, but at the same time, materiality exists for humanity in Christ. Rather than being an obstacle, material reality "is indispensable for our service and knowledge of Christ."[8] The material world is redeemed by using it for Christ's service, and similarly, by our actions we can assist in realizing a universe where all things are recapitulated in Christ. Humanity's vocation, therefore, is not to escape the world, it is instead to be "in the world" but not "of the world" by "being Christ" in the world and offering the whole world—including one's own work of whatever sort that is and whoever one might be—to the Father. Even though Teilhard's thought is supremely Christocentric, in a country built on the myth of hard work and love of the material, these themes are tantalizing beacons indeed.

In an era of immense scientific, social, and intellectual creativity, Merton continues, many in the United States could also resonate to Teilhard's declaration that we are to share the aspirations, "in essence religious," of those people who strongly feel the beauty and potential of the world and the "sacred value of every new truth." This we do not for the sake of progress itself, but because these living

6. Ibid., 172.

7. Merton, "Christian Humanism," in *Love and Living*, 137.

8. Merton, "Universe as Epiphany," 176.

developments are clues to God's will for our future direction. They manifest, each in their own way, an expectation of the Parousia. Not to act in this manner is to exhibit infidelity and distrust in God.[9]

These insights of Merton's offer many clues as to why Americans of this era were so taken with Teilhard's work. That interest is exemplified by what was happening in New York City. At the very beginning in the early 1960s, the locus of Teilhardian studies in the United States was at Fordham University in New York. These focused studies started slowly at first, as Dr. Louis Marks in Biology and Joseph Donceel, SJ, in Philosophy introduced Teilhardian thought in their classes. J. Franklin Ewing, SJ, a former associate of Teilhard, began a "Teilhard Circle," the objective of which was to encourage critique of his work through an anthropological lens. Ewert Cousins, another contributor to Francoeur's book, went to Fordham in 1960 to teach in the Classics Department and discovered an already active interest there.[10] Francoeur himself, in part as a result of his Teilhard ties, did graduate studies in biology at Fordham from the summer of 1962 through 1964, after first teaching biology in Baltimore.

Even before Francoeur's *The World of Teilhard de Chardin* was published, a sign of the growing Teilhardian interest was a television program on Teilhard's thought sponsored by the Knights of Columbus in Baltimore in early spring, 1960. Teilhard had already gone multimedia! Gustave Weigel, SJ, J. Franklin Ewing, SJ, Dr. John Walsh, and Robert Francoeur all took part, and Walter Burghardt, SJ, acted as commentator. The transcript of the show "Evolution, Science and Religion" was later published in *Jubilee* magazine.[11] Burghardt posed three questions to his panelists: (1) What is the present state of scientific knowledge regarding evolution? (2) What has Teilhard added to that knowledge? (3) Is Teilhard simply a scientist in a restricted sense of the word, or is he more? How did he link his science to the other elements of his thoughts?

9. Ibid., 183.

10. *ATA*, 3.

11. "Evolution, Science and Religion," *Jubilee*, May, 1960, 48–51. Thomas Merton, Edward Rice, and Robert Lax were the original editors of *Jubilee*, which was the first monthly pictorial magazine for a Catholic audience in the United States, published initially in 1953.

In response to question 2, Francoeur in particular commented that Teilhard was a combination of both the old and the new; Francoeur noted that even Paul of Tarsus spoke about the world as being directed toward some supernatural goal. Teilhard has the same Christological viewpoint as Paul, Francoeur argued, but he also incorporates contemporary scientific knowledge. Walsh responded to question 3 by stating that Teilhard's greatest achievement was his synthetic ability, "gathering together several lines of convergence—scientific, social, historic, and also religious—and seeing them in a common vision, perhaps for the first time on this scale by a Christian thinker who was also a very great scientist."[12] It is his vision therefore, that sets Teilhard apart.

Francoeur added that Teilhard had gone so close to philosophy and theology at times in his writing that you "have to watch your step in reading the book!"[13] For Francoeur what was of major significance in Teilhard's efforts was the discovery of a direction and goal for evolution: the world evolves not just by chance, but in a purposeful manner that involves Point Omega, Christ. For Ewing, it was Teilhard's genius that he could take scientific thoughts and reconsider them in terms of humanity and God and "inspire them with poetic enthusiasm." Teilhard gives people hope that "one can be a modern man, one can be an evolutionist, and one can be a Christian."[14]

This discussion shows that by early in 1960, a few people were aware of and were attempting to disseminate the Christ-centered focus of Teilhard's thought. Unfortunately, as the popularity of his work grew, those who could understand the Christology located within the evolutionary science and so contextualize Teilhard's spirituality accordingly would prove to be limited in number.

This television show was at least in part commissioned and viewed by many as a result not only of articles found earlier in the secular *Time,* but also because of essays found in journals such as *Catholic World, Commonweal, America,* and the more academic *Theological Digest*

12. Ibid., 49.

13. Ibid., 50.

14. Ibid., 51. In regard to his comments about hope, Ewing specifically mentions the people of France.

and *New Scholasticism,* which were at the forefront of the deluge that would become Teilhard.

In the first months of 1960, J. Edgar Bruns, who also contributed to Francoeur's later volume, wrote an article on Teilhard for *Catholic World.*[15] One highlighted point was that "Teilhard de Chardin claimed that the only God we can worship 'in spirit and truth' is a synthesis of the Christian 'God up above' and the Marxist 'God up ahead.'" Additionally, Bruns asked, "Can the new evolutionism of Chardin win back the dechristianized intellectuals of the space age by liberating theology from the old cosmology?"[16]

The author noted the hostile trepidation in the Catholic world concerning Darwin, as well as Copernicus and Galileo. Yet, he commented, the church, even as it was faced with challenges to traditional concepts and insisted on a doctrine of special creation, had to admit that the idea of evolution was not new at all. Gregory of Nyssa, after all, had noted that "all things were virtually in the first Divine impulse for creation, existing as it were in a kind of spermatic potency sent forth for the genesis of all things."[17] But this line of thought, which built upon the Apostle Paul's own writing, did not gain ascendancy in the ancient church. Teilhard, Bruns pointed out, used these ancient texts, particularly 1 Corinthians 15:28 and Colossians 1:15–20. Unfortunately, he noted, when the theory was reintroduced in the nineteenth century, it was complicated by the work of the materialists, who desired to discredit God and the Spirit. "It is perhaps only a man entitled to include Pascal and Voltaire among his ancestors," he wrote, "who could reconcile in himself so many disparate vocations and who could conceive of a synthesis of materialism and religion that is impressive enough to be labeled 'seductive' by its opponents."[18]

Bruns conveyed three concepts in this article that he considered vital to understanding Teilhard (and that he feared many would miss): (1) Teilhard's understanding of the essential unity of all life;

15. J. Edgar Bruns, "God Up Above, or Up Ahead?" *Catholic World,* April 1960, 23–30.

16. Ibid., 23.

17. Ibid.

18. Bruns, "God Up Above, or Up Ahead?," 24.

(2) the continual evolution of the universe; and (3) the convergent direction that this evolution has been and is taking. He also added that Teilhard's phenomenology can be reduced to one word "Spiritualization. 'Spirit' is the 'stuff of the universe.'"[19]

In April of 1960 one of Teilhard's dearest friends, the Jesuit priest François Russo, wrote a review of *The Phenomenon* in *America* magazine.[20] He mentions in his article that *The Phenomenon* was one work Teilhard really wanted published, as it brought together the essential, guiding ideas of his worldview; these first dated from 1916, but Teilhard continued to refine them throughout his life. Russo gives a brief overview of Teilhard's primary principles, then stresses how it is impossible to overemphasize how important is this effort at synthesis, as it is certainly necessary to bring together scientific data, but also to permit the integration of man into cosmology. Teilhard's is not a mere intellectual game, but "is also poetry, which in this case is a genuine method of the phenomenological study of reality. His thoughts might be daring, but are rooted in fact and reality." One can compare Teilhard's work to Descartes or Leibnitz, as he is "haunted by the desire to grasp reality in a truly profound new way," as were they.[21]

Indeed, Teilhard's idea of transformation is a major contribution to thinking about cosmology, and opens "great windows to faith" for people of a new age. And it must be pointed out, Russo insists, that in contrast to the Marxists, Teilhard is adamant that science "cannot find its fulfillment except in a spiritual dimension."[22]

Finally, in *Commonweal* early that same year, John Whitney Evans also wrote on Teilhard's efforts.[23] Yes, he agrees, Teilhard was pious,

19. Ibid.

20. François Russo, SJ, "The Phenomenon of Man," *America*, April 30, 1960, 185–89. Russo was a much younger friend and correspondent of Teilhard's during his New York years, and was also the editor of the French Jesuit review *Les Études*.

21. Ibid., 187. Russo notes that Teilhard relies mightily upon the scientific method, but not in the same way as it is used in scientific treatises. In this work, one cannot neatly distinguish between the scientific and the philosophical, as it is an attempt to understand life itself, which is in itself both scientific and philosophical. He most definitely does not rule out the transcendence of God.

22. Russo, "The Phenomenon of Man," 189.

23. John Whitney Evans, "Dilemmas and Limitations," *Commonweal*, 1960, 439–41. Father John Whitney Evans was a priest, historian, and long-time professor at Duluth College and St. Scholastica in Minnesota.

loyal, courageous, patient, and brave, as well as a great scientist with an extraordinary power of insight and a gift for expression. Still, Evans argues that questions can be asked about the value of his work. Teilhard wrote on the level of phenomenology, with its restricting view of reality as to what could be involved in a system of space and time. If one wants to write of "the whole phenomenon of man," is this not an impossible task, Evans questions. That task would involve earth, humanity, thought, God, destiny—the sum total of which goes far beyond the merely phenomenological. So instead, Teilhard "hedged at his own stated limits and has offered more than a mere inspection of reality."[24]

As a result, Evans concludes that Teilhard is employing poetic expression, and should not be discussed too logically. One must realize: "His thought is impelled by a greater force than that which arises simply from "the logic and coherence of facts."[25] Still, Teilhard is more than simply a naturalist arriving at conclusions that could be described as "transparently Christian."

One important conclusion expounded by Evans in this review is that "man is greater than any science alone."[26] To understand mankind, it is necessary to unify all given truths and to work toward synthesis. What results, Evans concludes, is the observation of Michael Polanyi, who wrote about the *Phenomenon* as "a text that is so ambiguous that people whose views on its subject matter are diametrically opposed can read it with equal enthusiasm cannot be wholly satisfying."[27]

Robert Francoeur responded to Evan's review in the same volume of *Commonweal.*[28] *The Phenomenon,* counters Francoeur, gives only an incomplete picture of Teilhard. The complexity and depth of his work ensure that it will take quite some time for the world to

24. Ibid., 439.

25. Ibid., 440.

26. Evans, "Dilemmas and Limitations," 441.

27. Ibid.

28. Robert Francoeur, "A Call to Greatness," *Commonweal,* 1960, 441–43. Francoeur begins with a contextualization of Teilhard with the biologist Jean Baptiste Lamarck, who published *Zoological Philosophy,* "the first 'complete' scientific study of evolution" in 1809. He also mentions the influence of Darwin and Henri Bergson's *Creative Evolution.*

understand his real vision. For Francoeur, the word "vision" is quite descriptive of his thought, for Teilhard was:

> one of those rare men who combined the attitude of the scientist with the visionary qualities of a mystic and the warmth of a great humanness....
>
> To study man and his place in the evolving universe and then to synthesize the findings of modern science with the light of supernatural revelation is the whole purpose of Teilhard's vision. To see man in his true place in our evolving world is the aim of *The Phenomenon of Man.*[29]

According to Francoeur, the basis of Teilhard's vision is the hypothesis now at the foundation of all modern scientific advancement: the general theory of evolution. Materialists have forced a one-sided theory of evolution that fails to synthesize the spiritual with the material and ignores the direction behind the random processes of Darwinian natural selection. By contrast, Teilhard tries to view the work of creation as a whole; he sought a perspective unifying all of the world's phenomena.[30]

Such a synthesis of knowledge must be incomplete, Francoeur insists, and must be the work of many scholars. Teilhard admitted his thought is tentative. Critics maintain his work is neither science nor phenomenology. Where is the theology, others ask? Where is the Scholastic terminology, with a worldview and a vocabulary they can understand? But we must remember, Francoeur notes, that Teilhard was writing as much (or more) for atheists and agnostics as for those well within the church.

Francoeur comments that what is especially significant is that Teilhard is the first since Aquinas to attempt a synthesis of human knowledge on such a scale. In that synthesis of scientific with spiritual, he sought the basis of the unity of the living universe. His discoveries explicated the ultra-sacramental nature of that same universe

29. Francoeur, "Call to Greatness," 441.

30. In so doing Teilhard found a law of recurrence—the law of complexity-consciousness. "With the birth of reflective thought with man—the course of evolution is involuted ... evolution begins now to converge on itself." However, convergence has to be focused on a point, and for Teilhard this is the Omega Point, the Incarnate Christ, "a point at which the whole Universe along with mankind is drawn into an ultrasynthesis where God, as St. Paul says, 'will be all in all'"; Francoeur "Call to Greatness," 442; 1 Cor 15:28.

and situated it in a Christology that has as its foundation the mystical body of Christ. Why is this significant? Francoeur observes that fifty years ago Bishop John Ireland said, "This age will not take kindly to religious knowledge separated from secular knowledge."[31]

From another perspective, in an essay for *New Scholasticism* published in 1960, Bernard Gilligan notes that *The Phenomenon* was widely acclaimed as "THE publishing event" of 1959.[32] "Reviewers predict it will remain a classic and be read assiduously for decades to come. The great publicity and fulsome praise it has received are well deserved. It affords the reader a unique opportunity for a great intellectual and emotional experience."[33]

Gilligan lavishly praises the book, commenting that it contains "a brilliant synoptic vision of total cosmic and human evolution," one that is quite consistent with traditional Christianity. This vision is completed only by what "the doctrine of the Mystical Body of Christ" supplies.[34]

Gilligan also affirms that Teilhard provides a synthesis of science and theology; the natural/supernatural question is suggested "implicitly" toward the end of the book, in a move that is bold but orthodox. He assures readers that "a profound spirituality can be discerned as inspiring [Teilhard's] scientific thought ... his thought and personality were completely Christocentric."[35] According to Gilligan, Teilhard's synthesis not only was between science and religion, the natural and the supernatural, but also attempted to bridge the gap between Christianity and the secular world. It is very much bilin-

31. Francoeur, "Call to Greatness," 442. Additionally, on page 443 Francoeur has French Cardinal Emmanuel Suhard noting, "Modern inventions (and knowledge) which have increased at an ever-growing pace cannot be for Christians just another news item or a mere scientific curiosity. They have their value as pointers and they must henceforth be integrated into the Christian's apostolic vision of Redemption. For they are something more than empty symbols: They are the making of a new universe. And this is the Universe we are called upon to save."

32. Bernard B. Gilligan, review of *The Phenomenon of Man*, *New Scholasticism* 34 (1960): 515.

33. Ibid.

34. Ibid.

35. Ibid. Also on page 515, Gilligan adds that the fact that Julian Huxley wrote an enthusiastic introduction to the volume is indicative of the almost universal esteem with which Teilhard was held by the scientific community.

gual by nature. As Gilligan writes, "The whole adds up to a mystical vision ranging over the entire universe with great intellectual acumen and profound emotional responsiveness."[36]

Weighing in with another theological opinion was the Jesuit priest Cyril Vollert, who in 1960 also commented on Teilhard's work in *Theology Digest.*[37] Teilhard, he writes, was above all a thinker and a prophet. His influence on contemporary thought is already great and is only bound to grow. What was Teilhard about? Vollert enumerates three points by which to understand Teilhard's achievement in *The Phenomenon.* First, that his methodology was scientific; his intention was to stick to experimental observation complemented by hypotheses. Second, that his interpretation of the past and future was presented in light of present knowledge. Finally, perhaps most important and also the source of much controversy, that he attempted to synthesize the conclusions of the scientific study of reality with Christian knowledge gained through faith and an experience of Christ. Teilhard's primary objective, according to Vollert, was simply to rescue evolution from materialism and return it to the spiritual realm.[38]

Another Jesuit, J. Franklin Ewing, wrote about *The Phenomenon* in *Theological Studies* early the following year.[39] Ewing, of Fordham, had taken part in the aforementioned Knights of Columbus show. He conjectures in this book that although Teilhard's books had excited vast numbers in Europe, most probably the same would not happen in the United States. This is so, he argues, as vast differences exist in the reading publics. In particular, the United States did not experience World War II and so cannot relate as Europe did to the message of hope so rampant in Teilhard's work. Still, Ewing notes that this is "a book which showed that one could be a modern (indeed, a scientist) and a believer in God."[40]

36. Ibid., 516.

37. Cyril Vollert, SJ, "Toward Omega: The Vision of Man," *Theology Digest,* 1960, 133–36.

38. Ibid., 133.

39. J. Franklin Ewing, SJ, "Notes: The Human Phenomenon," *Theological Studies* 22, no.1 (March 1961): 86–102. Although Ewing made the decision not to contribute to Francoeur's book, he did write a favorable review of it in *American Anthropologist* 64, no. 5 (October 1962): 1132.

40. Ewing, "Notes," 86. Ewing notes that *The Phenomenon* is selling very well in the

Ewing is another who believes that the most profound influence of Teilhard for many is his attempt at a synthesis of "various areas of reality, with evolution as the prime key to an appreciation of the workings of God and His universe."[41] Ewing would like the reading public to remember that Teilhard was a prose poet and a mystic. For many, Teilhard's conversation would be ennobling, if overly original. Still, Ewing believes Teilhard's work exhibits the extreme empathy that was characteristic of the man himself.[42]

Ewing recognizes that these personality traits and the story of a life spent primarily in exile have tended to sacerdotalize Teilhard's work and make of him a missionary. As Teilhard's friend George Barbour also noted, he "suffered greatly, and could not understand why others might not follow his manner of acting and thinking." Ewing observes that at the present time many have tremendous empathy for Teilhard and his life story, and this too feeds interest in his writings. As he concludes, "Perhaps the author did not succeed in being a twentieth-century Aquinas, but no one else has come so close to achieving this enviable position."[43] Teilhard's efforts are therefore, Ewing believes, a powerful incentive for modern people to rethink our ideas about the universe.

A quick review of these articles/essays shows that already early in the decade several common themes can be discerned regarding the

---

United States. In particular, teachers of philosophy and theology should know about the book, as most likely they will be asked about it at some point in the near future.

41. Ibid., 87. Ewing comments, however, that because Teilhard was not permitted to publish during his lifetime, his work is very experiential, rather than scholarly. For example, many of his doctrines come close to those of biblical scholars, but Teilhard apparently never read these as he never references them. Doubt about his orthodoxy was only exacerbated in the minds of the authorities when his work was published outside the norms of the Jesuits and the church after his death. Yet this too has drawn many to his writings.

42. Ewing includes a quote here from Teilhard's coworker and friend George Barbour: "Most accounts of his life fail to mention Teilhard's most striking characteristics—his humility and his warm sympathetic humanity. He was utterly without conceit or self-interest, and had a marvelous sense of humor. He found it well-nigh impossible to think ill of any man, at least for long, even when others took advantage of his forbearance and generosity. He just continually gave himself away"; George Barbour, memorial to Pierre Teilhard de Chardin, SJ, *Proceedings Volume of the Geological Society of America: Annual Report for 1955* (July 1956), quoted in Ewing, "Notes," 170–71.

43. Ibid., 102.

reception of Teilhard's thought in the United States. His work was variously regarded as poetry, mysticism, and philosophy. The synthetic quality of it was easily recognized and both this and his love for both Christ and the material world appreciated. His life itself was an example of how a modern contemporary attempting to balance work and faith might manage this.

Popular Media

Journalists in the broader popular press had also encountered this burgeoning fascination with Teilhard and were beginning to explore facets of his life and work. An article in *Time* magazine on February 1961 was the first of several to do so.[44] The opening lines quote the *Divine Milieu*: "Is the Christ of the Gospels, imagined and loved within the dimensions of a Mediterranean world, capable of still embracing and still forming the center of our prodigiously expanded universe?"[45] It is interesting to note that the unidentified author of this piece, in beginning with this quote, appears to already comprehend the Christocentric nature of Teilhard's cosmology. The article then suggests that one person who not only asked but answered those questions well was Teilhard. The author comments that the recent publication of some of his "philosophical writings," in particular *The Divine Milieu*, has sparked a posthumous cult of "Teil-hardism" in France.

The *Time* article also notes that the book's audience is not primarily fast and true Christians, but "the waverers, both inside and outside" the church, "whose education or instinct leads them to listen primarily to the voices of the earth." After all, his book's dedication is "for those who love the world."[46]

The article concludes that Teilhard most certainly would have placed himself within this category, for Christianity, Teilhard be-

44. "Passionate Indifference," *Time*, February 10, 1961, accessed July 11, 2012, http://www.time.com/time/magazine/article/0,9171,872124,00.html#ixzz1QKfKPjDF.

45. Teilhard, *The Divine Milieu* (New York: Harper and Row, 1960), 46, quoted in "Passionate Indifference."

46. "Passionate Indifference."

lieves, teaches that the things of the world all play their role in the continuing work of God with humanity through the spiritualization of the universe. As the article points out, even the evils of the world have their part in this process, for God "transfigures them by integrating them in a better plan—provided we trust lovingly in Him."[47]

Publication Data

A letter dated February 7, 1961, from Hugh Van Dusen of Harper and Brothers to "Friends and Admirers of Father Teilhard de Chardin" shares the news that on Sunday, February 19, at 1:00 p.m. there would be a half-hour television program devoted to Father Teilhard, his life, and writings.[48] The script for this program was written by Michael Novak, "a brilliant young Catholic at Harvard."

Additionally, Van Dusen adds that the Harper edition of *The Divine Milieu* (formerly titled *The Realm of the Divine*) had already sold almost 9,000 copies since publication at the end of October, and *The Phenomenon* was almost at 30,000 and had been selling much more briskly since the appearance of *The Divine Milieu.*[49] *The Phenomenon* was planned to be published as a paperback that next August.[50]

Subsequent to the distribution of these two, according to Van Dusen, the next volume scheduled for publication in English was

47. The true Christian, according to Teilhard, does not renounce the world, nor does he embrace it wholly; he neither puts his trust in action nor resigns himself to acceptance. Instead, the Christian rejoices in all the world's potentials, including that of surrender; if any words might best describe the "intoxication" felt for the world, those would be "passionate indifference." Hence the title chosen for this examination in *Time;* Teilhard, *Divine Milieu,* 118–20, quoted in "Passionate Indifference."

48. Hugh Van Dusen, notice of February 7, 1961, Harper and Row correspondence, Robert Francoeur collection, Box 1, Folder 6, Lauinger Library Archives, Georgetown University (hereafter LLA).

49. The English translation of the title of this book was hotly debated, as is indicated in a letter in late 1960 from George Barbour, Teilhard's dear friend of many years, to Robert Francoeur, which asks, "Have you seen the just published English version of the *Divine Milieu,* for which they apparently adopted the title I suggested as an improvement on Cuénot's wording 'Divine Environment,' which misses the point entirely"; "Wednesday Night, November 1960: From Cincinnati," George Barbour Letters, Robert Francoeur Collection, Box 1, Folder 3, LLA.

50. The paperback edition of *The Phenomenon* was actually finally published as a Harper Torch book in 1965.

the *Letters*, possibly combining the two volumes of *Lettres de voyage.* Other books by Father Teilhard already published in France were in the process of translation into English at that time. Books and articles about Teilhard continued to appear in France and Germany. Van Dusen notes that in a recent Blackwell's catalogue he noticed four more. Additionally, Claude Cuénot's biography of Teilhard was still being translated and was expected to appear from Helicon Press later in the year.[51]

In closing, Hugh Van Dusen notes that "we are still hoping for a feature article on Father Teilhard in LIFE." Mention of Teilhard's thought and influence did occur numerous times through the years in *Life* (although not in a feature article)—the first in an editorial, "The Spirit Is at Work," on March 31, 1961.[52] In a few paragraphs, the editor comments in regard to Teilhard that whereas his friends knew him for his "selfless charm," and the scientific community for his admirable work, only today is "his influence spreading wherever men take seriously the ultimate questions of their origin, nature and destiny."

This article in *Life* notes that Teilhard was not only a Christian mystic, but also a French rationalist, proud to be related to Voltaire. It comments, "Teilhard used Darwin and genetics the way Aquinas used Aristotle, weaving them into the fabric of a comprehensive theology." Along the way, he reconciled science and church dogma by transcending both. Slowly the realization is dawning in both church and society that he is "one of the 'great thought shapers' of the century, because he could find the poetry hidden in science's dustiest facts." In an age of technology, the article notes, Teilhard has helped to place man back at the center of God's creation.

51. Published as Claude Cuénot, *Teilhard de Chardin: A Biographical Study*, ed. René Hague, trans. Vince Colimar (Helicon, 1965).

52. "The Spirit Is at Work," *Life*, March 31, 1961, 30. Actually, Teilhard is made note of—either in passing or extensively—ten times in *Life* between 1961 and 1972. However, no feature article was ever written.

INCREASING CONTROVERSY AND REPERCUSSIONS

Despite this generally positive assessment of Teilhard's impact, others were not so quick to promote his theories. Father Robert Francoeur, for one, was already feeling heat over his espousal of Teilhard's thought in conjunction with his desire for change within the church. Mention of his forthcoming *The World of Teilhard* was made in a footnote to an article that appeared in early 1961 in the *American Benedictine Review*, a small magazine with a circulation of perhaps 800. As a result of that citation, however, even before the book was in print, a *monitum* concerning it was issued by the apostolic delegate to the United States, Archbishop Egidio Vagnozzi, prohibiting its reading by American seminarians. After much correspondence with the apostolic delegate, the book was finally published. Although it was well received, it never did receive an *imprimatur.*

This small battle was indicative of the greater turmoil surrounding the publication of Teilhard's writings as well as subsequent expositions. A cover story concerning Teilhard, which Francoeur penned in September 1961 in the popular journal *Catholic World*, well illustrates this.[53] Titled "For Teilhard, No Flight from Time," Francoeur addresses Teilhard's critics, some of whom Francoeur comments condemned him as "an inventor of a new gospel." He notes that reviewers tend to consider *The Phenomenon* as either "pure charlatanism" or a "truly masterful vindication of the spiritual in a materialistic world."[54]

Francoeur contends here that many of Teilhard's critics harbored nostalgia, or a desire for regression back to a premodern, prescientific society, and some way to escape from the passing of time that ushers in change. By contrast, Teilhard views time as a way to

53. Robert T. Francoeur, "For Teilhard, No Flight from Time," *Catholic World*, September 1961, 367–73. This was the cover story for this particular issue. From 1961 to 1962, Francoeur was a professor of biology at Mt. St. Agnes College in Baltimore. There he became friends with Gustave Weigel, SJ, and John Courtney Murray, SJ, both of whom would be influential spirits in the Vatican Council.

54. The quote that begins the article is "The trend that gained momentum with Darwin finds its apex in Teilhard." One might argue that to highlight such a quote was perhaps not a politically expedient move, at least if one is attempting to soothe ruffled feathers!

reach the infinite and speaks a language the contemporary world can understand.

In the article, the author notes that *The Phenomenon* sold over ninety thousand copies in France and over fifty thousand in thirty months in both England and the United States. In the five years since its first publication in France, over five hundred articles and thirty books had been written in French concerning Teilhard and his work. Obviously, his work was meeting some need in contemporary society.[55]

Francoeur perceives that Teilhard has taken the traditional synthesis of Catholic knowledge and woven into it new concepts and ways of expressing that knowledge so that some readers see his work as "an entirely 'new gospel.'" This in itself has caused consternation and fear among the more conservative.[56] Still, the overwhelming spiteful reaction of some gives Francoeur pause. The reactions have "run the gamut of emotion and sense and it will be a hundred years before we will be able to sift the diamonds of critical study from the rubble of nonsense. But even with this fact in mind and allowing for it, there is still a very disturbing element in some of these reactions which can be quite dangerous to the true progress of our understanding of this world of ours."[57]

Francoeur questions: do these reactions indicate a craving for an escape from time, or a desire on the part of some to avoid forward progress in both society and the church?[58] He argues that attempting to hide from the possibilities created by science and research is "not a healthy sign of a vigorous intellectual life." If truth exists in new vistas, it must be found; if it is in error, it must be corrected. However, this can only be done by moving forward. Teilhard saw all time, work, and research as ascending to an end point, not standing still. In contrast, many of his critics' reactionary stances against Teilhard offer no alternative answer to the problems he raises.[59]

55. Francoeur, "No Flight from Time," 367.
56. Ibid.
57. Ibid., 368.
58. Ibid., 373.
59. Ibid.

Francoeur quotes Nicholas Corté, one of Teilhard's friends and biographers, as suggesting two types of reactions: critics and "sympathetic voices." However, Corté himself finds not much distinction between the two: "When you add it up, there is not, perhaps, a very great distance between the two positions, but only, to put it thus, a change in perspective."[60] In other words, as proposed already in chapter 1, Corté suggests that certain people are simply better able to "see" and to accept the movement of time as described by Teilhard.

So, Francoeur concludes in turn, the refusal to follow the course of knowledge as it moves onward and an obstinacy in the notions of the past, or "the flight from time and history itself, are points which seem to play a large role in some of the more violent and bombastic criticism of Teilhard."[61]

He ends his article by suggesting that simply because a reviewer does not find Teilhard's writings, approach, or treatment helpful does not mean they are not perfectly orthodox. Indeed, it "will take patient, serious, honest and courageous study along with the prudence of a Solomon to separate the wheat from the chaff. But the results thus far obtained clearly indicate that the effort is well worthwhile."[62]

THE TEILHARD CONTROVERSY IN EUROPE

Although Francoeur might write publicly that the effort was worthwhile, as pressure from church authorities mounted in these years before the Second Vatican Council against the further pub-

60. Nicholas Corté, *Pierre Teilhard de Chardin: His Life and Spirit* (New York: Macmillan, 1960), 371.

61. Francoeur, "No Flight from Time," 373. See also chapter 1 of Garry Wills's *Bare Ruined Choirs: Doubt, Prophecy and Radical Religion* (Doubleday: New York, 1972) for a further exemplification of the arguments of those exasperated with Teilhard's vision, particularly in regard to the Roman Catholic Church. A quote from page 18 particularly seems appropriate here: "[The Church] belonged to no age or time, but was above them all; it had a 'special dispensation' from history. History was a thing it did not have to undergo." The development of historical consciousness, particularly the deep historical consciousness that Teilhard was advocating, was an immense struggle for many within the Church—hierarchy and lay people both.

62. Francoeur, "No Flight from Time," 373.

lication of Teilhard's work and vitriolic criticism grew, at times he must have privately wondered if this was truly so. Francoeur's struggle however, was an indication of the dissonance brewing in the universal church, particularly in Europe. This disharmony did involve Teilhard, but he was only one small piece of the inevitable jerky movement being taken toward opening the church to the modern world. It seems worthwhile then, to discuss through the lens of two particular people, Henri de Lubac and Dorothy Poulain, the European background of some of the Teilhardian controversy and their own contributions to the reception of Teilhard in the United States.

The Role of Henri de Lubac

De Lubac was first contacted by Monsignor Bruno de Solages in April 1936 about some of Teilhard's writings and the need to gather all these in a publication of some kind before they were lost.[63] He notes, however, that after Teilhard's death in 1955 the Jesuits did not wish to publish anything of Teilhard's, except some very select and carefully chosen texts. Publishers considered this impractical to manage, however, so initially nothing was done on the matter.

In 1957, de Lubac was taken to the Teilhard gathering at Cerisy-la-Salle in La Manche, a gathering with which Dorothy Poulain was involved, and where he gave an impromptu talk on *Le Milieu Divin.* This then led to a written text, *Du bon usage du milieu divine,* which was copied and distributed around Europe. A similar article was later published in Paris and was signed by Father Eugene d'Oncieu, the Jesuit national chaplain, breaking the "law of silence" under which de Lubac had been forced to live.

By 1961, however, everything had changed. In April of that year the Jesuit Provincial of the Lyon Province, Blaise Arminjon, reminded de Lubac of the interdiction against writing about Teilhard; how-

63. Henri de Lubac, *At the Service of the Church: Henri de Lubac Reflects on the Circumstances that Occasioned His Writings,* trans. Anne Elizabeth Englund (San Francisco: Ignatius Press, 1998), 103f. De Lubac notes here that he considered the editions he provided of the works of several people, including Father Auguste Valensin, Maurice Blondel, and Teilhard de Chardin, "one of the most useful tasks ever given to me to accomplish."

ever, later that same summer, he was called into Father Arminjon's office and received a very different message. The Society of Jesus was concerned that all sorts of "nonsense" was being written about Teilhard, both in support of and against him. With the publication of several of his books already by Les Amis de Teilhard, the Jesuits (including at least the four provincials of France and the general superior) had decided it was necessary that "one who knew him well, who has followed his thought, bring his testimony to bear about him [Teilhard]; there are very few left in this world who can do so; we have decided on you." As a result, de Lubac was to free himself from his other occupations and set to work quickly on a text of his own conception.[64]

The immediate result was *La Pensée Religieuse du Pere Teilhard de Chardin.*[65] Concerning relations with Rome in writing about Teilhard, de Lubac later noted that "I gave my opinion clearly, and I was not asked to suppress or change a single word."[66]

Cardinal Ottaviani of the Curia asked to have this Teilhard book of de Lubac placed on the *Index,* but when the matter was brought before Pope John XXIII, the papal response was "No." A condemnation was not going to happen. De Lubac saw this response as in line with a public *monitum* that had very "vague formulas." However, the book was immediately attacked by Philippe de la Trinité, editor of *l'Osservatore Romano,* a conservative mouthpiece, and one at least in part responsible for the *monitum* itself. As a result, at the end of June de Lubac was informed that any new editions or translations of his book were forbidden.[67]

64. Ibid., 104. As regards the "nonsense" being written about Teilhard, this will continue to be an issue for years with many of those who knew Teilhard well and who saw his thought being used in a manner inconsistent with the beliefs and attitude of the man they knew. Consider, for example, the comments of George Barbour, and later his son Ian, in the chapters following.

65. De Lubac, *La Pensée Religieuse du Pere Teilhard de Chardin* (Paris: Aubier, 1962), trans. René Hague, published in the United States as *The Religion of Teilhard de Chardin* (New York: Desclee, 1967).

66. De Lubac. *At the Service of the Church,* 105. For example, de Lubac included a comment by Teilhard "about the integrist theologians." Teilhard had written that "they keep us from adoring and loving *deeply,* they would like to keep God from growing in our eyes" (112).

67. De Lubac, however, was somewhat mollified by a note of support from the

This ban on any new editions of his initial book required de Lubac to produce yet another volume to correct further misconceptions on Teilhard, *La Priere du Pere Teilhard de Chardin,* published in 1964.[68] After 1961 and throughout the next dozen years, de Lubac became increasingly involved in controversies surrounding Teilhard as he published or edited another seven volumes concerning Teilhard.[69] He later commented that "all these works on Teilhard, which were not of passionate interest to me, took much of my time over a period of twelve years or so and brought me many difficulties."[70]

He noted later, though, that in regard to his efforts in this matter:

> In order to understand certain orientations and emphases of his thought, in order to do justice to what was both most daring and most timely in it, a work of historical reconstruction had become necessary.... Neither the denigrators nor the admirers of Teilhard ordinarily per-

---

Jesuit father general, who stated that in regard to Trinité's review, "it is not hard for me to understand that his article was painful for you; but *for the moment* an intervention on my part with the Holy Office seems inopportune. At this time, the cause of truth will be better served by our silent suffering than by untimely clarifications. In a little while—a few months?—we shall see. Many here and elsewhere are hoping for a change.... I am fully in agreement with you; your book constitutes a first, very important elucidation of the work of Father Teilhard, and in the very spirit of the *monitum,* a 'warning' against possible extrapolations of Father's thought, not in conformity to the doctrine of the Church"; de Lubac, *At the Service of the Church,* 106.

68. De Lubac, *La Priere du Pere Teilhard de Chardin* (1964; repr. Paris: A. Fayard, 1967. An English translation by René Hague was published in London by Burns and Oates in 1965 as *The Faith of Teilhard de Chardin.*

69. These include de Lubac, *Teilhard: Missionaire et apologist* (1966), from conferences given in Rome; and two collections of letters: *Lettres d'Égypte 1905–1908* (Paris: Aubier Éditions Montaigne, 1963), and *Lettres d'Hastings et de Paris 1908–1914* (Paris: Aubier, 1965). The first of these was translated into English by Mary Ilford and published in New York by Herder and Herder in 1965 as *Letters from Egypt: 1905–1908*; the second was translated by Judith de Stefano as *Letters from Hastings: 1908–1914,* with an introduction by de Lubac, and published by Herder and Herder in 1968. In addition, he was involved with *Écrits du temps de la guerre 1916–1919* (Paris: B. Grasset, 1965) with an introduction by Bruno de Solages and de Lubac. He also contributed a chapter to *Teilhard de Chardin* in the Réalités series (at the last moment five pages written concerning the Christology so crucial to understanding Teilhard's thought were suppressed), and a commentary on *The Eternal Feminine: A Study on the Poem by Teilhard de Chardin, Followed by Teilhard and the Problems of Today* (New York: Harper and Row, 1971). Several of these publications will be discussed later in this work. The last of the series was de Lubac, *Lettres intimes à Auguste Valensin, Bruno de Solages, Henri de Lubac, 1919–1955* (Paris: A. Montaigne, 1973).

70. De Lubac, *At the Service of the Church,* 109.

ceived the historical importance of his effort to establish ... a spiritual interpretation of universal evolution that included the transcendence of man, the value of personal being, freedom, openness to God, and consummation in Christ.[71]

The Role of Dorothy Poulain

Madame Dorothy Poulain of France was one who both knew Henri de Lubac and remained in correspondence with Francoeur throughout these years, sharing her own concerns from Europe. As was mentioned in chapter 1, she was an American married to a French writer and living in Paris at this time, was very active in Catholic Church circles, knew Madame Mortier well, and was a member of the French Les Amis de Teilhard. In the years to come, her support of both Robert Francoeur and the American Teilhardians would prove crucial.

In October 1961, she wrote Father Francoeur from Paris to thank him for a copy of the September issue of *Catholic World*.[72] She noted that she appreciated his article with its analysis of the "conservative reaction to Teilhard." Surely, she wrote, he would succeed in making those who criticize Teilhard in this manner "look very much like a certain long-eared species!"

The following January, 1962, she wrote to Francoeur, "Your account of the 'coup de frein' launched against Teilhard or writings on him in the U.S. is simply following a consecrated pattern—exactly the same as that in France where even today none of his works are allowed in the seminaries or houses of study."[73] How, though, she

71. Ibid., 110. As additional commentary on this point, de Lubac notes on the same page that in his journal in 1963 Mircea Eliade wrote in regard to Teilhard, "What a joy to rediscover in a Western theologian, a 'man of science,' the optimism of the Rumanian peasants, who were themselves Christians but who belonged to that 'cosmic Christianity' that has long since disappeared in the West. The peasant believes that 'the World is good,' that it became so once again after the Incarnation, death and Resurrection of the Savior"; Eliade, *No Souvenirs: Journal, 1957–1969*, trans. Fred H. Johnson Jr. (New York: Harper and Row, 1982).

72. Dorothy Poulain to Father Francoeur, September 24, 1961, from Paris, Madame Poulain correspondence, Francoeur Collection, Box 1, Folder 9, LLA.

73. Dorothy Poulain to Father Francoeur, January 23, 1962, Box 1, Folder 9,

asks, was *Commonweal* or *Catholic World* able to publish their articles? She mentions that she has a letter from Father John Sheerin, the editor of *Catholic World*, that mentions that although *The World of Teilhard* had aroused little popular interest, it had irked some of the hierarchy, particularly the apostolic delegate.[74]

She goes on to remark that since the Holy Office knew nothing of science and even less of Teilhard, they asked for judgment from others, including Monsignor de Journet of Fribourg. As those of his like are still rampant, Poulain notes, until they disappear or are "converted" by those more qualified and understanding, "we can periodically expect this sort of thing." She then encourages Francoeur (and mentions that Madame Mortier feels the same) not to be downcast, but to lie low. After all, "remember what happened after 'Humani Generis' when Congar, de Lubac & Co. all went into the silence ... well, behold them up and coming right into the Vatican Council preparations!"

On February 1, Poulain wrote again with the news that Cardinal Ottaviani had decided "*not* to crack down on Père Teilhard as someone has evidently convinced him that Teilhard brought so many into the Church."[75] About a week later, a follow-up missive explains that the papal legate to Senegal learned of Teilhard's anti-Marxist influence in his country.[76] This has apparently made Rome feel that if Teilhard is a sort of "anti-communist bulwark" maybe their restrictions and concerns are for naught. She also mentions that during one of the Crespy conferences on Teilhard held annually in France, in response to a question from a participant as to why Teilhard's works were forbidden in seminaries, a priest present explained that the concerns of the hierarchy did not necessarily imply a *condem-*

Madame Poulain correspondence, Robert Francoeur Collection, LLA. The phrase "coup de frein" might literally be translated as a sudden "putting on of the brakes."

74. In this same letter, Poulain also shared that apparently numerous eyebrows were raised over the lack of an imprimatur. However, she asks, why was one imperative, as the book was a collaboration between Catholics and non-Catholics alike?

75. Dorothy Poulain to Father Francoeur, February 1, 1962, from Paris, Box 1, Folder 9, Madame Poulain correspondence, Robert Francoeur Collection, LLA. Emphasis is the author's.

76. Dorothy Poulain to Father Francoeur, February 10, 1962, from Paris, Madame Poulain correspondence, Francoeur Collection, Box 1, Folder 9, LLA.

nation of Teilhard's works. It was simply considered more prudent to expose seminarians to the more classical systems ("Thomism of course"). This would give them a solid foundation, as Teilhard's ideas were not yet able to be classified in this category.

CONTROVERSY CONCERNING AN AMERICAN TEILHARD ORGANIZATION

Francoeur and others primarily at Fordham were quite interested in starting an official Teilhard organization patterned along the lines of Madame Mortier's Amis in Paris. By this point, Francoeur had been in correspondence with Poulain and Mortier concerning this possibility for at least two years. Finally, in late February of 1962 Poulain wrote Francoeur to let him know that she had obtained permission for him to "organize the American branch of the Association des Amis de Pierre Teilhard de Chardin."[77] For the first time, an organization would have the "right" not only to publish, but also to call official conferences concerning Teilhard and his work.

Francoeur responded to both Madame Poulain and Madame Mortier expressing his interest and pleasure in his development, but also again his concerns regarding the direction the U.S. hierarchy appeared to be traveling concerning Teilhard.[78] Madame Mortier replied in very early March with the news that in her view the situation appeared to "be less strained with Rome since Father Danielou was able to put out his article on Teilhard in *Études* without restrictions."[79] Also, Père de Lubac suddenly received authorization to publish his book *La Pensée réligieuse de Teilhard* after an earlier refusal.[80]

Madame Mortier also spoke of a former provincial of Paris, a Father Bith, who commented to a friend:

77. Dorothy Poulain to Father "Bob" Francoeur, February 26, 1962, from Paris, Madame Poulain correspondence, Francoeur Collection, Box 1, Folder 9, LLA.

78. This letter is not extant in the correspondence at Georgetown; however, Poulain's letter in return makes note of Francoeur's comments.

79. Madame Mortier to "My Father," March 4, 1962 from Paris, Robert Francoeur Collection, Box 1, Folder 7, LLA.

80. This book would be published in summer 1962 in France as de Lubac, *La Pensée réligieuse de Teilhard* (Paris: Aubier, 1962). It was later translated into English and published as *The Religion of Teilhard de Chardin* (New York: Desclee, 1967).

We are witnessing a veritable Teilhard tidal wave and we Jesuits are the first to be surprised by it; in Africa, all the independent States are asking us for colleges and praising us among their own people; they tell us that it is because of our Teilhard; we must realize that Fr. Teilhard knew how to speak the language of our time, that of human hope; he brings a concrete ideal; we are going to have to adapt to this need that we did not understand—we underestimated Teilhard.

As an example of the volatility of this position, however, only two days later Madame Poulain informed Francoeur via letter that "*for the time being you will have to wait until the Council gets well underway before attempting anything in the U.S.*"[81] Concern about the refusal to issue imprimaturs for anything to do with Teilhard had confirmed for many in France that this was not yet "le moment juste." Therefore, Francoeur was to "*halt all proceedings and not put any machinery in motion.*" Continue to think about it, of course, she wrote, and to pray. Poulain noted that Father Ong would be in Paris soon and more discussion concerning this would take place then, as he could give a clearer picture of what was happening in the United States. For "penance," she suggested "an attentive reading of *Americanism: A Phantom Heresy*—it's most instructive. You will understand."[82]

The capricious nature of the debate was further illustrated in a letter in late April from Madame Mortier to "Mon Père Francoeur."[83]

81. Dorothy Poulain to Robert Francoeur, March 6, 1962, Madame Poulain correspondence, Robert Francoeur Collection, Box 1, Folder 9, LLA. Emphasis throughout this letter is hers.

82. Félix Klein, *Americanism: A Phantom Heresy* (Cranford, N.J.: Aquin, 1951). Reference is to the book that was the primary text fairly recently published at this time concerning Americanism. It was the fourth volume of the autobiography of Klein and was translated into English by the Paulist Joseph McSorley. In so doing, McSorley enlisted the aid of Dorothy Poulain, who translated chapter 25 of *The Phantom Heresy*. Through McSorley, Poulain became a sort of "guardian angel" to the old Abbé Klein (1862–1953). She helped him transcribe letters, organize his materials, and secure needed information for the English version. McSorley frequently asked both of them to check various points for accuracy; from Margaret Reher, "Phantom Heresy: A Twice-Told Tale," in *The Americanist Controversy: Recent Historical and Theological Perspectives*, special issue of *U.S. Catholic Historian* 11, no. 3 (Summer 1993): 93–105. See also Dorothy Poulain, "Evening Star," *Ave Maria*, January 31, 1953, 135–41.

83. Madame Mortier to "Mon Père," April 30, 1962, Robert Francoeur Collection, Box 1, Folder 7, LLA: "Le P. de Lubac, qui revenait de Rome, semble espérer que les interdictions d'imprimateur en Amérique émanent des anciennes directives

She relates that Father de Lubac, who had just returned from Rome, seems to hope that the prohibition of the imprimatur in the United States to anything Teilhard is from some old directives of just a few Cardinals. De Lubac expects a loosening of this after the Council. At the moment the Jesuit fathers can publish on Teilhard and take part in conferences concerning his work, which until now had been forbidden.[84]

At the same time, George Barbour was writing Francoeur concerning the same organization.[85] He was interested in this idea, but what would such a group do, he asks: "If an American branch had been alive before the two publishing houses of Helicon and Harper got into the business for commercial reasons it might have done something of the kind Cuénot and the Fondation were able to do." Instead, things in the United States are scattered everywhere with no oversight, and "McManus is sticky and afraid of the hierarchy. Otherwise he would never have asked whether my story could somehow recall whether Père Teilhard ever said Mass!"[86]

Barbour also tells Francoeur that he had been informed in a letter that *The World of Teilhard* had attracted the attention of the bishops and made the Vatican excited. Most likely, he concludes, it is because the book's essays were not all written by Catholics, and so the book could not wholesale be given an *imprimatur.*

---

de quelques cardinaux. Il present un allegèment de ses measures dès après le Councile – Déja les Pere Jésuites peuvent publiers sur Teilhard et participer des conférences, ce qui leur était défender jusqu'ici"; English translation my own.

84. Less than a week later, however, Walter Ong wrote "Bob" from Paris and suggested that in regard to establishing an American branch of Les Amis, it would be best to move slowly. "Worthwhile ideas" concerning this project could continue to multiply while they waited; a formal organization was not yet really necessary, "especially if there is serious opposition"; Walter Ong to "Bob" Francoeur, May 5, 1962, from Paris, Ong Letters, Robert Francoeur Collection, Box 1, Folder 7, LLA.

85. George Barbour to Father Francoeur, May 4, 1962, from Duke University, George Barbour letters, Robert Francoeur Collection, Box 1, Folder 3, LLA.

86. David McManus was founder of and editor in chief of Helicon Press of Baltimore from the late 1950s through the 1960s.

THE *MONITUM* AND ITS INTERPRETATION

The controversy over Teilhard reached its apex on June 30, 1962, when a *monitum* was issued by the Sacred Congregation of the Holy Office of the Vatican.[87] The admonition warns that Teilhard's recently posthumously published works contain numerous ambiguities and errors. As a result, the Holy Office was exhorting superiors of religious institutes, rectors of seminaries, and university presidents to protect minds from the "dangers presented by the works of Father Teilhard" and his followers.

The aftermath of this was a flurry of letters flying between the United States and France. Just a few days later, the Jesuit J. Franklin Ewing wrote Father Francoeur, "I am just as much in the dark as you. All I know is that the thing happened. And all I have seen is what appeared in the newspaper. I am waiting to get the exact wording."[88]

He mentions that a rumor is going around about a letter prohibiting any new editions or translations of Henri de Lubac's book on Teilhard. This would hold up the American edition. On the other hand, he expounds, it could always have been worse! After all, the works were not placed on the *Index*.[89]

Madame Mortier also wrote Francoeur within the week to let him

87. *Warning Considering the Writings of Father Teilhard de Chardin*, Sacred Congregation of the Holy Office, June 30, 1962. The full text reads, "*Admonition*: Several works of Fr. Pierre Teilhard de Chardin, some of which were posthumously published, are being edited and are gaining a good deal of success. The above-mentioned works abound in such ambiguities and indeed even serious errors, as to offend Catholic doctrine. For this reason, the most eminent and most revered Fathers of the Holy Office exhort all Ordinaries as well as the superiors of Religious Institutes, rectors of seminaries and presidents of universities, effectively to protect the minds, particularly of the youth, against the dangers presented by the works of Fr. Teilhard de Chardin and of his followers"; signed by Sebastianus Masala, Notarius. This *monitum* was specifically addressed in *L'Osservatore Romano* in a long article in the December 29, 2013, issue, which eulogized Teilhard and his thought.

88. Franklin Ewing, SJ, to Father Francoeur, July 1, 1962, Robert Francoeur Collection, Box 1, Folder 5 J, LLA.

89. Ewing closes his letter by sharing that he did send de Lubac a note of congratulations on his book, hoping that might cheer him up some. Also, his "remaining hope is that there will be a very large number of missionary, more open-minded Bishops at the Council! Keep in there fighting!"; Franklin Ewing, SJ, to Robert Francoeur, July 1, 1962, Robert Francoeur Collection, Box 1, Folder 5 J, LLA.

know that the *monitum* was all over the news in France and it was impossible to send all the clippings.[90] She added, "Let me say on the best authority that this new onslaught is simply the same old theme song that we have had over here like a recurring fever for the past seven years. There is really nothing new in it." She also comments that this latest action "represents the 'revenge' of the conservative *Divinitas* group who are boiling because of Père de Lubac's book (he definitely has his enemies)."[91] Apparently, reference to *Divinitas* in the book raised their ire. Madame Mortier claims this is the usual "thomist reaction," but a bit nastier than in the past. Those who do not realize the history are "understandably perturbed and troubled—which is exactly what the group is aiming at. On the positive side, Teilhard's works have sold astronomically as a result; still this is the time for prudence."

In regard to prudence and any American branch of the Amis, Madame suggests that Father Francoeur must exercise even more patience. Not only that, but "to say it plainly, Father, you will simply have to disappear into the weather for quite a while for the Apostolic Delegate's letter of last September has made of you a marked man. You are too young and inexperienced and without titles and authority to cover you (see what has happened to Père de Lubac!) and if you don't heed *my* warning, you may get yourself into serious trouble."[92]

In July, Francoeur also heard from J. Edgar Bruns.[93] Bruns seems

90. Madame Mortier to Robert Francoeur, July 6, 1962, Robert Francoeur Collection, Box 1, Folder 7, LLA.

91. *Divinitas* is a conservative theological journal published in Rome. The reference is in de Lubac's *The Religion of Teilhard de Chardin* to a quote in the chapter "The Basis in the Tradition" from Teilhard's "The Priest" (1918) about allowing God to grow within us. Apparently, someone at *Divinitas* ([1959]: 344) commented that this was "trusting to the resources of one's will to power." De Lubac saw this response as "a gross misconception"; de Lubac, *Religion of Teilhard de Chardin,* 56n3.

92. She also notes that both Father Ong and Claude Cuénot agree that great prudence is now necessary in planning for an American organization. It should not have a single priest's name on the organizing committee; it should be comprised only of laymen and continue to "plug away quietly and prayerfully." She sends her encouragement and tells Francoeur to realize "you are only seeing and having the experience that ... the veterans of Teilhard know only too well."

93. J. Edgar Bruns to "Bob" Francoeur, July 14, 1962, George Barbour Letters, Robert Francoeur Collection, Box 1, Folder 3, LLA. Bruns begins his letter with the comment that he missed the news item about Teilhard; unlike in Paris there was little

to think the *monitum* was inevitable, as "the die-hards seem to be winning out." Like Ewing, however, he finds it important to consider the kind of censure involved; it would have been almost as easy just to put all his works on the *Index*. Still, the censure does make it difficult to defend Teilhard on the grounds, "which are true," that his work is misunderstood. Look at all those, like the Jansenists, Bruns exclaims, who have claimed this in the past! If those interested in salvaging Teilhard could join together in petitioning the pope for dialogue on what the specific concerns are, that might prove to be useful, but "who is going to suggest that they stick their necks out?" Now, though, that the "ultras" (ultra-conservatives) have "succeeded in putting Teilhard's works under a cloud," perhaps the matter will subside.

Bruns continues to reassure Francoeur that just as his previously mentioned article in *Catholic World* noted, those responsible for the admonition would like to put back the clock; still, this will not come about. They would like to pretend Teilhard never existed, but "the deeper they dig the grave the more their efforts are noticed and mocked." He too suggests that Francoeur be more discreet in his writings, "but with those who honor the pursuit of truth, your devotion to Teilhard will be a recommendation." Additionally, as the furor grows, so are the curious attracted!

The next day Ewing wrote again, with the heading: "Last Minute Flash!"[94] He reports that he had a phone conversation with an old friend from Rome who is now a Vatican official visiting in New York City. He said that "he thinks the censure of the Holy Office is all thunder and no lightning and that probably, in ten years Teilhard will be hailed as the new Aquinas."

The *Catholic Messenger* of Davenport, Iowa, published an explanation of the *monitum* on July 26, 1962, by theologian Gregory Baum, OSA.[95] Baum had attended a conference at Rosary College in Riv-

---

fuss about it, most likely because they did not "know what it was all about (or is that an unpardonable provincialism?)."

94. Franklin Ewing to Robert Francoeur, July 15, 1962, Robert Francoeur Collection, Box 1, Folder 5 J, LLA.

95. Gregory Baum, OSA, "Warning on Teilhard," *Catholic Messenger*, Davenport, Iowa, July 26, 1962. Source incomplete, page number missing.

er Forest, Illinois, and was then a consulter to the Secretariat for Christian Unity. He commented that Teilhard's *monitum* perhaps marked a new way of handling the censorship of books for the Catholic Church. When people were forbidden to read certain books with dangerous tendencies, they could not profit from the positive elements in those works and did not understand the problems or reason that they were considered dangerous. Baum criticized the *Index* as an inadequate educational device, failing to make Catholics critical readers. Perhaps then, in his mind, this new process would be more satisfactory, as the author is not accused of unorthodoxy or bad will, and without totally rejecting his thought, certain tendencies of concern are singled out as dangerous and described in detail.

In Teilhard's case, Baum remarks, even the writers who shared some of his interests would agree that the theological details for much of what he wrote had not been worked out or the scriptural basis established. Since "modern Catholics are only beginning to reflect on the meaning of the world," too much emphasis on Teilhard's approach may veer too far away from the gospel itself. This then, "is what the warning asserts." Rather than forbidding Catholics to read Teilhard, they are asked to read critically and to search for new solutions for the problems raised by him. This warning then "combines the Church's concern for protecting truth with the modern ideal of academic freedom and inquiry."

In early August, Francoeur also heard from George Barbour, who was now in Cincinnati.[96] Barbour comments that he was glad to hear the recent news about the censorship taking place. He adds, "I assume that you have followed in Teilhard's steps and suffered for your beliefs ... others have before now had to suffer in like fashion. I pray that the road ahead be revealed to you. Wherefore I am sure you will find yourself in good company."[97]

96. At the time of this letter, Francoeur had been recalled to Steubenville by his bishop due to the controversy swirling around his Teilhardian involvement; George Barbour to Father Francoeur, August 3, 1962, from Cincinnati, Robert Francoeur Collection, Box 1, Folder 3, LLA. Barbour's "booklet" eventually was published as *In the Field with Teilhard de Chardin* in 1965 by Herder and Herder of New York.

97. Barbour shares his own news that he has been working on putting together for publication a dozen letters or so from Teilhard, with explanatory text and

In regard to further inquiries from Francoeur about a possible book, Barbour wrote again in mid-August that Charles Raven had been urging him to write a full-length biography.[98] Barbour hesitates at this, though, as in his opinion much of what had thus far been written had been done too hastily. "I do not wish to be doing that kind of shoddy job again. It is not right to Père Teilhard." Especially since he is working with some of Teilhard's original letters, rather than Barbour's own thoughts and interpretations, he does not wish to throw it "out of focus," as has occurred with some of the other letters.[99]

---

historical context, which speak of the obstacles Teilhard encountered in his own life and his reactions to these. "A booklet of this kind would be in a sense an American contribution to the growing literature on Teilhard, almost all of which, except your own booklet, came out in Europe and first in French." He mentions too that he has been in touch with Father Ewing about what should or should not be included, in order to avoid any more confrontation with Rome; George Barbour to Father Francoeur, August 3, 1962.

98. George Barbour to "Father" Robert Francoeur, August 18, 1962, from Northfield, Minnesota, Robert Francoeur Collection, Box 1, Folder 3, LLA. Charles Raven himself published *Teilhard de Chardin: Scientist and Seer* (Oxford: Blackwell, 1968). Eventually George Barbour went ahead with plans for a book of Teilhard's letters, as he discusses in a letter to Francoeur on November 20, 1962. First, he praises Charles Raven's "marvelous book," which he considered quite the best "from the pen of any man who did not know Teilhard personally." Still, he worries that so much is being published about Teilhard "in snippets by all and sundry." Barbour himself strongly feels that the most important letter in his collection is the one Teilhard wrote on the eve of his departure for Rome in 1947 to discuss what would be necessary for publication of the *Phenomenon.* That should not be buried in the midst of a collection, Barbour comments, as it says so much about Teilhard's personality and dedication.

99. In early December, Barbour wrote Francoeur once again, offering to him the letter of Teilhard mentioned earlier—the one written just before his final trip to Rome to plead for publication of *The Phenomenon.* Barbour hopes that whoever else it was that wrote about Teilhard's relationship with Rome has sensitivity and spiritual insight, someone who knew Teilhard and will not just analyze what others have said. "The enclosed letter is something very precious, that almost needs to be handled with reverence." Nothing else like it exists in print, except the one from which Pierre Leroy quotes. He notes hesitation in allowing it to be published in *CrossCurrents,* Francoeur's vehicle of choice, as that journal is primarily considered a Catholic publication, whereas Teilhard also hoped to touch the non-Catholic world. Barbour also is concerned with having the letter combined with work by other authors, some of whom stress aspects of Père Teilhard involving ideas he himself would most likely not espouse—for example, some of the psychological stuff that "seems written primarily to let the authors exploit their own little egos by pinning them to a great soul who despised such doings"; George Barbour to Father Francoeur, December 4, 1962, from Cincinnati, Robert Francoeur Collection, Box 1, Folder 3, LLA.

This concern by one who knew him well over what is published about Teilhard should be noted, as it will prove important for his future reception. Indeed, unlike the others, a copy of the response of Francoeur to this and Barbour's subsequent letter was available, which perhaps shows its importance.[100] Francoeur replied that he too is concerned about the "junk" appearing on Teilhard. He commented, "It was shocking as I went through my files and saw the dull repetition and nonsense in the majority of 'Teilhardiana.'" He also mentions that the latest news is that Père de Lubac gave a "private" talk on Teilhard de Chardin at one of the Roman churches during the Council. The "private" talk was reported in the newspapers. This development Francoeur speculates, perhaps exemplifies the attitude of Pope John XXIII against Cardinal Ottaviani.[101]

100. Robert Francoeur to George Barbour, December 5, 1962, from St. Peter's Church, Steubenville, Ohio, Barbour Collection, Box 2, Woodstock Library, Georgetown University.

101. In his *Memoires*, Henri de Lubac noted that both John XXIII and later Paul VI expressed favorable opinions of Teilhard de Chardin, an opinion shared in a speech he gave entitled "Tradition and Innovation in the Position of the Problem of God in Father Teilhard de Chardin," before an assembly of theologians at the Sixth International Thomist Congress, in the Roman Pontifical Academy of St. Thomas Aquinas in October 1965. In *Teilhard Posthume*, de Lubac writes, "I referred to a conference that I was asked to make on him in Rome in 1965. The invitation had been extended to me by Fr. Charles Boyer, Prefect at the Gregorian, at the bequest of Pope Paul VI. I have just come across his letter. When we realize that Fr. Boyer was formerly Teilhard's greatest adversary in Rome (and just as much mine!), this letter takes on its full meaning"; from de Lubac, *Teilhard Posthume: Réflexions et Souvenirs* (Paris: Fayard, 1977. The letter, addressed from "The Roman Pontifical Academy of St. Thomas Aquinas and of the Catholic Religion" and dated June 10, 1963, states, "Reverend Father, Pax Christi. You must have already received the notice concerning the sixth International Thomistic Congress. I well understand that your various occupations have prevented your taking any interest in it. But here is the reason that I venture to bring it to your notice once again. Having been received by the Holy Father [Paul VI] in the last few days, I have had the opportunity to see for myself the high esteem he has for yourself and for your writings. At the same time, he expressed, albeit with certain reservations, an opinion on Fr. Teilhard (de Chardin), which would not have displeased you. Further considerations on this matter have led me to think that, at this Congress, we should hear an exposition casting a favorable light on Teilhard de Chardin's thought on our theme ('de Deo'). No one could do this better than yourself. I beg you, therefore, to simply participate in our congress which will take place just prior to the opening of the fourth session of the Council.... (If you prefer), you could come for the last days (of the congress), and if too pressed for time, you could merely read a paper on the subject"; from de Lubac, "Memoirs Concerning My Works," in *At the Service of the Church*, 451.

In the meantime, Father Francoeur continued to be under scrutiny due to his past work with Teilhard and association with others who were similarly involved, including Dorothy Poulain. In a letter dated mid-September 1962, she makes note of Francoeur's problems with Vagnozzi, the papal legate to the United States, as well as Father Francis Fenton.[102] What about hopes for the Council to start in just a few weeks? "The general impression of everyone returning from Rome is rather pessimistic. I had a private talk with one of the big figures at the Secretariat, whose name I naturally can't disclose, but someone I've known for a long time, and he intimated that if things continue as at present we may be heading for a real 'crise dans l'Église.'" Additionally, she comments, the French, because of fears of a recurring Gallicanism, aren't trusted, and so leadership in opposition is falling to the Dutch and German, followed by the Africans and French. "We'll see what we'll see ... what a time to be alive! Convergence? Or the opposite?"

Edgar Bruns wrote Francoeur just a few days later, also noting the general disillusionment of the times.[103] He comments, "What a life! Everyone seems to be dispirited these days and little is expected from the Council. Lyonnet & Zerwick have both been forbidden to teach at the Biblical Institute in Rome (you can add their names to your list of victims).... I can assure you that neither one is, or even resembles, a radical!"[104]

Those negative thoughts were followed, though, just a week later by a short note from Poulain, who wrote, "I have a hunch that having tossed a few bones to the hunting dogs they haven't the slightest intention of really cracking down on Teilhard's works."[105]

102. Dorothy Poulain to Robert Francoeur, September 16, 1962, from Paris, Madame Poulain Letters, Robert Francoeur Collection, Box 1, Folder 9, LLA.

103. J. Edgar Bruns to Robert Francoeur, September 20, 1962, from St. Michael's College, Robert Francoeur Collection, LLA.

104. Fathers Stanislas Lyonett and Maximilian Zernick were biblical scholars at the Biblical Institute at this time who were questioned and accused for their use of form criticism in regard to the historicity of the gospels, particularly the Annunciation and primacy of Peter. Both were suspended from teaching responsibilities in biblical studies in 1962, a decision not revoked until October 1964.

105. Poulain to Francoeur, September 22, 1962, Madame Poulain correspondence, Robert Francoeur Collection, Box 1, Folder 9, LLA.

Dorothy Poulain also was preparing a piece on Teilhard for publication, this one in *Jubilee.* In a letter to Francoeur in late 1962 she notes, however, that at the moment *Jubilee* was withholding publication.[106] The editors insist that no problem exists concerning Teilhard, as people continue to read him. However, as the controversy concerning his work had finally calmed down in the States, "it would seem unwise to make an issue of it at the time."[107]

FINAL THOUGHTS

Despite any "editorial rabbitry" that may have existed, it is obvious that millions in the United States were attracted to Teilhard's thought during this time period. As this chapter has attempted to explicate, these readers and scholars were overwhelmingly attracted to his synthetic worldview, a meta-narrative that managed to integrate science with a Catholic mystic's spiritual poetry. Additionally, in Teilhard's work they saw an affirmation of the value of the natural world and the importance of everyday life for humanity's progress, both of which were especially prized by the American populace.

Those in the United States, like people worldwide, were fascinated by his optimistic sense, fostered by his Christology, that progress toward an organic whole, toward some form of greater unity is inevitable, even when that progress is marred by apparent stumbling blocks, such as the difficulties described in this chapter. Not only his writing, but also his life, were a lived example of Christian hope prevailing against all odds, even in times of war, exile, and darkness. As several of the letters quoted in this chapter indicate, Teilhard's character, his warmth, and compassion, as much as his ability to "speak the language of our time," attracted people.

106. Poulain to Francoeur, November 30, 1962, Madame Poulain correspondence, Robert Francoeur Collection, Box 1, Folder 9, LLA.

107. Concerning this, Poulain comments that "my personal feeling is that Price (editor of *Jubilee*) has had an attack of what a well-known writer friend of mine calls 'Editorial Rabbitry' (just plain cold feet!)." Note that she is here referring to Edward Rice. She continues on to ask how the "Committee" who gave permission for her to write the article can take American Catholic publishing seriously, after such a way of acting? Apparently, Cuénot is not the "only one to complain of U.S. editors, many of whom coolly cut a text or 'fix' it in order to avoid censorship."

As Teilhard was not a Thomist and had no use for scholastic concepts, controversy raged over his thought. His Christology diluted boundaries between the natural and supernatural, the secular and the sacred. In addition, Teilhard was a man of innate historical consciousness, serving and writing in a church that was not yet quite sure it wished to admit to any historical development. The wisdom of Teilhard, particularly since it was presented in idiosyncratic terminology, "could not fail to disturb some members of the Catholic hierarchy."[108] This thus impeded its positive acceptance. Teilhard's work remained a "hot potato," successively praised and condemned by the Jesuits, the church hierarchy, and independent scholars. That controversy itself drew interested readers to his publications. Ironically, the *monitum* concerning Teilhard's writing that was issued by the Holy See during these years also encouraged many among the curious to seek out his works.

Yet, changes in the structure of society and the church were inevitable and rampant during this decade. Those changes, as discussed in chapter 3, will lead to a shift in the reception of Teilhard both in the church, as well as in the larger Catholic and non-Catholic U.S. population.

108. Merton, "Universe as Epiphany," 176.

3 ~ AMERICAN TIES AND RECOVERY

THIS CHAPTER explores several societal movements that begin in earnest during these years and their significance for the reception of Teilhard. In addition, noteworthy journal essays, academic or public conferences, and literary works that speak to the growing attention to and the recovery of Teilhard in the United States in the years following the issuance of the *monitum* will be examined.

Several recurring themes appear in regard to the reception of Teilhard during these years. As mentioned, primary among these is the appreciation in the United States for his love of the material world. In a complementary sense, this also pertains to his views regarding the secular world and everyday life. For Teilhard, what happens in daily life, the work people do and their response to what comes along, really does matter in a spiritual and evolutionary framework. Also, Teilhard's positive stance toward progress and science is crucial for his popularity in this time period; this attitude correlates powerfully with the American proclivity toward an almost naive optimistic trust in pragmatic scientific progress and human endeavor. For American Catholics a propensity toward the latter as it pertains to the church manifests itself in what at times has been termed "Americanism"; Teilhard's thought, if not actually favorable toward Americanism, was interpreted in this way by many. A reason for this interpretation is Teilhard's evolutionary understanding of change. In his worldview, change is intrinsic to ongoing life. Therefore, for the church to survive, for example, it must indeed change and evolve. In an era when a new historical consciousness is rocking the bastions of the Catholic Church, this awareness is both vital and threatening.

During the years discussed in this chapter, the emphasis begins to shift to methods by which to make use of his ideas within a practical, humanistic standpoint. These tactics are particularly useful not only in academia, their original area of application, but also in light of the American political and social milieu; for example, they are used by the administration in the call to service and in the battle for racial justice.

A select few will also comprehend and attempt to convey the mystical foundations of Teilhard's Christological worldview and its possibilities for both being church and "doing" church. For this group of people, rather than evidencing solely confidence in certain scientific or social progress, his mystical relationship with Christ is understood as the source of Teilhard's ever-present optimism.

THE SOCIAL CONTEXT OF THE UNITED STATES IN THE EARLY 1960S

Considering the social context, the first years of this time period in many ways continued to be a carryover of the themes of the fifties, and those concerns addressed in chapter 1 certainly still prevailed. However, earlier religious motifs were also under increasing pressure from the civil rights movement, the Kennedy presidential years and later assassination, and the eagerly anticipated changes of the Second Vatican Council. Robert Ellwood, for one, considers the decade of the 1960s as the era the apocalyptic "children of light" were in battle with the "children of darkness."[1] Dualisms abounded; consider for one, the Cold War image of communism versus Americanism. This apocalyptic battle is symbolized well in the civil rights crusade of African Americans against "Bull" Connor and George Wallace. In

1. Robert S. Ellwood, *The Sixties Spiritual Awakening: American Religion Moving from Modern to Postmodern* (New Brunswick, N.J.: Rutgers University Press, 1994), 20.

just a few years, the "children of light" will be transformed into the communities of light and unity active in the antiwar movement, the counterculture, communalism, and the post–Vatican II church.

American society was transformed by these crusades and movements as public interest in Teilhard increased. So many thought that new doors were opening, that innovative ways of being were becoming available; one sees this, for example, in the hope that the Second Vatican Council will bring a fresh manner of the church's presence in the world, something more than "the dead inertia of merely conventional Christianity" against which both Teilhard and Thomas Merton protested.[2] Teilhard's vision was perceived as one that offered a pathway by which dualisms could be resolved and the future obtained.

Francoeur's attitude toward Rome, as discussed in chapter 2, seems typical of some in American Catholic circles at this time. Jay Dolan would have us believe that by the early 1960s, being Catholic was "compatible with being American," and "reasons for Catholic pride" and confidence were everywhere.[3] Although perhaps not the universal truth, it is undeniably true that a new age and a new people were demanding a new Catholicism. The calls for reform and renewal were coming more frequently from around the world, and certainly from progressives in the United States. They rejoiced when Pope John XXIII in January 1959 declared, "We announce to you, indeed trembling a little with emotion, but at the same time with humble resolution of intention ... an ecumenical council for the Universal Church." However, already the American Catholic world was not in agreement as to whether such a happening was desirable.[4] This division will certainly not disappear in the years to come.

2. Thomas Merton, "Teilhard's Gamble," in *Love and Living*, ed. Naomi Burton Stone and Patrick Hart (1979; repr. New York: Harcourt, Brace Jovanovich, 1985), 185.

3. Jay Dolan, *The American Catholic Experience: A History from Colonial Times to the Present* (Notre Dame, Ind.: University of Notre Dame Press, 1992), 417.

4. Pope John XXIII's speech was given to seventeen cardinals in the Basilica of St. Paul-Outside-the-Walls on January 25, 1959; accessed February 22, 2015, http://www.vatican2voice.org/91docs/announcement.htm. Although Jay Dolan writes that the majority of American Catholics eagerly anticipated any changes an ecumenical council might bring to update the church, by contrast Patrick Carey, in *Catholics in America*, suggests just the opposite. "Neither American bishops nor laity had any clear

Those Catholics seeking change, though, similarly rejoiced two years later in January 1961 when the Catholic John F. Kennedy took the presidential oath of office. He spoke of a new frontier, of the necessity of sacrifice for the good of the country, and of the strength of America. He especially stirred up the idealism of the young people—what we today would call the oldest "baby boomers" born after World War II—who appreciated his vision, intelligence, and wit. Kennedy did not hesitate to tackle the religious issue head-on, and at a meeting of Protestant ministers in Houston, he stated that he would take orders from the people of the United States, rather than from the pope. He would accept and operate as president within the parameters of separation of church and state.[5]

Although Kennedy won the election, he did so by the slimmest of margins; still, he put to rest the notion that a Catholic could not be elected to high office. Additionally, his obvious education, poise, wealth, and admired wife were all signs that American Catholics truly had come of age and were now well integrated into American society.[6]

To begin this section I consider the implications of three already mentioned major American events upon the reception of Teilhard—the election and subsequent assassination of John Fitzgerald Kennedy, the popularity of Pope John XXIII and his commencement of the Second Vatican Council, and the civil rights movement. All these, however, are placed within the context of a 1960s rendition of Catholic "Americanism" that must first be examined.

---

ideas of what to expect from a council, and perhaps few saw the necessity for one in the first place. Catholicism in America was strong institutionally. Like Cardinal James McIntyre of Los Angeles, many American Catholics saw 'no need for change'"; Carey, *Catholics in America: A History* (Westport, Conn.: Praeger, 2004), 112. The final quote is from Philip Gleason, "A Browser's Guide to American Catholicism, 1950–1980," *Theology Today* 38 (October 1981): 375; see also Dolan, *American Catholic Experience,* 417–18.

5. John F. Kennedy, "Address to the Houston Ministerial Association," in Houston, Texas, in September 1960 can be found in Elizabeth McKeowan and Steven M. Avella, eds., *Public Voices: Catholics in the American Context* (Maryknoll, N.Y.: Orbis, 1999): 361–64.

6. Dolan, *American Catholic Experience,* 422.

CONCERNING AMERICANISM

It is not the purpose of this study to examine in detail the issues and historiography of Americanism as it has been understood over the last century.[7] What follows, therefore, is a succinct background for an understanding of how Americanism influenced the reception of Teilhard in the United States in the 1960s. As was mentioned in chapter 2, Dorothy Poulain, friend of Teilhard, Henri de Lubac, and Robert Francoeur, was more than aware of the concept and its history and without provocation shared the parallels she saw between Americanism and Teilhard's thought, as well as the manner in which both were received, at least by some, in the United States.[8]

The original leaders of the movement that eventually would be labeled "Americanism" were not, according to the scholar Thomas McAvoy, consciously pursuing a national American Catholicism.[9] They were instead attempting to "solve the problem of Catholics in the United States." They initially wished to adapt Catholic practices, especially those foreign traditions that had accompanied the recent Catholic immigrants to this country during the mid-nineteenth century. The question, one might say, was "how to acclimatize Catholic practices to the American milieu."[10] Those who favored adjustment were the Americanists, while those opposing felt this move was heretical. Ultimately, as McAvoy asserts, this became a theological and cultural battle.[11] During the nineteenth century American Catholi-

7. A good place to start that study would be *The Americanist Controversy: Recent Historical and Theological Perspectives*, special issue, *U.S. Catholic Historian* 11, no. 3 (Summer 1993), or John Farina, ed., *Hecker Studies: Essays on the Thought of Isaac Hecker* (New York: Paulist Press, 1983).

8. The French ties of the Americanists are another reason to not only examine the similarities between their thought and Teilhard's, but also discuss both Poulain and Henri de Lubac's involvement in Teilhard's American reception. With thanks to William Portier for the comment that in many ways Teilhard's reception in America is the reversal of Isaac Hecker's reception in France.

9. Thomas McAvoy, *The Great Crisis in American Catholic History, 1895–1900* (Chicago: Henry Regnery, 1957), 20.

10. Ibid., x.

11. Ibid. Additionally, McAvoy comments later at 354 that without a doubt, "American Catholicism has been always essentially the same as any European, Asiatic, or African Catholicism, but at the same time it has almost always had some qualities brought about by circumstances of time and place which make it American."

cism became quite different from Catholicism in England and Europe, as the governmental, geographic, and economic culture of the new country was singular.

Abbé Bricourt, editor in the late nineteenth century of the journal *Revue du Clergé Français*, wrote that what defined American Catholicism was, first, love of science, and second, love of democracy.[12] The "Americanist" bishops of the late nineteenth century dreamed of evangelizing American culture, even while trying to convince the surrounding culture that Catholicism could be more than simply an alien force in a democratic, pluralistic society. Instead, they and millions of other immigrants implicitly recognized that the freedom of the United States gave them "a chance to live their Faith to the fullest," thus making of American Catholicism something quite distinct in the church.[13]

When *The Life of Father Hecker*, a biography written by Isaac Hecker's disciple and fellow Paulist Walter Elliot, was translated into French and published in 1896, it set off a heated controversy, particularly in Europe.[14] Abbé Felix Klein asserted in his preface for the translation that Hecker was the exemplary priest for the times

12. J. Bricourt, "Américanisme," *Revue du Clergé Français* 15 (June–August, 1898): 416–35, quoted in McAvoy, *Great Crisis in American Catholic History*, 359.

13. McAvoy, *Great Crisis in American Catholic History*, 365.

14. In his book *New Experiment in Democracy* (Kansas City: Sheed and Ward, 1987), Dennis McCann comments that the Hecker biography came under Vatican surveillance primarily because the French translation (and Klein's introduction) were taken so seriously by French liberals (the "Gallicans" to whom Poulain refers elsewhere) seeking to work out an accommodation with the new French Republic. They were in turn opposed by the conservative Catholic French monarchists (10). Teilhard was a firm believer in progress and evolution, yet in a resolutely Christian manner, similar to that of the Americanists of the late nineteenth century. One might recall the writings of Walter Elliott, friend and disciple of Isaac Hecker, himself founder of the Paulists, who consistently claimed Christ as the culmination of the providential workings of history. Christ's activity was centered not above and beyond time, but in, through, and at the final end of it. The links that Elliott made among creation, humanism, and the unifying aspects of Christ's love were common among the Americanists. Teilhard would have been studying among the Jesuits in 1897 when Elliott's biography of Hecker was translated into French. Most likely he heard, and maybe participated in, the intense discussions concerning *l'Americanisme.* Possibly, he later incorporated some of the same general themes into his own work. Perhaps, then, it is these underlying, if unrecognized, similarities between the Americanists and Teilhard's work that American Catholics in particular found so intriguing and satisfying.

and suggested that the church should adapt itself to "the age." As a result, in 1899 Pope Leo XIII issued the Apostolic Letter *Testem benevolentiae*, addressed to Cardinal James Gibbons of Baltimore.

Catholic leaders in the United States denied at the time that they held the views addressed in this letter. The Americanists at whom the letter was aimed stated that the condemned doctrines were "phantoms" created by their enemies and had no basis in fact. However, we must also be aware that at the turn of the twentieth century many Americans still viewed the United States as the shining city on the hill, a blessed nation full of optimism and teeming with opportunity.

That understanding of their country as providentially chosen for a special divine destiny has deep roots in the American past, beginning with seventeenth-century New England Puritans.[15] Whether Puritanism evolved into or greatly influenced political Americanism, the cultural worldview of Americans as God's new chosen people, living in God's new promised land—in short, as God's new Israel—remained rampant throughout the first half of the twentieth century.[16]

This disputation, coupled with the encyclical *Pascendi dominici gregis* of 1907, which condemned the heresy of modernism, encouraged any inherent American Catholic tendencies toward Americanism to instead become focused on the "practical and concerned with the everyday, and this practicality became sacramental. It was not dogmatic or even too liturgical."[17] As Joseph Chinnici has discussed, the reaction from Rome subsumed the Americanists' and especially Hecker's holistic worldview to neo-Scholasticism's "two perfect but separate orders" of church and society. This fractured view held sway in the American Catholic Church until the 1960s, at which time due at least in part to the work of Teilhard whose work was itself so well-integrated, movement toward synthesis became more pronounced.[18]

15. See, for example, Conrad Cherry, ed., *God's New Israel: Religious Interpretations of American Destiny*, 2nd ed. (Chapel Hill: University of North Carolina Press, 1998).

16. Consider David Gelernter, "Americanism—and Its Enemies," *Commentary* 119, no. 1 (January 2005): 41–48.

17. McAvoy, *Great Crisis in American Catholic History*, 365.

18. Joseph P. Chinnici, OFM, ed., *Devotion to the Holy Spirit in American Catholicism* (Mahwah, N.J.: Paulist Press, 1985), 78–84. Chinnici suggests that *Testem benevolentiae*

For David O'Brien, among others, the tradition associated with Hecker and Ireland continued in modified form in the work of liberal Catholics like John Burke, John A. Ryan, Michael Williams, John Courtney Murray, and George Shuster. He suggests that although they offered considerable ethical reflection on economics and politics, for them it was a matter of pragmatic philosophy and ethics, rather than of theology and grace.[19]

Still, as Philip Gleason has written, most of these Catholics, in addition to many other Catholic scholars of the 1950s, supported the policy that deprecated Catholic "separatism" and encouraged them to instead "break out of the ghetto" and immerse themselves into the mainstream of American life. He comments, "The congruence between this policy and the views of the Americanists of the 1890s is obvious." As Gleason additionally noted, the sudden outpouring of scholarship regarding the Americanists during the 1950s provided the historical precedent for midcentury Catholic liberalism, the acceptance of the Vatican II reforms, and the future rapprochement between American Catholicism and modernity.[20] In so doing, they helped to set the stage for a positive reception of Teilhard and for the secular Catholic John Fitzgerald Kennedy.

Throughout the rest of this chapter, four central Americanist

---

forced the severance of Isaac Hecker's doctrine of the Holy Spirit from any connection with everyday social activity or even ecclesiastical reform. As a result, his holistic belief in the unity of personal, social, religious, and political reform through the guidance of the Spirit was lost to Pope Leo XIII's pronouncement of church and society as two perfect but quite separate orders. See also Chinnici, *Living Stones: The History and Structure of Catholic Spiritual Life in the United States* (New York: Macmillan, 1989), 119–36 and 120, where he contrasts the vision of the "Immigrant Church" with the "Americanist Vision." See also Margaret M. Reher, "Phantom Heresy: A Twice-Told Tale," in *The Americanist Controversy: Recent Historical and Theological Perspectives,* special issue, *U.S. Catholic Historian,* 11 no. 3 (Summer 1993): 93–105.

19. David J. O'Brien, "The American Laity: Memory, Meaning and Mission," *America,* March 7, 1987. Scott Appleby would also include in this number Charles Curran, George Weigel, Rosemary Ruether, William F. Buckley Jr., Michael Novak, Mary Jo Weaver, James Hitchcock, Dennis McCann, and Carl Anderson; see Appleby, "The Neo-Americanist Center and the Limits of Conservative Dissent," *Americanism and Americanization: Essays in Honor of Philip Gleason,* special issue, *U.S. Catholic Historian* 17, no. 1 (Winter 1999): 13–27.

20. Philip Gleason, "The New Americanism in Catholic Historiography," *The Americanist Controversy: Recent Historical and Theological Perspectives,* special issue, *U.S. Catholic Historian* 11, no. 3 (Summer 1993): 1–18.

themes will be referred to often and will serve our purposes well. They are: (1) The world is in an era of radical change; (2) America is at the cutting edge of change and is indeed the very embodiment of the future; (3) the Catholic Church is obliged to change with the times; and (4) the Catholic Church in America has been given a divine mission to point American society toward Christ and the church.[21]

THE CULTURAL SITUATION IN THE UNITED STATES

The Election and Death of JFK

Despite Vatican denouncements, pragmatic Americanism continued underground throughout the early and into the mid-twentieth century, culminating in the election of the first Roman Catholic president, John Fitzgerald Kennedy, in 1960. With the rise of the two "Johns," the other being Pope John XXIII, American Catholics found the "shining city on the hill" image once again quite apt.[22] The understanding of many that they had been given a special mission to point American society toward Christ and the church was greatly heightened.

Robert Ellwood suggests that at first the sixties were the ultimate expression of modernism.[23] If one agrees with Lyotard's two metanarratives of modernity, which are the emancipation of humanity by progress both political and scientific and the unity of knowledge in a way amenable to rational, scientific abstraction and technological implementation, then the late 1950s brought examples of the fulfillment of both.[24] Certainly, for American Catholics the election

21. Rory Conley, *Caelum et Terra* (Winter 1993), quoted in Russell Shaw, "Americanism: Then and Now," accessed June 22, 2012, http://www.ewtn.com/library/ISSUES/AMERICAN.TXT.

22. The "two Johns" reference is from Garry Wills, *Bare Ruined Choirs: Doubt, Prophecy and Radical Religion* (New York: Doubleday, 1972), chap. 4, "The Two Johns: Rome and the Secular City."

23. Ellwood, *Sixties*, chap. 1.

24. In *Jazz Age Catholicism: Mystic Modernism in Post-War Paris 1919–1933* (Toronto: University of Toronto Press, 2005), Stephen Schloesser suggests the idea of modernity as the invention of linear time: of a setting of oneself over and against "traditional" visions of the world and embracing the notion that the world is (a) materialist; (b) fated

of Kennedy, the space race, the immense increase in attendance at Catholic universities, and John XXIII's announcement of the future Second Vatican Council could be construed as the fulfillment of these metanarratives. The first Americanist theme, that the world is in an era of radical change, certainly appeared to be true. Additionally, the increasing drive to complete a progressive agenda through civil rights, the space race, even the Vietnam War with its democratic concerns in Southeast Asia were seen as expressing a "universal" commitment to American-style democracy. America was indeed at that moment at the cutting edge of change and embodied the future; JFK and Martin Luther King Jr. were the elites devoted to the high ideals of modernism, symbols of progress, and a communal, spiritual awakening.[25]

When he chose to run for the Democratic nomination in 1960, Kennedy knew that his Catholic background would be a problem. His campaign speeches emphasized that his religion, a private matter for him, would not get in the way of his public office. Certainly, a significant moment occurred when, in September of 1960, he addressed a group of Protestant ministers in Houston, Texas, and received a standing ovation after stating, "I believe in an America where separation for church and state is absolute."[26] He pledged that if ever he encountered a situation when he felt unable in conscience to carry out his political duty, he would resign.

Garry Wills maintains that the Catholic liberalism that was on the rise at this time contended that church teaching properly understood was identical to American political ideas—*individualist,*

---

to be always progressing (that is, an inversion of the "Great Chain of Being"); and (c) composed of autonomous individuals. In contrast, although Teilhard embraced temporality, his conception of progress hinged upon the understanding that free will allows each person to contribute toward the "Christification" of the universe (the ultimate teleology of "progress") or its dissolution. In a similar fashion, the apex of the world is the unity of individuals in solidarity. "Our hope can only be realized if it finds its expression in greater cohesion and greater human solidarity"; Teilhard de Chardin, *The Future of Mankind* (New York: Harper and Row, 1959), 9.

25. Ellwood, *Sixties,* 19.

26. Wills, *Bare Ruined Choirs,* 79. See the text of Kennedy's Address to the Houston Ministerial Association in September 1960, in McKeowan and Avella, *Public Voices,* 361–64.

because based on the rights of each man's conscience; *pluralist*, protecting all consciences as the way to protect any one person's; and *secular*, making the division between church and state a matter of conscience.[27] Catholics who supported Kennedy were delighted that others now recognized that separate spheres for action made Catholic politics the most American kind of politics as well as the most effective kind and that they had an educated, secular, and affluent Catholic who exemplified this so well.[28] The affluence of the Kennedys spoke to all those other upwardly mobile, young, and newly suburban Catholics of the age of the endless possibility of progress, of making all things new and shucking off the old. Kennedy's ability to compartmentalize his religious faith from his politics speaks not only to the separation of church from state resulting from *Testem benevolentiae*, but also to the increasing secularization already seen at the beginning of this decade. It also assumes the third Americanist theme: that the Catholic Church is obliged to change with the times and that it will at the same time encourage American Catholics to adopt that same assumption.

During his inaugural address, Kennedy acknowledged that the Cold War era had pitted America against her ideological rivals but insisted also that the nation's real common enemies were "tyranny, poverty, disease and war itself." The young were to serve their country and all of humanity in order to progress toward a better America.[29]

The impact of this "Ask not" speech derived not so much from

27. Wills, *Bare Ruined Choirs*, 84.

28. Ibid., 88. Another, similar perspective on the importance of President John F. Kennedy to some American Catholics can be found in Andrew Greeley, *The Catholic Experience: A Sociologist's Interpretation of the History of American Catholicism* (New York: Doubleday, 1967), 280–98. Greeley first suggests in this last chapter of his book that "in another age . . . John Kennedy would be hailed as a saint" (280). However, as that was not likely to happen today, perhaps instead he could be acclaimed as a "hero of the Church" (281). Or, he asks, what of naming him a "Doctor of the Universal Church?" (282). In another nod to the Americanist thesis explored in this chapter, Greeley notes numerous similarities between John Kennedy and Bishop John England. He argues that the "election of a Catholic president offers an opportunity of the sort found only in 1820 with John England and in 1885 with the Americanists." Kennedy's presidency, however, might have been the last such opportunity (298).

29. David M. Haugen and Matthew J. Box, eds., *Examining Pop Culture: The 1960s* (Detroit: Greenhaven, 2005), and Mark Lytle, *America's Uncivil Wars: The Sixties Era from Elvis to the Fall of Richard Nixon* (New York: Oxford University Press, 2006).

what was said, but the manner in which it was said and the visual portrayal of the media. "There, coatless and hatless on a bitter January day, stood a vibrant young leader looking steadfastly into the future and challenging the nation to realize its destiny. That was the kind of authenticity so many young Americans yearned for."[30] Similarly, the new space program reasserted American technological supremacy. Through this, Kennedy reaffirmed the American sense of possibility, progress, and promise implicit in the first two Americanist assumptions.[31]

Then he was dead. Would the country feel confidence and hope for the future ever again? Perhaps even more than his election, Kennedy's assassination was the decisive watershed that marked the real beginning of the sixties for many.[32] When he was murdered on the streets of Dallas in 1963, it was not just Catholics who wept at his passing. This event was just the first in a series that would temporarily decimate the Americanist optimism about historic destiny still building in 1962. It also, according to Mark Lytle, galvanized the youth of the age, who in increasing numbers now began to look for answers to the question of "Why?" In both the optimism and the seeking, Americans would turn to Teilhard for inspiration.

30. Lytle, *America's Uncivil Wars*, 106.

31. Ibid., 139. Again, those two Americanist assumptions were that the world is in an era of radical change and that America is at the cutting edge of change and is indeed the very embodiment of the future. Therefore, for example, America must win the space race. Some within the Kennedy administration, particularly Sargent Shriver, his brother-in-law, found Teilhard's thought so amenable to Kennedy "Camelot" politics that Robert McNamara, secretary of defense, put Teilhard's name on a list of most valued authors for the administration; see Wills, *Bare Ruined Choirs*, 98. In recognition of the ready reception of Teilhard's thought by the Kennedy administration, Wills also notes later in his book that "this strange priest in the French army [Teilhard] was preparing the rationale for a weird American optimism, voiced ... a decade after Teilhard's own death. He became the posthumous theologian to Camelot" (117).

32. Ellwood, *Sixties*, 102. See also Philip Jenkins, *Decades of Nightmares: The End of the Sixties and the Making of Eighties America* (New York: Oxford University Press, 2006), and Lytle, *America's Uncivil Wars*.

Moving toward Vatican II

In the early 1960s, at least officially, a neo-Scholastic dichotomy between the sacred and the secular, religion and science, clergy and laity still existed on each side of the Atlantic. John XXIII had already changed the atmosphere, though.[33] This was still the age of faith, despite all the talk of secularity. As Ellwood commented, the decade did not so much "secularize the sacred as sacralize the secular." It turned "its causes into crusades and its activism into liturgies ... the [young] especially knew no dearth of sacraments and sacramentals."[34]

Then "Pope John's Revolution" began. Four centuries after Trent, the Counter-Reformation epoch came to an end. Two great encyclicals, *Mater et magistra* and *Pacem in terris,* in conjunction with the Second Vatican Council, would again open the conversation with the modern world that had been stifled for almost a century.[35]

Certainly, the dominant religious figure in the world at this time was Pope John XXIII. His calls for *aggiornamento,* or updating the life of the church, gladdened all hearts; the true revolution, Ellwood writes, was in his warm, spontaneous, natural personality. Suddenly the emphasis became love over legalism, grace over gravity.[36] In 1959 the pope called for a general council, a "New Pentecost" that was to eventually radically change the face of Roman Catholicism, just as Martin Luther King's words would for black Americans.[37] This council was to deal with the relationship of the church to the mod-

33. An examination of the pre–Vatican II church can be found in Gregory Baum, OSA, ed., *The Twentieth Century: A Theological Overview* (Maryknoll, N.Y.: Orbis, 1999), particularly chapter 2 written by Victor Consemius, "The Condemnation of Modernism and the Survival of Catholic Theology," 14–26; and Robert Schreiter, CPPS, "The Impact of Vatican II," 158–72. An examination of the lived spirituality of the Catholic population during these decades can be found in James P. McCartin, *Prayers of the Faithful: The Shifting Spiritual Life of American Catholics* (Cambridge, Mass: Harvard University Press, 2010), 71–138.

34. Ellwood, *Sixties,* 19.

35. *Mater et magistra,* written by Pope John XXIII, was on the topic of "Christianity and Social Progress." *Pacem in terris* (Peace on Earth): *On Establishing Universal Peace in Truth, Justice, Charity and Liberty* was John XXIII's other encyclical, issued in April, 1963. *Pacem in terris* was the first encyclical that a pope addressed to "all men of good will," rather than only to Catholics.

36. Ellwood, *Sixties,* 66.

37. Ibid., 85.

ern world, eventually including liturgical reform, the relationship between church and state, religious freedom, greater collegiality between bishops and Vatican, and perhaps even ecumenical reunion.

For Catholics around the world, the Second Vatican Council was yet another spark of optimism that was to grow into a full-fledged fire.[38] For the first time the Catholic Church's leaders were attempting to come to grips with the issues of modernity in a positive, constructive manner. Numerous American Catholics of the past, particularly those Americanists such as John Carroll, Isaac Hecker, and John Ireland, had made the same attempt. By the 1960s, however, Catholics were much readier to accept the Americanist idea that the church must change with the times, whether in theology, liturgy, or attitude toward the world. It is no surprise that Teilhard, who had eagerly pursued the integration of modern science with Catholicism and who had especially intended his book *The Divine Milieu* for modern people who "loved the world," would be caught up in this catholic revolution.

Additionally, far more pastoral than the popes of the recent past, John XXIII also pleaded for movement toward Christian unity. As a result, when the Council opened in the fall of 1962, Protestants for the first time ever attended an ecumenical council as invited observers. This was a small step, but one that pointed in a far more dramatic way to a new perspective. The neo-Scholastic worldview was slowly, often reluctantly (as obvious from the impatient comments about particular Council bishops in the letters to Francoeur that are discussed later in this chapter) opening to one with a more modern, historical perspective. This could only bode well for those like Teilhard who saw and wrote in this manner forty years before the Council even began.

Although both Johns died within five months of each other in 1963, Pope John's successor, Paul VI, took up where his predecessor left off and brought the Council to a successful conclusion in the fall of 1965. The Council produced sixteen documents that together sought to revitalize both church and world.

38. Dolan, *American Catholic Experience*, 424.

In terms of controversy, as the previous chapter alluded, the Council showcased the emergence of dissent and change within the church. At the very first session of the Council in 1962, a number of bishops protested the proposed agenda, the people selected for major committee positions, and the initial prepared documents. John XXIII did so also. The newspapers covering the Council were quick to pick up on this and expounded upon fissures within the foundations of what had previously seemed a static, unchanging institution. "Divine Providence is leading us to a new order of human relations," expounded Pope John in his opening message; it was time for the church "to bring herself up-to-date where required."[39] *Aggiornamento* would occur in the church. Rather than consider what the future might bring as something to fear, "we feel that we must disagree with these prophets of doom, who are always forecasting disaster as though the end of the world were at hand."

As Wills noted, many considered Vatican II as the vindication of Teilhard.[40] Chapter 4 will further explore how his themes of unity, progress, and hope were rampant in the final documents of the Ecumenical Council.

39. Pope John XXIII, "Opening Speech of the Second Vatican Council," October 11, 1962, accessed April 2, 2013, http://conciliaria.com/2011/12/john-xxiii-convokes-council/.

40. The entirety of the quote from Wills is, "Many call Vatican II the vindication of Teilhard, considering him its absent but presiding genius"; Wills, *Bare Ruined Choirs*, 99. Note that Wills does not reference who the "many" are. It should also be explained here that Wills's purpose in writing on Teilhard was certainly not to justify his thought, but instead to note his proclivity to the Kennedy administration, the Americanists, and the Vatican II era. The title for his chapter on Teilhard is, "Omega, the New Frontier," and he begins it with the quote from John F. Kennedy's nomination speech: "I tell you the New Frontier is here whether we seek it or not.... I believe the times demand invention, innovation, imagination, decision." An underlying thesis throughout the chapter is his argument that in a large sense Teilhard glorifies war and that his primary spiritual formation came not from his Catholic faith and religious experience, but from the novels of the author Robert Hugh Benson. Teilhard read these during World War I, and Wills argues he later incorporated Benson's primary themes into his own work; see Wills, "Omega, the New Frontier," in *Bare Ruined Choirs*, 97–117.

Civil Rights

Another sign of progress toward unity and optimism was the civil rights movement. By 1960, civil rights became imperative for many, who saw the years of nonviolent sit-ins and the Freedom Rides of 1960–61 as the movement's greatest glory. Certainly one could also include in this category the March on Washington under Martin Luther King in 1963, leading up to the Civil Rights Act of 1964 and the Voting Rights Act of 1965. Ellwood would argue that the civil rights movement itself began as an upsurge of modernity fed by the belief in progress. As the movement progressed, however, certain achievements were won, and consequently more demands arose; the then prevalent modernist agenda could not respond adequately to the demands of the population.[41] The result was inner-city riots, the rise of the Black Panthers, the assassinations of Martin Luther King, Malcom X, and Robert Kennedy, a splintering into factions of previously united groups, and a subsequent loss of hope.

Still, Martin Luther King Jr.'s "I have a dream" speech at the March on Washington in 1963 touched many hearts. His call for a new form of unity for all, a new, greater vision for the future, a brotherly love healing all wounds of race and slavery and bringing all peoples together—even if much anticipated—especially spoke volumes to the younger generations.[42] It was a time when a sense of unity prevailed, if only briefly. Even the Beatles rhapsodized about a new feeling of love that had to do with spiritual well-being; it was love as an existential quality.[43] That kind of love "brought to the world a higher sense of harmony and goodwill, a sense of brotherhood and communal feeling not unlike the ethos advocated by the integrationist faction of the civil rights movement."[44]

41. Ellwood, *Sixties*, 71.

42. Lytle, *America's Uncivil Wars*, 136.

43. A soundtrack remix album of music recorded by the Beatles in the 1960s, and actually given the title "Love," was released in November 2006. It features tracks such as "Eleanor Rigby," "Because," "I Want to Hold Your Hand," and "Here Comes the Sun," which were compiled and remixed for the Cirque du Soleil show *Love.* Producers were George and Giles Marin.

44. Lytle, *America's Uncivil Wars*, 146.

As Mark Silk has commented, the civil rights movement itself was often tied up with religion.[45] The religion of the civil rights movement, Ellwood also contends, was in some ways very distinct from the rest of the sixties religious scene. It was rooted in the traditions of the Black church and was not theologically adventurous like the more secular theologies, but was instead biblically rooted, emotional, and communal. Unlike the later mysticism of the counterculture, it was more interested in the practical than in transcendental visionary experiences. Participants preferred to reflect upon how their faith lives were to be a force for social and inward freedom, for salvation from social oppression.[46] A quote from Martin Luther King expresses this well: "If today's church does not recapture the sacrificial spirit of the early church, it will lose its authenticity, forfeit the loyalty of millions, and be dismissed as an irrelevant social club with no meaning for the twentieth century."[47] Teilhard wrestled with this same concern for decades before his death, questioning what his Christological worldview might have to offer the beloved people of his church who so often found Christ and faith superfluous to their life. Indeed, he had written in 1953, "Christianity still to some degree provides a shelter for the 'modern soul,' but it no longer *clothes* it, nor *satisfies* it, nor *leads* it. Something has gone wrong—and so something more in the area of faith and religion, must be supplied without delay on this planet."[48]

45. Mark Silk, *Spiritual Politics: Religion and America since World War II* (New York: Simon and Schuster, 1988), 3.

46. Ellwood, *Sixties*, 80.

47. Dr. Martin Luther King Jr., quoted in Silk, *Spiritual Politics*, 3.

48. Teilhard de Chardin, "God and Evolution," in *Christianity and Evolution*, trans. René Hague (New York: Harcourt, 1971), 237. In another essay from the same volume, titled, "What the World Is Looking for from the Church of God at this Moment: A Generalizing and a Deepening of the Meaning of the Cross," Teilhard argues that it is time that a new meaning for the cross and the Paschal mystery of Christ be found for the contemporary world, one that moves away from a mistrust of humanity and matter and a "catastrophic conception" of the world because of original sin, toward one that can coexist with a human nature very much at home in a changing world. "This cross should present itself to us as a sign, not merely of 'escape,' but of progress." It must be not just about purification, but a sign of the ongoing evolution or cosmogenesis of the world. This cross is not a sign that minimizes the role of sacrifice but adds to the "already existing pain of expiation" the yet more demanding pain of sharing in what Teilhard calls "the universal labor which is indispensable to its

RECONCILIATION AND THE RECOVERY OF TEILHARD

Even before anything explicitly concerning Teilhard's influence on the Council or any official "softening" of the powers that be toward him was published, those aware intuitively understood that movement toward reconciliation was occurring. A letter from Dorothy Poulain to Robert Francoeur in March of 1963 suggests just this. Poulain is delighted that some "rumpus" like Americanism is at last occurring again in the States. This, "plus the U.S. Bishops' eye-openers at the Council, maybe will start what all Europe has been yearning for: The breaking of the spell under which the 'American Giant' has been sleeping for so long! And may he ROAR! This, my fellow-countryman is your 'Gold Opportunity.' Every enlightened Catholic everywhere will be cheering you heartily."[49] One must suppose that the "all Europe" to which Poulain refers here is primarily her fellow French Teilhardians; it is interesting that at this point in Catholic history it appears she and her fellows themselves acknowledge an aforementioned implicit Americanist tenet: in some fashion, American Catholics have a divine mission to lead the global Catholic Church in a particular direction.

Indeed, as the year 1963 went along its way, the rumpus did increase. As preliminary news of the proposed Council reforms leaked out into the general population, interest in these Teilhardian themes exploded across the United States, and not solely within the Catholic population. In a sense, Americanist Teilhardians did indeed point the larger U.S. society toward the Catholic Church.

As an early example, in the fall of 1963, the first formal conference on Teilhard occurred at Fordham University. Sponsored by the newly formed "Human Energetics Institute," six lectures by Maurits Huybens on "Teilhard de Chardin and the Future of Man" averaged an amazing weekly attendance of six hundred people.[50]

---

accomplishment." Thought of this way, he writes, even more weight must be given to Jesus' summons: "If any man would come after me, let him deny himself and take up his cross daily and follow me [Lk 9:23]" (216–19).

49. Dorothy Poulain to "Bob" Francoeur, March 7, 1963, Madame Poulain letters, Francoeur Collection, Lauinger Library, Georgetown University (hereafter LLA).

50. Maurtis Huybens, SJ, was the Belgian editor of the *International Philosophical*

The vast interest in this lecture series in turn prompted a plethora of responses.[51] One of special significance to Robert Francoeur and the Teilhard disciples in the United States was a letter from Madame Mortier written in October that speaks of the sacrifices Francoeur has already made for "the cause" and the current, optimistic state of Teilhardian studies in the church. Mortier thanks Francoeur for his perseverance and patience, and pledges to send money to help create an American branch of the Teilhard Amis.[52]

Another example of the increasing interest expressed by the larger U.S. society regarding Teilhard was a *Saturday Evening Post* article that appeared that same month of October 1963, by which thousands more were introduced to Teilhard's work.[53] John Kobler, in "The Priest who Haunts the Catholic World," wrote that "over eight years after his death, Teilhard's many books are creating fierce controversy and influencing thousands, including numerous princes

Quarterly. Father Huybens was a philosopher working on his dissertation on Teilhard. He had suggested to Beatrice Bruteau, managing editor of *IPQ* and a doctoral candidate in philosophy, that he give some lectures to introduce Teilhard's thought to American students. The chair of the Philosophy Department at Fordham, James Somerville, SJ, agreed, and the overwhelming response startled everyone involved; see *ATA*, 6.

51. Halfway across the country from Fordham, a similar initiative was under way at tiny Clarke College in Dubuque, Iowa. An article written by a Sheila O'Connor in the *Clarke Alumna* newsletter of 1964, under the title of "The Phenomenon of Man," mentions that during the academic year of 1963–64 a group of female junior and senior chemistry and biology majors, with faculty members from those departments in addition to the departments of philosophy and theology, met every three weeks to discuss *The Phenomenon of Man*, "one of the most controversial books of the current intellectual life." Those participating, Miss O'Connor writes, found the time spent quite worthwhile and their understanding of life "vastly expanded"; from the Barbour Collection, Box no. 2, Woodstock Library, Georgetown University.

52. Madame Mortier to Robert Francoeur, October 16, 1963. Robert Francoeur Collection, LLA. The initial group that formed consisted of Francoeur, as well as Dr. Theodosius Dobzhansky, Dr. Loren Eiseley, Dr. Pierre Dansereau, and Dr. Alexander Wolsky, among others both at Fordham and outside the university. This was a very informal group. They had stationery printed that used as a logo the reverse of the Teilhard medal struck by the French government. Due to the ongoing controversy of the time concerning Teilhard, it was decided to elect a layman, Dr. John Walsh, as president. Meetings were held every four to six weeks at a restaurant near Pace College in New York City. At each meeting, one of the members read a paper and led the resulting discussion; *ATA*, 5–6.

53. John Kobler, "The Priest Who Haunts the Catholic World," *Saturday Evening Post*, October 12, 1963, 42–51.

of his church presently meeting in Rome."[54] Kobler notes that two extremes existed regarding Teilhard: at one end he is "acclaimed as 'the St. Thomas Aquinas of our age ... a new Galileo,' whereas at the other extreme he is denounced as 'the Trojan horse of Catholicism,' or 'a man with dangerous theories in which maximum seduction coincides with maximum aberration.'"[55] The article also mentions that while the Second Vatican Council never openly referred to "the forbidden Jesuit," his influence definitely lurked beneath. Kobler adds, "An Italian expert on the council goes so far as to predict that the outcome will either reflect the Teilhard spirit or it will accomplish nothing of influence."[56]

Kobler writes that at this time bibliographies concerning Teilhard already list more than 1,200 titles globally. This torrent of books, he believes, is the largest stimulus to Teilhard's name recognition. According to the article, Louis Marks, then associate professor of biology at Fordham, contended that "Teilhardism will become the Church's new philosophical system." Still, Marks cautioned, as the *monitum* suggests, students should approach Teilhard's writings with prudence and some education.

The article also comments that despite what might appear as deviations from orthodox Christian doctrine or scientific logic, both theologians and scientists agree that Teilhard fills an urgent need in both areas. Scientific materialism, at least for now, is on the wane as is religious isolationism.[57] At the same time, progressive clergymen,

54. Ibid., 43.

55. The "Trojan horse" reference concerns theologian Dietrich von Hildebrand's statements and later book *Trojan Horse in the City of God: The Catholic Crisis Explained* (Chicago: Franciscan Herald Press, 1967) regarding, at least in part, Teilhard. The book is principally a defense of conservative, neo-Scholastic Catholicism and an indictment of "progressive" or "liberal" Catholicism. The author exposes the "progressive" Catholic agenda and the dangerous heresies it promotes finding these contrary to traditional Catholic truth. The book also condemns Teilhard's influence on the Vatican Council, particularly his inability to separate the secular from the sacred, the natural from the supernatural, and his abuse of Scholastic concepts and his "misuse of language" in general.

56. Kobler, "Priest Who Haunts the Catholic World," 45. This was perhaps the first public affirmation that Teilhard's thought was indeed influential at the Council.

57. Kobler notes that as science more thoroughly probes nature, the less likely it seems that it can explain everything. It becomes more difficult to state convincingly that "superhuman power" plays no part; ibid., 48.

including those at the ongoing Vatican Council, feel "the church must readjust its outlook to the discoveries of modern science, if it is to remain a vital influence."

As a specific example of Teilhard's influence in the popular sphere, Kobler's article mentions that the French mint has recently struck a medallion with the inscription "Everything that rises converges." Kobler also quite interestingly mentions in this widely read article that in contrast to Europe, in the United States no official Teilhard organization yet exists, principally because of pressure by the apostolic delegate Archbishop Egidio Vagnozzi. The article suggests that Robert Francoeur, the primary proponent behind efforts for such an organization, has been obliged to abandon his efforts to create a Teilhard center; Francoeur's own book, *The World of Teilhard*, has been forbidden in seminaries in this country. When questioned about this by Kobler, Francoeur's response was the quote from Teilhard concerning those who do not understand: "They're not ripe yet!"[58]

Almost concurrently, another article entitled, "Teilhard de Chardin: A Cathedral for the Wasteland," appeared in *Show* magazine, a popular journal of the arts.[59] The author, Mary Lukas, with her sister Ellen Lukas, would fifteen years later write one of the American biographies on Teilhard as well as several articles defending him against accusations brought concerning the Piltdown Hoax.[60] The

58. Ibid., 50. Kobler closed his article on the same page with a hint of Teilhardian optimism: "Let truth appear but once to a single soul, and nothing can ever stop it from invading everything and setting everything ablaze."

59. Mary Lukas, "Teilhard de Chardin: A Cathedral for the Wasteland," *Show: A Magazine of the Arts*, December 1963, 100–11, 162–63. *Show* was published from at least 1961 through 1971, although its publication history was rocky throughout that entire period.

60. Mary Lukas and Ellen Lukas, *Teilhard* (New York: McGraw-Hill, 1977). See also Mary Lukas, "Teilhard and the Piltdown 'Hoax,'" *America*, May 1981, 424–27. This was Lukas's response to Stephen Jay Gould's essays "Piltdown Revisited," *Natural History* (March 1979): 86, and "The Piltdown Conspiracy," *Natural History* (August 1980): 8–28, concerning Teilhard's possible involvement in the Piltdown man hoax. Lukas commences her article by noting that *The Phenomenon* had sold over 75,000 copies in the United States alone by December 1963. Within less than a decade since its first publication in France, it had been translated into eight languages, including Finnish, Russian, and Japanese. Additionally, Teilhard study groups were springing up everywhere, including in Lisbon and Melbourne.

article questions the source of Teilhard's attraction for people; that, Lukas concludes, is a complex issue. Almost everyone would agree, however, that at its heart is the thought of this religious man who was an evolutionist, and one who sought to integrate faith and science.[61] With this in mind, Lukas concludes that it is probably most accurate to account for this attraction to qualities within Teilhard himself, especially "that ardent hunger which made him reach beyond forbidding surfaces for the coherent, the beautiful and the lovable in the cosmos." These attributes were formed "by resistance, pain and loss, like the upward-striving earth he wrote about."[62]

Additionally, his intuitive powers were immense and "were prior to his rational synthesis." He had always been one of those natural mystics whose consciousness was subject to an overwhelming unitive force.[63] But, Lukas comments, an understanding of this way of looking at the world is difficult for modern readers, who are far more used to "getting their science in the laboratory, their poetry at the ladies' cultural society and their religion—what there is of it—in an hour at church on Sunday. Our age is definitely not used to mystics."[64]

Lukas notes that Teilhard wrote out of the natural mystic's unitive impulse toward everything. He had that Christian perception that "behind the impersonal appearance of things there was a 'Face' and 'Heart' that could be found." He also urgently desired to heal

61. Lukas adds a note here, however, that others, including Gerald Heard and Lecomte du Nouy, had similar visions. Henry Fitzgerald Heard (1889–1971), commonly called Gerald Heard, was a historian, science writer, educator, and philosopher. Heard was also a guide and mentor to numerous well-known Americans in the 1950s and 1960s, including Clare Boothe Luce and Bill Wilson, cofounder of Alcoholics Anonymous. His work was a forerunner of, and influence upon, the consciousness development movement that has spread in the Western world since the 1960s.

62. Mary Lukas, "Teilhard de Chardin," 100. As we shall see later in this project, this last point will prove to be quite important, for it is an understanding that Teilhard's inherent optimism owes to something more than an easy life and amenable personality and is, perhaps, more than simple "optimism."

63. Ibid., 101. Lukas also suggests that perhaps Teilhard's most distinctive characteristic was a certain honesty and vulnerability that made prevarication and hesitation almost impossible for him. He did not shrink from addressing scientific and religious (as well as personal) problems with a transparency and an almost innocence that most found unique.

64. Ibid.

the agony he saw in those around him. Teilhard was trying to work out a viable alternative to the results of exposure to an increasingly complex, impersonal, and bureaucratic world.[65] He wished to share his vision of a Christian optimistic hope, his understanding that mankind was in its infancy, "man is young," and that the potential achievements of humanity were only beginning.

Another publication from about this same time frame, one of the first to explore Teilhard's mystical nature, was R. C. Zaehner's *Matter and Spirit: Their Convergence in Eastern Religions, Marx and Teilhard de Chardin.* Zaehner argues that *The Phenomenon* supplied an antidote to the existentialist disease too often prevalent at the time; it encouraged man to look out upon the world of which he was part rather than just contemplating the "nasty mystery of his own individual being." Teilhard urged the reader to think less about his own salvation than that of the entire world, especially the need to build up the mystical body of Christ here on earth through daily tasks and participation in the Paschal mystery. His mysticism is not just about visions and transports of individual souls but is the mysticism of the integration of souls with all things through God. For Zaehner, the greatest service of Teilhard is that he has put the concept of growing into the fullness of the mystical body of Christ in his church into the forefront of all the concepts of Christianity. He has therefore diverted attention from a focus on one's own soul to the communal roles we must all play. In a decade in which social activism is an omnipresent reality, as for example in the racial justice movements already discussed in this chapter, it is not difficult to understand why a mystical worldview would be found attractive. This is particularly true during a time period that views these roles as crucial and necessary for Christians.[66]

65. Ibid., 162.

66. R. C. Zaehner, *Matter and Spirit: Their Convergence in Eastern Religions; Marx and Teilhard de Chardin*, ed. Ruth Nanda Anshen, Religious Perspectives (New York: Harper and Row, 1963). Zaehner stresses that with the publication of Teilhard's work religion can no longer be seen as the enemy of science, but its culmination instead; science itself is now "tinged with mysticism and charged with faith." In Catholic terms, what Teilhard writes of here is the Communion of Saints (16). According to Zaehner, "His was an integral and therefore 'Catholic' vision of reality," corresponding to a very real need that conventional religion had failed to supply (18).

Just a month or two later, in December 1963, the popular Catholic journal *America* published an article titled, "The Importance of Matter," by Robert J. Roth.[67] The opening blurb for this article states it is "an assessment of Pierre Teilhard de Chardin's appeal for the American mind," and it explored the ties between Teilhard's thought and the concept of materialism as essential to the American experience.

Perhaps Roth also had recently read *Americanism: A Phantom Heresy*, since parallels between the Americanist precepts and Teilhard's themes abound in his analysis. He notes that the people of America find tremendous confidence in their involvement with matter, which they overwhelmingly consider to be good, especially now that evolution has reached its culmination in man. The affinity they have for Teilhard must spring from this contemporaneous emphasis. Roth states that Americans concur that all future progress will be made in relation to humanity's personal growth, and such growth, "though moving along moral and religious lines, will depend on man's continued interaction with the world."[68] This world includes inorganic matter, as well as social institutions, cultural development and, of course, science. So, Roth finds that respect for matter, not as in sensual gratification but as a means of human growth, is essential to the American experience. In this, Americans find great affinity with Teilhard's message.

As he concludes, "The thought of a man like Père Teilhard is more congenial to the American temperament than to that of any other people. We do not need to have the importance of matter proved to us. This orientation has been native to us from our beginnings."[69] One might add that the orientation toward matter has been native to the people of the United States, for they are a nation established in modernity and with therefore a modern mindset.[70]

These three articles in the popular press had numerous ramifi-

67. Robert J. Roth, "The Importance of Matter," *America*, December 21, 1963, 792–94.

68. Ibid., 793.

69. Ibid., 794.

70. "Modern" in this context refers to those descriptors of modernity provided by Stephen Schloesser in note 24.

cations. A letter from Robert Francoeur to George Barbour in early December 1963 elucidates several of them. Francoeur mentions that the lecture series had been held at Fordham in the fall of 1963, coinciding with the *Post* article. The results of both the lectures and the article "were so phenomenal that it was decided to take advantage of the resulting explosion here."[71] As a result, with the aforementioned encouragement of Madame Mortier in Paris, the American Association of the Friends of Teilhard became more visible, and a Teilhard Research Institute at Fordham, a five-week summer research institute, and an international congress on Teilhard scheduled for August 14–21, 1964, were all planned.

Barbour replied to Francoeur almost immediately, encouraging the formation of an American Teilhard association of some sort and noting his honor at being requested to serve on the scientific committee.[72] Several days later Barbour also wrote Dr. John Walsh of Pace College. He offered his thanks and his congratulations in finally getting an "American Père Teilhard society" off the ground. He himself felt the time was appropriate, as until that point American interest had lagged badly behind that of Europe, but the previous ten months, particularly since the start of the Council, had shown the beginning of a change.[73]

In the same letter, Barbour mentioned that he intends to send a provisional draft of his book in progress, *In the Field with Teilhard de Chardin.* He had been writing this because it bothered him that

71. Robert Francoeur to George Barbour, December 20, 1963, Barbour Collection, Box 2, Woodstock Library, Georgetown University.

72. Barbour to Francoeur, December 11, 1963, George Barbour letters, Robert Francoeur Collection, Box 1, Folder 3, LLA. Barbour suggests that Francoeur be cautious as to who is likewise asked, as certain biologists have "strong attitudes" and could easily sway the opinions of the American public and even of Catholic bishops. Dobzhansky and Hallam Movius should be included, as well as John T. Robinson of Wisconsin. Barbour found the Lukas article far more discriminating than Kobler's. A few months later, on April 16, 1964, Barbour again wrote from Cincinnati to "Father Francoeur." By this time, Francoeur had received a graduate assistant position at Fordham and was traveling around the country talking about Teilhard. Barbour, then chair of the Geology Department at the University of Cincinnati, comments that he himself had promised to "speak about Pierre" at Earlham, the Quaker school in Richmond, Indiana, in May, "if I have the courage!"

73. Barbour to John Walsh, December 15, 1931, from Cincinnati, Robert Francoeur Collection, Box 1, Folder 3, LLA.

almost everything of significance regarding Teilhard had started overseas, and he felt it was time it was recognized that people on the North American continent also were aware of and embraced Teilhard's work. Additionally, before it became too late, someone who personally knew Teilhard needed to write some things about him firsthand rather than just another article about what Teilhard did or did not mean. Barbour commented, "As I have some dozen and half personal letters which have not yet been printed, I can speak to this in a way others cannot." He suggested that if it met with Walsh's approval and seemed worthy of Teilhard, perhaps the association would want to sponsor this book in the publication series they would eventually no doubt create.[74]

In addition to the fall lecture series in 1963 previously mentioned, a year-long series of university-wide faculty seminars scrutinizing Teilhard's thought was already underway at Fordham.[75] The Human Energetics Institute arranged with Fordham's radio station to broadcast all these lectures and then sponsored yet another Spring Lecture Series from January through May 1964 to examine the possible trajectories of the Teilhardian vision.[76]

74. Barbour to John Walsh, December 15, 1931, from Cincinnati, Robert Francoeur Collection, Box 1, Folder 3, LLA.

75. This discussion was held every three weeks in the faculty lounge. Each session introduced papers given by representatives of various fields of knowledge. This continued into the spring of 1964. Beatrice Bruteau, the doctoral student already mentioned, suggested to her chairperson at Fordham that an interdisciplinary research institute be founded "to illuminate our experience of an evolving reality in a way that is appropriate to the evolutionary process itself." Her resulting proposal suggested the institute was to make a critical study of Teilhard's work and then "pass on to 'new questions, new criteria, and new fields of investigation'"; *ATA*, 7. Information regarding all these initiatives also was explained in more detail in a mimeographed brochure produced by the Human Energetics Institute found in the Barbour Collection, Box 2, Woodstock Library, Georgetown University.

76. The brochure that discusses these initiatives in more detail mentions that the Fall–Spring faculty workshop was restricted to professionals who wish to explore critical problem areas in Teilhardian thought. This workshop would serve as a pilot project for other long-range research programs. A representative from each of six disciplines served on the initial executive committee of the Human Energetics Institute: Robert O'Connell, SJ (philosophy); Dr. Joseph Budnick (Physics); Richard Zegers, SJ (psychology); Robert Namara, SJ (sociology); Dr. Louis Marks (biology); and Ewert Cousins (theology). Robert Francoeur, who represented the American Teilhard Association, was also a member of the executive team, as was Beatrice Bruteau. As publicity was going out for the spring lecture series, a difficulty arose again in that the Jesuit

In contrast to the later faculty workshops, the August convention was open to the public via prior registration. The Summer Institute was taking place in collaboration with the American Teilhard Association, and prominent specialists were being invited to come spend three or five days in a discussion about the possible synthesis of Teilhard's thought. The first week would deal with "pre-life," the second with the biosphere, the third with man, the fourth with an attempt to determine man's future, and the fifth with some overall evaluation of the synthesis. In addition, a team of some ten representatives from around the country, experts in various fields, would engage in ongoing discussion and research to provide continuity during this process.[77]

The purpose of this institute is "to achieve some coherent vision of man and of his place in reality, some 'public philosophy' to guide the concerted action the age requires of us. The institute would concern itself with the rift between 'two cultures, the scientific and the humanistic—between the secular and religious.'" This rift displays the fervent need for cross-disciplinary study, which is "*the first aim of this institute.*"[78] The second is to promote a reciprocal understanding and cooperation between the university and the world at large, and the third to provide a permanent institute where ongoing collaborative research can take place. The focus of some research might be on

---

provincial forbade the use of the name *Teilhard* for the Institute. This was a direct result of the Vatican *monitum* issued earlier. The executive committee was therefore required to choose another name quite quickly. Remembering Teilhard's own words, "We need and are irresistibly being led to create, by means of and beyond all physics, all biology and all psychology, *a science of human energetics*" (*The Phenomenon of Man*, 283), the obvious solution appeared to be an institute in concentration on 'Human Energetics"; *ATA*, 8.

77. The American Teilhard Association could operate under this name because it was not associated with a religious educational institution and because it had a layman, Dr. John Walsh, as its president. Those who participated in the conference in August included J. Franklin Ewing, SJ; Robert Johann, SJ; Father Thomas Berry, who spoke on "The Threshold of the Modern World"; Barry Ulanov, speaking on the humanist expression of Teilhard; Petro Bilaniuk, on Teilhard's Christology; Werner Stark, presenting on Teilhard and human autonomy; Gwen Garrigan, on "Chemical Evolution," and John Page, SJ, speaking on "The Phenomenon of Urbanization and Teilhard." The conference was financed by contributions, including one from Henry Luce, who attended; *ATA*, 9.

78. Emphasis found in original brochure.

such topics as the interdependence of technology and culture, the role of business as a carrier of culture, ethical questions about nature and ecology, and international and intercultural communication.

Just about the time the August conference was ending, an influential article appeared in the Religion section of *Newsweek* magazine. It noted that the conference had taken place and that it focused on the theory that man through technology, culture, and his power to love advances evolution. In so doing, man is engaged in an essentially religious act.[79]

Following a discussion of some of Teilhard's writing and the publishing history of his work, the article argued that when Teilhard died he left behind a foundation for "an extraordinary new synthesis of knowledge based on an original Christian understanding of evolution." Unlike many materialistic evolutionists, the article explains that Teilhard, a radically committed Catholic, asserted that man is the crown rather than the accident of evolution and that, through man, evolution is humanizing the entire cosmos.

The article details that the previous week at Fordham twenty-seven scholars from philosophy, theology, science, and literature concluded a five-week intensive workshop on Teilhard. As the article put it, they "reverently dissected Teilhard's cosmic system." And what emerged from all the "cerebration" was the feeling that Teilhard's thought "may ultimately lead to the most radical re-dressing of Catholic philosophy since St. Thomas Aquinas introduced Aristotle to the medieval church seven centuries ago."

Josephine Wtulich, a sociologist from Baltimore's College of Notre Dame, noted in the article that applying Teilhard's evolutionary synthesis to American social problems "raises as many questions as it answers." Certainly Teilhard was aware of the many difficulties facing contemporary society, but "he didn't realize all the implications of his theories."

Another presenter, theologian Petro Bilaniuk of St. Michael's College in Toronto, stressed Teilhard's Christocentric vision. Teilhard placed everything, he argued, in relationship to the mystery of

79. "The Noosphere around Us," *Newsweek*, August 31, 1964, 70–71.

Christ, as well as to evolution. This is in contrast to the static, ahistorical vision common in the past. "From Teilhard on, theologians cannot any longer ignore evolution in their thought or work."

The closing comments in the article are from Robert Francoeur, who notes that almost everyone educated in the Catholic tradition is trained to think in static categories, but Teilhard challenges them to "think in evolutionary terms—and the challenge is just starting." Indeed, already in 1963 the torrent of publications concerning Teilhard is just beginning, and will not peak until 1968. Note that those already discussed in this work were found in both the popular press and academic journals; the intended audience was both Catholic intellectuals and those with no Christian background whatsoever. Teilhard's ecumenical appeal was already immense.

LITERARY RESPONSES TO TEILHARD

Catherine Aller

The Summer Institute previously discussed was the first sizable conference on Teilhard in the United States, and the coincidental journal articles spurred yet more interest.[80] Attesting to its ecumenical appeal, the conference itself attracted many from outside the university population, including those from beyond Catholicism. One such person was Catherine Aller, a published poet, housewife, and non-Catholic Christian from Connecticut. She first made contact with George Barbour in August 1963; at that time she was attempting to write an explanatory statement for the general public concerning *The Phenomenon* and was looking for feedback regarding her efforts. Barbour in turn referred her to Robert Francoeur, who was then updating a Teilhardian bibliography. This action precipitated a several-year correspondence among the three as well as Aller's ongoing association with the later efforts at Fordham and the American associations.

80. A large percentage of the papers read at this conference were published by the Human Energetics Research Institute as *1964 Fordham Conference Proceedings* (Bronx, N.Y.: Fordham University, 1964). As chapter 4 will discuss, the Research Institute continued under this name and in this direction for a few more years before its reconfiguration.

In September 1963, Aller wrote Francoeur directly and commented that the kind of friendship she felt with Dr. Barbour was typical, she believed, of the "gradually drawing together to be found amidst the 'Les Amis de Teilhard.'"[81] She was creating her own work, which was "meant to go out to Christians who do think but would not be likely to study Teilhard as they must, to get his deep meaning. As I am an unknown it is a bit difficult to find a reliable publisher."[82] Aller comments that after coming to know Teilhard, she thinks it difficult to find any other writer who can compare for insightful and incisive statements, as well as inspiring suggestions. She also notes that the situation with Teilhard is perhaps only to be expected, for it is "a movement of Evolution surely as we think on these things."[83]

She also questions the "Tout ce qui Monte" insignia that Francoeur uses on his stationery.[84] She notes that it puzzles her more than it illumines. "It is individual ascent towards God—but individuals who converge. Can that be put in any geometric pattern? It seems necessary, for those who are not theologians or philosophers, to have some sort of pictorial representation of these things!"

Found within the Catherine Aller letters in the Francoeur Collection was a Christmas card to Francoeur dated December 1963.[85] This card perhaps exemplified the desire for a visual representation of Teilhard's work as noted in their previous correspondence as well as the interest in the general public in incorporating Teilhard's concepts into their own daily lives. The card is small, perhaps 2.5

81. Catherine Aller to Robert Francoeur, September 15, 1963, Robert Francoeur Collection, Box 1, Folder 2, LLA. She also noted that she was very interested in the formation of an American "Friends of Teilhard" and knew many others who would be, also. On stationery imprinted with "Mrs. Howard Lewis Aller, Lane's End, Lakeville, CT" Catherine Aller also published a book of poetry in 1948 titled *Lane's End.*

82. This work by Catherine Aller was initially published in 1964 as *The Challenge of Pierre Teilhard de Chardin* (New York: Exposition). A second edition was published in 1967.

83. Underlined comments here are the author's.

84. "Tout ce qui monte" translates as "everything that rises," a reference to the famous Teilhard quote "Everything that rises must converge," from Teilhard de Chardin, *The Future of Man* (New York: Harper and Row, 1964), 186.

85. In the Catherine Aller letters, Robert Francoeur Collection, Box 1, Folder 2, LLA. Although very professional, the card and contents gave the impression of having been designed by Aller herself.

inches by 3 inches, stamped with a colored print of three kings on camels. The opening verse reads, "As with gladness men of old did your guiding star behold, So the wise men of today seek the truth in their own way; Bringing it to human sight, less in cloud and more in light; All that is made one in Thee. Blessed are the eyes that see." What follows is:

> SEEING—THE WHOLE OF LIFE LIES IN THAT WORD. Today we are seeing the sweep of a movement infinitely transcending all human knowledge. To it all theories, all hypotheses, all systems must bow if they are to remain from henceforth true and worthy of research and adoration.
>
> EVOLUTION IS A LIGHT conquering one after another all the fields of science and uniting them with religion. To the Christian it is offering today a more magnificent means of discovering his God in all the length and breadth of creation; in every inch of space every instant of history, every idea in consciousness. It draws man toward a great Presence, a supreme Personality, infinite in love, power and intelligence.[86]

The annotation follows: Teilhard de Chardin, from *The Phenomenon of Man*. The card is signed simply "Catherine Aller."

In late December 1963 Aller again wrote to Francoeur in response to what must have been an intervening, no longer extant letter. She writes, "I am sorry to learn of law suits and deviations of various kinds, but I suppose in this stage of our way such things must be expected. There is of course only one way to meet them as did Teilhard—to walk in love, without personal condemnation."[87]

Aller notes that her own book is now off the press. "My whole intent was to spread the thought of Teilhard further in a very simple way to those who will want it simply explained. I hope I have not mis-interpreted Teilhard's words. Of course I know he does go far deeper, wider, higher than as simple a work as mine could discuss." Still, she believes that as interest in Teilhard continues to grow in so many walks of society, among so many different groups of people, the need for such a work seems immense.

86. Capitalization as found on the card.

87. Catherine Aller to Robert Francoeur, December 31, 1963, Catherine Aller letters, Robert Francoeur papers, Box 1, Folder 2, LLA.

Aller also comments about the implication of Teilhard's thought regarding one recent national event:

It struck me as most significant that the thought of all the world was focused for a while on the tragedy of Kennedy's death. For at least an hour there were millions of minds virtually *in* that emergency room. That means something in the Noosphere! That never has happened in history—could not happen until the inventions of modern science made it possible. Does this not mark a definite move forward in Evolution?

The final letter from Aller to Francoeur in these years was written in February 1964 while the lecture series was underway at Fordham. She comments that she had attended with her son and a friend and thoroughly enjoyed the discussion of all the many scientists, theologians, and philosophers who were the catalysts for Teilhard's thought. Still, "he is the one who has finally alerted word [*sic*] thought and brought us to our present stage of comprehension. Even I recognize this!"[88]

Aller believes that Teilhard's flame burns brighter and stronger as more are drawn to it. "None who see this can go back to yesterday's individualized circles of science, religion or activity." As to her book, she realizes it is a very simple primer for beginners, but it continues to steadily make its way, humble though it is. The letter is signed "Faithfully yours for every move toward ecnumenical [*sic*] stability."[89]

Finally, several months later in a letter addressed to "Mr. Francoeur," Aller commented on the "inevitable revolution in Christian thinking" toward which the United States was heading. In all the lectures and discussions she attends, she listens with hunger for mention of Teilhard, and is seldom disappointed. Without the precision

88. Catherine Aller to Francoeur, February 2, 1964, Catherine Aller letters, Robert Francoeur collection, Box 1, Folder 2, LLA. In the last paragraph, she notes with poetic imagery that "he stands out against the background of all world thinking as an eagle against a stormy sky ... his thinking ... is confined to no present circle." We grope for what he presents, she writes, and "that groping is the cutting edge of God's law of Evolution." The letter is addressed to "Mr. Francoeur—or should I say, rather, Father Francoeur?" Elsewhere Aller comments that the latter is an address that "is rather foreign to my way of thinking."

89. Ibid.

of his thought, the discipline of his words, and above all, without the spiritual élan and depth of his personality, for her everything else seems diluted and weak, or overburdened with the human intellectuality. "Surely," she contends, "the Holy Spirit is leading these efforts." Her short note ends with the comment "Thank God for Teilhard and those who love him."[90]

Flannery O'Connor

Another published female U.S. author who found herself increasingly influenced by Teilhard's thought in the early 1960s was Flannery O'Connor. Following her mounting difficulties with lupus and the subsequent return to her Milledgeville, Georgia, home, Teilhard's writing brought her both solace and hope for the future. In particular, Teilhard's ideas about diminishment helped her progress through the last stage of her life and her preparation for death.[91]

O'Connor wrote a review of *The Phenomenon of Man* (February 20, 1960) and of *The Divine Milieu* (February 4, 1961) in the *Bulletin*, the local Catholic diocesan newspaper.[92] She suggested that these should be read in just this order, noting that:

After reading both books I doubt his work will be put on the Index, though I think some of the people who latch upon his thought and distort it may cause certain propositions in it to be condemned. I think myself he was a great mystic. The second volume [*The Divine Milieu*]

90. Catherine Aller to "Mr. Francoeur," May 8, 1964. At this time, Francoeur was starting the process of laicization; Catherine Aller letters, Robert Francoeur correspondence, Box 1, Folder 3, LLA.

91. Steven Watkins, *Flannery O'Connor and Teilhard de Chardin: A Journey Together Towards Hope and Understanding about Life* (New York: Peter Lang, 2009), 11. O'Connor was introduced to Teilhard via her editor, Robert Giroux from Farrar, Straus, who mentioned in May 1959 that he had known Teilhard in New York before he died and that a book on his thought would be published shortly. Giroux suggested that O'Connor would be "very impressed." Over the next five years, as she conducted an intensive study of Teilhard's thought, his influence upon her became increasingly evident (11).

92. By the time of her death, O'Connor owned copies of all Teilhard's books thus far published, as well as studies and biographies by Nicholas Corté, Oliver Rabut, Charles Raven, and Claude Tremontant. She wrote reviews of all these books and in fact reviewed more of his works than any other writer between 1959 and 1964; Watkins, *Flannery O'Connor and Teilhard de Chardin*, 23.

complements the first and makes you see that even if there were errors in his thought, there was none in his heart.[93]

In regard to his influence on her own life, in a letter of February 1963, Flannery O'Connor wrote that "Pere Teilhard talks about 'passive diminishment' in *The Divine Milieu.* He means those afflictions that you can't get rid of and have to bear. Those that you can get rid of he believes you must bend every effort to get rid of. I think he was a great man."[94]

In addition to Teilhard's concept of diminishment, she was fascinated with his ideas of convergence and the relationship between the two. They offered Flannery a "positive" and intriguing perspective of discerning God in a new and illuminating way in her illness; they offered an answer to the crisis of lupus in her life and provided material for her varied stories in her last collection. The title of that posthumously published collection, *Everything That Rises Must Converge,* is a phrase of Teilhard's that he uses in describing his theory of continuing evolution.[95]

For O'Connor the focus on diminishment points us toward the

93. Flannery O'Connor, *Habit of Being,* ed. Regina O'Connor (New York: Farrar, Straus and Giroux, 1979), 430.

94. Ibid., 509, from a letter to Janet McKane, February 5, 1963. *The Habit of Being* is a selection of O'Connor's letters written primarily to Sally Fitzgerald. Steven Watkins suggests that rather than "passive diminishment," O'Connor preferred to use the term "progressive diminishment" for this process, as she saw it as part of learning all possible information about a situation, including how to best deal with or how to eventually accept what cannot be changed; Watkins, *Flannery O'Connor and Teilhard de Chardin,* 21.

95. O'Connor, *Everything That Rises Must Converge* (New York: Farrar, Straus and Giroux. 1965), published posthumously. This is a collection of nine short stories with an introduction by O'Connor's longtime friend Robert Fitzgerald. Patricia Dineen Maida, in her essay "Convergence in Flannery O'Connor's *Everything that Rises Must Converge,*" states that "in a commentary on *The Phenomenon of Man* Miss O'Connor tells why the work is meaningful to her.... 'It is a search for human significance in the evolutionary process. Because Teilhard is both a man of science and a believer, the scientist and theologian will require considerable time to sift and evaluate his thought, but the poet, whose sight is essentially prophetic, will at once recognize in Teilhard a kindred intelligence. His is a scientific expression of what the poet attempts to do: penetrate matter until spirit is revealed. Teilhard's vision sweeps forward without detaching itself at any point from the earth'"; Maida, "Convergence," *Studies in Short Fiction* 7, no. 4 (Fall 1970): 552, quoted in in Watkins, *Flannery O'Connor and Teilhard de Chardin,* 25. See also note 87 in this chapter for the derivation of this title.

limitations of life. Our existence is about progress, growth, and spiritual and intellectual development. Teilhard, however, also reminds us that this process includes physical limitations, disabilities, aging, and disease, all of which he would term "diminishments." Even these, however, depending upon how we struggle with and view physical decline, when linked with the Passion of Jesus can lead to progress and evolution for humanity. It is interesting that O'Connor, suffering terribly from an incurable disease, recognized this as crucial to understanding Teilhard's work; as we shall see, numerous others will overlook or refuse to understand that this underlies his ever-present optimism.

As an example, her *Everything That Rises Must Converge* introduces readers to a variety of characters who suffer from one physical or psychological malady or another. These physically imperfect, eccentric characters have idiosyncrasies that differentiate them from the surrounding society, and expose them to pain and discomfort. O'Connor's emphasis spotlights their responses to this pain and its possible positive implications for humanity as a whole.

Additionally, like so many others, O'Connor admires Teilhard for the fact that he had elucidated that it is not possible to escape matter, and yet matter and spirit are intrinsically intertwined. She saw that in motivating and encouraging humanity forward in development it is necessary to deal with the concrete and the material world while recognizing how essential and intrinsic the spiritual is. As she wrote, "As a novelist, the major part of my task is to make everything, even an ultimate concern, as solid, as concrete, as specific as possible. The novelist begins his work where human knowledge begins—with the senses; he works through the limitations of matter."[96]

O'Connor also recognized, through Teilhard's influence, that the forces of upwardly rising energy move to a convergence together that culminate in a community of knowledge and love. Diminishments of all kinds represent the opportunity for humans to transform the usual dichotomy of body/soul, matter/spirit into a unitive

96. O'Connor, *Flannery O'Connor: Mystery and Manners*, ed. Robert Fitzgerald and Sally Fitzgerald (New York: Farrar, Straus and Giroux, 1969), 155, quoted in Watkins, *Flannery O'Connor and Teilhard de Chardin*, 39.

whole, a whole that allows the participant to "cleave to God hidden beneath the inward and outward forces which animate our being and sustain it."[97] This was the same movement that at least some analysts believe she sought in her own final years of writing.[98]

FINAL THOUGHTS

As this chapter has shown, by the beginning of the mid-1960s escalating acceptance and even wild enthusiasm for Teilhard's work existed in the United States. An increasing number of scholars and authors were not only expounding upon his work, but acknowledging his influence in their own writing; additionally, the desire to better understand and to engage in discussion about his thematic points is spurring growing numbers of conferences, classes, and study groups.

By late 1964, blatant opposition to Teilhard's premises had decreased greatly. This decline in hostility was in part due to the realization that Teilhard's thought was in increasing favor at the Vatican and at the Council. Fundamental paradigm shifts were occurring not only within the Catholic Church, but in society as a whole. In addition, the JFK presidential years and the civil rights movement placed earlier social, political, and religious motifs under pressure. As this era of transformation in American society gained momentum, so too did public interest in Teilhard.

Several propositions were suggested in this chapter as to why Teilhard's thought was received in this manner during these years. Primary among these was the ongoing appreciation in the United States for his stance toward the material world, the secular, and daily life. For Teilhard, rather than viewing these as inconsequential, they are instead essential within his evolutionary framework. In addition, Teilhard's positive stance toward progress, particularly scientific progress, was crucial for his popularity in this time period. In Teilhard's thought no disjunction exists between science and religious faith;

97. Pierre Teilhard de Chardin, *The Divine Milieu: An Essay on the Interior Life* (New York: Harper and Row, 1960), 52.

98. Watkins, "The Enduring Chill," in *Flannery O'Connor and Teilhard de Chardin*, 29–55.

they are instead flip sides of the same coin. For Americans who have traditionally held a deep trust in human endeavor and the value of scientific progress, Teilhard was the man of the hour.

In regard to the church itself, this optimistic hope in progress and change intersected quite favorably with the Americanist stance long a part of the American Catholic culture. Even if Teilhard never used the term "Americanism" in his own writing, his evolutionary understanding of change, an implicit tenet of the Americanist tendency, certainly encouraged others to interpret his thought in this way. Additionally, as chapter 4 will show, the Second Vatican Council would foster an unprecedented understanding of the role of historical consciousness within the church and the world. Teilhard's worldview lent itself easily not only to an appreciation of these concepts, but as a schema by which they might be applied elsewhere.

This chapter noted that several commentators and authors from this time period began to see the possible implications of Teilhard's emphasis on convergence and unity in terms of real-life possibilities. The question arises as to how his thought and methodology might be applied to sociology, psychology, political science. Conferences and articles explored this theme. Beyond this, a few writers note their fascination with Teilhard's synthetic, Christocentric mysticism and its possibilities for the future of religion and the spiritual life. The primary themes of Teilhard's thought are creeping out into the wider, non-Catholic, population as exemplified by his influence upon the sample of poets and literary works given here.

THE YEARS OF HOPE

1965–1967

4 ~ THE SOCIAL CONTEXT

FOR AT LEAST A FEW HISTORIANS, the escalating trends of hope and progress that dominated the early 1960s were tempered during the middle years of that decade by radical theology, countercultural movements, a search for new life styles, and serious dissatisfactions with traditional religious expressions. In addition, widespread questioning of long-accepted views on the church, the university, the state, and societal expectations was increasing. These public, societal developments definitively put the 1960s into sharp contrast with the previous, postwar period.[1]

This chapter and the next will explore these themes and their relationship to Teilhard's reception during the years 1965–67. Teilhard, with his vision of man as the pinnacle of evolution and of organic global unity, truly exploded onto the scene during these years. It seemed that a new volume or periodical article concerning some aspect of his thought was published every week. Henri de Lubac's commentaries on many of Teilhard's works became available in the United States during this time period, and these also increased interest in his thought among the Catholic population. In general,

1. See, for example, Sydney Ahlstrom, "The Radical Turn in Theology and Ethics: Why It Occurred in the 1960s," *Annals of the American Academy of Political and Social Science*, special issue, *The Sixties: Radical Change in American Religion* 387 (January 1970): 1.

this was an iconoclastic age, and a particular generation (or perhaps several generations) was transfixed by the possibilities inherent in the Civil Rights Act, in new forms of interpersonal relationships and sexual mores, in the spiritual effects of psychedelic drugs, in a theology and a church opening to the world. The counterculture was rising, and the counterculture adored Teilhard.

TEILHARD'S INFLUENCE ON VATICAN II

This chapter first explores the potential impact of Teilhard's thought upon the Second Vatican Council. Also, a perusal of the Teilhardian concepts found in the documents of Vatican II will provide a framework by which to look at the social and political history of this time period and hence further an understanding of the positive reception of Teilhard in the United States during these years.

The Second Vatican Council called between two thousand and twenty-five hundred bishops, more than 150 superiors of religious orders, and thousands of observers, auditors, sisters, laymen, and laywomen to four sessions at St. Peter's Basilica between 1962 and 1965. From these gatherings came sixteen documents in total.[2]

The most immediate result of Vatican II as seen by the laity was the Constitution on the Sacred Liturgy, *Sacrosanctun Concilium.*[3] It presented an agenda for change that in 1965 was already dramatically altering the way Catholics in the United States worshipped. Even more important, however, was the new perception of the church originating in the first moments of the opening message given by Pope John XXIII and continually reinforced by the Council's efforts.[4] Over the following decade, the centuries-old understanding of a juridical, institutional church would be modified by a new model

2. Pope John XXIII, who died of cancer on June 3, 1963, was succeeded by Pope Paul VI (1963–78), who advocated that the church (and therefore the Council) focus both inwardly and outwardly. The Council closed on December 8, 1965.

3. Pope Paul VI promulgated the *Constitution on the Sacred Liturgy, Sacrosanctum Concilium,* on December 4, 1963. The primary aim of this first document of the Second Vatican Council was to achieve greater lay participation in the liturgy of the Catholic Church.

4. Bill Huebsch, *Vatican II in Plain English: The Council* (Allen, Tex.: Thomas More, 1997), 84.

of servant church, located in the scriptural paradigm of the People of God. The ecumenical efforts of the Council advocated work toward unity; religious freedom was another key, controversial issue.

The debate over the continuity of the Council with what had gone before, particularly in light of the *ressourcement* and *nouvelle théologie* of many theologians of the mid-twentieth century, has at times been intense. In an article in *America* magazine in 2005, John O'Malley noted three "trends" in considering Vatican II: the Council as an aberration, the Council as continuous with what occurred before, the Council as discontinuity.[5] In O'Malley's opinion, nothing frightening exists in any discontinuity that may have occurred, for "even the most radical discontinuities in history take place within a stronger current of continuity." Change, as part of the human condition is necessary to life, and so cannot be "un-Catholic." O'Malley maintains that "change, moreover, does not necessarily entail loss of identity. In fact it is sometimes necessary to assure identity, especially of a living organism."[6]

Some would claim that it was Teilhard, one of those scholars writing in the early- to mid-twentieth century, who made this kind of evolutionary and progressive worldview unavoidable for those of intelligence within the Catholic Church.[7] Chapter 3 showed that the implied condemnation of the *monitum* of 1962 was already being overlooked just a year later; to consider, therefore, that Teilhardian thought might strongly influence and even be integral to the documents of the Council does not seem inconceivable.[8] Teilhard's

5. See, for example, John O'Malley, *What Happened at Vatican II* (Cambridge, Mass.: Harvard University Press, 2010); also O'Malley, "Vatican II: Did Anything Happen?" *Theological Studies* 67 (2006): 3–33.

6. O'Malley, "The Style of Vatican II," *America*, February 24, 2003, 6. Note that one could consider these comments themselves as quite Teilhardian in nature!

7. Leo Donovan, SJ, "Was Vatican II Evolutionary? A Note on Conciliar Language," *Theological Studies* 36 (1975): 494.

8. Even none other than Pope Paul VI himself expressed interest and support during this time period. On February 24, 1966, in a speech to employers and workers of an important pharmacy company, Paul VI praised the basic theories of Teilhard concerning the evolution of the universe and pointed toward them as a model for science compatible with faith. Although the pope included some qualifications in his praise, it seems a strong endorsement of Teilhard's theses; Pope Paul VI, Speech to Employers and Workers of a Pharmacy Company, February 24, 1966, in *Insegnamenti*

evolutionary consciousness and unifying, optimistic worldview are particular qualities that several commentators on the Council point to in regard to his possible impact. Especially it is in *Gaudium et spes*, the "Pastoral Constitution on the Church in the Modern World," that they agree that Teilhardian notes are visible.

Teilhard's contribution to the Council primarily appeared to occur through the efforts of his own great friend and supporter Father Henri de Lubac. De Lubac was appointed by John XXIII as consultant to the Preparatory Theological Commission and was later named as *peritus* to the Council itself. In the years surrounding Vatican II de Lubac intervened on Teilhard's behalf numerous times, providing both written and verbal explications of his works at various gatherings. De Lubac later agreed, although with some reservations, that Teilhard's impact amounted to "a certain influence, at least indirect and diffuse, on some orientations of the Council." In particular, *Gaudium et spes* expressed "precisely what Père Teilhard sought to do." In a later article written in 1968, de Lubac extensively examined issues concerning the "goodness of the world," the separation between the natural and supernatural, and the Christian vocation in the world. In his explanation of how the Christian anthropology of *Gaudium et spes* evolved, he quoted Teilhard several times. Only a few years after the closing of the Council, however, de Lubac was already expressing his concerns that the Christological heart of *Gaudium et spes* was being subsumed within a secularism concerned solely with the urgent problems of the world and with human progress.[9]

---

di Paolo VI (Vatican: Poliglotta Vaticana, 1966), 992–93, accessed March 25, 2013, http://www.traditioninaction.org/ProgressivistDoc/A_035_Paul6Teilhard.htm.

9. Henri de Lubac, *Athéisme et sense de l'homme: Une double requête de "Gaudium et spes"* (Paris: Éditions du Cerf, 1968), 130. This article was translated by D. C. Schindler as "The Total Meaning of God and the World," *Communio* 35 (Winter 2008): 613–41. According to Dr. Mathias Trennert-Helwig, Teilhard's thought had a "polarizing effect" right up to the Council's last debates. For those Council fathers who did not know his writings or only knew them superficially, he was, as Cardinal Döpfner commented on September, 22, 1965, the symbol for a "superficial," "triumphant," or "poetical optimism" that dangerously played down the reality of sin. Archabbot Benedikt Reetz and Archbishop Marcel Lefebvre offered similar views. (See "Teilhard de Chardin and Vatican II—and the Monitum," *British Teilhard Association Newsletter* 23 [February 2007]). In regard to de Lubac's interventions with this population, on September 11, 1965, shortly before the opening of the final session of the Second Vatican

Theologians Robert Speaight, Leo Donovan, Bishop Otto Spülbeck, Sigurd Martin Daecke, Cardinal Joseph Ratzinger, and John Haught are among those who concur, if only in passing, that this Teilhardian influence exists. Speaight's biography of Teilhard mentions in the foreword that "nothing that Teilhard said in public or in private ... was left unsaid at the Second Vatican Council. Much that he had clamored for was implied or incorporated in its decrees."[10]

According to Leo Donovan, "Protestant and Catholic alike have commented on [Teilhard's] influence at the Council." Donovan argues that although Teilhard's name was never explicitly mentioned

Council and a consideration of the final draft of *Gaudium et spes*, Father de Lubac presented a report titled "Tradition and Innovation in the Position of the Problem of God in Father Teilhard de Chardin" to the sixth International Thomist Congress in Rome, at the aforementioned request of Father Charles Boyer, SJ, secretary of the Academy of Saint Thomas Aquinas and organizer of the Thomist Congress, under the direction of Pope Paul VI. His report began with an examination of what de Lubac calls the "Initial Postulate" in the "goodness" or "value of being," or "in the goodness of the world" as a "point of departure" for faith in all that surrounds us. He includes in his report an explanation of Teilhard's orthogenetic evolution; the spiritualization of all matter and its convergence toward Omega; the attributes of this Omega; the revelation of the Christic Omega to mankind; Teilhard's synthesis of science and philosophy; and numerous pages on his optimism. Just over a month later, in mid-October 1965, he wrote a "Letter to a Council Father from Whom I Had Just Heard, in the Aula of Saint Peter's, an Intervention Unfavorable to Teilhard." In particular, his letter concerned the lack of understanding many had at the time concerning Teilhard's optimism and apparent lack of perception of the evil in the world. De Lubac refers the priest addressed to the *Milieu divin*, noting that "no contemporary religious writer ... has spoken of the dogma of hell with so much courageous firmness as Father Teilhard." He notes that Teilhard's "optimism" is first opposed to all forms of atheistic pessimism. But Teilhard most certainly does not deny the sufferings and misaligned choices of humanity. De Lubac ends with the note that his "testimony ... comes from someone who is not particularly 'Teilhardian,' but who has sufficiently known the person and work of the Father to have had the opportunity not to be seriously mistaken about them"; de Lubac, *Theology in History*, with a foreword by Michael Sales, SJ, trans. Anne Englund Nash (San Francisco: Ignatius Press, 1996), 505–40, 565–66. See also William Portier, "What Kind of a World of Grace," *Communio* 39, no. 1–2 (Spring–Summer 2012): 136–51, for an explication of the initial article of de Lubac's mentioned here concerning *Gaudium et spes*, as well as his contribution to the Council.

10. Robert Speaight, *The Life of Teilhard de Chardin* (New York and Evanston: Harper and Row, 1967), 14. Speaight also notes here that when Teilhard wrote of revelation in a letter to Père Auguste Valensin on October 20, 1919, "it is not limited to the composition of a text, but it envelops that text and *lives* in it to the extent that the Church very slowly understands it," he was stating what is now accepted as a theological commonplace.

in the conciliar documents or the official proceedings, it was well known how *Gaudium et spes* was shaped by theologians from the University of Louvain, as well as the French bishops and *periti*, who were especially familiar with Teilhard's work.[11] However, Donovan also notes that if a Teilhardian influence is to be claimed, it is a diffuse one dealing more with orientations than with specific teachings. A Teilhardian "school," he notes, does not seem to exist.[12]

Spülbeck of Meissen noted four occasions when Teilhard's name was specifically mentioned in the Council hall during the discussion of the *Pastoral Constitution*.[13] It was his own view "that Teilhard's optimism in judging the world process, his effort on behalf of developing all concealed possibilities, his 'Yes' to the entire creation in all its stages of evolution, his struggle for a unified and inclusive conception and view of the world in which every spiritual endeavor of mankind would be integrated, all this accompanied the writing of the text from the very beginning."

Spülbeck thought that chapter 3 of the *Constitution*, "Man's Activity throughout the World," has perhaps the most clearly defined Teilhardian characteristics. He also saw articles 13 and 14, on original sin and the role of the body, as attempting to balance Teilhardian optimism in regard to the problem of evil.

Daecke, a German Lutheran theologian, on the other hand believes that Teilhard's themes are found in the *Pastoral Constitution* only in those areas on the threshold of theology, such as in anthro-

11. Donovan, "Was Vatican II Evolutionary?," 494. For another opinion on how this occurred, one might want to review http://www.sspxasia.com/Documents/SiSiNoNo/1994_April/They_Think_Theyve_Won_PartV.htm, by the Pius X Society.

12. Donovan, "Was Vatican II Evolutionary?," 497. He also notes that Charles Moeller, in *Commentary on the Documents of Vatican II*, ed. Herbert Vorgrimler (New York: Burns and Oats, 1967 ff), 5:72, as well as in Sergio Bonato's unpublished thesis "La presenza del pensiero di Teilhard de Chardin nei lavori del Concilio Vaticano II" (University of Genoa, 1967), 207, all speak to Teilhard's influence on Vatican II.

13. Otto Spülbeck, "Teilhard de Chardin und die Pastoralkonstitution," in *Die Autorität der Freiheit*, ed. Johann Christoph Hampe (Munich: Kosel, 1967), 3:86–87, as cited in Donovan, "Was Vatican II Evolutionary?," 495. Donovan also refers the reader to Spülbeck's essay "Fortschrittsglaube und Evolution," in *Der Fortschrittsglaube: Sinn und Gefahren*, ed. Ulrich Schöndorfer (Graz: Verlag Styria, 1965), 85–107; and he comments that Giovanni Caprile, SJ, notes seven references to Teilhard in the Council aula *Il Concilio Vaticano II: Cronache del Concilio vatincano II*, ed. Giovanni Caprile, S.J. (Rome: La Civiltà cattolica, 1966), 4:257, 263, 25, 278; 5:76, 105, 153.

pological and sociological issues. In the theology about God, Christ, the church, and God's relationship to the world, he finds Teilhardian thought completely absent. Daecke laments that "Where Catholic interpreters must falsify Teilhard's thought in order to be able to affirm it at these central theological passages, there is no trace left in the Constitution of an influence of Teilhard's thinking."[14] In particular, Teilhard's distinctive cosmic Christology was bracketed off from any significant influence upon the Council; what was left was a whitewashed version of his vision. This opinion obviously is quite different from Spülbeck's; in Daecke's view the change in attitude toward Teilhardian themes resulted from "oversimplifying interpretations." That simplification is what permitted Teilhard to be considered orthodox and useful for the purposes of the Council.

Much later Cardinal Joseph Ratzinger wrote similarly in speaking of Teilhard's influence upon the documents of Vatican II and the optimistic stance toward the world found in these. He believed that Teilhard encouraged an understanding of evolution "as a type of technical and scientific development in which Matter and Spirit, the individual and the society constitute a global ensemble, a divine world. The conciliar Constitution on the Church and the Modern World [*Gaudium et spes*] followed the same train of thinking."[15]

One who later agreed with this opinion was John Haught, formerly of Woodstock Theological Center.[16] Haught notes that *Gaudium et spes* is revolutionary in particular for two statements: "The human race has passed from a rather static concept of reality to a more dynamic, evolutionary one. In consequence there has arisen a new series of problems ... calling for efforts of analysis and synthesis,"[17]

14. Donovan, "Was Vatican II Evolutionary?," 495. For Siguard Martin Daecke's own interpretation, see his *Teilhard de Chardin und die evangelische: Theologie Die Weltlichkeit Gottes und die Weltlichkeit der Welt* (Göttingen: Ort Verlag, 1967).

15. Joseph Cardinal Ratzinger, "*Gaudium et spes* took its notion of Christianity from Teilhard de Chardin," in *Les Principes de la Theologie Catholique: Esquisse et Materiaux* (Paris: Tequi, 1982), 374–75, accessed May 5, 2012, http://www.traditioninaction.org/ProgressivistDoc/A_034_RatzTeilhard.htm.

16. John F. Haught, "More Being: The Emergence of Teilhard de Chardin," *Commonweal*, June 5, 2009), 17. This article is included as a chapter in the book *Reclaiming Catholicism: Treasures Old and New*, ed. Michael Daley and Thomas Groome (Maryknoll, N.Y.: Orbis, 2010).

17. *Gaudium et spes*, no. 5, in *The Documents of Vatican II*, ed. W. M. Abbott, SJ

and, "A hope related to the end of time does not diminish the importance of intervening duties but rather undergirds the acquittal of them with fresh incentives."[18] Haught contends that it is almost impossible to read these words and not recognize Teilhardian thought in them, particularly that about the necessity of building the earth. He comments that when we recognize that the universe is still a work in progress, true Christian hope orients our life and efforts toward participation in that ongoing work of creation; it is then we also realize with Teilhard that "our hope for final fulfillment is not a reason for passivity here and now."[19]

Finally, not long after the Council ended, Cyril Vollert wrote extensively on how Teilhard's influence is directly evident in the conciliar documents. His thought is used here as a means by which to give a far more specific schema for considering what influence Teilhard may have exerted upon the Council.

Vollert's essay "Teilhard in the Light of Vatican II" was published in 1968 in the United States in an edited volume of works on Teilhard. Vollert has no reservations in arguing that Teilhard's influence was immense and significant. Several of the speakers, he states, including the future Paul VI, referred to Teilhard during the last three sessions of the Council.[20] However, along with others already mentioned, he contends that although Teilhard's influence was tremendous, to claim that the Council deliberately or systematically incorporated any of his theses into the constitutions would be "an exaggeration."[21] Still one could argue, as does Vollert, that Teilhard's spirit and fingerprints are all over the debates and documents of the Council, and these therefore speak of the role he played and the "influence he exercised" on Christians during these decades.

(New York: American Press, 1966), 203. All quotations from the constitutions and decrees of the Council henceforth in this section of the chapter will be taken from this volume.

18. Ibid., no. 21, 219.

19. Haught, "More Being," 18.

20. Cyril Vollert, "Teilhard in the Light of Vatican II," in *Dimensions of the Future*, ed. Marvin Kessler, SJ, and Bernard Brown, SJ (Washington, D.C., and Cleveland: Corpus, 1968), 147. Vollert includes a quote from Paul VI: "Teilhard is an indispensable man for our times: his expression of the faith is necessary for us."

21. Ibid.

To render this point, Vollert compares phrases from the Council's teachings with corresponding themes from Teilhard's own work in five different areas: building the earth; the unification of mankind; the ecumenical spirit; faith and science; and new theological investigations. A brief synopsis of Vollert's argument follows in hopes of also establishing that so early in the 1960s Teilhard's influence on the ecclesial hierarchy was already quite substantial, in the United States and globally. These themes will prove useful later in this chapter in considering the influence of Teilhard upon the general U.S. population of the time and as a way to consider his reception in light of social events.

In the section "Building the Earth," Vollert first points to the statements in *Gaudium et spes* previously mentioned: "Today, the human race is involved in a new stage of its history."[22] Then later, "The human race has passed from a rather static concept of reality to a more dynamic, evolutionary one."[23] The reference to dynamic, evolutionary forces was recognized immediately by those reading about the Council as revealing the influence of Teilhard.[24] This constitution encourages Christians to respond to the spirit of the gospel by performing their earthly duties conscientiously.[25] Additionally, although the sacred and the profane must not be confused, they are not to be separated, as the sacred is "the deepest dimension of the profane, and every human task has a sacred aspect."[26] Every one of our actions can serve to build up Christ's body. All work "takes on the form and greatness of a sacred duty."[27]

22. *Gaudium et spes*, no. 4.

23. Ibid., no. 5, *in Abbott, Documents of Vatican II*, 203.

24. Vollert, "Teilhard in the Light," 149.

25. "The Christian who neglects his temporal duties neglects his duties toward his neighbor and even God"; *Gaudium et spes*, no. 43, in Abbott, *Documents of Vatican II*, 243. Also, "When, by the work of his hands or with the aid of technology, man develops the earth ... he carries out the design of God"; ibid., no. 57, 262. Vollert also directs the reader's attention to Teilhard's *Divine Milieu*, which explicitly argues that the new, evolving world "must be built by man himself. Man must guide the direction of history; he must make a map for the future"; Vollert, "Teilhard in the Light," 151.

26. Vollert, "Teilhard in the Light," 152. As Teilhard wrote, "Nothing here below is profane for those who know how to see"; Teilhard de Chardin, *The Divine Milieu* (New York: Harper and Row, 1960), 35.

27. Teilhard de Chardin, *L'Énergie humaine* (Paris: Éditions du Seuil, 1962), 215.

Concerning the unification of mankind, Vollert's second category in his essay, he writes that the documents of Vatican II emphasize the reasons that unity among humankind is important for the church.[28] All those who perform their work in a way benefitting society are correct in thinking "that by their labor they are unfolding the Creator's work … and contributing by their personal industry to the realization in history of the divine plan."[29] This becomes even clearer "if we consider how the world is becoming unified" and how all have the responsibility to build a better world together. This is a witness to the birth of a new humanism.[30] The increasing sense of solidarity among all people is a sign of our times, argues Vollert.[31]

The evolutionary vision of Teilhard de Chardin is obviously not static; the cosmos is a cosmogenesis that necessarily includes humanity in anthropogenesis. As a result, humanity is beginning to act in a more unified fashion. The prejudices of old have to be transcended, for "the age of nations is past."[32] Human unity consists of the achievement of oneness with Christ, but without the loss of one's own personality.[33]

Vollert notes that Teilhard called unceasingly for a "common front of all those who believe that the world is still advancing" and who understand that humanity has the responsibility of making it progress; Teilhard de Chardin, *The Future of Man* (New York: Harper and Row, 1964), 81.

28. Also, consider that "the conditions of this age lend special urgency to the Church's task of bringing all men to full union with Christ"; *Lumen gentium: Dogmatic Constitution on the Church,* no. 1, 15. The thought behind these quotes could only serve as further encouragement for those Christian devotees of Teilhard who saw the work for civil rights and/or various antiwar efforts as divinely inspired.

29. *Gaudium et spes,* no. 34, in Abbott, *Documents of Vatican II,* 232.

30. Ibid., no. 55, in Abbott, *Documents of Vatican II,* 260–61.

31. Vollert also suggests that the document *Decree on the Apostolate of the Laity* reinforces this sense, as for example in the statement "It is a function of the lay apostolate to promote this awareness zealously and to transform it into a sincere and genuine sense of brotherhood"; *Decree,* no. 10, in Abbott, *Documents of Vatican II,* 501.

32. Teilhard de Chardin, *Building the Earth* (Paris: Éditions du Seuil, 1958), 60. The entire quote, "The Age of Nations is past. It remains for us now, if we do not wish to perish, to set aside the ancient prejudices and build the earth," appears above the stairs leading down to the auditorium at the Bunn Intercultural Center (completed and dedicated in 1982) at Georgetown University, Washington, D.C.

33. Teilhard de Chardin, *Hymn of the Universe* (New York: Harper and Row, 1965), 89. The kind of unified socialization that Teilhard sought was personalist; perfection of self occurs through reciprocal love. It is with and through this love that humanity will achieve a state of "ultra-humanity"—that is, of social unification; from Teilhard de

Vollert recognizes that the goal of the unification of humankind as broached by Vatican II both requires and fosters the ecumenical spirit, another great theme of the Council, and one also encouraged by Teilhard. That spirit is dependent upon an appreciation of the dignity of the human person, which "has been impressing itself more and more deeply on the consciousness of contemporary man."[34] As with unification, successful progress of the ecumenical movement requires dedicated action on the part of all Christians.[35]

As with the age of nations, Teilhard thinks that eventually humankind will leave the ages of religions and enter the age of religion; without any doubt the ecumenical movement points in this direction. Of all the world religions, it is Christianity that is best suited to anthropogenesis. Evolution therefore will follow along the lines of Christianity, and other world religions will converge on this axis.[36]

In regard to the intersection of faith and Teilhard's evolutionary theories, *Gaudium et spes* stressed that science and faith (the next

---

Chardin, *Future of Man*, 275f. Consider also that whereas in the past anthropogenesis took place "naturally" without much involvement on humanity's part, now that we better understand what is occurring we realize the choices of our free will can guide the future of evolution. The most important event of that future is the movement up toward Someone, the mystical Christ; ibid., 279.

34. *Declaration on Religious Freedom*, no. 1, in Abbott, *Documents of Vatican II*, 675.

35. Consider: "Concern for restoring Christian unity pertains to the whole Church, faithful and clergy alike. It extends to everyone, according to the potential of each ... and it leads toward that full and perfect unity which God lovingly desires"; *Gaudium et spes*, no. 23, in Abbott, *Documents of Vatican II*, 222. Vollert adds that this action includes the explanation of Catholic belief in forms and with terminology that all can better appreciate, including the "separated brethren." Vollert also notes that a portrait of the ideal missionary for this work is found in *Ad Gentes*, a portrait that strikingly reminds one of Teilhard himself: "He must be ready to take initiatives ... persevering in difficulties, patient and strong of heart in bearing with solitude, fatigue and fruitless labor ... he needs a noble spirit for adapting himself to strange customs ... he needs an empathetic mind and a responsive heart for cooperating with his brethren and with all who dedicate themselves to a common task"; *Decree on the Missionary Activity of the Church*, no. 25, in Abbott, *Documents of Vatican II*, 615.

36. Vollert, "Teilhard in the Light," 159; see also Teilhard, *The Phenomenon of Man*, trans. Bernard Wall, introduction Sir Julian Huxley (New York: Harper), 1959, 297f. Through his theory of evolution, Teilhard offered a goal—that of Omega, Christ the *Pantocrator*—that greatly spurred ecumenical progress. Teilhard himself thought that almost all theists, philosophers, and humanists offered truth of some sort. As Vollert points out, he was fond of saying, "Let us take care not to reject the least ray of light from any side. Faith has need of all the truth"; Teilhard de Chardin, *The Appearance of Man* (New York: Harper, 1965), 32; Vollert, "Teilhard in the Light," 158–60.

grouping in Vollert's essay) are not in opposition.[37] The church wanted all branches of knowledge to be studied in a spirit of freedom, since in scientific research "faith and reason give harmonious witness to the unity of all truth."[38]

Vollert points out that Teilhard's theories offered aspects that even nonbelievers, such as Julian Huxley, could accept: "It seems to me that the bond Teilhard established between evolutionary biology and Christian theology is his single most important contribution to modern thought.... It traces the road for an eventual reconciliation between science and the faith."[39] Still, Vollert makes an extremely important point in noting that for Teilhard it is the Christian vision alone that gives meaning to matter and to evolution. He saw no reason to refute the arguments of the materialists; he was instead satisfied to show that evolution was far better explained within the perspective of the faith. After all, when science is "probed deeply, it reveals the hidden countenance of God who is Love."[40]

Finally, Vollert considers the goal of *aggiornamento* as espoused by the Second Vatican Council. Theological updating, he comments, requires "new investigation" into the faith through "use of the tools of the present moment."[41] Still, the centrality of Christ must continually be stressed, for Christ is "the key, the focal point, and the goal

37. See, for example, "If methodical investigation within every branch of learning is carried out in a genuinely scientific manner and in accord with moral norms, it never truly conflicts with faith. For earthly matters and the concerns of faith derive from the same God"; *Gaudium et spes*, no. 36, in Abbott, *Documents of Vatican II*, 234.

38. *Declaration on Christian Education*, no. 10, in Abbott, *Documents of Vatican II*, 648.

39. Julian Huxley, "Message," *Europe* 43 (1965): 12f. See also Huxley's introduction to Teilhard's *Phenomenon of Man*, which is much along the same line. Huxley also argues that the most essential feature of Teilhard's work is "that of having built the bridge between science and religion." Of course, Huxley comments, Teilhard's own life points to that bridge. He did not separate his two callings into discrete compartments but lived them in perfect unity. How many men "intoxicated by science and technology," asks Vollert, did Teilhard lead to consider the religious depths of matter? Vollert, "Teilhard in the Light," 162. See also Paul Chauchard, *Teilhard de Chardin: Un modèle et un guide pour notre temps* (Paris: Éditions du Levain, 1963), 11f, for a similar argument.

40. Vollert, "Teilhard in the Light," 163.

41. As *Gaudium et spes* notes, "Recent studies and findings of science, history and philosophy raise new questions which influence life and demand new theological investigations"; *Gaudium et spes*, no. 62, in Abbott, *Documents of Vatican II*, 268.

of all human history."[42] Christ "is drawing all men to himself."[43] Teilhard was a reformer who worked for a rejuvenation of Christianity, "not by structural alteration but by assimilation of new elements."[44] His primary focus, as has been noted before in this work, is that he wished to show that only Christ is the apogee of evolution, toward which all is converging. In a point that perhaps many today, as well as the social activists and others working for "human progress" during the 1960s, might argue, Teilhard numerous times claimed that it is Christ who "reveals himself as the form of faith most suitable to modern needs, a religion for progress ... the very religion of evolution."[45]

A REFLECTION ON U.S. HISTORICAL EVENTS 1965 THROUGH 1967

This chapter now examines the phenomenon of a growing tension in the United States. Fissures grew in the confidence of the nation as a whole as a result of sporadic violence between those for whom this continued to be a time of intense optimism and progress and those who experienced the reality of the difficulty of change and preferred to maintain traditional forms of life. The ongoing utopian hopes of some and the militant conservatism of others will increasingly create "an atmosphere of intense expectation alternating with despair which gave this decade a truly unique flavor."[46]

The pertinent historical events briefly discussed here are three: the movement for racial equality, the escalation of the Vietnam War with the resulting antiwar movement, and the rise of the counterculture. The sixties were a time of hope, despite ongoing divisiveness, excess, and incivility. Activists both within and outside the Catholic Church had confidence in the resilience of the national fabric and

42. Ibid., no. 10, in Abbott, *Documents of Vatican II*, 208.

43. *Lumen gentium*, no. 48, in Abbott, *Documents of Vatican II*, 79.

44. Teilhard de Chardin, *Christianisme et Evolution* (Paris: Éditions du Seuil, 1969); quoted in Vollert, *Dimensions*, 165.

45. Teilhard de Chardin, *Science et Christ* Paris: *Éditions du* Seuil, 1965), 164; quoted in Vollert, *Dimensions*, 166.

46. Hugh McLeod, *The Religious Crisis of the 1960s* (New York: Oxford University Press, 2007), 129.

felt free to test the limits of the nation. Their trust in the ultimate good sense of the American people gave them faith that conservatives did not seem to share.[47] Additionally, their belief in possibility and progress strongly paralleled a primary theme in Teilhard's thought, as well as in the documents of Vatican II. An examination of these events will give a further understanding of why, as transformation in American society gained momentum, so too did public interest in Teilhard continue to increase. An aspect of this interest to consider, however, is whether societal belief that human progress in solving the social problems of the world included a mistakenly shifted understanding of both Teilhard's focus and the basis of his optimistic hope.

Civil Rights

Without a doubt, the civil rights movement and the work of Dr. Martin Luther King Jr. were of tremendous importance during these and subsequent years. Mark Silk situates his book *Spiritual Politics* on the premise that civil rights was often a religious affair. Dr. Martin Luther King Jr. himself noted that "if today's church does not recapture the sacrificial spirit of the early church, it will lose its authenticity, forfeit the loyalty of millions, and be dismissed as an irrelevant social club with no meaning for the twentieth century."[48] Indeed, the March on Selma of 1965 brought to the forefront a new wave of quite visible nonviolent troops, many of them clerical activists. On January 2 of that year, King told a rally in Selma that a new voter registration drive would be launched from there. Two weeks later the United States sued the state of Alabama for making voter registration too difficult for its citizens.

As the registration drive got under way in February, thousands of blacks were arrested as they demonstrated against the registration requirements. On February 10, 1965, state officials attacked black

47. Mark Hamilton Lytle, *America's Uncivil Wars: The Sixties Era from Elvis to the Fall of Richard Nixon* (New York: Oxford University Press, 2006), xiv.

48. Mark Silk, *Spiritual Politics: Religion and America since WWII* (New York: Simon and Schuster, 1988), 3.

protesters in Selma with nightsticks and cattle prods; another confrontation in early March involved the use of tear gas and clubs.

The March from Selma to Montgomery, Alabama, on March 21, 1965, involved twenty-five thousand protesters from across the nation. Three who were involved died as a result of these protests. Still, unlike the Mississippi Summer just a year earlier, suspects in the civil rights murders were at least brought to trial. The Voting Rights Act of 1965 was passed on August 6 as a direct response to Selma and further racial violence. At long last, segregation and discrimination appeared to be dying; progress in the civil rights front was happening.

The civil rights movement introduced nonviolent resistance to the nation and emphasized the importance of community. What became clear, though, was the necessity of building and maintaining a community of activists if any ongoing progress for humanity were to be had.[49] The movement speaks to several of the Teilhardian themes elucidated by Vollert, particularly those of building the earth and the unification of peoples. In addition, the ecumenical spirit of the civil rights movement fit nicely with that espoused by the Second Vatican Council. Teilhard very much discerned that it was the work of the people to create progress in the world, which would include a deep appreciation of the dignity of every person and the unity of all the races. Ahlstrom comments that "new cosmic signs *were* being read in the 1960s. The decade *did* experience a fundamental shift in American moral and religious attitudes. It is no accident that phrases such as 'post-Puritan, post-Protestant, post-Christian, postmodern and even post-historical were commonly used to describe the American scene.'"[50] Presuppositions held for centuries were widely questioned; the nation was evolving. From Teihard's viewpoint, "to cooperate in total cosmic evolution is the only deliberate act that can adequately express our devotion to an evolutive and universal Christ."[51] The United States may have been evolving; the question however, was, what was the evolutionary endpoint?

49. Robert Ellwood, *The Sixties Spiritual Awakening: American Religion Moving from Modern to Postmodern* (New Brunswick, N.J.: Rutgers University Press, 1994), 80.

50. Ahlstrom, "Radical Turn," 1–13, 2.

51. Teilhard, *Science and Christ* (New York: Harper and Row, 1969), 68.

This question was on the minds of many when the violence of Selma escalated into the Watts riots in Los Angeles not even six months later. From August 11 to August 16, 1964, primarily black Americans rioted in the streets; eventually thirty-four people died, over one thousand were injured, and four thousand were arrested. Riots spread across the nation until in 1967 they took place in Detroit, Michigan, where 7,000 National Guardsmen were called in to protect the city. Riots also erupted in Rochester, New York, the Spanish Harlem section of New York City, and Birmingham, Alabama. The result was widespread confusion and discouragement.

Teilhard had written, however, that a generalized desire for progress and unity, for movement toward convergence is not in itself sufficient. Instead, what is needed is to develop a relationship with others in terms of Christ; Christ was to be loved not just for him, but as the heart of the universe. For Teilhard, this center of the universe, this Omega Point, not only gives meaning to each person, but each person, through loving Christ, also loves those with whom they live and strive. In working to build the earth and to progress, man then sees "that he can love by his activity, in other words he can be directly united to the divine center and to others by his every action, no matter what form it might take."[52] Without that center, convergence and love cannot survive. One might wonder how many of those reading Teilhard, while striving at the time for racial equality or in antiwar protests, understood this about his thought. In any case, these riots basically brought an end to the civil rights movement. The unity that had existed around the issue deteriorated in the midst of the violence and was never recovered. It must be admitted, though, that at least in part the cessation of activism in this area occurred because energies aroused by civil rights were shifting instead toward the Vietnam War situation.

52. Ibid., 170ff.

The Vietnam War and Antiwar Protests

The demographic developments during these years that created almost simultaneously both an urban crisis and a racial crisis are critical to the decade that became the sixties. What is also significant is that the public's former confidence in and allegiance to the American system was undermined by the transition of governmental concern from peace and reconstruction during the previous decade to the pursuance of the war in Vietnam. What could have been a gradual transition became sudden and traumatic.[53]

In 1962, President Kennedy sent American "military advisors" to Vietnam to help train the South Vietnamese army, but quickly concluded that the Diem regime was unsalvageable. As a result, the following year the United States backed a coup that overthrew that regime and installed a new leader. Unfortunately, the new U.S.-backed leaders proved just as corrupt and ineffective.

Kennedy's successor, Lyndon B. Johnson, pledged to honor Kennedy's commitments but hoped to keep U.S. involvement in Vietnam to a minimum. After North Vietnamese forces allegedly attacked U.S. Navy ships in the Gulf of Tonkin in 1964, however, Johnson was given carte blanche in the form of the Gulf of Tonkin Resolution and began to gradually send U.S. troops to Vietnam.

Within a week of Martin Luther King Jr.'s initial protests in Selma, Alabama, and only a month after President Johnson's "Great Society" State of the Union speech in January 1965, the war in Vietnam suddenly escalated with the regular bombing and strafing of North Vietnam by the United States—operation "Rolling Thunder." At the end of March, a car bomb exploding in front of the U.S. Embassy in Saigon killed twenty-two people and injured another 183. The following day the United States ordered the first combat troops to Vietnam. The conflict escalated. By the end of 1966, Johnson's Americanization of the war led to a presence of nearly 400,000 U.S. troops in Vietnam.

American involvement began optimistically enough, with the

53. Ahlstrom, "Radical Turn," 2.

belief that it would be quick and minimal. As the United States increasingly mired itself in Vietnam, it pursued a strategy of attrition, attempting to bury the Vietnamese Communist forces under an avalanche of casualties. However, the Viet Cong's guerrilla tactics frustrated and demoralized U.S. troops, while its widely dispersed, largely rural presence left American bomber planes with few targets. The United States consequently relied upon the use of unconventional weapons such as napalm and the herbicide defoliant Agent Orange. Still, little headway toward ending the war occurred.

In 1968, the North Vietnamese Army and the Viet Cong launched a massive campaign called the Tet Offensive, attacking several dozen U.S. targets and the major cities in South Vietnam at one time. Although the United States pushed back the offensive and won a tactical victory, American media coverage characterized the conflict as a defeat, and U.S. public support for the war plummeted. Morale among U.S. troops also hit an all-time low.

What were the results of the escalation of the war in Vietnam? Historian Sydney Ahlstrom believes that it prevented a concentrated assault on the nation's social justice problems of poverty and urban dislocation as well as showing the "terrible inequities in military conscription."[54] The optimism spawned during the Kennedy years was dampened by the escalation and hardened the beliefs of many that military considerations were determining American priorities. As a result, this activated the student dissent movement and led to a major loss of confidence in American institutions. The entire American system came under suspicion.

The antiwar movement within the United States consisted of student protesters, countercultural hippies, and those from middle-class suburbs, labor unions, and government institutions. The movement gained national prominence in 1965, peaked in 1968, and remained powerful throughout the duration of the conflict. As it encompassed political, racial, and cultural spheres, the antiwar movement exposed a deep schism within 1960s American society.

In the late 1950s, a New York socialist, Michael Harrington,

54. Ibid., 13. This topic will be discussed in more detail in chapter 6 of this work.

had revived the League for Industrial Democracy as a forum for laborers, African Americans, and intellectuals.[55] Within the year the organization was taken over by the student radicals Al Haber and Tom Hayden of the University of Michigan and reformed as the SDS—Students for a Democratic Society. In June 1962, fifty-nine SDS members met with Harrington at Port Huron, Michigan, in a conference sponsored by the United Auto Workers. From this meeting materialized the manifesto the Port Huron Statement, from the group that came to be known as the New Left. Written by Hayden, the document expressed disenchantment with the then current military-industrial-academic establishment. The students bemoaned the ambiguity of life in Cold War America as well as prejudice against African Americans as examples of the failure of modern American ideologies. They also called for a reconsideration of academic compliance. In regard to the latter, many claimed a widespread conspiracy existed, the purpose of which was to maintain a sense of apathy among American youth.[56]

For the first several years of its existence, the SDS focused solely on national concerns. The students actively supported Lyndon Johnson in his 1964 campaign against Barry Goldwater. Following Johnson's victory, they concurred with the social programs of the Great Society. Not yet an antiwar organization, the SDS actively participated in the civil rights struggle and later proved an important link between the two primary causes of the decade.

Another bridge between the civil rights and antiwar crusades was the Free Speech Movement (FSM) at the University of California at Berkeley. Students who had participated in Mississippi's "Freedom Summer" began the organization in December 1964. After several skirmishes with university president Clark Kerr, the FSM and its dynamic leader Mario Savio publicized the close ties between academic

55. Mark Barringer, "The Anti-War Movement in the United States," in *The Oxford Companion to American Military History* (New York: Oxford University Press, 1999), online at *Modern American Poetry*, accessed July 11, 2013, http://www.english.illinois.edu/maps/vietnam/antiwar.html.

56. Barringer, "Anti-War Movement." Tom Hayden grew up Catholic in an Irish family in Royal Oak, Michigan, as did Mario Savio in a Sicilian-Catholic neighborhood in New York City. Savio initially intended to become a priest.

and military establishments. By the beginning of 1965, the foundation of the antiwar movement was already coalescing on campuses and lacked only a significant catalyst to bring wider public acceptance.

Early in February 1965, when the United States began bombing North Vietnam, that catalyst appeared. The pace of the protest immediately increased; in both February and March, the SDS organized marches on the Oakland Army Terminal, the departure point for many troops heading to Southeast Asia. On March 24, faculty members at the University of Michigan promoted a series of "teach-ins," on the model of successful civil rights seminars. These sought to educate the student population about the moral and political implications of U.S. involvement. The teach-in format spread to campuses around the country and brought faculty members into active antiwar participation. In March, the SDS extended the scale of dissent to a national level, calling for a march on Washington to protest the bombing, one that would mirror civil rights protests. Between 15,000 and 25,000 people gathered at the Capitol on April 17, 1965. The turnout shocked not only the organizers, but the media and subsequently the nation as a whole.[57]

A significant development between 1965 and 1968 was the emergence of civil rights leaders as active proponents of peace in Vietnam. In a January 1967 article that appeared in the *Chicago Defender*, Martin Luther King Jr. first expressed support for the antiwar movement due to moral grounds.[58] He expanded his views in April of that year at the Riverside Church in New York by asserting that the

57. The SDS movement gained new allies over the next two years. "Vietnam Day," a conference held at Berkeley in October 1965, drew unexpected thousands to debate the moral basis of the war. In the spring of 1967, over 1,000 seminarians from across the country wrote to Secretary of Defense Robert McNamara promoting recognition of conscientious objection as a form of alternative service on secular, moral grounds. Within just two months, 10,000 students wrote, demanding this alternative for those who opposed violence. Another two-day march on the Pentagon in October 1967 once again attracted nationwide media attention, while leaders of the war resistance called for young men to turn in their draft cards. Underground railroads funneled draft evaders to Canada; churches provided sanctuary for those attempting to avoid conscription.

58. Mark Barringer, "The Anti-War Movement in the United States," *Modern American Poetry*, http://www.english.illinois.edu/maps/vietnam/antiwar.html.

war was draining much-needed resources from domestic programs.[59] King's statements rallied African American activists to the antiwar cause and established a new dimension to the moral objections of the movement. By this time, the entire nation was aware that the administration's foreign policies were being widely questioned.

As the antiwar movement's ideals spread beyond college campuses, doubts about the escalation of the war began to appear within the Johnson administration itself. As early as the summer of 1965, Undersecretary of State George Ball counseled President Johnson against further military involvement in Vietnam. In 1967, Johnson fired Defense Secretary McNamara after the secretary expressed concern about the moral justifications for war.[60] Many more in government offices simply believed that the cost of winning was too high. However, widespread opposition within the government did not appear until 1968 during the presidential campaigns. That year Johnson faced strong challenges from peace candidates Eugene McCarthy, Robert Kennedy, and George McGovern, all Democrats, as well as his eventual successor, Richard M. Nixon. By March 31, after learning that his closest advisors now opposed the war, he withdrew from the presidential race.

As was expressed in the introduction to this work, World War I was a point of conversion for Teilhard and in many ways the catalyst

59. Reverend Martin Luther King Jr., "Beyond Vietnam: A Time to Break Silence." This was a speech delivered by Dr. Martin Luther King Jr. on April 4, 1967, at a meeting of Clergy and Laity Concerned at Riverside Church in New York City. Included in the speech are these words: "Even when pressed by the demands of inner truth, men do not easily assume the task of opposing their government's policy, especially in time of war. Nor does the human spirit move without great difficulty against all the apathy of conformist thought within one's own bosom and in the surrounding world.... And we must rejoice ..., for surely this is the first time in our nation's history that a significant number of its religious leaders have chosen to move beyond the prophesying of smooth patriotism to the high grounds of a firm dissent based upon the mandates of conscience and the reading of history. Perhaps a new spirit is rising among us." Additionally, he asserted that "the promises of the great society have been shot down on the battlefields of Vietnam, making the poor, white and Negro, bear the heaviest burden both at the front and at home." About a week later, he addressed a major anti-war rally in New York City; accessed on July 17, 2013, http://www.hartford-hwp.com/archives/45a/058.html.

60. McNamara's appreciation for Teilhard's work has already been mentioned; in chapter 6 his concerns over the Vietnam War will be discussed again.

for his later writing and further mystical experiences. Although Teilhard saw war as evil, it was still potentially an opportunity to build the earth, to promote convergence of humanity toward Omega, and to unite in a common cause. The civil rights movement, the antiwar protests, the groups of student activists, even Johnson's War on Poverty, not mentioned in this work, were all possible opportunities for Teilhard's form of evolutionary progress to occur. This is not to imply that all those who thoroughly perused his *Phenomenon* understood Teilhard's perspective as to how this progress was to happen, for the work and his categories were easily reinterpreted as the reader wished. As has already been expressed by some, it was perhaps the easily transportable quality of his basic ideas, particularly when divorced from his Christological center, which permitted them both to percolate into an increasingly pluralistic American society and to be transformed as the carrier desired. It is just this phenomenon with which de Lubac, Francoeur, and Barbour took issue.

The Rise of the Counterculture

Both the civil rights and the antiwar protest movements contributed to the growth of the counterculture; however, it was also a phenomenon that simultaneously developed and existed on its own. The segment of the counterculture most associated with a rejection of mainstream values was that of the "hippies," a movement springing from the Haight-Ashbury district in San Francisco.[61] The hippies were theoretically nonmilitant, espousing peace and love as alternatives to violence and racism, embracing long-held taboos as a way to revisualize and reform established society. They defied racism by adopting the idea of a general unifying brotherhood that drew all peoples into their fold. Through the philosophy and lifestyle of the hippie culture, the personal became political.

Those who could not travel to San Francisco had the music of their generation as an inspiration. Haugen and Box, for example, consider the Beatles as the beginning of the counterculture in the

61. David M. Haugen and Matthew J. Box, eds., *Examining Pop Culture: The 1960s* (Detroit: Greenhaven, 2005), 15.

United States. Some see the Beatles as redefining the sense of love for a generation, although some music critics would contend that their work had more to do with establishing identity and a general sense of spiritual well-being.[62] It had, however, a strongly existential quality. The love about which they (and similar bands) sang "brought to the world a higher sense of harmony and goodwill, a sense of brotherhood and communal feeling not unlike the ethos advocated by the integrationist faction of the civil rights movement," similar to the ethos many found in Teilhard's thought.[63]

Anyone could aspire to hippie ideals with nothing more than a change in ethical or aesthetic views; through advances in media millions of young whites could dabble in the music, dress, and philosophy of the counterculture without giving up the comforts of mainstream life. Once this option spread to the affluent and mainstream, it could not be ignored and was instead marketed. Scholar Mark Hamilton commented that at this point "hippieness had finally been subsumed by mainstream pop culture, but the essential message was not entirely lost in the process."[64] Ongoing questions over the war in Vietnam, the paradox of the loss of civil rights for some in a democracy, and the notion that perhaps pleasure might exist outside of economic well-being helped to liberalize mainstream American culture. Certainly, the organized protest movements were more influential in pointing out and confronting injustice, but hippies were important in the overall cultural shift. As Barry Miles writes, "It was only by stepping outside society that people were able to look at it objectively—to see what was wrong with it, to see how they'd like to change it."[65]

The *International Times*, a periodical founded in the fall of 1966 for and by the London counterculture, defined "hippiedom" as an inner-directed movement, so that those involved share a common viewpoint, one that could not be suppressed by force.[66] They be-

62. Lytle, *America's Uncivil Wars*, 146.

63. Ibid.

64. Ibid., 16.

65. Barry Miles, *Hippie* (New York: Sterling, 2004), 18.

66. *International Times* was launched on October 14, 1966, at the Roundhouse in London at a gig featuring Pink Floyd. The *IT* event was important because it marked

lieved that the individual should be free from any hindrance of external law so long as their actions did not impinge on another. This was not a movement of protest but of celebration, futuristic in nature, interested in having a good time or "pleasure now." The new movement was essentially optimistic, with a "happy view of man and his potential, based mainly on his creativity ... the new approach is to make changes wherever you are, right in front of your nose. The weapons are love and creativity."[67]

The counterculturalists saw Christianity and the churches as far too dogmatic, interested primarily in laying down too many moral rules. At the same time, a strictly secular wisdom was criticized as also too dogmatic, reflecting a narrow conception of life and the universe.[68] The hippies were ready to accept the supernatural even as they rejected Christian ethics. McLeod considered them within a tradition that went back to the latter half of the nineteenth century, members of that middle way between orthodox religion and orthodox science, desiring a way of life that was spiritual without being exclusive, one that took "experience" seriously and considered phenomena that the mainstream rejected as a matter of course, including mystical experience.

As Timothy Leary wrote in the 1980s, "Everything we did in the 1960s was designed to fission, to weaken faith in and conformity to the 1950s social order. Our precise surgical target was the Judeo-Christian power monolith, which has imposed a guilty, inhibited, grim, anti-body, anti-life repression on Western civilization. Our assignment was to topple this prudish, judgmental civilization. And it worked!"[69]

"the first recognition of a rapidly spreading socio-cultural revolution that had its parallel in the States" as explained by Daevid Allen of the band Soft Machine. Hugh McLeod enumerates the themes of "hippiedom" as: (1) the use of drugs; (2) an advocacy of free love and rejection of the nuclear family; and (3) a rejection of the traditional work ethic, so that many perceived hippies as "parasites" upon the larger society; McLeod, *Religious Crisis,* 125.

67. McLeod, *Religious Crisis,* 129.

68. Ibid., 132.

69. Paul Harvey and Philip Goff, *The Columbia Documentary History of Religion in America Since 1945* (New York: Columbia University Press, 2007), 94–95. In the early 1970s then-President Richard Nixon called Leary "the most dangerous man in

From about 1965 onward a variety of esoteric religious ideas began to reach a much wider audience, flowing especially from the San Francisco countercultural area. Sociologist Robert Wuthnow saw a strong correlation between the counterculture involvement and a rejection of Christianity.[70] As is noted with Dr. Leary, the movement included the nonreligious and "mystics" interested in knowledge of and belief in astrology, extrasensory perception, and Native American religions. Consistent with their overall stress on the experiential and on individual freedom, the counterculture, in terms of spirituality, emphasized the need for personal exploration, highlighting the subjective, the emotional, and intuition rather than rational argument.

The mystical, ecumenical qualities of Teilhard's thought would on the surface appear to be quite appealing to those in the counterculture. For those seeking union not only with each other, but with the cosmos and the spiritual in general, someone who wrote of his own mystical experiences was quite alluring. Teilhard's conception of what was later known as "deep time" would have also found favor with those seeking something beyond a dogmatic view of history and culture. In addition, of course, those who advocated love for all would have been quick to embrace one who spoke of love as the ultimate force of life. For Teilhard, however, as stated above, this "love" was first found in a love of Christ. Repeatedly, he notes that "it is impossible to love Christ without loving others ... it is impossible to love others without moving nearer to Christ."[71] It would seem, then, that to reject Christ along with Christianity was to reject that which would bring about exactly what at least seemed to be most desired by the counterculture—a community of love. And, especially for the mystics in their midst, Teilhard notes that rather than individual spiritual ecstasy, "the only subject ultimately capable of mystical transfiguration is the whole group of mankind forming a single body and a single soul in charity" through Christ.[72]

America"; from "Timothy Leary, Pied Piper of Psychedelic 60s, Dies at 75," *New York Times*, June 1, 1996, accessed September 5, 2013, http://www.nytimes.com/learning/general/onthisday/bday/1022.html.

70. McLeod, *Religious Crisis*, 134.

71. Teilhard de Chardin, *Divine Milieu*, 125.

72. Ibid., 126.

THE FORMATION OF THE AMERICAN TEILHARD ASSOCIATION

It was in this turbulent atmosphere and intense interest in Teilhard's thought in both church and world that an official U.S. Teilhard association finally came into being. As prior chapters detailed, repeated attempts at the same thing earlier in the 1960s had not succeeded. However, as an indication of the increasing influence of at least some portion of Teilhard's thought on the general American population, the American Teilhard Association was officially launched on February 24, 1965. Twenty people met for this purpose in New York under the initial leadership of Robert Francoeur, Pierre Dansereau, and John Walsh.[73] They had finally been authorized by the French Teilhard Association to form a counterpart in the United States. The ATA, as it became known, was incorporated as a nonprofit with tax-exempt status in April 1967.

The front page of the first membership brochure for the ATA remarks that "throughout the modern world the writings of the French Jesuit paleontologist Pierre Teilhard de Chardin are inspiring hope and a sense of direction, zest for life and love of the world. Many thoughtful readers find that he speaks to the deepest problems of our troubled time."[74] Also included are comments that typify the decade:

> As the process of creative union continues, aided by sophisticated modern communications, human persons will be united in a timeless and richly diversified universal community. The force that propels us from below that works in us and through us, that draws us up from above, is known and named. It is love. Thus, Teilhard challenges us to do our utmost to increase consciousness, union, love.

73. ATA Brochure, Barbour Collection Box no. 2, Woodstock Library Archives, Georgetown University; also Winifred McCulloch, *A Short History of the American Teilhard Association* (Chambersburg, Pa.: American Teilhard Association for the Future of Man, 1979).

74. The address given on the first membership brochure for the ATA was 157 East 72nd Street, New York, New York. This location was a room in a former Anglican theological library, the Library of St. Bede's, which had been founded and administered for over thirty years by a group of women from the Episcopal Church. It was also about three blocks away from the neighborhood in which Teilhard had spent his last several years and the apartment in which he died.

The purpose and plans of the ATA are enumerated as: (1) to extend knowledge and understanding of the thought of Teilhard; (2) to encourage critical study of his work and to further develop lines of thought indicated by this work; (3) to provide a focus for the integration of developments in science, sociology, religion, and philosophy; (4) to organize meetings of those interested in such studies; and (5) to promote fellowship and cooperation among those interested in the life, work, and thought of Teilhard.

As a means of accomplishing these aims, the association planned to maintain a Teilhard Center that would include a reference and lending library as well as space for meetings and seminars. Additionally, they were organizing an advisory board, membership association, and newsletter for the purpose of exchanging information. This board would also sponsor lectures and conferences on the thought of Teilhard and related issues. Finally, they wished to encourage research and interdisciplinary projects.

On the final fold of the ATA brochure is the comment:

Among the seminal thinkers of our century Pierre Teilhard de Chardin holds a pre-eminent place. He is one of the few scholars to make a creative contribution both to science and to theology. His distinction was to combine precise, analytic observation with a brand new synthetic vision and deep-rooted faith at a time when these three elements of human endeavor were divided and opposed to one another.

Rejected at first by positivistic science as well as by traditional theology, Teilhard nevertheless pioneered and summed up the dynamic and integrative approach of modern thought in theology, history and the natural and social sciences. Despite the scope of his thought, however, Teilhard did not aim to construct a closed or finished system. Rather, he sought to open the way through research and dialogue to an evergrowing knowledge of man, society and the world as parts of one organically related and developing universe whose fundamental characteristic is not atomic matter but mind, and whose supreme product, looking towards the future, is the full flowering of spirit. It is this search, initiated by Teilhard, that the ATA hopes to continue.[75]

75. Initial membership costs were regular membership $10, student $3, sponsoring $100. This included a subscription to the biannual *Teilhard Review* and to the newsletter. The members of the initial board of directors with their association positions

Finally, three years after interested parties initially gathered, the first annual general meeting took place in April 1968.[76] Within a year, membership in the ATA stood at 1,117, and subscriptions to the *Teilhard Review* climbed to 135 nonmembers.

The reader should note, however, that once again, although "love" was mentioned in numerous places on this initial brochure, any mention of the Christological focus of Teilhard's own love and thought is neglected here. Rather than a personal Omega, the final point of humanity's effort and love is an amorphous "full flowering of spirit."

---

and credentials (included here to indicate the already interdisciplinary nature of those interested) were Pierre Dansereau, president (Cranbrooke Institute—Department of Ecology, N.Y. Botanical Garden, and professor of botany, Columbia, Fordham, and NYU); Michael H. Murray, vice president (Episcopal minister and communications officer, Joint Urban Program, the Episcopal Church); Beatrice Bruteau, vice president (executive secretary, Foundation for Integrative Education—first convener of the 1964 Teilhard Conference at Fordham); Minna Cassard, secretary-treasurer (lay Episcopal member); Ewert Cousins (professor of theology, Fordham); Theodosius Dobzhansky (professor of genetics, Rockefeller University); Henry Elkin (psychotherapist and Jungian analyst, New School for Social Research); Bob Francoeur (assistant professor of biology, Fairleigh Dickinson University); Louis Marks (chair of Biology Department, St. Joseph's College, Philadelphia and then Fordham); Alexander Wolsky (chair of Natural Sciences Department, Marymount College, Tarrytown, N.Y.). The advisory board included George Barbour (chair of Geology Department, University of Cincinnati); Sister Margaret Mary Bach (chair of Philosophy Department, Marymount); Thomas Berry (associate professor, Asian Religions Department, Fordham); Donald J. Bloom (founder of the Phenomenon of Man (POM) Project, Canoga Park, California); J. Donceel, SJ (professor of philosophy, Fordham); Loren Eiseley (professor of anthropology, University of Pennsylvania); W. H. Kenney, SJ (professor of philosophy, Bellarmine School of Theology, Louisville, Kentucky); Hallam Movius (professor of anthropology, Harvard); Mildred Mann (leader, Society of Pragmatic Mysticism, New York, N.Y.), Jean Houston (director, Foundation for Mind Research, New York, N.Y.), J. V. Langmead Casserley (Theologian, Seabury-Western Seminary, Evanston, Illinois).

76. The meeting took place on Saturday, April 27, 1968, from 10 a.m. to 5 p.m. First on the agenda were instructions given to attendees to pronounce the name as "Tay-yahr." In response to the question as to why this was his surname was the explanation that Teilhard's grandfather—Pierre Cirice Teilhard—married in 1841 into the de Chardin family, whose name was then appended onto his own, a custom not uncommon in Europe. As to the membership itself, the New York reading room had eighty-six visitors that first year, with numerous ongoing study groups. The first editions of the *Teilhard Review* went to three hundred printings.

FINAL THOUGHTS

In light of the cumulative impact of the Second Vatican Council and the civil rights, antiwar, and countercultural movements, it seems Sydney Ahlstrom was correct in writing that "the full significance of these several compound events will not be knowable until the end of time, but it was perfectly clear to any reasonably conscious American historian that the postwar revival had completely frittered out, that the nation was moving rapidly towards a *crise de la conscience* of unprecedented depth."[77] It is appropriate here to remark that Teilhard commented more than once that phenomena, whether natural or chronological, can only be explained from a "God's-eye" or highly bird's-eye view. As is noted in his *Pantheisme et Christianisme*, "Not a thing in our changing world is really understandable except in so far as it has reached its terminus."[78] Even today historians debate the interaction of these movements in the "perfect storm" that was the 1960s.

One must wonder again, then, in the midst of that storm of the mid-sixties, why it was that Teilhard was so readily embraced. In large part it was perhaps, as he wrote in *Hymn of the Universe*, that he was one "whom the Lord had drawn to follow the road of fire," whose calling led him away from the road of abandonment of the life of matter into the world of people, action, and the "stuff" of the universe.[79] These years in the decade were certainly about people, action, and the stuff of life. They were also replete with passion, and Teilhard was undoubtedly a man of passion who became a model for many others.

The passion that drove Teilhard led him not only in the fire of love for and union with God, but toward union with a world of people of all types, participating in many different events. One of those events that so greatly shaped his vision and thought was World

77. Ahlstrom, "Radical Turn," 2.

78. Teilhard de Chardin, "Pantheisme et Christianisme," in *Comment Je Crois* (Paris:Éditions du Seuil, 1969), 8.

79. Teilhard de Chardin, *Hymn of the Universe*, 62, quoted in Ursula King, *Spirit of Fire* (Maryknoll, N.Y.: Orbis, 1996), 58.

War I.[80] In a new way, he realized at that time that the matter of the earth was indeed charged with life and with spirit. As a result, the passion that so permeated his life was intensified, and the love he felt for the world, the need he felt to choose life, only grew stronger. He became more convinced that each of us is bound together by all our being—materially, organically, psychically, and mentally—with all around us. We are, like all other beings, cosmic by nature. All humanity together is in the process of forming that new entity, the cosmic Omega, which is far more than merely a collection of individuals, but the very body of Christ. For Teilhard, perceiving this as happening at the war front was very much a redeeming and hopeful quality of the war. He wrote that "I brought back from it the very definite conviction that, among other results of the war, will be that of mixing and welding together the peoples of the earth in a way that nothing else, perhaps, could have done."[81]

In the United States during these years, many who were fighting the war on racial inequality and what they perceived as the curtailing in any way of personal freedom rejoiced in the sense of community and future hope fostered by this battle.[82] Additionally, in Teilhard's essay "Cosmic Life," a motto written on the first sheet of the essay and later crossed out, read, "To those who feel; To those who will understand me," an existential expression that thousands of people struggling for their voice in the mid-1960s might well have appropriated as their own salutatory plea.[83]

As for those in the counterculture who aspired to peace, love, and personal freedom, Teilhard's words that "at the rate the consciousness and the ambitions of the world are increasing, it will explode unless it learns to love. The future of the thinking earth is organically bound up with the turning of the forces of hate into forces

80. See the discussion of Teilhard de Chardin, *The Making of a Mind: Letters from a Soldier-Priest* (New York: Harper and Row, 1965) in chapter 5.

81. Ibid., 125.

82. One might recall the lyrics of the Beatles' opening track on the album *Abbey Road*, "Come Together," released in October 1969.

83. From the first essay in French found in Teilhard de Chardin, *Érits du temps de la guerre* (Paris: Grasset, 1965), quoted in Ursula King, *Spirit of Fire*, 55 and n. 49.

of charity" were truths they were delighted to discover and attempt to put into action.[84]

Those involved in the aforementioned movements, therefore, could be excused for thinking that Teilhard's thought paralleled their own efforts quite nicely. What many appeared to overlook in their appropriation of his work was the thoroughly integrated mystical Christian vision that required him to also write, with sincerity, "To live the cosmic life is to live dominated by the consciousness that one is an atom in the body of the mystical and Cosmic Christ. The man who so lives dismisses as irrelevant the host of preoccupations that absorb the interest of other men; his life is projected further, and his heart more widely receptive."[85] For Teilhard, the promised unity and ongoing hope existed only within the context of, and a life lived in, adoration of Christ. By no means did all those who appropriated his work understand it was this Christocentric focus that fueled the faith, hope, perseverance, and love that were keystones of his life and his thought.

84. Ibid., 138.
85. Teilhard de Chardin, *Cosmic Christ,* quoted in Ursula King, *Spirit of Fire,* 55.

5 THE "DEATH OF GOD"

THIS CHAPTER, like the previous, attempts to delineate the increasing influence of Teilhard in the United States during the mid-1960s. As we have seen, the dominant trends of the time such as civil rights, radical theology, and various countercultural movements fed the increased interest in his work and were in turn influenced by it. Teilhard's thought truly exploded onto the scene during these years, as the escalating numbers of publications verify.

This chapter explores the themes of hope, optimism, and progress inherent to this time period and their relationship to Teilhard's reception as expressed in conferences, journal essays, and books. The hope and excitement generated by the civil rights movement, the changes mandated by Vatican II, and the various student movements led to intense expectation. Even the radical theology and "Death of God" movement optimistically presumed that dispensing with moribund images of the sacred, the church, and religion would permit the evolution of something positive and improved.

In particular, the emphasis in the United States in the early to mid-1960s was on hope for humanity and new possibilities for human progress. Harvey Cox's *The Secular City* was indicative of the national mood during this time, as Cox articulated what so many were expressing in other forms: "Man, seen as the steersman of the cosmos, is the only starting point we have for a viable doctrine of

God."[1] This thought strongly parallels Teilhard's own conviction that humanity is the apex of God's creation. The line between the secular and the sacred, the natural and the supernatural became thinner still during this time period in the minds of quite a few, and Teilhard was in the midst of that adjustment.

As chapter 4 showed, these may have been years of hope, but the aftershocks of the race riots and the escalation of the Vietnam War also constrained that hope. One pertinent Teilhardian question is how hope in evolutionary progress might be sustained when all seems to have been lost, or at least quite stymied. This work has argued that for Teilhard, the promised unity of all humanity and ongoing hope despite suffering existed only within the context of, and a life lived with, a Christocentric focus. As has already been shown, far too many did not understand that about him and so were eager to facilely label him as scientific humanist, mystic, or poet.

The chapter begins by examining numerous publications out of the school of "radical theology," including Harvey Cox's *Secular City*, to determine their intersections with Teilhard's writings. It then looks at a selection of the conferences on Teilhard's work that took place during this time period, as well as publications from both the public and academic press concerning Teilhard and his work.

TEILHARD, THE "DEATH OF GOD," AND THE SECULAR CITY

Perhaps the most widely publicized aspect of this decade's religious history was efforts made to meet the needs of the world's new age. The Second Vatican Council was certainly one of those. Additionally, Dietrich Bonhoeffer's earlier demand for a "secular interpretation" of scripture was answered by some with the emergence of radical theology. This entailed, like Teilhard's writing, yet another major reappraisal of the basic Judeo-Christian doctrinal consensus.

Radical theology was explored in Harvey Cox's 1965 *The Secular City*, in H. Richard Niebuhr's essay *Radical Monotheism* from

1. Harvey Cox, *The Secular City* (New York: Macmillan, 1965), 199.

1960, and in Gabriel Vahanian's *The Death of God: The Culture of our Post-Christian Era* in 1961.[2] Numerous theologians and scholars noted the correspondences between some aspects of radical theology and Teilhard's work, and for that reason alone it would be worthwhile to explore those parallels. Consider however, how several of the documents of Vatican II focused on the world, the role of the laity in the world, and the secular; this appears to be a topic very much in the forefront of the minds of many. It was a theological topic that "grew legs," so to speak, giving momentum and agency to the ongoing efforts of those actively involved in the various social and racial justice movements of the time. Even if they had not read or even heard of either Teilhard's thought or "the death of god" movement, they lived it at this time. Hence, radical theology is a necessary topic for discussion in this work. Note too, that the Human Energetics Research Institute, the first official Teilhard-inspired organization formed at Fordham and discussed in chapter 3, sponsored one more conference following its successful seminars of the summer of 1964. In 1966, the institute explored the similarities between Harvey Cox's newly published book, *The Secular City*, and Teilhard's thought.

Cox, of Harvard Divinity School, developed in a particular trajectory the contemporary thesis that the church is primarily a people of faith and action, rather than simply an institution.[3] An ordained Baptist minister, he argued that "God is just as present in the secular as the religious realms of life."[4] With this so, the church should therefore be found in the forefront of change in society, discovering

2. Hugh McLeod, *The Religious Crisis of the 1960s* (New York: Oxford University Press, 2007), 8. Other best sellers included H. Richard Niebuhr, *Radical Monotheism and Western Culture* (Louisville: Westminster John Knox Press, 1960); Gabriel Vahanian, *The Death of God: The Culture of our Post-Christian Era* (New York: George Braziller, 1961); John A. T. Robinson, *Honest to God* (Louisville: Westminster John Knox Press, 1963); Cox, *Secular City*; and Pierre Berton, *The Comfortable Pew: A Critical Look at Christianity and the Religious Establishment in the New Age* (Philadelphia: Lippincott, 1965).

3. Harvey Gallagher Cox Jr. (1929–) served as Hollis Research Professor of Divinity at the Harvard Divinity School until his retirement in October 2009. *Secular City* could definitely be classified as a "run-away bestseller," as it sold over a million copies.

4. "Theology: Life in a Defatalized World," *Time Magazine*, April 2, 1965, accessed May 2013, http://www.time.com/time/magazine/article/0,9171,941039,00.html#ixzz2Br7yBowP.

and celebrating the new ways religion was finding expression in the world, rather than hiding from the world.

Cox was specifically attempting to move beyond existentialism and "demythologization" to reprogram theology for what he saw as a new era in the history of humanity: the age of urban secularization. For the practical "technopolitan" dweller, "life is a set of problems, not an unfathomable mystery." This particular population is too busy dealing with the realities of this life to have much concern for the next. The world, in other words, has been "defatalized," and life is now the task and responsibility of mankind alone. According to Cox, rather than deploring this trend, the church should welcome and assist it by supporting rapid social change.[5]

For Cox, John Fitzgerald Kennedy was the perfect presidential type for this time period, as he was "the first really urban President," one whose style was urbane, cool, detached, yet mobile and appreciative.[6] Kennedy was of "the world." Cox chose the then newly mar-

5. Ibid. Regarding secularization, Cox reiterates the definition of Dutch theologian C. V. Van Peursen: "[Secularization is] the deliverance of man, first from religious and then from metaphysical control over his reason and his language. It is the loosing of the world from religious and quasi-religious understandings of itself, the dispelling of all closed worldviews, the breaking of all supernatural myths and sacred symbols. It represents the 'defatalisation of history,' the discovery by man that he has been left with the world on his hands, that he can no longer blame fortune or furies for what he does with it. Secularization occurs when man turns his attention away from worlds beyond and towards this time"; Cox, *Secular City*, 1–2. Also, Michael Novak's article "Harvey Cox's Secular City," in *First Things* on March 5, 2007 (accessed June 4, 2012 at https://www.firstthings.com/web-exclusives/2007/03/harvey-coxs-secular-city), states that *The Secular City* caused such a sensation that by 1966 both *Christianity and Crisis* and *Commonweal* had published symposia on the book, in each of which Cox replied to his critics. These symposia, plus a set of the outstanding critical reviews that had already appeared and a set of essays newly commissioned for the occasion, appeared in the volume *The Secular City Debate*, edited by Daniel Callahan (New York: Mcmillan, 1967). To this volume, too, Cox added "a vigorous rejoinder." In addition, Cox issued a new and revised edition of *The Secular City* in 1966, "to correct some of the more egregious overstatements, tone down an occasional vivid passage, and respond at points to helpful criticisms the book has elicited."

6. Garry Wills, *Bare Ruined Choirs: Doubt, Prophecy and Radical Religion* (New York: Doubleday, 1972), 89. Wills commented later on that "many felt on November 22, 1963 that God or fate or history had taken 'the very best' away." Although the public and the government of the United States tried to solve that problem, they could not, and little solace, simply sadness was subsequently found. In the mid-1960s one might consider that "God's death had been the death of mystery ... but Kennedy's death signaled the rebirth of mystery— the mystery of evil" (95–96). If the years of the

tyred Kennedy as the model of his newly identified pragmatic, secular mind, for John F. Kennedy had assertively attacked old questions of civil rights, poverty, and crime with an innovative spirit, inspiring the younger generation to fresh ways of thinking. Additionally, Kennedy was an ideal example of the secular man who compartmentalizes his life in order to survive at work, at play, and at home. Cox contends that the anonymity of city living helps preserve the privacy essential to human life; urban man "wants to maintain a clear distinction between private and public."[7] Kennedy, in his mind, did this quite well.

Cox's book gave John F. Kennedy the "secular canonization" liberal Catholics wanted; in turn, his paperback was a standard part of the teaching equipment of Catholic theologians. Carrying the theology of *The Secular City* one step further, "God is Dead" proponents cheered the news of God's death.[8] God *had* to be dead if, in "the

---

Kennedy administration were years of great hope and the beginning of the Americanist appeal of Teilhard's thought, the death of the Kennedys spoke to another aspect of Teilhard's thought, one that was more difficult for most Americans to understand, much less to find of comfort.

7. Cox, *Secular City*, 40.

8. The "death-of-God" movement meant different things to different theologians, as Cox himself admitted; Cox, "Afterword," in Callahan, *Secular City Debate*, 195–97. Yet, the movement hardly began with Cox and is instead a widely quoted statement by the German philosopher Friedrich Nietzsche that first appeared in *The Gay Science* (German: *Die fröhliche Wissenschaft*) in 1882. It is also found in Nietzsche's work *Thus Spoke Zarathustra* (German: *Also sprach Zarathustra*, 1883–85), which is most responsible for popularizing the phrase. The idea is stated in "The Madman" from *The Gay Science* as follows: "God is dead. God remains dead. And we have killed him. How shall we comfort ourselves, the murderers of all murderers? What was holiest and mightiest of all that the world has yet owned has bled to death under our knives." By the early 1960s, however, the movement was garnering a great deal of contention, and numerous books were published around the subject. In 1961, Gabriel Vahanian argued in his book *The Death of God* that modern secular culture had lost all sense of the sacred, lacking any sacramental meaning, and had no sense of teleology. He concluded that for contemporary society a transformed post-Christian and postmodern culture was required to resurrect God. Therefore, according to the norms of then contemporary modern thought, God *was* dead.

Another significant contribution to the "death of God" movement is found in *Honest to God*, written by the Anglican bishop John A. T. Robinson, which criticized traditional Christian theology and aroused a storm of controversy on its publication. The dominant theory of *Honest to God* is the idea that having rejected the idea of "God up there," modern secular man also needs to recognize that the idea of "God out there" is also an outdated simplification of the nature of divinity. Rather, Christians

marketplace," John F. Kennedy left religion behind, sealed up privately. If the world was truly to be secular, "God must die to it, and release his claim on it."[9]

Therefore, God had to die, Cox concludes, to give us "Technopolis," so that we might become the pragmatic men necessary to the age.[10] Cox though, also outlines in his book the linkage of secularization with religion since even before the time of Christ. He also discusses how religion, particularly Christianity, has encouraged a secular response to change throughout the ages. A few have especially plumbed these ideas, he concludes, including Teilhard. Teilhard, one might argue, merged the religious with the secular even more than Cox, who calls him one of the most important teachers of the future because of his emphasis on "man as 'that point where the cosmos begins to think and to steer itself."[11] In *The Secular City Debate,* Cox refers to Teilhard as a "pariah" whose efforts to transcend

should recognize in the existentialist theology of Paul Tillich that God is "the ground of our being." Dietrich Bonhoeffer's notion of religion-less Christianity is also a major theme in this book, as it is in Cox's own later volume. Robinson claims that secular man requires a secular theology. That is, God's continuing revelation to humanity is one brought about in culture at large, not merely within the confines of "religion" or "church." It is thus not a surprise that the cover of the April 8, 1966, edition of *Time* magazine asked the question, "Is God Dead?" The accompanying article addressed the growing atheism in America of the time. Cox's *Secular City* therefore falls at least somewhat into this same theological discussion. Where, these authors are asking, is God to be found in a culture that is rapidly secularizing and reexamining the concepts of nature and grace? For some, Cox contended, the "death of God" meant the disappearance of the abstract divinity on which rested "our classical metaphysical systems." For others this concept referred to the disappearance of the numerous culturally acceptable ways that the numinous of our ancestors was apprehended. As he notes, religious experience is shaped by cultural patterns, and when these change, so too do the means by which we discern and approach the holy. Hence, he writes, "the experience of the 'death of God' correlates with a rapid dissolution of traditional cultural patterns and is a frequent characteristic of societies in abrupt transition."

9. Wills, *Bare Ruined Choirs,* 91.

10. Ibid., 92. The world is where one works, and religion therefore must also go into the secular, where the "action is." Wills notes that the death of God resembled Marshall McLuhan's "death of print" and his concept of "Rejoicing in the non-word!" McLuhan (a convert to Catholicism) argues that print had to die to give us TV. McLuhan was another who took inspiration from the thought of Teilhard. In a 1952 review of McLuhan's *The Mechanical Bride* (London: Routledge, 1967), Father Walter Ong, who happened to have studied under McLuhan, drew connections between McLuhan's theories and Teilhard's "noosphere."

11. Wills, *Bare Ruined Choirs,* 98.

metaphysical dualism with a secular theology, or more than that a Christian cosmology, are poetic and only accidentally scientific. This is a cosmology, Cox notes, that is "the first in some time to truly engage the imagination of modern man."[12]

What Cox discerns as key to humanity's being is the future and the understanding of man as a "creature who can hope."[13] Hope is essential to Teilhard's discussion of transcendence. For Teilhard that hope is at least in part discovered in humanity's growing capacity to apply science in the shaping of that future; the future then becomes not just that for which humankind is responsible, but that for which we now *know* we are responsible.[14]

In an article in *Continuum* in 1965 on this very topic, Charles Thompkins notes that some are claiming Teilhard's thought is already a passing fad, supplanted not just by the "Death of God," but by Bonhoeffer's emphasis upon secularization. Thompkins argues that for the most part, Teilhard's and Bonhoeffer's thought are identical. He gladly sees these as spelling an end to what some called "Christian culture" as well as "wholesale condemnations of the secular world." The realization has dawned that secularity is instead where personhood is found. "We are less distressed by a church of the diaspora because we see the destruction of Christendom and of the myth of Christian Culture, as a sign that Christianity is growing in self-awareness; it is becoming more Christian."[15]

What radical theology attempted to do, therefore, was to update Christian language to make it more meaningful to a modern, scientific age. These authors wished to create what might be termed a "religionless Christianity," for "Christianity had been separated off into a compartment labeled 'religion,' which had little relationship

12. Callahan, *Secular City Debate,* 197.

13. Ibid., *Secular City Debate,* 198.

14. Donald Gray, "The Phenomenon of Teilhard," *Theological Studies* 36, no. 1 (March 1975): 19–51. Gray suggests that Teilhard's work represents an attempt on hope's part to achieve understanding of the sweep of cosmic evolution and of man's place in it. "Teilhard hopes in order to understand." Gray, therefore, writing several years after the last period covered in this work, places a great deal of emphasis on Teilhard's Christology as his source of hope.

15. Charles Thompkins, "Fads upon Fads," *Continuum* 3, no. 3 (Autumn 1965): 396–98.

with the rest of life, and might offer means of escape from the tragic or mundane."[16]

In regard to these topics Donald Gray later reaffirmed in an essay in *Theological Studies* that Teilhard's spirituality is decidedly secular in that it is directed to finding God in and through the "evolving world" and in "building the earth." No dichotomizing tendency between sacred and secular exists for Teilhard. The future of the world is humanity's responsibility; left solely to scientific evolution, the world would devolve from what order and unity presently exist into chaos and multiplicity.[17]

In terms of Teilhard's hope, Gray believes it becomes for him a way of seeing. Teilhard, Gray argues, is writing against (1) those who have no hope whatsoever, the pessimists of contemporary society; (2) those Christians whose hope is too individualistic and focused overly much on the eschaton, and who therefore have no hope for the successful building of the earth; and (3) those humanists who do hope, but whose hope does not go far enough, and hence does not break through the barriers of death and suffering. Gray contends that for Teilhard neither Christianity nor humanism as they now stand is sufficiently optimistic; instead those whose stance is that of the absolutely optimistic draw their sustenance from a hope that embraces all of cosmic evolution, matter and spirit, nature and grace, through the power of the Paschal mystery and especially the Resurrection of Christ. Teilhard's hope, therefore, is in the Cosmic Christ. This is an explanation that those who later shunned Teilhard for too facile an optimism would have done well to make note of at the time.

16. McLeod, *Religious Crisis of the 1960s*, 85.

17. Religion for Teilhard is not an enemy of evolutionary humanism but can be a compatriot and is certainly a dialogue partner. Religious faith therefore is not opposed to humanism, but its "complement and completion"; Gray, "Phenomenon of Teilhard," 19–51. See also Thomas Oden, "Contemporary Theology and Psychotherapy," *Philadelphia* (1967): 51–52; Charles Hegarty, "Boenhoeffer and Teilhard on Worldly Christianity," *Science et Esprit* 21 (1965): 35–70; and Hegarty, "Boenhoffer and Teilhard: Christian Prophets of Secular Sanctity," *Catholic World* 207 (1968–69): 31–34.

CONFERENCES AND SYMPOSIA

The fact that the decidedly non-Catholic "Death of God" theologians would include an analysis of Teilhard's work alongside Dietrich Bonhoeffer's shows that for those outside the Catholic Church as well as those staunchly within it, Teilhard's thoughts were proving increasingly fascinating during these years. This argument can also be illustrated by what was becoming an increasingly common occurrence—namely, special courses, conferences, and "Teilhard Days" for both universities and the general public. To demonstrate this point, what follows is a summary of a few symposia from areas located apart from the previous Teilhard strongholds in the northeastern United States; those referenced here occurred in non-Catholic institutions in Chicago and Pennsylvania, in the stronghold of the counterculture in southern California, and in the midst of middle-class, midwestern America.

The earliest of these was an ecumenical lecture series by Georges Crespy at the University of Chicago titled, "Evolution and Its Problems."[18] This was one of, if not the first, large conference concerning Teilhard given in the Midwest and the first outside Catholic walls. These ecumenical talks were attended by over five hundred people and were to be televised weekly by the Church Federation of Greater Chicago as "The Future of Man—a Discussion of Teilhard de Chardin."

Additionally, February 10 was designated "Teilhard Day" at the university. An all-day conference on Teilhard's thought and writings took place, and over one hundred philosophers, theolo-

18. Dave Meade, "Evolution: A Scientific New Gospel," *Chicago Daily News*, January 9, 1965, 19. Georges Crespy's thought is significant, as he was one of the leading Protestant interpreters of Teilhard, particularly in Europe. He presented eight lectures on Teilhard between January 6 and February 24, 1965, at the University of Chicago. The titles for these were: "Teilhard's Concerns and Questions"; "The 'Christology' of Teilhard"; "The Question of Evil in Teilhard's Thought"; "History and Eschatology in the Mind of Teilhard"; and "Theology after Teilhard." Crespy had already written *La Pensée Théologique de Teilhard de Chardin* (1961), and in 1965 would author *De la Science à la Théologie: Essai sur Teilhard de Chardin* (Neuchâtel: Delachaux et Niestlé, 1965), later translated into English as *From Science to Theology: An Essay on Teilhard de Chardin* (Nashville, Tenn.: Abingdon Press, 1968).

gians, and doctoral candidates attended. Most certainly that such a well-attended, wide-ranging event with internationally known Teilhard experts would occur, much less be sponsored by an ecumenical religious organization, implies a great deal not only about the interest in, but also the respect accorded, the subject matter.[19]

Yet another example of ecumenical interest can be found in the “Teilhard de Chardin Seminar,” which took place at Friend’s Central School in Overbrook, Pennsylvania. About 130 teachers from high schools and higher education attended to learn about and better understand Teilhard’s thought and what it meant for their own scholarly discipline. The day concluded with a panel discussion by Haverford professors from biology, philosophy, and religion on the impact of Teilhard’s thought.[20]

A third conference on Teilhard at a non-Catholic school was held at Claremont Men’s College in December 1966. The question of Teilhard’s popularity was broached by the main presenter, a Benedictine scholar. His conclusion was that Teilhard appeals especially to contemporary youth because of “a great intellectual curiosity, a very genuine creativity, a deep sense of and love for matter, a thorough understanding of man’s development, a fresh enthusiasm in research, an unshakable optimism in man’s goodness, a limitless confidence in the co-existence of spirit and matter, faith and reason to the point of some ‘mystical fusion,’ that was of great interest to many at the moment, particularly in the local area.”[21]

19. Additional essays presented included, among others, George Barbour’s “In the Field with Teilhard de Chardin” and “Teilhard’s Philosophical Affirmations,” by Ernan McMullin, professor of Philosophy at Notre Dame.

20. The teaching day took place November 12, 1965. The keynote speaker was Henry Van Dusen, former president of Union Theological. Georges Barbour once again also spoke about his friendship with Teilhard; Barbour Collection, Box 2, Woodstock Library, Georgetown University.

21. “Thoughts on Teilhard,” *Claremont Collegian*, November 30, 1966. Although held at a private, non-Catholic college, the conference chose for its keynote speaker the Benedictine Eleutherius Wilnance. In preparation for the presentation and resultant discussions, an issue of the *Claremont Collegian* was dedicated to the topic of Teilhard’s work in late November. Father Wilnance was giving an overview of “Chardin’s” life in order to acquaint the students with a powerful mind who might be able to shine a new light on everyday life within the context of faith. The presenter noted that while Teilhard follows the Greek scientific methodology of rationality, logic, and accuracy, he also belongs to the mystical tradition emphasizing union with the absolute.

Of local significance was another, much anticipated lecture on Teilhard that was to take place at Mount St. Mary's of the West for the Athenaeum of Ohio in February 1966. Due to unprecedented interest, the Teilhard lecture was moved to Wilson Auditorium at the University of Cincinnati. The presenter, the Dominican scholar Michael Stock, began his talk by discussing some of the controversy concerning Teilhard—in particular, whether his thought would endure and whether he was either a "new Thomas Aquinas" or alternatively a heretic.[22]

Why, Stock asked, the interest in Teilhard in America? His own response was that Teilhard's vision is very modern, and so it naturally appeals to the modern mind. Beyond that, Stock believes this interest exists because it is based on a scientific theme and confirms the strong present-day trend toward communal action. Additionally, it is optimistic in an age of increasing anxiety, and it encompasses spirituality that, while very Catholic, emphasizes "the sacredness of the world and the need for commitment."[23] Still, however attractive Teilhard's ideas might be, and however much they may stimulate new thought, Stock believes the essential vision is not likely to endure.[24]

Another public presentation on Teilhard in Cincinnati took place at Xavier University in February 1967 at the annual "Thomasfest" of the Philosophy Department.[25] Like that at the University of

22. "Teilhard de Chardin," *The Record*, February 1966, 1, 5–6. The *Record* is the newspaper of Mt. St. Mary's of the West at Norwood. This was one in the Leblond Lecture Series in Science, Philosophy, and Religion, and this lecture took place on January 14, 1966. Michael Stock was the then Dominican president of St. Stephen's College in Dover, Massachusetts.

23. Ibid., 5. According to Stock, because science is respectable and successful, any vision that can claim a scientific basis is more easily accepted. Also, in Teilhard's vision, "it is inevitable that men will pool their resources and move into closer and closer cooperation on a planetary level." Eventually language, customs, and racial and creedal barriers will dissolve, and problems will be solved based on fraternal love and mutual respect—a theme most convivial to the hopes of the activists of the 1960s.

24. What Teilhard has done is to see and create a vision "at the level of phenomenon." Teilhard "was an artist," Stock argued. "The theologians and philosophers and scientists are engineers. They cannot accept the artist's picture for their purposes; they have to check the terrain by their own methods"; ibid., 6.

25. From a flyer found in the George Barbour collection, Box 2, Woodstock Theological Library, Georgetown University. Father Raymond J. Nogar, OP, of Aquinas Institute and Father W. Henry Kenney of Xavier presented on "Teilhard de Chardin:

Cincinnati, this talk was also exceedingly well attended. Apparently not just students and faculty, but the public wanted to understand what the implications of Teilhard's work were for their own lives; this was particularly true for Catholics in light of the *aggiornamento* of the Second Vatican Council.

What this array of symposia shows us is the ongoing distribution of Teilhard's ideas into the general population of the United States. His thought was now no longer contained solely within the intellectual settings of New York and environs; instead, it had transcended academic and Catholic settings and had become almost distilled, one might say, into the very air breathed throughout the country during these years. The word "distilled" is used here purposely; the question remains as to how his thought was truly understood and utilized by those who read or heard it. Did they actually grasp the incarnational, personal, and very Christological spirituality that was its heart? A look at a representation of publications from these years may assist in answering this question and furthering understanding of Teilhard's reception during this time.

PUBLICATIONS BY AND ABOUT TEILHARD

Not only symposia, but also the numbers of published manuscripts and journal essays concerning Teilhard continued to swell during these years. The number of books alone increased from 50 in 1961 to 399 in 1967, and the majority of these publications occurred in the United States.

Obviously, the constraints of this project make it impossible to converse about even fifty of the books published in the United States during this time. Instead, a significant few of these publications, in addition to periodical articles that are representative of several categories of interest, have been selected for further discussion. The publications of this time in the main fall into four broad groupings that will be used for the purposes of this chapter: (1) four general introductions to Teilhard, particularly for those who are encounter-

---

Pro and Con." It seems much of the interest in and around Cincinnati was due to the Barbours's influence.

ing him for the first time; or for those already familiar with his work, additional help in understanding his thought; (2) five commentaries that attempt to analyze how Teilhard should be read, or why his popularity is so widespread; (3) a consideration of Teilhard's innate optimistic hope and his response to suffering, consisting of three publications; and (4) five publications of a more theological nature that consider Teilhard's doctrinal points and Christology, particularly in light of Vatican II.

Group 1: Who Is Teilhard de Chardin?

As Teilhard's popularity spread across the United States and into increasingly diverse populations, the need remained for additional introductions to Teilhard's life and thought. The following publications, all books, assisted in fulfilling this need both for those encountering Teilhard for the first time and for the well-read who desired yet more information. They are presented here in order of increasing sophistication.

First, a pictorial life of Teilhard de Chardin was probably inevitable; *Album*, edited by his literary executrix Madame Jeanne Mortier, certainly fulfilled this requirement. Two hundred and twenty pages of black-and-white photographs cover every phase of Teilhard's life, from his childhood to his death. In addition to the photographs are brief texts taken from Teilhard's writings and letters. The book ends with a chronology of his life as well as a bibliography of publications to date. Altogether, the *Album* is more a coffee-table type of book—but the fact of its publication in the United States shows the high level of interest in Teilhard's life that existed at this time.[26]

In contrast, a small book by Hugh McElwain, OSM, *Introduction to Teilhard de Chardin*, by Argus Communications was published with the express purpose of making Teilhard accessible to the masses and

26. Jeanne Mortier, with Marie-Louise Aboux, *Teilhard de Chardin Album* (New York: Harper and Row, 1966). Jeanne Mortier was at the time the director of the Paris Les Amis de Teilhard and Teilhard's former secretary. The book begins with a foreword by André George that was actually written for a memorial on the tenth anniversary of Teilhard's death.

in particular to those who were not university-trained in either the sciences or theology.[27] The book begins with a preface that stresses Teilhard's search for meaning in the universe and then relates this to one's own existential quest and the need to "grasp the reality of change," to see change "as virtually the only constant" in our lives.[28]

The vocabulary and writing level of the book are quite obviously lower than those of, for example, either Mooney's or Balthazar's efforts discussed later in this chapter, but perhaps what really sets it apart are the multicolored graphical images of Teilhardian quotes scattered throughout—for instance, "Love is the only strength which makes things one without destroying them," paired with a photo of a tree. "Nothing is profane for those who know how to see," with a black-and-white image of river gravel. However, no citations are given for these quotes.

In an era when change—it seemed most suddenly—was a driving factor of life in the United States, McElwain's emphasis on Teilhard's acceptance and anticipation of the same must have been reassuring. The addition of "sound bite" quotes as further assurance could only have been of assistance.

A more traditional, but still accessible, biography is Robert Speaight's *The Life of Teilhard de Chardin.* Speaight begins with the comment that any new book about Teilhard requires an explanation or an excuse, as so many already exist.[29] What Speaight desires most

27. Hugh T. McElwain, *Introduction to Teilhard de Chardin* (Chicago: Argus Communications, 1967). McElwain presented a paper, "Comparing Teilhard de Chardin's *The Human Phenomenon* with John Stewart's *Evolution's Arrow,*" at the 2005 conference *Teilhard's Legacy: Rediscovering Fire,* commemorating the fiftieth anniversary of the publication of *Le Phénomène Humaine.* He published a chapter, "Teilhard and John Stewart: A Metaphysics of the Future," in *Rediscovering Teilhard's Fire,* ed. Kathleen Duffey, SSJ (Philadelphia: St. Joseph's University Press, 2010).

28. McElwain, *Introduction to Teilhard de Chardin,* 3. The introduction to this book notes that the work will concentrate on three areas: (1) Teilhard the man; (2) a basic orientation to Teilhardian thought; and (3) broad implications of an evolving world for theology.

29. Robert Speaight, *The Life of Teilhard de Chardin* (New York: Harper and Row, 1967). Speaight's work also contains a glossary of terminology, as well as an extensive bibliography and index of names and topics. When asked in January 1963 to write a biography, the English translation of Claude Cuénot's book was not in the works, and the 1965 flood of books by and about Teilhard was "only a modest stream." That said, this present book includes much yet unpublished material. In addition, Speaight

is to write from his own personal relationship with Teilhard and his recognition that Teilhard's appeal "is a dramatic vindication of his own claim to speak to, and for, the men and women of his own time." He also notes that if Teilhard as mystical "seer" is suspect to the scientist, this is almost as true for the theologian. Critics of Teilhard from both sides have thus impugned his personal integrity, and as this distresses Speaight, he hopes to correct it.

Additionally, he notes that if Teilhard has been the object of suspicion and scorn by his opponents, "he has also suffered from his more uncritical advocates. A bold exponent of the Gospel has been treated as if he were the Gospel himself. This is the last thing he would have wanted!"[30] Speaight acknowledges that many more books will most likely yet be written on the application of Teilhard's theories; this book, however, deals with Teilhard "in his habit as lived," in his dual vocation of priest-theologian and scientist. He counts Teilhard as a "passionate apologist," out to persuade others of Christ's ongoing involvement in the world.[31]

In Speaight's opinion, the great sadness in Teilhard's life was a result of the prohibition against addressing the larger public; this was then coupled with the heroic humility with which he bowed to this refusal. This humility was not easily achieved, just as his optimism was not a facile cheerfulness. Although his outward serenity and humility may have belied it, to continue to hope was at times a hard-won struggle. The struggle was eased, however, by his "robust optimism," which he regarded as "the secret of all activity and all success," and which was, most importantly as Speaight sees, rooted in his dynamic faith and Christocentric vision.[32]

---

comments, Teilhard's true nature was still hidden at that time: "Between the smoke raised by his critics and the smoke raised by his thurifers his true stature tends to be obscured." That point was sufficient, Speaight believed, for a "less ambitious" and perhaps more accessible biography than Cuénot's; Speaight, *Life of Teilhard de Chardin*, 11; Claude Cuénot, *Teilhard de Chardin: A Biographical Study*, trans. Vincent Columore, ed. René Hague (Baltimore: Helicon, 1965).

30. Speaight, *Life of Teilhard de Chardin*, 12. Speaight considers Teilhard as both cause célèbre and casus belli.

31. "What you cannot deny is the fact that Teilhard has brought many people to a belief in Christ who would otherwise have had no belief in him at all"; ibid., 13.

32. Ibid. See also Teilhard's letter to Pierre Lamare, March 29, 1932.

The last book to be considered in this category is de Lubac's *Teilhard: The Man and His Meaning*. The frontispiece to the Mentor-Omega edition notes that as the number of Teilhard's readers has grown and his work brings hope to humanity, elements of his work still remain unclear for many. Once again, in this book de Lubac attempts to eliminate the obscurity and show how Teilhard's deep originality is steeped in traditional wisdom.[33]

Additionally, in the preface de Lubac notes that his book tries to explicate Teilhard's "life-long vision," as Teilhard first described in a twenty-five-page essay initially entitled *Forma Christi*. As de Lubac's view is that Teilhard's approach is more existential than most assume and is situated in a personal witness to his mystical faith in the Cosmic Christ, he hopes that in writing about the vision that nourished Teilhard he will also explain its strength and its attraction for many of Teilhard's readers.[34] The book concludes with an assertion that although Teilhard would admit his faith was obscured by the shadows of not knowing, this is the same as for all other Christians; in de Lubac's opinion these shadows didn't much affect Teilhard's belief, as he always had hope in God.

In conclusion, the five biographical books presented here,

33. Henri de Lubac, *Teilhard de Chardin: The Man and His Meaning* (New York: New American Library, 1967), 38–44. De Lubac also argues here that Teilhard at least in part adopted this Christology from his early Jesuit training. For example, Père Yves de la Brière, who taught Teilhard theology at Ores Place, Hastings, gave a lecture on May 21, 1907, for which the printed summary included the statement "Thus the whole of theology may be summed up in what St. Paul said of Christ, '*Omnia in Ipso constant*'"; Teilhard, *Letters from Hastings: 1908–1912*, ed., with an Introduction by Henri de Lubac, trans. Judith de Stefano (New York: Herder and Herder, 1968), 1:42.

34. De Lubac's *Teilhard: The Man and His Meaning* is divided into two studies. The first explores Teilhard's spiritual development, looking at his thoughts on a personal God, the Cosmic Christ, the meaning of death, and the role of the Ignatian tradition in his work. The second is Teilhard's "Defense of Christianity" and, beyond exploring Teilhard's apologetics and methodology, also discusses his use of revelation and the impact of Rome on his work. The final chapter, "Other Interpretations," refutes those critics who attempted to place Teilhard outside orthodox Christianity, through the rebuttal of such arguments by not only himself, but also Père Roger Leys, SJ, and Pastor Georges Crespy. These critics would include Ernest Kahane and Philippe de la Trinité, mentioned elsewhere in this chapter. De Lubac also carefully considers Teilhard de Chardin, *Comment je Crois* (Paris: Seuil, 1969). These essays, which set forth Teilhard's vision of the Christian mystery and the evolving cosmos, include the famous one on Original Sin, which was the cause of his banishment to China.

therefore, vary from the "sound bite" variety through another of de Lubac's carefully constructed apologetic works. They represent the diversity of the population that was finding Teilhard's thought of vast interest during these years. Additionally, several of them do indeed at least appear to recognize as crucial the Christological underpinnings of Teilhard's theories and life.

Group 2: How Should Teilhard Be Read, and Why Is He Received as He Is?

In contrast to these books, the next five publications considered in this chapter are essays or articles and are primarily concerned with the question of why Teilhard's reception is what it is at this time. All of these authors pursue an answer to this question by analyzing, as we already saw in chapters 2 and 3, how one might classify, and therefore interpret, Teilhard's work. These particular essays and articles are included here because their responses provide us with more information as to what scholars of the time believed was the impetus behind his popularity.

In the first article, published early in 1965 in *America,* Donald Campion finds opposition to Teilhard slight, despite the *monitum,* and primarily generated by ultraconservative mouthpieces.[35] He also suggests that the oppositional rhetoric has attracted people to Teilhard. He affirms that "today, we witness a world-wide phenomenon: an interest in Teilhard that mounts with the years and reveals itself in new and often unexpected quarters. Teilhardism in the United States is a fact established beyond question."[36]

35. Donald R. Campion, SJ, "The Phenomenon of Teilhard," *America,* April 10, 1965, 480–81.

36. Campion takes as an example that the French ambassador to the United States was at Teilhard's Requiem Mass in 1955. Surely, he believes, this points to the respect with which the man and his work were already held. Additionally, according to Campion, sales of the American editions of his books certainly show this. The paperback edition of *The Phenomenon* had passed the 95,000 mark already by 1961, with over 37,000 copies of the *Divine Milieu* by the same point. Similarly, both *Letters from a Traveler* and *Future of Man* have sold incredibly well. *Hymn of the Universe* went on sale this month, as did the English translation of Claude Cuénot's biography of Teilhard.

Campion discerns five distinct groups in 1965 to whom Teilhard appeals:

1. Young Catholic intellectuals are drawn to his work, as for them, Teilhard "offers a serious intellectual alternative to the secular ideologies, world view, or personal philosophies otherwise available."[37]

2. Teilhard appeals to men of science who admire his gifts as a field paleontologist or researcher and as one who attempts to breach the religion-science divide.

3. He has already influenced the writing of statesmen and international affairs people. Consider, Campion writes, Louis Halle's article in the *New Republic,* which states that one can best grasp the major political currents of the day, particularly those regarding European unity, by first perusing *The Phenomenon.*[38] Another who could be included here is Robert S. McNamara, appointed as defense secretary by John F. Kennedy, who, as already noted, was also an avid reader of Teilhard.

4. Teilhard is of major interest to religious thinkers, Catholics as well as Protestants, as can be illustrated by the dozens of books and hundreds of scholarly essays published annually.[39]

5. Thomas Corbishley notes in the *Wiseman Review* of England that it is "the educated layman who has found in these writings inspiration and hope," perhaps even more than formal theologians, as the unity and convergence of the sacred and the secular allow God's presence to penetrate all aspects of life. Particularly now, post–Vatican II, Campion finds this group is seeking to understand how to better live this on a daily basis.[40] Catherine Aller and Flannery

37. Consider, Campion suggests, the then recent choice of *Omega* as the name for the new Catholic student center at New York University's Washington Square campus.

38. Louis Halle, "Ariadne's Thread," *New Republic,* December 22, 1962, 17–22.

39. Both Teilhard and Pope John XXIII, Campion believes, had a "bold simplicity of spirit grounded on an unshakeable sense of Church." It was this, perhaps, he argues, that enabled them to understand "the meaning of contemporary convergence as a God-given sign of the times." The author contends, however, that without a doubt opposition to both exists. Consider the activist group "Catholics for Better Libraries" on the West Coast, who are attempting to purge their libraries of works by people such as Karl Rahner and Teilhard; Campion, "Phenomenon of Teilhard," 480.

40. Ibid.

O'Connor, both mentioned in chapter 3, come to mind as examples here.

Members of all these interested groups have been introduced in previous chapters, and more will yet follow. Although the scientific community will continue to be part of the mix, it is now especially the newly visible and vocal young who are the focus of many of those writing about Teilhard during these years.

Additionally, as we have already seen, many of the religious thinkers who advocated for Teilhard tried almost desperately to explain his method of synthesis to others who were determined to classify it. One of these advocates, the Jesuit Christopher Mooney, wrote an article concerning this for the *Saturday Review*, this one in early 1966. The debate as to where Teilhard's work should fit was obviously not yet resolved. Mooney's "A Fresh Look at Man" noted that although Teilhard had little use for scholasticism and did not use scholastic language, he has been called by no less than the modern scholastic Joseph Pieper "one of the boldest and most spiritual of the theological thinkers of our time."[41] The paradoxes surrounding the reception of Teilhard, Mooney argued, derive from paradoxes in the man himself, and their acceptance by the reader depends "in large measure on the extent to which a given individual shares Teilhard's own intellectual and spiritual experience."

Teilhard's search for unity, he writes, is from beginning to end the expression of a personal spiritual experience; a quest that concerns the desire to find some meaning and outcome for human life and the corresponding conviction that Jesus Christ is the only true foundation for all universal life.[42] Finally, Mooney suggests that if

41. Mooney, "A Fresh Look at Man," *Saturday Review*, February 26, 1966, 21–25. Christopher F. Mooney, SJ (1925–93), was at the end of his life a professor of religious studies at Fairfield University in Connecticut and the winner of two national Catholic book awards, including for "Teilhard de Chardin and the Mystery of Christ," which won the National Catholic Book Award in 1966.

42. Mooney, "A Fresh Look at Man," 22. Mooney repeatedly asserts that if one believes Teilhard's analysis of man as phenomenon is all he is about, one is wrong. Instead, Teilhard the Jesuit priest had to rethink evolution within the context of Christianity. Evolution itself was a theological issue of immense importance, especially as it concerned the relationship of the cosmos to Christ. This relationship was actually the focus of Teilhard's attention, in Mooney's opinion. Mooney is one of the "religious

Teilhard has a special mission in the church, it is perhaps a removal of the belief that no compatibility whatsoever can be found between modern scientific thinking and traditional church teaching. Only the Christian faith "can grasp the full meaning of the obscure human searching present in every scientific achievement."

Another essay concerning Teilhard's synthetic ability was also one of the first in the new interdisciplinary journal *Zygon.* It was authored by Theodosius Dobzhansky, an early founder of the American Teilhard Association and a nationally recognized scientist. Dobzhansky believed that Teilhard was very much a humanist and therefore the ideal scientist for his age.[43] He was a scientist who spoke often about the ineffable, which required the use of poetic imagery. Too often, however, his poetic imagery was mistaken for scientific discourse. What is most interesting and significant about Teilhard's thinking, according to Dobzhansky as for Mooney, is the synthesis that he was able to achieve.

Dobzhansky sees Teilhard's vision as that of both scientist and religious mystic, a mystic not only familiar with evolutionary doctrine but one to whom this is of paramount importance. Evolution incorporates for Teilhard that which in his vision is the source and the endpoint of all life—Jesus the Christ.[44]

What is perhaps most noteworthy about this particular essay is the fact that it is in itself an example of the synthetic methodology of Teilhard; it is written by a scientist who speaks of the value of poetry and mysticism for elucidating a vision, within a journal conceived to bridge the synapse between religion and the sciences. Most importantly, it is written by an eminent scientist who grasps the foundational qualities of Teilhard's Christology for understanding his vision.

Perhaps Mooney and Dobzhansky were writing in reaction to Jo-

---

thinkers" who appears to have consistently understood the importance of Teilhard's Christology.

43. Theodosius Dobzhansky, "An Essay on Religion, Death, and Evolutionary Adaptation," *Zygon: Journal of Religion and Science* 1, no. 4 (1966). Dobzhansky has been introduced elsewhere; *Zygon* will be discussed in chapter 6.

44. "I think that the proponents and the opponents are equally in error because they mistake a part for the whole. The greatest interest of Teilhard's work is that it represents a synthesis of science, metaphysics, and theology; this synthesis is stated, as such a synthesis can only be stated, in a language of poetic inspiration"; ibid., 329.

seph Collignon, who just a few months earlier had asked in the *Christian Century*, "Is there room in the church for Teilhard?" Collignon's response: perhaps someday there may be, but as of right now, this was not likely.[45]

In contrast to several writers who had suggested that Teilhard is a second Thomas Aquinas, Collignon asserts that nothing could be further from the truth. In his view Teilhard's vision is not another theology, but an entirely new look at Christian living. It is new, though, only in the sense that it provides a trajectory coherent to modern times from the model that is Christ. In contrast to Aquinas, his vision solves no theological point; it only points to a direction, "a goal in the Omega point."[46]

Collignon also notes his fear that in time those intoxicated with Teilhard's thought will border on cultism. He claims the trajectory among the young is in that direction already, and that some aspects of Teilhard's life in fact encourage this. Better then to be sure, he argues, that reliable discussions concerning his thought occur now, especially with young people.[47]

One who would agree with this particular statement was Stephen Toulmin, a British philosopher, who wrote the last essay here, which

45. Joseph Collignon, "The Phenomenon of Teilhard: In Man's Past This Priest-Paleontologist Found Truths Which Show a Direction for Man's Future," *Christian Century*, November 1965, 426–28. Collignon does concede that "both the man and his books have caused intense concern among Christians both in and outside the Catholic Church." Collignon had written a previous article on Teilhard, "The Christian's Dilemma," for *Saturday Review*, June 27, 1964, 14–16, in which he asked which direction the future contemporary Christians would choose: that of Dostoevsky, B. F. Skinner, or Teilhard.

46. Collignon, "Phenomenon of Teilhard," 428. He claims that unlike Aquinas, in Teilhard's work there is only the existential process, the ascent toward spirit.

47. Ibid., 426. Collignon points to the following as potential reasons for Teilhardian "cultism": Teilhard's "total unconcern for death; his trip to Rome to offer the ideas of a life-time's search, the agony of the denial; the aura of the mystic about him, culminating in the fulfillment of his wish to die on Easter Sunday." Despite his concern, Collignon comments that it is difficult to discover anything controversial about Teilhard or his writings. His life as a scientist, Christian, and Jesuit were exemplary. His overwhelming love for God, which reflects in his love for the world in the evolution of man, "is manifested on every page of *The Divine Milieu*." Still, the *monitum* should have been expected. Questions exist still as to whether a Catholic can reconcile his beliefs with the "scientific mysticism" of *The Phenomenon*. In Collignon's mind the question remains, "Do Teilhard's works constitute a denial of the existing dogma in the Church?"

is concerned with analyzing Teilhard's work in this way. Toulmin argued that what Teilhard was proposing was simply another and not even very sophisticated version of natural theology. He writes, "Teilhard's *Phenomenon* is one further attempt in a long series to re-establish a place for natural theology within the new, evolutionary view of nature."[48] Toulmin contends that Teilhard's concept of humanity as "the cosmic standard-bearer," alone fulfilling the purpose of evolution, is less about science than it is simple human pride. It is primarily the young, he believes, acting out of the naïve pride of youth, who have been captured by Teilhard's thoughts.

As was Collignon, Toulmin also is concerned that since Teilhard's ideas will "survive as something more than a fad," it is necessary to discern how his work is to be read and judged. He argues that in the two subjects on which Teilhard is most dependent, Catholic theology and evolutionary biology, Teilhard's standing was only that of "an enthusiastic amateur."[49] Therefore, caution must be taken in espousing his theories, for how are these not just scientific humanism? Is this the synthesis, he laments, toward which contemporary Christianity is moving?

It is interesting that the preceding two scholars note the interest of young people in Teilhard's thought, as well as concern over how they are interpreting his thought. That at least these two, in addition to Campion, found it necessary to remark upon this should be a sign to us that his popularity was high among the youth, perhaps especially the counterculture, and that these concerns about his reception were at least somewhat present in the larger population.

48. Stephen Toulmin, "On Teilhard de Chardin," *Commentary* 39 (March 1965): 50–55. In particular, Toulmin notes that Teilhard's ideas on evolution are not Darwinian but hark back to an older continental tradition that leads from Lamarck back to the early idealist philosophers, especially to Herder. For these authors, "evolution" is always the name "of a cosmic process with a unique, recognizable direction and providential overtones." The teleological theories of Teilhard in *The Phenomenon of Man* are, therefore, not scientific theories, but the "current exposition" of the tradition of "natural theology" (54).

49. Ibid., 50. Despite the charm and sincerity of Teilhard's personality and writing, Toulmin finds "something reckless about Teilhard's theology."

Group 3: Teilhard, Hope, and Suffering

The next category of four publications to be considered in this chapter address the issue of what for some seemed to be Teilhard's naïve optimism and neglect of evil and suffering. As has been touched upon before, this issue is in many ways of paramount importance when examining the reception of Teilhard in the United States during these years.

First, a special issue of *PRJ* in 1967 addressed "Optimism or Pessimism in Our Brave New World—Teilhardian Perspectives."[50] A note from the editor Máire Compe commented that "when accused of naivety and a facile optimism Teilhard would counter that 'the depth of the abysses between the peaks are obvious enough not to need stressing.'" What, the contributors ask, about nuclear war, though? Or the use of science and technology? The Brave New World?[51] It is granted that many who do not share Teilhard's religious convictions "share his optimism, the hunger for more-being (as opposed to well-being) and recognize the vital force which is asserting itself ever more strongly in our world." This particular issue did not deny that suffering is a necessary part of the spiritual life for everyone but argues that it is love that gives meaning to the anguish of humanity. In a phrase well-suited to the mid-1960s, the essay ends with the claim from Teilhard that the darkness of the shadows of suffering will disappear "for those who in an ideal or a cause discover the secret of collaboration and identification with the universe in formation"—certainly a claim that the activists of the time could possibly take as their own.

A book published on very similar subjects and with comparable conclusions was a Paulist Press translation from the French of Paul

50. *Optimism or Pessimism in our Brave New World: Teilhardian Perspectives*, ed. Máire Compe, special issue of *PRJ* 2 (1967). Seven contributors were included in this issue.

51. The reference here is to *Brave New World*, a novel written in 1931 by Aldous Huxley (1894–1963) and published in 1932. Set in London of 2540 (632 A.F. in the book), the novel anticipates developments in reproductive technology and sleep-learning that combine to change society. The future society is an embodiment of the ideals that form the basis of futurology. Huxley's brother, Julian, an evolutionary biologist, wrote the foreword for the first English edition of Teilhard's *Phenomenon of Man* (1959).

Chauchard's *Teilhard de Chardin on Love and Suffering.*[52] Chauchard begins his small book with the argument against the then recent work of Roger Garaudy and Ernest Kahane, who assert that to understand the world scientifically all that is necessary is a historical analysis of nature like that of Teilhard's that proves the uselessness of God.[53] No, Chauchard emphatically asserts, this is not what Teilhard says; in fact, this interpretation could almost in no way more misunderstand Teilhard's meaning.

Instead, he counters, "What is essential is not the historical analysis of nature. It is rather that such analysis, sometimes claimed as atheistic, necessarily leads the reason not to agnosticism or vague religious sentiments ... but straight to a mystic encounter with Jesus Christ, the god of love."[54] Teilhard is neither a scientist who is a believer nor a priest who does scientific research, but a whole man, one who had a deep relationship with God. It is this relationship, Chauchard asserts, that sustained him throughout a life often full of suffering. In the evolutionary Christian sense, however, Teilhard realized that our suffering was minimal in contrast to Christ's. Chauchard writes that "his work was precisely that of reinserting Christianity in the world ... with an 'optimism' convinced that nothing else could turn the world aside from self-destruction. Humanity is as much in danger from the opium of a disincarnate religion, which could not be that of Christ, as from the new opium of a science which denies the spirit its full dimensions." Instead, Chauchard contends, like Mooney and Barbour elsewhere in this chapter, that Teilhard knows how to belong to the worlds of both science and religion. These worlds think that, because they speak different languages and are ignorant of each other, they are enemies.[55] Although this synthetic ability of Teilhard's, like his scientific yet incarnational

52. Paul Chauchard, *Teilhard de Chardin on Love and Suffering,* trans. Marie Chène (Glenn Rock, N.J.: Paulist Press,1966).

53. Ernest Kahane was a biochemist, born in Romania and a naturalized citizen in France. He was president of the Union of Rationalists in Paris for many years while he was a professor at Montpellier. He cowrote with Roger Garaudy—who knew Teilhard from his Paris days in the early 1920s—the book *Teilhard de Chardin* about this same time. This was published in Budapest by Kossuth Könyvkiadó in 1967.

54. Chauchard, *Teilhard de Chardin on Love and Suffering,* 9.

55. Ibid., 10.

worldview, often confounded then and continues to confound many today, it was obviously immensely enticing to the population of the time and certainly remains so today in the United States.

The third article that examines Teilhard's optimism is also significant, as it was written by another scientist, George Barbour's son, Ian. In late 1967, Ian Barbour penned an article called "The Significance of Teilhard" for the *Christian Century*. Although he, like many others, found it difficult to classify Teilhard, he believed that much of Teilhard's appeal in "a day of widespread anxiety and despair lies in his message of hope, a hope seemingly derived by projecting into the future the long ascent of the past."[56]

Although Teilhard's writings can be read in a variety of ways—and this is indeed one reason for their widespread popularity—as science, poetry, natural theology, process philosophy, and Christian spirituality, Barbour suggests that what is most original and important in Teilhard is his "exploration of the nature of man and the meaning of creation, redemption and eschatology in an evolving world."[57] Barbour emphasizes again that it is Teilhard's stress upon the hopeful possibilities of the direction of the evolving universe that will continue to draw people to his work.

Even in war, Teilhard saw hopeful possibilities. Indeed, "of the outside events in Teilhard's life the war was probably the most decisive of all. It had a profound effect on his whole being," writes Marguerite Teillard-Chambon in her introduction to the remaining

56. Ian G. Barbour, "The Significance of Teilhard," *Christian Century*, August 30, 1967, 1099. Dr. Ian Barbour (1923–2013) was born in Beijing, China, while his father, George, was a member of the geologic expedition to which Teilhard was also attached. He was awarded the Templeton Prize in 1999 (nominated by John Cobb) for Progress in Religion in recognition of his efforts to create a dialogue between the worlds of science and religion. Although Barbour can't accept *The Phenomenon* as "straight science," neither can he dismiss it simply as "mere poetry." He compares Teilhard's metaphysics to those of the philosopher Whitehead, both with their reliance upon Henry Bergson. Both men, he notes, "stress the continuity of evolutionary history and of the levels of life today."

57. Ibid., 1101. Additionally, Barbour believes that Teilhard's refusal to abandon the quest for synthesis, even if it is only partly successful, and his refusal to assign ideas to watertight compartments, are a criticism and contrast to the contemporary world's settling for a plurality of "totally unrelated languages.... Teilhard's conviction of the coherence of truth and the unity of the universe can inspire our hope of compassing even so modest a goal as honest dialogue between the disciplines."

book considered in this section, *The Making of a Mind: Letters from a Soldier-Priest (1914–1919)*.[58] This work of Teilhard's consists of a series of letters sent by Teilhard to his friend and cousin Marguerite Teilhard-Chambon, who was a schoolteacher in Paris during World War I. In this collection are included Teilhard's "most extraordinary observations on suffering and death," as well as those "on prayer, on detachment and Christian hope and above all on the need to rethink the Christian message in terms of modern man's outlook on the world."[59]

Additionally, within the letters one finds Teilhard's touching spiritual counsel to Marguerite. This counsel to Marguerite and many others is, perhaps, along with the overall sense of trust in God and optimism for the future even in a time of war, what has made this book and Teilhard himself so popular. That optimism, though, as this book shows, and indeed as all these works attempt to elucidate, is not simply the outlook of a happy disposition, but a difficult victory of faith in the Paschal mystery. The letters included in this book explicate how that victory was achieved; as Christopher Mooney wrote in one review of the book, because of this perhaps they are the best of all introductions to "the many-chambered edifice of Teilhard's thought, as well as the complex spiritual experience that was its source."[60]

Teilhard's optimism then, was not one rooted solely in the belief that humanitarian, communal activism in the world was sufficient. Teilhard's "optimism" was instead a hopeful understanding that all of humanity, all the matter of the world, all the effort expended on a daily basis, and all our own suffering are redeemed through the power of the Paschal mystery and especially the Resurrection of Christ. With this in mind we have no reason, therefore, not to hope.

58. Teilhard de Chardin, *The Making of a Mind: Letters of a Soldier-Priest 1914–1919* (New York: Harper and Row, 1965), 23.

59. Christopher Mooney, review of *The Making of a Mind*, by Pierre Teilhard de Chardin, *America*, October 23, 1965, 473–74.

60. Ibid., 475.

Group 4: Teilhard's Theology and Christology

The last five publications discussed in this chapter are concerned with the theology and particularly the Christological thought of Teilhard. They are all scholarly books, intended for a theologically knowledgeable audience. As Campion suggested earlier in this chapter, Teilhard continued to draw the intense interest of the Catholic intellectual.

The first, Michael H. Murray's *The Thought of Teilhard de Chardin: An Introduction*, attempts to relate Teilhard to traditional Christian doctrines such as revelation, Incarnation, and evil. In addition, it presents Teilhard's response to secularism and discusses Teilhard's methodology, including the "conjunction of science and mysticism," as well as his attempts to fuse the natural, the supernatural, and God with the everyday.[61]

The next two books heavily concentrate specifically on Teilhard's Christology. They are included here as a reaffirmation of the recognition, contrary to some detractors, of Teilhard's orthodoxy, as well as the centrality of his Christocentrism. His vision of Christ might have been one often overlooked in the Western church, but, as these scholars comment, it is most certainly Pauline and New Testament in nature.

The first is *Teilhard de Chardin and the Mystery of Christ*, by Christopher Mooney, SJ.[62] Mooney, introduced previously in this work, had

61. Michael H. Murray, *The Thought of Teilhard de Chardin: An Introduction* (New York: Seabury, 1966). The book is dedicated to Murray's wife, as well as Father Robert T. Francoeur. It appears to be a published dissertation, but this could not be definitively discovered. The opening quotation is from William Blake's *Jerusalem*, which speaks of the vision of "Past, Present and Future existing all at once," and the need to see the Divine in the "Minute Particulars" of the everyday. The introduction provides a short biography of Teilhard, emphasizing the political, religious and social context of France in the late nineteenth century as the foundation for Teilhard's later thought. The book also includes a Catholic theological response to the "Death of God" theologians.

62. Christopher Mooney, *Teilhard de Chardin and the Mystery of Christ* (New York: Harper and Row, 1967). See also Mooney, "The Body of Christ in the Writings of Teilhard de Chardin," *Theological Studies* 25, no. 4 (December 1964): 576–610; also "Teilhard de Chardin and the Christological Problem," *Harvard Theological Review* 58, no. 1 (January 1965): 91–126. Additionally, Mooney wrote on Blondel's influence on Teilhard in "Blondel and Teilhard de Chardin," *Thought: Fordham University Quarterly* 37

already explored Teilhard's Christology in at least two essays prior to the publication of this book, and so this text is both a summary and a further exploration of his salient points.

Although he claims he is not "captured" by Teilhard's jargon, Mooney gives careful explanations of what the neologisms mean so that Teilhard's own texts can be approached more intelligently; he also attempts to systematize Teilhard's thought in a straightforward manner. He emphasizes that for Teilhard there are two sources of knowledge: the evidence of the world to be understood scientifically and the content of revelation; revelation confirms the scientific hypothesis.[63] The Omega Point, which Mooney asserts is for the most part a Pauline depiction of Christ, is the teleology of Teilhard's evolution. For Teilhard and Mooney, the mystical body of Christ must be interpreted in a worldly, even physical sense. Christ is a growing force in the world, leading all to union in his own body; the body of Christ is the world evolving to the point of unity where God will be all in all.

What is perhaps the apogee of explanations of Teilhard's Christology, however, is also the first published offering in English to explore what Teilhard's thought might mean for the church of Latin America. Francisco Bravo's *Christ in the Thought of Teilhard de Chardin* is, as Ivan Illich comments in the preface, "a prime opportunity for English readers to become aware of the unsuspected importance this author has assumed in a world which is conscious of its growth yet often called 'underdeveloped.'"[64]

In this particular study, Bravo outlines and analyzes Teilhard's

(December 1962): 543–62; also "Anxiety and Faith in Teilhard de Chardin," *Thought: Fordham University Quarterly* 39 (December 1964): 510–30; and "Teilhard de Chardin and Christian Spirituality," *Thought: Fordham University Quarterly* 42 (Fall 1967): 383–402.

63. Mooney, *Teilhard de Chardin and the Mystery of Christ,* 18.

64. Francisco Bravo, *Christ in the Thought of Teilhard de Chardin* (Notre Dame, Ind.: University of Notre Dame Press, 1967), vi. The overleaf reports that Francisco Bravo, with a doctorate in Theology from the University of Salamanca, has been associated with the Center of Intercultural Formation at Cuernavaca, Mexico, working in pastoral renewal in Panama and Mexico. This particular study not only adds a new dimension to the Teilhardian corpus, it exemplifies the interest in Teilhard throughout the New World.

interaction of Pauline doctrine and Darwinian evolution, God and the world.[65] These two converge in Christ, and Bravo presents them as two articles of a single creed, for he argues that no longer can we dichotomize matter versus spirit or science versus faith. Instead, he contends that it is now imperative, in a time just past Vatican II, to acknowledge the personal presence of Christ in the world as a stimulus for pastoral and communal renewal.[66]

In fact, the next book to be discussed here, Robert Faricy, SJ,'s *Theology of the Christian in the World,* considers just this. The preface to the book states that "the purpose of the work is to present on a central theme in Teilhard's writings: "the relation between human endeavor and Christian revelation."[67] Like Teilhard, Faricy is interested in exploring a theology of human effort in the context of an evolving world directed toward its salvation. Faricy notes that this theme is scattered throughout Teilhard's works; probably the closest complete statement is found in *The Divine Milieu,* which, rather than being theological is more "a spiritual essay," without the necessary theological underpinnings.[68] So, the book is an articulate presentation of the point that Teilhard has revived Christian endeavor in a way that has not been paralleled in recent times.

Similar to Teilhard's *The Divine Milieu,* however, Faricy begins his effort with a discussion of the difficulties contemporary people find in possessing both "faith in the world" and "faith in God." Or, how does one live both a secular and a spiritual life simultaneously? This certainly was a question that proponents of the Secular City were attempting to answer, as well as many of those newly involved in social justice movements and in implementing the Vatican II documents.

65. Ibid., viii.

66. Bravo comments in his introduction that it is with apprehension that he takes up the task of interpreting Teilhard, as so much has already been written so well about his work. He perceives that his role is to point out the possibilities of the Teilhardian vision of Christology, a field that has been "practically stationary" since the Council of Chalcedon; ibid., xv.

67. Robert L. Faricy, SJ, *Teilhard de Chardin's Theology of the Christian in the World* (New York: Sheed and Ward, 1967). The book opens with a dedication to Jeanne Mortier, "who has done so much for the Church in making known the ideas of Father Teilhard de Chardin."

68. Ibid., viii.

These difficulties are discussed in Faricy's book within the context of Teilhard's vision of evolution and teleology, the meaningfulness of the universe and Christ-Omega, and the Eucharist. In particular, Faricy unites a theology of human effort and activity with the Eucharistic offering, including that found in Teilhard's *The Mass on the World.*[69]

The question of the relation between nature and grace addressed in both Murray's and Bravo's books also appears in the last one discussed in this chapter. Eulalio R. Baltazar explores what he considers "the crucial problem" in *Teilhard and the Supernatural,* for he regards the efforts of scholars such as de Lubac, Claude Tresmontant, and Christopher Mooney as incomplete in this area.

Baltazar identifies quite precisely, at least in his own mind, the problem between traditional Christians and Teilhardian Christians: If evolution is a natural process that tends toward Christ, then it would seem that this natural process is able to attain Christ-Omega as supernatural by its own natural powers. However, this view would appear to be in opposition to the irrevocable teaching of the church that the supernatural is not attainable by humanity's natural powers or by the natural evolutionary process. Therefore, Christ cannot be the teleological fruit of the evolutionary process. Baltazar examines this integral question regarding Teilhardian thought and subsequently finds the scholastic formulation unsatisfactory.[70]

In response, Baltazar reconstructs Christian theology strictly within the orientation and worldview of process philosophy; in so doing he utilizes an operational definition of process and con-

69. Teilhard de Chardin, "Mass on the World," in *Hymn of the Universe* (New York: Harper and Row, 1961).

70. The pertinent quote is: "The scholastic formulation is unable to explain how the supernatural is the highest perfection of man, for it cannot show that it is at the very core and center of his being, constitutive of his nature, and the goal towards which his nature is intrinsically ordained. It is unable to resolve the tension in the modern Christian whose new awareness is that time is redemptive, creative, positive, for this formulation tells him that value is in the extra-temporal, transphenomenal, metaphysical, metaempirical. And finally, it is unable to meet the needs of naturalism and secularism, because it is unable to present the truths about the supernatural in a meaningful and significant way, or in a way that is harmonious with the other truths of Christian faith"; Baltazar, *God within Process,* 71.

verts the dynamism of being from act and potency to the dynamism of love. He is, one might succinctly say, strongly critical of the Aristotelian-Thomistic context of the then prevalent Catholic theology. What is most significant about this work of Baltazar's is that it is one of the first to label Teilhard's thought as "process theology," a label that has tended to haunt it ever since.[71]

FINAL THOUGHTS

These last two chapters have attempted to explicate the increasing influence of Teilhard in the United States during the mid-1960s. Trends such as civil rights, radical theology, countercultural movements, and new lifestyles and religious expressions helped increase interest in his work. At the same time, these developments were all influenced by it. Teilhard's name was everywhere. As this chapter has further illustrated, articles, books, and other media regarding Teilhard were published constantly during these years.

This chapter especially explored the themes of hope and progress inherent to this time period and their relationship to Teilhard's reception as expressed in journal essays, conferences, and written publications. Many of these discussed in this chapter affirmed that although Teilhard's writings were optimistic, his hope was predicated by his relationship with and understanding of the Cosmic Christ at work in the world and maintained by both his Christology and his tremendous faith in the Paschal mystery of Christ. Indeed, a large number directly examined that Christology and the intensely Chris-

71. Process theology or process thought is a school of thought influenced by the metaphysical process philosophy of Alfred North Whitehead (1861–1947), later developed more fully by Charles Hartshorne (1897–2000). Most who move in that direction would agree that Teilhard's "process theology" is similar to but unrelated to the work of Whitehead. For both Whitehead and Hartshorne, an essential attribute of God is to be fully involved in and affected by temporal processes. This is a concept in conflict with traditional theological thought that holds God to be eternal, immutable, and impassible. Also check out Eulalio Baltazar, *God within Process* (New York: Newman Press, 1970); Ian Barbour, "Teilhard's Process Metaphysics," *Journal of Religion* 49 (1969): 136–59, which is also in *Process Theology: Basic Writings*, ed. Ewert H. Cousins (New York: Newman Press, 1971), 323–50; Norbert O. Schedler, ed., *Philosophy of Religion: Contemporary Perspectives* (New York: Macmillan, 1973), 440–60.

tocentric nature of his thought; this was explicated by authors and speakers both as a means by which to stress his orthodoxy and to establish it as Teilhard's foundational spirituality.

Finally, we must remember that we have not yet come to the end of the sixties, and the optimism of this time will not last. In the difficult years yet to come in the United States, the accusations that Teilhard was merely a facile optimist who neglected to account for the inevitability of human failing will increase. So, in regard to America's Teilhard, one primary question remains unanswered: How was it that just when it was so very much needed, so many of those Teilhard inspired failed to catch the importance of his cosmic Christology?

THE BITTER YEARS

1968–1970

6 THE SOCIAL CONTEXT

IN HIS *The Sixties Spiritual Awakening*, Robert Ellwood contends that 1968–70 were bitter years in the United States, as the hoped-for social and cultural changes did not occur easily, if at all. Instead, society found itself further polarized by war, assassinations, riots, and overall violence. The counterculture, founded on the budding optimism of the mid-1960s, lost its sheen.[1]

Mid-1960s theology had expressed the increasing interest in the secular prevalent throughout the country, as well as in the documents of Vatican II. The waning years of the decade, however, articulated the concerns of some that an ongoing cheerful secularism rooted in the Incarnation and God's immanence was improbable.[2] These were years in which there simply was less to be jovial about. Society, young people especially, turned against both secularism and mainstream churches.

Concomitantly for many these were the years in which doubt about the optimistic Teilhardian worldview took hold; the movement toward progress and unity that Teilhard saw as inevitable instead appeared increasingly elusive. For some populations his writing simply

1. Robert Ellwood, *The Sixties Spiritual Awakening* (New Brunswick, N.J.: Rutgers University Press, 1994), 249–325.

2. William L. O'Neill, *Coming Apart: An Informal History of the United States in the 1960s* (Chicago: Quadrangle, 1971), 314–15.

became a source of support for personal beliefs. For those numerous factions who attempted to appropriate Teilhard's thought for their own purposes during this decade, whether as justification for their actions or to force their agenda, his work was suddenly found wanting, and his influence waned.

All too often, however, those inspired by his teaching had caught the flavor and not the true substance of his conviction in the future. Rather than the patient, persevering faith rooted in a deep relationship with Christ that Teilhard himself exemplified, what dominated was an expectation of progress centered primarily on the efforts of humanity itself. This was progress certain to be waylaid, if not destroyed, by the political and cultural upheavals taking place. For Teilhard's brand of evolutionary progress to actually occur, willingness for a personal as well as societal Christ-focused transformation was critical. As Teilhard wrote in *The Divine Milieu*, "The supernatural awaits and sustains the progress of our nature. But it must not be forgotten that it purifies ... in the end only in an apparent annihilation."[3] For the Christian, hope and progress are found in the willingness to die and change; many of those who advocated change during this era were apparently still in need of this message.

These tumultuous remaining years of the decade thus resurrected long-debated questions concerning the effectiveness of human engagement with the world. How does one distinguish between justified optimism and Christian hope? What is the role of science and rationalism in contemporary life? Of what does "progress" truly consist? Is human unity actually possible? Where lies the distinguishing line, if any, between the sacred and the secular? These questions and more will be explored in this chapter and the next within the context of the reception of Teilhard during the years 1968–70.

3. Pierre Teilhard de Chardin, *The Divine Milieu: An Essay on the Interior Life* (New York: Harper and Row, 1960), 76. This quote precedes Teilhard's section on "The Mystery of the Cross."

POLITICS AND CULTURE

The cultural and religious movements detailed in these final two chapters transformed American politics and society. What was previously considered simply a social or cultural norm, such as racial or gender discrimination, became part of the public debate. At the same time, groups never previously considered oppressed—for example, the economically disadvantaged and ethnic Americans—also adopted specific identities and value politics. The inevitable disagreements that resulted over the goals and strategies of these groups, as the moderate ideas of the founding members faced the conservative, liberal, or radical suggestions of later additions, further accelerated the fragmentation of the times. After 1968, politics was an area for division, not consensus.[4] By 1969, especially, the great affluence boom seemed to be over. Inflation rose due to the war, and the stock market sagged. Corporate dominance increased, with a shift toward escalating demands for efficient, impersonal operations. The movement toward a global, rather than local, economy was making itself felt. In response, conservatives began to dominate in the White House and in state legislatures.

Yet, in early 1968 everything still seemed possible—whether new ways of living, distinctive worldviews, or nonviolent confrontation. As author Hugh McLeod later commented, "Every tradition had been thrown in the melting pot. A new age was dawning."[5] The times were exhilarating, liberating, and replete with transcendental experiences, and "the feeling of being part of a great movement also fed the belief that real and fundamental change was possible—even inevitable."[6] Many active in the movements of the age believed an apocalyptic battle between good and evil was happening before their very eyes.

The remainder of this section of the chapter will briefly examine

4. Mark Hamilton Lytle, *America's Uncivil Wars: The Sixties Era from Elvis to the Fall of Richard Nixon* (New York: Oxford University Press, 2006), 271.

5. Hugh McLeod, *The Religious Crisis of the 1960s* (New York: Oxford University Press, 2007), 143.

6. Ibid., 143.

the playing out of that battle through the lens of several events and their results. These include the assassinations of Martin Luther King Jr. and Robert F. Kennedy, the Vietnam War, and the radicalization of the youth culture. It will end with a look at the overall U.S. culture at the end of the 1960s.

Martin Luther King Jr.

The last few years of Dr. Martin Luther King's life could be read by some as an apocalyptic battle. By 1968, despite Sargent Shriver's best efforts, the Johnson War on Poverty appeared to be a failure, neglected in favor of military expenditures for the Vietnam War. In response, beginning in the late summer of 1967, the Poor People's Campaign, as envisioned by King and the Southern Christian Leadership Conference, hoped to raise nonviolence to a new level in order to pressure Congress into passing an Economic Bill of Rights for the impoverished of the United States. In particular, organizers sought to address poverty in income and housing by dramatizing the needs of the impoverished and by uniting all races through the common hardship of economic struggle. The battle for economic justice, therefore, would also challenge the Vietnam War. At the preliminary planning conference, King suggested a shift from "reform" to "revolution" and stated, "We have moved from the era of civil rights to an era of human rights."[7] The Poor People's Campaign was intended as the initiatory incident in the second phase of the civil rights movement. King proclaimed, "We believe the highest patriotism demands the ending of the war and the opening of a bloodless war to final victory over both racism and poverty."[8]

The March 1968 National Advisory Commission on Civil Disorders study led by Illinois governor Otto Kerner was highly praised but deemed controversial for blaming recent violence on white rac-

7. Martin Luther King Jr., "To Chart a Course for Our Future," Frogmore, S.C., May 21, 1967, quoted in Amy Nathan Wright, "Civil Rights 'Unfinished Business': Poverty, Race, and the 1968 Poor People's Campaign" (Ph.D. diss., University of Texas at Austin, August, 2007), 151.

8. Stewart Burns, *To the Mountaintop* (New York: HarperCollins, 2004), 404–5.

ism and calling for "massive" governmental programs to allay black discontent.[9] The study, which reached the second position on the *New York Times* bestseller list, also accused the news media of exaggerating the violence and underreporting on the poverty of America's inner cities. It noted, "A new mood has sprung up among Negroes, particularly among the young, in which self-esteem and enhanced racial pride are replacing apathy and submission to 'the system'"[10]

The commission called for drastic increases in federal spending while recognizing that such an action was in direct competition with the cost of the expanding Vietnam War. New York City mayor John Lindsay was noted along with Robert Kennedy as "complaining that the cost of the war was keeping the country from its social responsibilities."[11] President Johnson buried the commission's study after calling it a "good report by good men of good will," adding that "they always print that we don't do enough. They don't print what we do."[12]

A month later, King was assassinated. By chance, he happened to be in Memphis, Tennessee. The AFL-CIO was supporting the strike by the Memphis sanitation workers, which had already lasted for over a month. Spontaneously, King came back to the city to bolster flagging spirits. In his speech of April 3 at the Masonic Temple, he called for unity, economic action, boycotts, and nonviolent protests.[13]

9. O'Neill, *Coming Apart*, 180. This study was also known as the "Kerner Commission Study." The final publication showed that the perceptions of whites and blacks regarding the state of the nation was widely diverging. Increasing numbers of whites felt that a great deal of money had been spent and much energy involved in attempting to allay not only the War on Poverty but racial tension, to no avail. Racial tensions and violence continued to increase. For their part, young African Americans perceived far less change. Jim Crow laws may no longer have been in use, but housing and education options had not much improved. James Reston concluded, "The main crisis is not in Vietnam itself, or in the cities, but in the feeling that the political system for dealing with these things has broken down"; quoted in Theodore White, *The Making of the President, 1968* (New York: Athenaeum, 1969), 109.

10. Mark Kurlansky, *1968: The Year that Rocked the World* (New York: Random House, 2004), 97.

11. Ibid., 97.

12. O'Neill, *Coming Apart*, 180.

13. At the end of the speech, Martin Luther King discussed the possibility of an untimely death: "It really doesn't matter with me now. Because I've been to the mountain top. I don't mind [if I die].... I just want to do God's will.... I've seen the

On April 4, he spent the day at the Lorraine Motel working with local leaders on plans for the Poor People's march to take place in Washington later that month. King was killed by one rifle round fired by a sniper on the balcony of that hotel and was declared dead just an hour later at St. Joseph's hospital.

President Johnson went on TV to call for public order: "I ask every American citizen to reject the blind violence that has struck down Dr. King, who lived by nonviolence."[14] Yet the president's attempt had little effect, as the Vietnam War had already undermined Johnson's authority as a foe of violence. Robert Kennedy, hearing of the murder just before he was to give a speech in Indianapolis, delivered a powerful extemporaneous eulogy in which he pleaded with the audience "to tame the savageness of man and make gentle the life of this world."[15]

Many considered the Poor People's Campaign that did occur, led by Martin Luther King's successor, the Reverend Ralph Abernathy, a flop. It appeared that nonviolence was now in retreat.[16] It seemed

---

Promised Land. I may not get there with you. But I want you to know tonight that we as a people will get to the Promised Land"; Martin Luther King Jr., "I've Been to the Mountaintop," April 3, 1968; accessed April 3, 2013, http://www.americanrhetoric.com/speeches/mlkivebeentothemountaintop.htm.

14. From the statement by Lyndon Johnson on the assassination of Dr. Martin Luther King on April 4, 1968; accessed April 3, 2013, http://www.pbs.org/wgbh/americanexperience/features/primary-resources/lbj-assassination/.

15. Robert F Kennedy, "Remarks on the Assassination of Martin Luther King, Jr," April 4, 1968, from http://rapgenius.com/Robert-f-kennedy-remarks-on-the-assassination-of-martin-luther-king-jr-lyrics#note-1420015, accessed April 4, 2013. Sunday, April 7, 1968, was designated as a day of mourning. At the end of his life King's popularity had declined, which was perhaps especially demonstrated by the failure of the open-housing campaign in Chicago in 1967. Black militants were calling him "de Lawd" and mocking his traditional speaking style. The hawks who had formerly supported him and nonviolence at home but not abroad turned against him when he began attacking the war in Indochina. Still, at his assassination, rioting erupted in Chicago and Washington, D.C. In the end, forty-six persons were dead, all but five of whom were black. One hundred cities suffered arson and looting. Over twenty thousand federal troops and thirty-four thousand state guardsmen were called out in civil emergency. The white backlash against what many saw as the results of the racial justice campaign, even in the North, ultimately reduced the effectiveness of civil rights; O'Neill, *Coming Apart*, 181.

16. Certainly the "Resurrection City" in the Lincoln Memorial reflecting pool area at the end of April 1968 received little media coverage. In many ways, the campaign exemplified the worsening of race relations throughout 1968. However, some

that the supposedly longed-for Teilhardian convergence of humanity would require far more patience and time than expected just a few years earlier. The question remained, however, as to whether the nonviolent civil rights campaign of Dr. Martin Luther King Jr., based upon a deeply held humanist reading of the Christian gospel stressing unity and equality parallel to Teilhard's own, would survive this time of great struggle.

Robert F. Kennedy

The assassination of Robert F. Kennedy just two months after that of Martin Luther King Jr. reemphasized the shift in the social, cultural, and political wind of the 1960s, as well as in the reception of Teilhard. Along with his older brother John, Dr. King, and Sargent Shriver, Robert Kennedy exemplified the movement toward racial and economic justice. With the violent death of Bobby Kennedy not only did the age of Camelot come to an end, but in a sense so too did the age of Teilhard, who at one time was deemed the "theologian" to Camelot.[17]

Much of the support for this and many of the other initiatives that occurred during President Kennedy's term in office from 1960 to 1963 actually was the result of the determination of his attorney general and younger brother, Bobby Kennedy.[18] It was the Tet Offensive in February 1968 that convinced Robert Kennedy he had to run

---

50,000 still participated in the reenactment of the March on Washington on June 19, 1968; O'Neill, *Coming Apart*, 193.

17. Garry Wills, *Bare Ruined Choirs: Doubt, Prophecy and Radical Religion* (Garden City, N.Y.: Doubleday, 1972), 117. Sargent Shriver found Teilhard's thought so amenable to Kennedy's "Camelot" politics that Robert McNamara, secretary of defense, put Teilhard's name on a list of most valued authors for the administration; ibid., 98. In recognition of the ready reception of Teilhard's thought by the Kennedy administration, Wills also notes later in his book that "this strange priest in the French army [Teilhard] was preparing the rationale for a weird American optimism, voiced ... a decade after Teilhard's own death. He became the posthumous theologian to Camelot"; ibid., 117.

18. Asked in an interview in May 1962, "What do you see as the big problem ahead for you, is it Crime or Internal Security?" Robert Kennedy replied, "Civil Rights"; from an interview conducted by Bob Spivack with then Attorney General Robert Kennedy, May 12, 1962, as quoted in Arthur M. Schlesinger, *Robert Kennedy and His Times* (New York: Ballantine, 1996), 313.

for president. Then President Johnson's unexpected "declaration of noncandidacy" in late March shook the entire nation and cleared the way for his campaign.[19]

As senator and then again as a party presidential candidate, Kennedy spoke forcefully in favor of the "disaffected," the impoverished, and "the excluded," thereby aligning himself with leaders of the civil rights struggle and social justice campaigners. His goal was to lead the Democratic Party to eliminate perceived discrimination on all levels more vigorously, thus seeking the further unity of all American peoples. His was indeed a very Teilhardian platform. During his speech at Ball State University in Muncie, Indiana, on April 4, 1968, following Martin Luther King's assassination, Kennedy asked the student body what kind of life America wished for; whether privileged Americans had earned the great luxury they enjoyed and whether such Americans had an obligation to those, in U.S. society and across the world, who had little by comparison? In a statement that recalled Teilhard's convergence toward the body of Christ, Kennedy asked when humanity will realize that we are "one world," and have responsibility for that entire world, and so violence has no place within it?[20] He demanded that each American take responsibility for the current disorder, and rather than react with more violence to the news of Dr. King's death, to react instead with love.

Robert Kennedy's campaign for the presidency included a continuation not only of his brother's programs, but an extension of

19. O'Neill, *Coming Apart,* 356.

20. John M. Murphy, "'A Time of Shame and Sorrow': Robert F. Kennedy and the American Jeremiad," *Quarterly Journal of Speech* 76 (1990): 402. One of the Kennedy administration's greatest efforts at promoting peace and unity, and one very Teilhardian in nature, was the Peace Corps, founded by John F. Kennedy in 1961 and headed by his brother-in-law, Robert Sargent Shriver, "Sarge," from the beginning. Another sign of Teilhard's influence upon the Kennedys was that in the very early years of the Peace Corps, book lockers were provided to all volunteers. These were to be left behind in the locations where volunteers were situated. Word was that Sarge himself, along with his wife, Eunice Kennedy Shriver, was behind the book lockers. In addition to reference books in the areas in which the volunteers were working, classics and paperbacks were provided. Also always included was spiritual reading, including books by Teilhard de Chardin; from John Coyne, "The Famous Peace Corps Book Locker, Part I," May 13, 2009, accessed December 7, 2013, http://peacecorpsworldwide.org/babbles/2009/05/13/the-fabulous-peace-corps-book-locker-part-i/.

those. A crucial element to his campaign was engagement with the young, whom he saw as being the future of a reinvigorated American society. He was willing to challenge the young people who supported the war while benefiting from draft deferments, for instance. He aroused rabid animosity in some quarters, with J. Edgar Hoover's deputy Clyde Tolson reported as saying, "I hope that someone shoots and kills the son of a bitch."[21]

On June 4, 1968, the night of the California primary, Kennedy addressed a large crowd of supporters at the Ambassador Hotel in Los Angeles. Around midnight he left the stage. While taking a shortcut through the hotel kitchen, Kennedy was shot by Sirhan Sirhan, a twenty-four-year-old Jordanian living in Los Angeles. The motive for the shooting was apparently anger at several pro-Israeli speeches Kennedy had made during the campaign. The forty-two-year-old Kennedy died in the early morning of June 6.

What followed were the by-now traditional post-assassination events. Cynicism, though, was the order of the day, particularly as Bobby Kennedy was liked, in the center and on the left, even by those who did not care for his politics. Numerous commentators reflected upon "what it was like to have this greatest of all modern electoral dramas end so tragically." And "the people who lined the tracks ... mourned not just the man but what in that moment he symbolized ... eyes thought to be drained of tears wept again."[22] A comment Edward Kennedy made during the eulogy he gave for his brother very much personified not only Bobby Kennedy, but the Camelot years in general: "As he said many times, to those he touched and who sought to touch him: 'Some men see things as they are, and say why. I dream things that never were and say why not.'"[23] Additionally, several commented that Robert Kennedy's greatest asset was his capacity for growth, for "he was always in the process of becoming."[24] Both of these statements are quite Teilhardian in na-

21. Clyde Tolson, quoted in Thurston Clarke, "The Last Good Campaign," *Vanity Fair*, June 2008, 173.

22. O'Neill, *Coming Apart*, 372.

23. The quote is a paraphrase of a line spoken by the devil (The Serpent) to Eve in George Bernard Shaw's *Back to Methuselah*, written during the years 1918–20.

24. O'Neill, *Coming Apart*, 374.

ture. With Robert Kennedy's death yet another "Teilhardian" man of unity, progress, and hope in the future had been destroyed by those who were unable to understand the teleology of his work. "Why?" asked those who mourned yet again. For those who turned to Teilhard, the answer given was that in the end, the issue of why evil happens must be transmuted into some very different questions. It is no longer important to know *why* something happened, but to, now that it has, how we plan to respond.[25]

Vietnam

The latter years of the 1960s saw an important shift in the perception of the Cold War consensus played by the United States in patrolling the remainder of the world. Thirty-eight countries benefited from U.S. military advisory teams, and major U.S. bases were found in twenty. This role was seen as even grander in the summer of 1967 when President Johnson claimed that America "had a whole world to guard."[26] Yet Congress was increasingly reluctant to do just this; the unspoken question was that if American military muscle could not stop the current war, how would they ever avoid future ones? Anti-interventionist, increasingly isolationist sentiments abounded.[27] Rather than convergence, it appeared that the United States at least was intent upon increasing separation.

By 1967, U.S. casualties in Vietnam had already reached the 100,000 mark. Most likely it will never be known how many hundreds of thousands of Vietnamese—troops or civilians—were killed. The country was bombed more heavily than either Germany or Japan in World War II; ground operations were equally destructive. Journalist Jonathan Schell of *New Yorker* magazine wrote in his book *The Village of Ben Suc* that "we are destroying, seemingly by inadvertence, the very country we are supposedly protecting."[28]

25. Teilhard de Chardin, *Divine Milieu*, 83–86.

26. President Lyndon B. Johnson, as quoted in O'Neill, *Coming Apart*, 345.

27. Ibid.

28. Jonathan Schell, *The Village of Ben Suc* (New York: Alfred Knopf, 1967); quoted in O'Neill, *Coming Apart*, 333. Schell found the level of self-delusion regarding this fact staggeringly high in both military leaders and the U.S. Senate.

The "Vietnam Summer," which took place during the summer of 1967, mobilized some twenty thousand young people to ring doorbells and "teach out" their neighbors regarding the issues surrounding the Vietnam War. The hope of the leaders was to encourage involvement by middle-class America in the peace efforts. Dr. Martin Luther King Jr. also agreed to participate. The effort was notable, for it exemplified the progressively real authority and agency flowing from the young. As we have seen already, the young, especially educated young people, were one of the primary groups interested in Teilhard's writing.

The Vietnam Summer effort was also a crucial turning point for the New Left. Many of those who would label themselves this way increasingly disdained this type of promotional, nonviolent activity and instead preferred radicalization. They considered anything else to accomplish little.

Similarly, their reaction to the October 1967 March on the Pentagon—which served as the culmination of the Vietnam Summer—was less than enthusiastic. Almost 100,000 people gathered to protest the American war effort in Vietnam. More than half of these then marched to the Pentagon to ask for an end to the conflict. The protest was the most dramatic sign of declining support for the administration's policies.[29] The New Left radicals, however, did not think it went far enough. The event also deepened the fissures between politically active hawks and doves.

Then, on January 30, 1968, the Vietnamese New Year or "Tet," pro–North Vietnamese Viet Cong troops assailed thirty-six provincial capitals and five major cities.[30] For the first time the U.S. public saw the war in action in almost "real-time" television coverage, along with images of U.S. soldiers panicked, dead, or dying. It was

29. Polls taken during the preceding summer had shown that for the first time American support for the war had dropped below 50 percent. The Johnson administration responded with a vigorous propaganda campaign to restore public confidence in the war effort.

30. Kurlansky, *1968*, 50. An illiterate farmer, Nguyen Van San, led fifteen men in attacking the U.S. Embassy in a suicide mission on the Vietnamese New Year, when it was least expected, and thereafter symbolized what became known as the "Tet Offensive."

a media success for the Viet Cong, as the U.S. military was at a loss in understanding suicide warfare. President Johnson himself was astonished.[31]

By 1968, television coverage reached more than eleven million American homes, and the government was no longer able to control all public images of this conflict. As Walter Cronkite observed in February, "The grim pictures unfolding in the last week cannot fail to leave the impression that the agony of Vietnam is acute and that the detached analyses of Secretary of State Dan Rusk and Secretary of Defense Robert S. McNamara could be incomplete."[32] This very public view of the hostilities encouraged yet more intense anti–Vietnam War demonstrations. On February 8, Robert Kennedy gave a speech stating the war was unwinnable. Between February 11 and 15, students from Harvard, Radcliffe, and Boston University held a four-day hunger-strike protest. Five hundred law professors nationwide signed a petition urging the legal profession to actively oppose Johnson's war policy.[33]

31. O'Neill, *Coming Apart,* 350.

32. Kurlansky, *1968,* 52. Walter Cronkite insisted on traveling to Vietnam to report on the war from a first-person perspective. His *Report from Vietnam by Walter Cronkite* aired February 27, 1968. Perhaps the most important statement from the report was, "To say that we are closer to victory today is to believe, in the face of evidence, the optimists who have been wrong in the past. To suggest we are on the edge of defeat is to yield to unreasonable pessimism. To say that we are mired in stalemate seems the only realistic, though unsatisfactory, conclusion." Cronkite's *Report* was a watershed mark in the reporting of opinion by news commentators. Additionally, within two days Secretary of the Defense Robert McNamara resigned from his position and instead became president of the World Bank, a post he held until 1981. In 1995, at the age of seventy-nine, he took a stand against his own conduct of the war, confessing that it was "wrong, terribly wrong"; quoted in Kurlansky, *1968,* 61. As another example of the influence of Teilhard upon the Kennedys, McNamara was recruited as secretary of defense for John F. Kennedy by Sargent Shriver. Although he initially had his doubts about McNamara, then newly hired chair of Ford Motor, when Shriver heard that McNamara was reading Teilhard's *Phenomenon of Man,* he exclaimed, "How many other automobile executives or cabinet members read Teilhard de Chardin?" McNamara had the job; from Scott Stossel, *Sarge: The Life and Times of Sargent Shriver* (New York: Other Press, 2011). 183. See also Peter Collier and David Horowitz, *The Kennedys: An American Drama* (New York: Summit, 1984), 1:466.

33. The only response from the administration to these actions was that the Selective Service raised the number of young men called in the draft from forty thousand to forty-eight thousand and abolished the student deferment for graduate students. The seven weeks ending February 18 broke the previous record for weekly casualties, with 543 Americans killed in battle.

Slowly, those in Congress who had previously been hawks recommended that the United States abandon hope for a military victory, deescalate the war, and try for negotiation. That particular shift, in addition to the advice given by new Secretary of Defense Clifford, forced President Johnson to realize the war could not be won at a reasonable cost. The administration could not win in Vietnam because it was politically impossible to send the million more troops victory would require; nor could the United States just withdraw, as this would require confessing errors that had already cost hundreds of thousands of lives. The only remaining alternative appeared to be eternal combat. Some would claim the Johnson administration ended in defeat—defeat in Vietnam, defeat in the war on poverty, defeat at the polls. His decision not to submit his name as a presidential candidate was in part a result of that sense of defeat.[34]

In a similar way, the great test of Richard Nixon's presidency was the war. The largest achievement in 1969 was that some troops did leave. The fighting scaled down, and casualties declined. But any hope for a quick end soon withered. "Vietnamization" went on, which meant a beefing up the ARVN so it could do most of fighting, accompanied by the slow withdrawal of American infantry. This withdrawal was imperceptible at first, as there were still over 400,000 troops in Vietnam at the end of 1969. Still, the war now was less expensive in terms of both lives and dollars. The change in the draft sharply reduced middle-class anxiety, so that opposition to the war continued, but it now lacked focus. In October 1969, MOBE's call for a Vietnam Moratorium was answered by millions.[35] In November of that year, 300,000 people gathered for a "March Against Death," the largest demonstration ever to take place in Washington, D.C. Unfortunately, the march had little effect on the administration; Vice President Agnew denounced the antiwar protestors as "effete snobs," "supercilious sophisticates," and worse.[36]

34. *Coming Apart,* 352.

35. MOBE is the acronym for the National Mobilization to End the War in Vietnam.

36. See, for example, "New Political Labels Confuse," *Kittanning Simpson Leader Times,* March 2, 1970, accessed October 4, 2013, http://newspaperarchive.com/kittanning-simpson-leader-times/1970-03-02/page-4. This is the newspaper of

Although Teilhard himself found some deeper meaning in war, as he considered it one of the primary forces by which to bring people together, the American public of 1968 obviously found it difficult to reconcile that belief with what was occurring in Vietnam. Instead, the war was proving to be quite divisive, particularly among the young who were in line for the draft. The difference perhaps was that for Teilhard times of war as much as periods of peace were opportunities for growth and progress; he believed that as people worked together in battling toward peace, convergence toward Christ was occurring. Still, Teilhard realized that peace would only happen when "men share a common understanding, at least as a first approximation, on what we should expect and hope for from the world's future."[37] It did not appear, at this point in the late 1960s, that such a common understanding yet existed.

The Youth Culture

As was discussed in chapter 4 of this work, the hippies of the 1960s counterculture were attempting to build alternative lifestyles to the corporate, suburban world of their parents. Against "hostile competitive, capitalistic values of bourgeois America they posed their own faith in nonviolence, love, and community."[38] The counterculture began when the ideological struggle between the young and elders was named the "generation gap." For the first time in American history social conflict was understood to be a function of age. Still, not all the young were rebellious—most were not, and

---

Kittanning, Pennsylvania. It appeared that the more Agnew abused blacks, intellectuals, and the young the more popular he became.

37. Teilhard de Chardin, *Letters from a Traveler* (New York: Harper, 1962), 278. He also wrote while on the Front in World War I, "Let them understand that . . . which was disclosed to them in the shell-holes and barbed wire, will never completely withdraw from the pacified world. There it will always remain alive, more difficult to detect though it may be. And that man will be able to recognize it, and once more unite himself to it, who devotes himself to the tasks of everyday existence . . . with the consciousness of forwarding, in God and for God, the great task of creating . . . a Mankind that is born . . . in hours of crisis but can reach its fulfillment only in peace"; Teilhard de Chardin, "Nostalgia for the Front," in *The Heart of Matter* (New York: Harcourt, Brace, Jovanovich, 1979), 178–79.

38. O'Neill, *Coming Apart,* 251.

many older people joined the rebellion; as many over thirty as not yet thirty were part of it.

"Hippieness" was often an individualistic journey; one did not "drop out" or "have to" take drugs to somehow "qualify" as a hippie. Being part of the counterculture was the result of a frame of mind, like being part of the Movement (the protest element of the counterculture).[39] As author Terry Anderson argued, "The hippie movement is not a beard, it is not a weird, colorful costume, and it is not marijuana. The hippie movement ... is a philosophy, a way of life, and a hippie is one who believes in this."

The counterculture was earnest in its pursuit of a new way of being from about 1965 to early 1967. One might remember Mario Savio, leader of the Berkeley Free Speech Movement, who made the connection between civil rights and the student movement in a famous speech in December 1964 at Sproul Hall at Berkeley.[40]

By late 1967 the names of those such as Savio, student and antiwar arrests, and headlines pertaining to the counterculture were legend to incoming university students. Unfortunately, what was most embraced by those same later students was the noise and hedonism; what was forgotten was the grace and civility that drove the originators. Consider, as an example of this, the time Mario Savio removed his shoes before climbing onto a police car.[41]

So hippiedom was consequently negatively affected by the influx of teenyboppers and runaways, attracted by media coverage, who some believe spoiled New York's East Village and San Francisco's Haight-Ashbury district for serious cultural radicals.[42] Although many of those who participated most likely read his work, the 1967 "Sum-

39. Terry H. Anderson, "The Hippies Reject Mainstream America," in *The Movement and the Sixties: Protest from Greensboro to Wounded Knee* (New York: Oxford University Press, 1995), 90.

40. "There's a time when the operation of the machine becomes so odious, makes you so sick at heart, that you can't take part, you can't even tacitly take part, and you've got to put your bodies upon the gears and upon the wheels, upon the levers, upon all the apparatus, and you've got to make it stop"; Mario Savio, quoted in Kurlansky, *1968*, 92–93.

41. W. J. Rorabaugh, *Berkeley at War* (New York: Oxford University Press, 1990), 19. Savio removed his shoes so as not to scratch the car.

42. O'Neill, *Coming Apart*, 251.

mer of Love" had little to do with Teilhard's concept of Omega-love. It certainly attracted thousands of young people to these two counterculture hubs, where rock bands, communities, "tribes," and "families" thrived for a while. But these "immigrants" also brought in their wake psychotics, drug peddlers, and criminals; rapes, muggings, and assaults became commonplace.[43]

Ultra-radicalism from the counterculture was more than just a calculated response. Kenneth Keniston wrote in *Young Radicals* that "the issue of violence is to this generation what the issue of sex was to the Victorian world." The youth of the 1960s were obsessed by violence; the massacres of World War II haunted them, and the prospect of nuclear war shadowed their youth. Resisting violence became central to life. They made great efforts, for example, through training in nonviolent confrontation, "to overcome in themselves any vestige of sadism, cruelty, domination, or power-seeking in human relationships." Hence, the Summer of Love, sit-ins, and teach-ins. However, these tactics aroused violence in others, which in turn increased their own intrinsic rage and hostility. When the slaughter grew in Vietnam, they began to think of American violence as so potent that only counterviolence would end it.[44] As Keniston commented, "For all his efforts to control violence, cataclysm and sadism, the young radical continually runs the danger of identifying himself with what he seeks to control, and through a militant struggle against violence, creating more violence than he overcomes."[45] It appeared that rather than working in harmony with others toward the evolution of the world, the radicals of the New Left were determined to force an evolutionary path of their own choosing. Unfortunately, they did not truly perceive, as did Teilhard, that "driven by the forces of love, the fragments of the world seek each other so that the world may come into being. Love alone is capable of uniting living beings in such a way as to complete and fulfill them, for it alone takes them and joins them by what is deepest

43. Soon, this became the first community in the world to revolve entirely around the buying and use of drugs, which were important as means to truth and as advancers of the pleasure principle. Simultaneously, violence greatly increased.

44. O'Neill, *Coming Apart*, 340.

45. Kenneth Keniston, *Young Radicals: Notes on Committed Youth* (New York: Harcourt Brace, 1966), 256.

in themselves."[46] For Teilhard and those who understood his vision, the unity the counterculture supposedly craved was not only necessary but was also possible only through participation in the Paschal mystery of Christ and hence also inherently involved suffering. Their true task, our true task, is simply to learn to see and work within this.

Still, patience with Dr. King's path of nonviolence and the associated "sit-ins" and "teach outs" was growing thin among not only the youth, but the more radical Black Panthers and the like.[47] The stage was set for a showdown among all these groups at the 1968 Democratic Convention.

Abbie Hoffman and his friends had formed the Yippies, the Youth International Party. They called themselves "revolutionary artists. Our concept of revolution is that it's fun."[48] The Yippies decided to stage a "Festival of Life" in Chicago to counterbalance the Democratic Convention, which they considered a festival of death. MOBE also planned to demonstrate. The joint Yippie-MOBE plan was heavily publicized in the underground press. All of this was designed—at least by some—to offend Chicago's provincial sensibilities and create the best possible confrontation. The thought of Yippies in his city goaded Chicago Mayor Richard Daley to rage. Presidential candidate Eugene McCarthy, running on the antiwar platform and hence well aware of at least some of the intent of the counterculture, encouraged people to stay home.[49] Only about twenty-five hundred Yippies came, but that was enough to cause the subsequent havoc.[50]

Mayor Daley meant to smash the protestors to bits. Consequent-

46. Teilhard de Chardin, *Phenomenon of Man*, 264 ff.

47. As with Teilhard's thought, the foundations of Martin Luther King's concept of nonviolence was at least in large part based upon the Christian New Testament, particularly the Beatitudes of Matthew 5.

48. Tom Buckley, "The Battle of Chicago: From the Yippies' Side," *New York Times Magazine*, September 15, 1968, 28.

49. Desire for an antiwar candidate led to Eugene McCarthy entering the race. He said that if no one else would, he would, because "there comes a time when an honorable man simply has to raise the flag"; quoted in O'Neill, *Coming Apart*, 361.

50. On August 26, 1968, Chicago Mayor Richard Daley opened the Democratic National Convention in Chicago. While the convention moved haltingly toward nominating Hubert Humphrey for president, the city's police attempted to enforce an 11 o'clock curfew. On that Monday night, demonstrations were widespread, but generally peaceful. The next two days, however, brought increasing tension and violence to the situation.

ly, the protestors were gassed, beaten, and maced. Police sergeants lost control of the police forces, who beat reporters, bystanders, and Yippies alike. The effect on the nation was ghastly. Although Hubert Humphrey was nominated, the Democratic Party lay in shambles.[51] The whole country had seen the violence in Chicago, some of which occurred in the convention hall itself.

American Culture at Large 1968–1970

The Democrats lost the 1968 election not just because of the riot in Chicago. These years also saw the start of what became known as the "silent majority" who desired to see hippies and their like beaten up. Law and order could hardly be too viciously applied to suit people who were demoralized by years of war, protest, and youthful contempt for middle-class life.[52] For example, the more the calls for repression came from society, the better off Richard Nixon was. Some would argue that despite his campaign slogan, "Come together," Nixon, in his calls for law and order, accelerated the fragmentation of American society.[53] Fragmentation flourished, not unity. Is it any wonder that vision of a united and unifying world seemed increasingly remote?

More campus outrages occurred in 1969 than in 1968, but the temper of public life seemed to ease a bit. Perhaps it was as historian William O'Neill wrote: "People can bear to address profound—therefore stormy and divisive—issues for only so long. When that time is up, regardless of what has been accomplished or not, private matters reassert their authority."[54]

51. Vice President Hubert Humphrey considered Shriver his first choice for running mate in the 1968 presidential contest, but the selection was effectively vetoed by the Kennedy family, according to Humphrey aides quoted in Stossel, *Sarge*, 515–19. Humphrey chose Senator Edmund Muskie of Maine instead; accessed November 12, 2013, http://www.theatlantic.com/past/issues/2004/05/stossel.htm. During the 1972 U.S. presidential election, Shriver was George McGovern's running mate as the Democratic Party's nominee for U.S. vice president, replacing Thomas Eagleton, who had resigned from the ticket. In contrast to his in-laws, Shriver's Catholicism appeared to be of the form of a deep discipleship.

52. O'Neill, *Coming Apart*, 387.

53. Ibid., 338.

54. Ibid., 396.

The closing of the 1960s saw the physical condition of Americans improving. Real income went up, especially among blacks, as did educational levels. The work force shifted toward skilled or white-collar occupations. As a result, not surprisingly, poverty declined. Black progress, though, was often accomplished by forceful tactics that offended whites. Many blacks felt cheated by the supposed wars on poverty, as their own lives did not reflect much growth.

Additionally, university populations grew as access to further education increased, but at the same time, students began treating what had been a privilege as a curse. University administrations were often damned as racists and authoritarians. The more people of color they recruited, the more discriminatory they were accused of being. White radicals claimed universities were imperialistic knowledge factories, while older adults turned against university administrators on account of their failure to control their students.

On top of all that, pollution was growing, and the environment was deteriorating. For the first time on a large scale, ecological preservation became a concern. John Muir, founder of the Sierra Club, argued quite vocally that nonmaterial values should have equal standing with economic ones.[55] O'Neill notes that "the abundance which had for so long been the American dream, now threatened the very hopes it was supposed to realize."[56] The situation was more ironic than many people could handle. Despite ongoing vociferous "discussion," the first Earth Day took place April 22, 1970, under the championship of Senator Gaylord Nelson of Wisconsin, who saw the day as an opportunity to promote teach-ins concerning the dangers of pollution. Even these attempts to preserve the earth were divisive, as some in mainstream America saw the call to work together to do so as yet another slogan by the spoiled counterculture. Conversely, young radicals believed that the argument for cooperation with "the man" in this effort was an argument "for the further consolidation of power and profit in the hands of those responsible for the present dilemma."[57]

55. Lytle, *America's Uncivil Wars*, 325.

56. O'Neill, *Coming Apart*, 422.

57. Lytle, *America's Uncivil Wars*, 331. The nascent environmental movement will

Again, the unity that had seemed such a sure thing in 1963 was not coalescing. Convergence appeared to be dead, and the question was, "Why?" What went wrong? Surely those who had given their lives to the work of social progress could expect to see movement in a positive direction by now. Teilhard, however, would counter that: "What paralyzes life is lack of faith and lack of audacity. The difficulty lies not in solving problems but expressing them."[58] From an evolutionary standpoint the roadblocks were temporary; what was perhaps needed was simply ongoing faith and perseverance.

RELIGIOUS ISSUES

Even if few in number, the hippies had a great effect on middle-class society, especially the youth. For one, hippies made spirituality socially acceptable. Interest in the supernatural was contagious; many of the communes in the late 1960s were actually religious fellowships practicing a contemporary monasticism.[59] Not coincidentally, courses in religion in higher education multiplied. For example, at Smith, the number offered grew from 692 in 1954 to nearly 1,400 in 1969, although the student population remained constant. In general, traditional religion was the point of departure rather than the final place for answers. Oriental theologies grew more attractive, as did mysticism of any ilk. Colleges were overwhelmingly asked for subjects like Zen, sorcery, and witchcraft.[60]

All of this points to the antipositivist, antirational, anti-science stance of many students. Science was now discredited as an agent of the military-industrial complex and made responsible for failing to make life more attractive. Additionally, the "establishment" was con-

---

be one direction in which Teilhard's work will be utilized in future decades by Thomas Berry and others.

58. Teilhard de Chardin, "The Evolution of Chastity" (1934), in *Toward the Future*, trans. René Hague (London: William Collins Sons and Harcourt, 1975), 86.

59. As an example, the "Cathedral of the Spirit" in western Massachusetts was the seat of a nineteen-year-old mystic who helped the commune members prepare for the Second Coming and a time when all men would be brothers. The "monastery" had strict rules against drinking, drugs, and "sex without love." The commune was essentially contemplative; O'Neill, *Coming Apart*, 254.

60. O'Neill, *Coming Apart*, 255.

sidered rational. This emotionally laden "fact" appeared to support the central thesis of many religions that "man is more than a creature who reasons."[61] During these years the interest in mysticism of any type was intense; rather than science and reason, young people especially sought union with the good, the beautiful, and the forces of nature. As Roszak notes in his *The Making of a Counter Culture*, young people wanted their life to exhibit "the beauty of the fully illuminated personality."[62] For many then, Teilhard's mystical qualities were very much a drawing point. The question will remain, however, just how his work is interpreted by those who, unlike Teilhard, chose to reject the Catholic and mainline Protestant churches in favor of the experimental.

This portion of the chapter will investigate how and why religion changed as it did in America in the years between 1968 and 1970. Changes in the Catholic Church will be examined first, then alternatives to organized religion—mysticism, magic, rebels, and dropouts—will be explored. Finally, we will return to the radical theology of the mid-1960s and the "God is Dead" movement as explored in the previous chapter to discern why a "Theology of Hope" was the next logical step and how this intersected with Teilhard's Christian hope.

Catholic Views

Prior to the mid-1960s Catholics in the United States in general were loyal and patriotic to a fault, equally devoted to both Washington and Rome. Since they perceived the church and politics as existing on different planes, they found no contradictions in serving both. Additionally, anti-Catholicism was finally declining due to the positive influence of Pope John XXIII and John F. Kennedy. Both men demonstrated that it was possible to "both be free and Catho-

61. Consider instead this statement from Teilhard: "We are not human beings having a spiritual experience; we are spiritual beings having a human experience"; paraphrased from Teilhard de Chardin, *Divine Milieu*, 20–25.

62. Theodore Roszak, *The Making of a Counterculture: Reflections on a Technocratic Society and Its Youthful Opposition* (New York: Doubleday, 1969), as quoted in O'Neill, *Coming Apart*, 255–56. Roszak is credited as the first to use the term "counterculture."

lic." During this decade, politicians like the Kennedys, Eugene McCarthy, and a host of nuns and clergymen dispelled the fears of the remaining population that the growth of Catholicism threatened American liberty.[63]

Changes in the institutional structure of the Roman Catholic Church resulting from Vatican II also attracted favorable attention. In 1966, the National Conference of Catholic Bishops (NCCB) was created, as was the United States Catholic Conference (USCC), both intended to better respond to the needs of the people within the church.[64] Additionally, special-interest groups, such as the National Black Sisters' Conference (1968) among many, began to be formed. The emphasis was on democratic procedures, even within the church.[65]

Despite these developments, by 1966 Catholics were drifting away from their church. A sign of this was that church attendance statistics for 1967 show a dramatic downward turn. Additionally, statistics from that time show a mass exit from the priesthood and a fall in clerical recruitment.[66]

63. O'Neill, *Coming Apart*, 307.

64. Patrick Carey, *Catholics in America: A History* (Westport, Conn: Praeger, 2004), 117. The National Conference of Catholic Bishops (NCCB) was an exclusively episcopal organization focusing on internal ecclesiastical issues, whereas the United States Catholic Conference (USCC) was an episcopal organization collaborating with lay Catholics and priests to address social and political issues of national and international concern.

65. As an example, the following organizations were formed in the indicated years: National Federation of Priests' Councils (1968); National Black Sisters' Conference (1968); National Black Catholic Clergy Caucus (1968); Priests Associated for Religious, Educational and Social Rights (Padres) (1969); Leadership Conference of Women Religious (1971); Las Hermanas (1971). Additionally, in 1969 the U.S. Catholic Bishops promulgated "The Resolution on Due Process" to protect "human rights and freedoms which should always be among the goals of the Church." Finally, the Bishops Committee for Ecumenical and Interreligious Affairs (BCEIA) had already been created in 1964. After 1966, diocesan ecumenical commissions were formed, and bilateral conversations increasingly took place. Unfortunately, by the mid-1970s most of these had died out.

66. Attendance at Mass was down from 71 percent in 1963 to 52 percent in 1971; participation in sacramental confessions was down from 38 percent in 1963 to 17 percent in 1971. Although the Catholic population increased (primarily due to immigration and an increased birth rate) by 17 percent between 1965 and 1988, the number of priests declined by 8 percent. This drop was due primarily to the 10,000 who left the priesthood and an 85 percent drop in the number of seminarians. The numbers

Catholic historical theologian Patrick Carey identifies four issues that appeared to be especially divisive in the U.S. Catholic Church at the time: (1) the nature and proper exercise of ecclesiastical authority; (2) sexual morality and abortion; (3) the definition and implementation of social justice; and (4) the role of religion in politics. These four points are considered in more detail later; however, what must be clarified is that although the conflict over issues was usual, what was new was the widespread, public, and substantive character of the conflict.[67] Suddenly, everyone and everything was open to questioning and criticism. The conflicts in the church reflected the general cultural revolution occurring in the larger American society. It was no longer presumed that tradition would necessarily prevail. The postconciliar battle was instead over defining what was and what was not continuous and changeable in that Catholic tradition.[68]

In regard to Carey's first point, despite the proliferation of new organizations and councils, it appeared that the consensus of the Second Vatican Council was more anticipated than real. As a result, in the United States the authority of the papacy and the Vatican bureaucracy was especially under attack. Statements on sexual ethics, jurisdictional debates between American theologians and the Vatican over the teaching authority of national Episcopal conferences, and the disciplining of some bishops created tensions and distancing between America and Rome. Pope Pius VI had already warned against excessive enthusiasm for change; later he and his successor, Pope John Paul II, would proclaim their supremacy in stronger terms. John XXIII had opened a door later pontiffs found hard to close, for freedom of conscience was proving irrepressible.

---

of women religious dropped 40 percent between 1965 and 1988. As addressed by David Rice in *Shattered Vows: Exodus from the Priesthood* (London: Fleming Revell, 1992), the decline in recruitment was primarily due to social and educational changes that provided alternative opportunities. In an age of "freedom," young men and women chaffed at being forced into a particular rigid mold. Accordingly, the role of celibacy began to be regarded with suspicion rather than as a witness of faith. Other factors contributing to the loss of clergy included loneliness, resentment toward authority, and the failure of the church to speak out on social issues.

67. Carey, *Catholics in America*, 122. This was new particularly for those whose experience of Catholicism was confined to the late 1940s and 1950s.

68. Ibid., 123.

As historian O'Neill wrote, "Change generated an appetite for more change."[69]

Much of the weakening of hierarchical authority occurred in regard to significant areas of Catholic moral life.[70] This took place simultaneously with the growing social mobility of the American Catholic people. Catholics were increasingly identified with the American middle class, achieving higher educational levels and greater prosperity and moving into the professional and business classes of society.

As we have seen, a revolution was taking place in society over moral and lifestyle issues, including those of artificial contraception, premarital sex, abortion, and homosexuality. All of these were generally more accepted in the church pews and in society; opinion polls of the time showed a growing divergence between official church teaching and the beliefs of ordinary Catholics.[71] *Humanae vitae,* in particular, became a cause célèbre. The 1968 encyclical reaffirmed the ban of the Catholic Church on artificial contraception and in so doing became a standard bearer for the postconciliar church. Although Pius VI intended to suppress the movement among Catholics for repeal of this ban, along the way he coincidentally further undermined papal authority.[72] The document provoked public opposition among theologians as well as a growing number of American Catholics. Unfortunately, the timing was terrible; the document was promulgated when Americans had a high expectation that the church would change the teaching on this issue.[73] As a result, for

69. O'Neill, *Coming Apart,* 308.

70. Carey, *Catholics in America,* 119.

71. Ibid., 131.

72. O'Neill, *Coming Apart,* 309.

73. John XXIII had created a papal commission on birth control in 1962 to reexamine the teaching; Paul VI had broadened its membership during Vatican II. The final encyclical, however, favored the minority who suggested retaining opposition to artificial contraception. In 1964, a sixty-member commission of laymen and married couples was appointed by John XXIII to study this issue, and in June of 1966 this commission advised that decisions regarding birth control should be left to married couples themselves. Sixteen prelates also endorsed this decision. This guaranteed that *Humanae vitae* would be disregarded in practice and challenged in principle. Nearly 800 theologians in the United States signed a statement against the encyclical. Loyal prelates counterattacked to no avail. By the late 1960s, over 70 percent of American Catholics approved the use of contraceptives within marriage; Carey, *Catholics in America,* 132.

the first time in American Catholic history, widespread public resistance occurred to an official church teaching. This was fueled by the prevailing cultural antiestablishmentarianism, the expectation of change created by the Second Vatican Council, and a new notion of ecclesiastical authority.

This last statement was also true in regard to the implementation of social-justice policies. The democratic surge within the church and the societal interest in racial justice and the war on poverty encouraged American bishops, the USCC, and Catholic theologians to become major advocates for social justice and civil rights.[74] The documents *The Challenge of Peace* from 1983 and *Economic Justice for All*, published in 1986, both address "postconciliar concerns to demonstrate the interrelated practical, political and social implications of Christian life." They present and represent the ideals to which the church aspired after Vatican II—very Teilhardian ideals, indeed.[75]

Additionally, the Catholic peace movement took a dramatic turn to radical protests against the Vietnam War in the late 1960s to early 1970s. From 1963 to 1972, the so-called Catholic Left, a group of more than two hundred Catholics, led high-profile, media-event protests against the war.[76] The Catholic Left felt no compulsion to demonstrate its Americanism or loyalty. The morality of conscience

74. Ibid., 124.

75. As an example of how important social justice issues became to the church starting in the late 1960s, of the 188 official public statements, resolutions, and pastoral letters of the American hierarchy between 1966 and 1988 some 52 percent were concerned with issues of national/international social justice. Only twelve discussed sexual morality and abortion. The remainder focused on internal ecclesiastical issues such as ecumenism, celibacy, Mary, charismatic renewal, and Catholic schools; Carey, *Catholics in America*, 124.

76. These protest groups were the Baltimore Four, Catonsville Nine, Chicago Fifteen, Minnesota Eight, New York Eight, and a host of other groups of local priests, women religious, and laity. They burned draft cards in defiance of federal legislation, poured blood on draft records, raided corporate headquarters, and destroyed federal documents, all to demonstrate the violence of the war. A few individuals—the Jesuit Daniel Berrigan, his brother the Josephite Philip Berrigan, Michael Cullen, and James Forest became national heroes. The 1968 Catonsville Trial against nine Catholic protesters who burned draft files became an international media event and a rallying point for the antiwar movement. The trial later became the subject of a book, a play, and a television documentary movie. Daniel Berrigan refused to turn himself in after the trial, instead becoming a fugitive who was not captured by the FBI until 1970; Carey, *Catholics in America*, 125.

and higher law they followed was not self-critical or drawn from the Catholic natural law tradition so much as it was a morality of prophetic witness. The reaction to their actions from American Catholics ranged from outright disdain to conditional support.[77]

Just as the Black Power movements challenged Martin Luther King's leadership in the black community, so too did the institutional Catholic Church experience a shift in its approach to racial justice. Leadership in this regard gradually passed to the black clergy and laity. On April 18, 1968, just two weeks after the assassination of King, more than fifty of the then 150 black U.S. Catholic priests met in Detroit to prepare "A Statement of the Black Catholic Clergy Caucus." The statement was a stinging criticism of existing racism in the church.[78] Without a doubt the church Teilhard loved, the church he believed would lead the world's people toward Omega, was in upheaval. No wonder the people of that church began to find it difficult to believe convergence toward Omega would happen via that means.

Mystics and Alternative Religions

From the mid-1960s onward, a variety of esoteric and unique religious ideas began to reach a much wider audience in the United States. Especially in the San Francisco Bay area, one of the homes of "hippiedom," a flowering of new forms of spirituality bloomed.[79] In his *Experimentation in American Religion*, sociologist Robert Wuthnow found a strong correlation between countercultural involvement and a rejection of Christianity.[80]

77. Ibid. Cardinal Spellman deplored these demonstrations and eventually exiled Daniel Berrigan. By 1971, 69 percent of American Catholics (by then over 50 percent were opposed to the war) believed Catholics who raided draft boards were not living their faith.

78. Ibid., 128. The formation of the National Black Catholic Clergy Conference (NBCCC) in 1968 attempted to create solidarity among black clergy. The NCCB also created within the USCC a National Office for black Catholics.

79. See, for example, McLeod, *Religious Crisis*, 134–45. At the time, the term "spirituality" was preferred by those who associated religion with an over-rigid body of dogmas and moral rules.

80. Robert Wuthnow, *Experimentation in American Religion: The New Mysticisms and Their Implications for the Churches* (Los Angeles: University of California Press, 1979), 129.

These new kinds of spirituality included all forms of mysticism, astrology, extrasensory perception (ESP), and Native American and tribal religions.[81] Readings from Eastern mystics were used by all faiths. Those who participated in these alternative spiritualities would constitute yet another group drawn to Teilhard's writing, particularly because of his mystical tendencies; in another fifteen years their practices would be labeled "New Age," and some would insist Teilhard be placed in their midst.[82]

Yet, even though church attendance declined from the high levels of the 1950s, this does not necessarily imply a corollary decrease in religious enthusiasm. It simply indicates that in the late sixties "faith" was instead expressed by *not* going to church.[83]

Especially for young radicals or "wanna-be radicals," experiential religious practice and alternative churches were the preferred mode. It is no surprise then that the peace demonstrations in 1969 were full of religious symbolism. By these years, many students regarded the war as a symbol of the absolute corruption of American society and consequently regarded their own involvement in antiwar protests as a moral and religious obligation.[84]

Sometimes alternative churches were known as "submarine" churches; their symbol was a yellow submarine with a cross, a peace symbol, and the word "ecumenical" in Greek. The symbol of the yellow submarine came from the Beatles' song "Yellow Submarine."[85] In the Beatles' movie of the same name, people of all types lived in the submarine loving each other "in a groovy way," love that gave them strength "to do battle with the Blue Meanies." The movie also showed "that a Church has to have flexibility and maneuverability." Submarine churches were one way the counterculture found God, did service, and loved one another.[86]

81. McLeod, *Religious Crisis,* 134.

82. See, for example, David Lane, *The Phenomenon of Teilhard* (Macon, Ga.: Mercer University Press, 1996).

83. O'Neill, *Coming Apart,* 257.

84. McLeod, *Religious Crisis,* 144.

85. The Beatles, "Yellow Submarine," 1966. *Yellow Submarine* was the tenth studio album by the Beatles in the United Kingdom. It was issued first as the soundtrack to the film *Yellow Submarine.*

86. Anonymous Free Church pastor in Edward B. Fiske, "Yellow Submarine Is

Some of the most important student leaders were strongly influenced by Christianity or Judaism, and Christian student organizations played a major role.[87] The "Jesus movement" was an umbrella term for a variety of Evangelical Protestant groups based in California from about 1967 on. It presented a theologically conservative gospel message in the language of the counterculture outside of conventional Christianity.

By the late 1960s, innumerable alternative possibilities were offered by mystics of all kinds. The growing interest in ecology was related to a revival of paganism, especially Wicca. Feminism and mysticism merged in the worship of the Goddess. Alternative therapies became mainstream; yoga was now understood as a form of spirituality as well as physical fitness.[88] The nomenclature of the "seeker"—one searching for one's spiritual path, and a characteristic figure of the "baby boom" generation—was born. Rather than the previous emphasis on orthodoxy and orthopraxy, the emphasis now was on the right and duty of all to follow their own path. The need for personal exploration was consistent with the societal stress on individual freedom.[89]

Symbol of Youth Churches," *New York Times*, April 20, 1970, a report concerned with Catholic and Protestant youth groups adopting the Beatles' yellow submarine as a religious symbol. The article discussed the aftermath of a three-day convention of so-called submarine churches held in St. Louis. The churches "combine heavy political involvement with new forms of liturgical celebration ranging from street parades to beer-and-pretzel eucharistic fests." The article reported that "submarine churches" grew out of the "free" or "liberated" churches that had developed across the country in recent years, most famously the Free Church of Berkeley, California, which claimed that there were about forty such churches around the country. Fiske wrote that some of the churches adopted the yellow submarine as a symbol after certain members of the peace movement used it as a symbol of social harmony and nonviolence. The Free Church of Berkeley added a cross to it.

87. For example, in Boston over one hundred thousand gathered before a gigantic cross on the Common, and lit candles were placed on the steps of St. Patrick's Cathedral in New York. Sometimes a shofar was blown. In the eyes of religious leaders, what was most important was that underground youth could relate to Jesus who also was a rebel, and who was also rejected by the citizens of the day. This is perhaps also one of the reasons for the acceptance of Teilhard among this group. He, too, was perceived as a rebel and an outcast; McLeod, *Religious Crisis*, 146.

88. Ibid., 244.

89. See, for example, Wuthnow, *After Heaven: Spirituality in American since the 1950s* (San Diego: University of California Press, 1998); also, Wade Clark Roof, *A Generation of Seekers: The Spiritual Journeys of the Baby Boom Generation* (San Francisco: Harper San

This highly subjective spirituality highlighted experience rather than doctrine, feeling and intuition rather than rational argument.

It is difficult to exaggerate the extent of the radical defeat or conservative resurgence in the world that was being created in the late 1960s. Christian radicalism suffered many casualties. Many left their churches, and those organizations most sympathetic to these events were severely disrupted, as disillusioned members dropped out of organized activity of any kind because of despair or exhaustion. Interest in Teilhard's thought waned as a result of that same disillusionment. It would appear that the mysticism that grounded him and strengthened his perseverance and fortitude did not do the same for them. What might be the difference? Teilhard did write that "it would be nursing a great illusion if the man of our times were to think ... he had no further need of religion ... in reality, for those who can see, the great conflict from which we will have escaped will only consolidate in the world the necessity of faith."[90] Most likely many of the sixties radicals and flower children would argue that it was indeed an interest in seeing as Teilhard did that drove them. At the same time, however, Teilhard's sight was focused on Christ. Everything in his life, including his mystical experiences and his scientific work, both pointed toward and was derived from the diaphony of Christ in the world. Perhaps it could be said, in light of expanding definitions of spirituality that for many "Christ" himself was too restrictive.

But Christian radicalism also left continuing legacies. Radical ideas now had an established place within the church, even if they were often contested. Social justice issues such as racism, Third World poverty and health concerns, ecology, and peace were now part of established church agendas. An enduring understanding of the interrelatedness of the human family and hope for ongoing unification, that strong Teilhardian concept, had taken root and would not so easily be quashed. These are among the many trajectories in Teilhard's thought that in the following years will be the subject of conferences,

Francisco, 1993); and Roof, *Spiritual Marketplace: Baby Boomers and the Remaking of American Religion* (Princeton, N.J.: Princeton University Press, 1999).

90. Teilhard de Chardin, *Building the Earth* (Paris: Éditions du Seuil, 1958), 58–59.

workshops, and the work of individuals, like Robert Mueller of the United Nations, which will ensure they are not forgotten.

The Death of God and the Theology of Hope

In the late 1960s, science and rationalism were losing ground; a concurrent decline was noted in the number of college science majors.[91] An exchange of interest in science for that of magic occurred; this could be considered yet another sign of a fascination with the everyday work of the divine immanence. In the minds of a good part of America, Christianity and science had been able to cohabitate, as each had its own, separate sphere; the visible, physical universe was the place of science, the invisible, of religion and the divine. Teilhard and the young of 1968 rejected this division, however. Under the influence of Teilhard and the counterculture many came to see the physical and spiritual universes as coexistential; actually only one reality existed, and that is where the divine dwelt.[92]

In chapter 5 of this book, "Death of God" theology was discussed. According to the theologians involved, the "death of God" was necessary for God's passage from transcendence to immanence. God's death was necessary to lead to a new humanity, a new world, a new life, and freedom. God became the evolving God and eventually the God of process theology.

Many saw this idea of the death of God as related to the work of Teilhard, for both theologies were focused upon the Incarnation as the key event in history. For Teilhard, at the moment of the Incarnation, God immersed himself in creation, unifying it, taking direct control, as it were, until, "having gathered everything together and transformed everything he will close in upon himself and his conquests there rejoining, in a final gesture, the divine focus he has never left."[93] At that point, then, "God shall be all in all."[94]

91. O'Neill, *Coming Apart*, 313.

92. Ibid., 313.

93. Teilhard de Chardin, *Phenomenon of Man*, 149.

94. "When Christ has assimilated all things unto himself, then he will himself also be subject unto him who put all things under him, that God may be all in all"; 1 Cor 15:18. This would appear to be Teilhard's favorite scripture passage, found repeatedly

All this meant that God really is not dead, simply that the traditional view of God has died. One might remark instead that God is "absent," or the ability to experience God is dead, or the word "God" is dead, obviating a continued search for his identity and nature. In summary, as Bonhoeffer wrote, man ought to act as if the Western idea of God were dead, while believing he is not.[95] So, human beings had become fully responsible for their own condition and must set about repairing it, particularly through modern social justice issues. Death of God theology was well received by both Protestant and Catholic activists who pushed back against obsolete and confining conditions in their churches. Rather than experiencing "God's death" as devastation, the proponents of this theology were instead overall an optimistic group.

However, by May of 1969 *Time* magazine was announcing the probable death of the "God is dead" theology.[96] This was not because of hostile publicity over the death of God, but because it became so much more difficult to foster the cheerful secularism springing from the Incarnation and God's immanence.[97] There simply was

---

in his writings. See, for example, *Let Me Explain* (New York: HarperCollins, 1970), 94; *Heart of Matter*, 104; *Hymn of the Universe* (New York: Harper and Row, 1965), 94; *Human Phenomenon*, trans. Sarah Appleton-Weber (Brighton and Portland: Sussex, 1999), 149; *Letters from a Traveler*, 302; *Human Energy* (New York: Harcourt Brace, Jovanovich, 1971), 69; and *Christianity and Evolution*, trans. René Hague (New York: Harcourt, 1971), 75.

95. Dietrich Bonhoeffer, *Letters and Papers from Prison* (New York: SCM, 1953).

96. "Is 'God Is Dead' Dead?," *Time*, May 2, 1969, 46. The article begins, "Whatever became of the death of *God*? Three years ago it was the most fiercely debated issue in American theology (consider the cover of *Time* on April 8, 1966). Scholarly journals were thick with discussions of it. No sermon topic was more popular; pulpits rang with denunciations." However, the article goes on to argue that it now appears that indeed the "God is Dead" movement is indeed dead. It was a shock, and it cleared away some of the simple-minded misconceptions of what it means to say "God is dead," but American theology has moved on and is ready for more creative thought. Death-of-God theologian Gabriel Vahanian contends that those who still want to believe, those who wait for God, need not be disillusioned. "The more a society becomes technological, the more it worries about spiritual questions," he explains. "After the death of *God*, man will be no less religious than before." German Protestant theologian Jürgen Moltmann agrees wholeheartedly. "'*God* is dead' is written on one side of the stone," he declares, "but when you turn it over, it reads 'everything is religion.'" Indeed, by December 26, 1969, seven months later, the lead article in *Time* was "The New Ministry: Bringing God Back to Life."

97. O'Neill, *Coming Apart*, 315.

less to be jovial about. Society turned against secularism and against institutional churches. None of it was working. As has been seen, young people especially were rejecting the secularized mainstream churches, which they found irrelevant for the age. They were going their own theological ways.

One of the responses to the time was the "Theology of Hope," proposed particularly by German theologian Jürgen Moltmann; this theology stated not that "God Is," rather, that "He is Not Yet."[98] God awaits man in the future. Hope was pointed away from the present and toward the future.

Indeed, in many ways this emphasis on the future, especially hope for the future, was consistent with revolutionary aspirations, where successful revolution was seen as the coming of God. This new theological emphasis, however, did not have the effect of "God is Dead." It was, to be blunt, ignored by most. Radical Catholics were especially still moving in a secular direction. Young people were still forming religious communes.

Yet in the minds of at least some Americans, religious life was more fertile and diverse by the end of the sixties than since the end of the nineteenth century.[99] Sunday morning congregations may not have appeared that way, but, compared to the 1950s, when religious life consisted solely in churchgoing, it certainly was. The religious revival in the traditional churches of the previous decade may have declined, but "religion" itself did not. As the established churches

98. Jürgen Moltmann, *Theology of Hope* (Philadelphia: Fortress, 1993), originally published as *Theologie der Hoffnung* in 1965. Moltmann is a German Reformed theologian. In this first book of his, written in 1965 during the period of West German reconstruction, Moltmann attempts to articulate Christian hope as a challenge to both the desperation and the official optimism of a reconstruction that sought only to return to the glory days of the past, rather than live in the hope of a completely new future that comes from God. This God lives not so much above us but in front of us, drawing us into God's own future for the world. Although his primary influences were Hegel and Bloch, his "God in front of us" sounds tremendously like Teilhard's "*Prime Mover ahead*"; see Teilhard de Chardin, *Phenomenon of Man*, trans. Bernard Wall, introduction Sir Julian Huxley (New York: Harper, 1959), 271, and *Science and Christ* (New York: Harper and Row, 1969), 179. Both are quite eschatological in nature. Some would also argue that both are panentheists.

99. As an example, see "The New Ministry: Bringing God back to Life," *Time*, December 26, 1969, 48–57.

became more secular, unchurched youths grew more spiritual. Mainstream churches may have been undermined by romantic, rigid, or utopian tendencies, but the example of the late sixties shows that "even in a technetronic age, perhaps especially then, men still have need of God, and that if the established churches cannot provide for it others will."[100] To continue to expect the future to look the same as it did thirty years in the past was to ignore the reality of the continuing evolution of all facets of life. Humanity, that spiritual creature, was moving in a spiritual direction, even if that direction was not yet clearly defined. We were not, perhaps, on the teleological track that Teilhard envisioned, but movement was definitely occurring.

THE AMERICAN TEILHARD ASSOCIATION

In the midst of the turmoil of these years, the American Teilhard Association (ATA), the organization created to spread Teilhard's thought in the United States, began with a great initial burst of energy. The first few years of 1967–68, which coincided with the peak numbers of books published about Teilhard, was a phase of great growth. Ultimately, though, the story of this organization mirrors the declension narrative that is Teilhard's reception during this decade.

Almost immediately upon the establishment in late 1967 of the American branch of the "Friends of Teilhard," plans began for various publications, conferences, and lectures. The hope of its founders was to operate on two levels—the academic and the popular. It was anticipated that the association would be useful in encouraging communication among scholars and students on topics relevant to Teilhardian studies. Another goal was to respond to the questions and demands of the public regarding "a wider understanding of the complex and subtle, and often confusing body of Teilhard's thought among those outside the academic community."[101]

December 1967 also brought the first of the lectures sponsored by the new association. Scholars presented at the universities of Fair-

100. O'Neill, *Coming Apart*, 317.
101. *ATA*, 18.

leigh Dickinson, Fordham, Rockefeller, and Seton Hall, as well as at Marymount-Manhattan College. These were very well attended.

But the association organizers realized they needed to attract more members. As a result, Harper and Row, the official publishers at this time of the Teilhard manuscripts in the United States, agreed to have postcards about the ATA's purposes and benefits of membership inserted in all the American Teilhard books published. This policy began with the 1969 publication of *Science and Christ.*

The official ATA secretary in March 1968 launched a newsletter that was published three times a year for five consecutive years. This was where those interested in Teilhard in America discovered information about the people and events dealing with his thought as well as book reviews concerning anything Teilhardian published in the United States and abroad.

The March 1968 newsletter advertised the fall conference of the organization, anticipated to be held at Seabury-Western Seminary.[102] It also encouraged members and others to attend the lecture program of five different talks yet to be held that academic year at Seton Hall and Fairleigh Dickinson universities in the New York City area. Finally, it made known that a new audiovisual program was available on the thought of Teilhard, as based on *The Phenomenon of Man.* This program, with text by Robert Francoeur, was illustrated with over two hundred colored slides created by the physicists and graphic artists involved in the POM project of Canoga Park, California.[103]

102. *American Teilhard Association Newsletter*, March 1968. The newsletter noted that at that time the ATA had 215 volumes in its library and had hired a part-time librarian who was creating a basic Teilhard bibliography. Additionally, the primary focus of this issue was the five-day conference to be held September 9–13, 1968, at Seabury-Western Theological Seminary in Evanston, Illinois. The theme of the conference was "Building the Earth, Hope for the Future," and the subject was "Teilhard de Chardin and the Future of Mankind." Invited speakers included the Rev. J. V. Langmead Casserlay of Seabury-Western, Robert Francoeur of Fairleigh Dickinson, Lynd Godson, Robert Wilshire from General Theological Seminary in New York, and Robert Speaight, a biographer and novelist of England. The conference was sponsored jointly by the ATA, Center for Christian Ministry at Christ Church, Winnetka, Illinois, and Seabury-Western Theological Seminary in Evanston, Illinois. Several of the papers from this conference were published in Robert Speaight, Robert Wilshire, and Julian Victor Langmead Casserley, *Teilhard de Chardin: Re-mythologization* (Chicago: Argus Communications, 1970), with an introduction by Thomas Oman Edmunds, of Seabury-Western Theological Seminary.

103. The AV program was seventy-five minutes long and was followed by a taped

The first annual meeting of the American Teilhard Association took place in April 1968 at the Harvard Club and was both a luncheon and a business meeting. The Reverend Michael Murray gave the address "Teilhard and the Nature of the Soul," which he had delivered at the Vezelay Conference in France the previous year. Sixty people attended this first meeting, including Dr. George and Mrs. Barbour from Cincinnati. They brought with them the Malvina Hoffman bronze bust of Teilhard, which now sits in the Woodstock Library at Georgetown University.

In September of 1968 the ATA, jointly with the Center for Christian Ministry, Christ Church, of Winnetka, Illinois, and the Seabury-Western Theological Seminary of Evanston, Illinois, sponsored their five-day ecumenical conference titled "Teilhard de Chardin and the Future of Man" for both clergy and lay people. Several of the papers from this conference were published in the book *Teilhard de Chardin: Re-Mythologization.*

The main speaker at the Second Annual meeting held at Essex House, New York, six months later in April 1969 was George Maloney, SJ, on the topic "The Cosmic Christ from St. Paul to Teilhard."[104] Although Teilhard may have originated the term "Cosmic Christ," Maloney wished to vindicate Teilhard by showing that the view of Christ he expressed was substantially that of St. John and St. Paul, who both understood Christ as immersed in and continually revital-

question and discussion period. The primary topics covered included: the process of cosmic evolution; the role of each particle and each human in this universal drama; the essential unity of science and religion; man's responsibility for shaping the future; the Omega Point. The POM Project is discussed further in chapter 7 of this work.

104. George Maloney pointed out in his talk that this same vision of Christ was developed by the early fathers, particularly those of the East: Irenaeus, Clement of Alexandria, Origen, and Athanasius, among others. The title of Maloney's later book was *The Cosmic Christ: From Paul to Teilhard* (Baltimore: Sheed and Ward, 1968). A review of the book states, "From a theological point of view, the value of Teilhard de Chardin's contribution to an understanding of the gospel ... rests on the validity of his Christology. Maloney is trying to prove the orthodoxy of that Christology—he relates it to the New Testament (Paul and John) as well as the ante-Nicene and post-Nicene Greek Fathers. The reviewer finds that Teilhard's thought, although absent from recent theology, is strikingly similar to that of the ancient Church, and contains elements–such as Christ the Omega—that had not been seen since the time of Maximus the Confessor"; Peter Fehlner, OFM Conv., Review of *The Cosmic Christ: From Paul to Teilhard*, by George A. Maloney, *Theological Studies* (March 1, 1969): 127–29.

izing the created, material world. However, Maloney also desired to illustrate the relevance and value of the "cosmic Christ" for modern society.

Later that same year, in November 1969, a two-day conference on "Process Thought: From Cosmogenesis to Christogenesis" was held at Drew University Theological School in Madison, New Jersey, with Pieter de Jong, Clarence Decker, Robert Francoeur, and Ewert Cousins. Teilhard was one of the primary foci of that particular conference. That month also saw the first of the evening series of discussions or seminars to be offered from that point forward at the ATA headquarters.[105] Additionally, due to public demand, the governing board approved, and several members created, a set of "Teaching Outlines" for explaining Teilhard's ideas to children, available for a minimal cost.

The 1970 ATA annual meeting had about 150 people attend to hear guest of honor Renee-Marie Parry, honorary secretary of the British Association, speak on "Teilhard and the Contemporary World Scene," as well as Dr. Theodosius Dobzhansky on "Evolution and Man's Conception of Himself." In September of that same year, Donald Gray gave a seminar on *The Phenomenon of Man,* and Larry Surget led a discussion on "Building Mankind" and "Human Energy." In Connecticut Professor Alfred Stiernotte conducted a workshop on "The Thought and Mysticism of Teilhard de Chardin," an inquiry into process theology, Teilhard's Christology, and the mysticism of process.

In late 1970 the distribution of members of the ATA showed numerous members in thirty-six states, as well as in five of the Canadian provinces. Additionally, members were represented in Burundi, France, Italy, Mexico, Peru, and Yugoslavia. The ages of the members varied between seventeen and ninety-two years old.[106]

105. Some of these from the late sixties included, "Exploring Teilhard," "Applying Teilhard's Insights to Contemporary Challenges," and "Church, Eucharist, Grace, Sin in the Thought of Teilhard."

106. *ATA,* 26–27. Volumes 6–7 of *Les Oeuvres de Teilhard de Chardin,* ed. Les Amis de Teilhard (Paris: Éditions de Seuil), published in Paris by the French Friends of Teilhard, had not been made available in the United States because by this time Harper and Row had allowed publication of the Teilhard works to lapse through declining

The 1971 annual meeting was held in New York at the St. Ignatius Loyola Community, where Teilhard lived the last several years of his life. Jean Houston gave the address "More Being and Being More—Teilhard and the Future of Consciousness." This was followed by an evening discussion with Ewert Cousins, Robert Francoeur, and Jean Houston on "The Transformation of Man: Towards the Year 2000."[107]

"Teilhard de Chardin: In Quest of the Perfection of Man" was later described by Robert Francoeur as "the best conference I ever attended." It was held in May 1971 in San Francisco at the Palace of Fine Arts; the cochairs were San Francisco mayor Joseph Alioto and Seymour Farber, dean of continuing education in Health Sciences, UCSF.[108] Mayor Alioto was impressed by the influence that Franciscan father N. Max Wildiers, the Dutch Teilhardian scholar, had already had on his son and other students at the University of San Francisco. Rather than watching young people "cop out" of society as so many were doing at the time, Wildiers offered them Teilhard's challenge to face their problems and "Build the Earth."[109]

---

sales. Then Harcourt Brace Jovanovich took over the publication rights of the remaining books; *Human Energy* and the *Activation of Energy* (New York: Harcourt, Brace, Jovanovich, 1971) appeared in February of 1971.

107. Jean Houston, born 1937, as a teenager lived in New York City, where she first met and later struck up a friendship with "Mr. Tayer" (the long French name was "unpronounceable") whom she met in Central Park in 1951, and who lived across the street from her in the Saint Ignatius rectory. Teilhard had a tremendous influence upon her later leanings; as an example, in 1965, she and her husband, Dr. Robert Masters, formed the Foundation for Mind Research. In one interview she recounted one of her conversations with Teilhard: "'We need to have more specialists in spirit who will lead people into self-discovery,' he told me. 'What do you mean, Mr. Tayer?' He said—and this is exactly what he said; I was taking notes because I knew I was in the presence of greatness—'We are being called into metamorphosis, into a far higher order, and yet we often act only from a tiny portion of ourselves. It is necessary that we increase that portion. But do not think for one minute, Jean, that we are alone in making that possible. We are part of a cosmic evolutionary movement that inspires us to unite with God. This is the lightning flash for all our potentialities. This is the great originating cause of all our shifts and changes. Without it there is nothing but struggle and decline'"; quoted in *EnlightenNext* magazine, accessed August 16, 2013, http://magazine.enlightennext.org/2010/11/03/a-chance-encounter-with-pierre-teilhard-de-chardin-think-about-this/.

108. *ATA*, 28–29. Alioto believed Father Wildiers inspired them much as Teilhard had inspired the worker priests and students of Paris earlier in the century.

109. *ATA*, 29. The speakers at this conference were Father Wildiers, Theodosius

The last American Teilhard Association event that this chapter will discuss was the "Hope and the Future of Man" conference held October 8–10, 1971. The theme is appropriate to a Teilhardian conference, for Teilhard had believed that hope was "the essential impetus without which nothing will be done" and that what was most important was the creation of the future.[110] Another purpose of the conference was to address the intersection between Teilhard's hope for the world and the aforementioned new Theology of Hope in light of what appeared to be the sometimes "overwhelming despair of the times."[111] The editor of the conference proceedings, Ewert Cousins, notes in the introduction that "nuclear weapons and the ecological crisis raise the basic question: Does man have a future? What kind of hope can he have for the future?" He also comments on the new prominence of "the future" in theology. "Instead of being viewed as outside time, God is seen as intimately involved in the temporal process, and Christ is viewed as the energy source of evolution. Eschatology has been singled out as the distinctive element in the Christian vision, and hope the central Christian virtue."[112]

The conference was conceived as a convergence of numerous innovative thinkers who were having a far-reaching influence on contemporary theology. It centered on three important Hope theologians from Germany: Joannes Metz, Jürgen Moltmann, and Wolfhart Pannenberg. In addition to the Hope theologians, American scholars were invited who would speak not only on the eschatological approach, but also on Teilhardian studies and process theology.[113]

Dobzhansky, Francoeur, Mooney, and Bernard Towers, as well as Dr. L. S. B. Leakey and Connor Cruise O'Brien. The conference papers were published by Fairleigh Dickinson University Press in 1973 as Joseph Alioto, Geraldine Browning, and Seymour Farber, eds., *Teilhard de Chardin: In Quest of the Perfection of Man* (Madison, N.J.: Fairleigh Dickinson University Press, 1973).

110. *ATA*, 29.

111. Ewert H. Cousins, ed. *Hope and the Future of Man* (Philadelphia: Fortress, 1972), vi.

112. Ibid., vii. The conference proceedings contain the six public lectures along with seven responses and concludes with an afterward by Daniel Day Williams. At this time Cousins was associate professor of theology at Fordham and president of the ATA. He was the editor of the anthology *Process Theology*.

113. Philip Hefner of the Chicago Lutheran School of Theology had helped to arrange for their attendance, and expenses for the Germans were underwritten by

For the first time they met for a mutual exchange over their understanding of the future, as well as of humanity itself and the values that could energize the people of the world in building the future.[114]

The conference consisted of six public lectures, in addition to private discussions between scholars that were to be open to students. Initial plans were to hold the public sessions in the Assembly Hall at Riverside Church, which held four hundred; aware of the potential large response to the conference, another local church was approached that held seating for fifteen hundred. In the end, well over twenty-five hundred attended. The conference was so well received that the *New York Times* had a feature story on it.[115] In fact, it was so well attended that before his presentation began Johannes Metz asked, "Who are all those people? How is it possible to assemble so many people for a Conference on Theology? And at 9:30 in the morning?"[116]

---

their government. The conference was sponsored by the ATA, Cardinal Bea Institute of Woodstock, Union Theological Seminary, Trinity Institute, and Goethe House in New York City. American scholars participating included: Carl Braaten of the Lutheran School of Theology in Chicago, representing the eschatological approach; John Cobb of Claremont, Daniel Day Williams of Union Theological, and Lewis Ogden of The Divinity School at the University of Chicago, who all presented on Process Theology; and Donald Gray then of Manhattan College, Philip Hefner of the Lutheran School of Theology at Chicago, Christopher Mooney, SJ, then president of Woodstock College, New York City, and Joseph Sittler of The Divinity School at the University of Chicago, who took a Teilhardian stance.

114. Cousins, *Hope and the Future of Man*, viii.

115. Actually, the *New York Times* printed two stories on the conference. The first, on October 9, 1971, mentioned the amazing turnout, and noted that all three theologies represented "acknowledge the massive problems of modern times, but with different approaches emphasize hope for the future"; *New York Times*, October 9, 1971, 33, accessed from ProQuest Historical Newspapers, *The New York Times* (1851–2009) with Index (1851–1993). The second, a feature story two days later, emphasized the need to move beyond society's frustration with the difficulties of the day to recognize God's ongoing involvement with the world and the positive possibilities available; George Dugan, "Theologians Find That Hope Survives," *New York Times*, October 11, 1971, 20, accessed from ProQuest Historical Newspapers: *The New York Times* (1851–2009) with Index (1851–1993).

116. Joannes Metz, in *ATA*, 31. In addition, over four hundred attended a special session for students held at Union Seminary at which the conference speakers answered questions. In addition to the public sessions, three working sessions took place, two at Woodstock College and one at Union Seminary. The purpose of these was to discuss in great detail the issues emerging in the public lectures. Not only were the twelve conference speakers present at these, but also some twenty other invited

The conference itself began with a public session of three presentations on the meaning of the future from a process, a Teilhardian, and an eschatological perspective. The process theologians argued, among other points, that no guarantee of progress exists in the short turn, but that the future will include a new kind of society beyond any collectivities of autonomous persons.[117] At the close of his discussion on this topic, the Teilhardian Philip Hefner concluded that "the activation of man's energy is the crucial question of the future, because if that energy is not activated in the proper direction, we will be only moments away from the abyss."[118]

Theologian Carl Braaten then took the eschatological approach. His primary thesis was that the future comes to us through two symbolic forms of consciousness: the utopian and the eschatological. "The utopian future is projected as another time *in* history; the eschatological future deals with the final fulfillment and end *of* history."[119] The eschatological provides hope as the future always offers the hope that the present can be reversed. Additionally, it can initiate new trends in which the reversal of the present becomes a new starting point. Braaten concluded with the thought that "ultimately what we mean by the future is what we mean by God. For God is our Future, the fulfilling power of the future in all things."[120]

---

specialists, including Charles Hartshorne, Theodosius Dobzhansky, Bernard Meland, and N. M. Wildiers. Schubert Ogden was the seminar leader for the first two sessions, and Daniel Day Williams for the third. Although most attendees were from the New York area, many traveled from across the United States and Canada.

117. John Cobb's argument was that process theology holds a mediating position in the tension between present and future; process itself does not assure progress. Although God's ongoing activity in the world provides for progress in addition to change, "there is no guarantee of progress in the short run, and in the long run it is inevitable that life on this planet will become extinct." For Whitehead "the penultimate value and meaning of history become ultimate in God." Cobb conjectured about a "post-personal future" in "which there would be a rich interpenetration of each into the other to the intensification and harmonization of the experiences of all." This future will create "a new kind of community," one beyond both collectivities and any form of voluntary associations comprised of autonomous persons. Process theology gives Cobb hope that humanity is able to discern its way through contemporary difficulties, but "it gives him no assurance that man *will* do so"; *ATA*, 31.

118. *ATA*, 31.

119. Ibid., 32.

120. *ATA*, 32. The three German theologians responded to the presentation by the Americans, and then each evening one delivered a lecture, followed by responses

During the second evening, Moltmann of the University of Tübingen spoke on "Hope and the Biomedical Future of Man." His primary thesis was that for the first time in the history of the world, "Human life in fact has become a moral task" that calls for a reassessment of illness, aging, and dying. Since medicine and biomedical research create hopes but do not guarantee happiness, it is essential that they be guided by a humane ethics. Moltmann ended his lecture with the comments that Hope Theology admittedly "sounds too good to be true. In light of contemporary history, things do not look too hopeful. The hopes of the early sixties have 'gone with the wind' and everywhere we hear words like 'frustration' and 'betrayal.'"[121] Yet, Dr. Moltmann concluded, the more humanity gains power over nature the less survival alone can be the sum total of what life is about.

On the final evening, Johannes Metz of the State University of Münster presented "The Future *ex memoria Passionis*," in which he contended that the future of our technological civilization is a political and social issue. He proposed "the memory of suffering" as a means by which political and social action might occur. This thought was that the memory of crucifixion "prevents us from ever becoming reconciled" to the realities of the everyday life of our societies. Memory should become "the ferment for that new political life we are now seeking on behalf of our human future."[122]

At an executive meeting held after the conference, Ewert Cousins reported that the conference evaluation showed it was positive for both the audience and the participants. Most felt that "important communication had occurred" and that significant exchange of knowledge and information had happened for all those who participated.[123]

---

from the Americans. On the first evening of the conference, Pannenberg of University of Munich spoke on "Future and Unity," exploring a diverse set of topics including the relation of God to the future, the interaction of the divine and the profane, the interaction of individual and society as well as religion and society, the probable significance of the resurrection, and "the meaning of the eschatological future as the future of God's kingdom in his eternal life and power," all through the lens of the thought of Teilhard and Whitehead. Donald Gray responded from a Teilhardian view, Williams from a process viewpoint.

121. Dugan, "Theologians Find That Hope Survives," 20.

122. *ATA*, 33.

123. Ibid.

In a reflection on the conference in the proceedings, Daniel Day Williams noted that all the theologians involved "see the meaning of the Christian faith as eschatologically determined. Life is understood through what we shall be." The Teilhardian perspective, he suggests, draws upon a general scientific understanding of the world, interpreted in a cosmic development toward final unity. The Teilhardians seem to put more emphasis upon the spiritual vision making it possible for people today "to live religiously through participation in the slow, painful growth of humanity toward unity." He further notes that what he found most impressive in the Teilhard contingent was "their continuing hopefulness about a significant ethical and religious life in the present age, despite the suffering that occurs."[124] Apparently, unlike many others at the time, this contingent understood and was comfortable with Teilhard's understanding that suffering points to a universe that is still unfinished, one that is emerging and becoming what God means it to be; along the way to completion, therefore, suffering due to imperfection will necessarily occur. The attribute of perfection can only be applied to some future cosmic unity that is currently and constantly being called into being by God from the future up ahead.[125] In the face of this becoming in God, then, hopefulness is quite justified.

This particular conference was to be the first stage in exploring the Teilhardian perspective set against the "Theology of Hope."[126] It is significant, both in terms of the reception of Teilhard in this time

124. Daniel Day Williams, "Hope and the Future of Man: A Reflection," in *Hope and the Future of Man* (Philadelphia: Fortress Press, 1972), 142–43. At the time of the publication of this work Williams was Roosevelt Professor of Systematic Theology at the Union Theological Seminary in NYC. He is the author of *The Spirit and the Forms of Love* as well as *God's Grace and Man's Hope.*

125. This concept of the purpose of suffering in an incomplete universe is explained well in John F. Haught, "Teilhard and the Question of Life's Suffering," in *Rediscovering Teilhard's Fire,* ed. Kathleen Duffy, SSJ (Philadelphia: St. Joseph's University Press, 2010), 53–68.

126. The second stage was to bring together the same group of theologians with future planners and thinkers in the fields of science, sociology, political science, and technology. For this second conference, a budget of some $25,000 was projected. Even though it never occurred, as a result of the "Theology of Hope Conference," by the end of 1971 the ATA boasted over five hundred members, the highest number ever in the history of the organization.

period and the preceding paragraph concerning hope, that due to a lack of financial backers and a concomitant lack of interest, the follow-up second conference never materialized.

FINAL THOUGHTS

The years of 1968–70 might be considered bitter years by some, as the social and cultural changes longed for earlier in the 1960s occurred only partially and with difficulty. Additionally, American society found itself increasingly divided by a multitude of political and societal events. As a result, those groups who had been attracted to Teilhard's work for its emphasis upon the ongoing progress of humanity, a movement toward organic unity, and a synthesis of the peoples of the world were themselves splintered between those who lost faith in evolutionary possibilities and those who, much fewer in number, kept their trust in a God who inexorably was drawing the world forward.

It would indeed seem that a positive reception of Teilhard's thought in the face of the collapse of promise appears predicated upon the ability of the reader to understand that the love about which Teilhard wrote, the foundation for his own hope in the face of suffering, is overwhelmingly experiential and religious in nature. This love, optimistic hope, and loyalty to the church rises out of his own experience of Christ, one that, although shaken at times by the experiences of his life, stayed true until the end. As Teilhard noted in 1951, "I can truly say—and this in virtue of the whole structure of my thought—that I now feel more indissolubly bound to ... the Christ of the Gospel than ever before in my life. Never has Christ seemed to me more real, more personal or more immense."[127] This statement was made shortly after learning his request to publish *The Phenomenon of Man* had again been denied, his faculty position at L'Institute Catholique in Paris revoked, and he had been sent in virtual exile to end his days in New York City. The suffering was immense, yet for him, faith and the hope remained.

127. Teilhard de Chardin, Letter from Cape Town to Father General, Jean-Baptiste Janssens, October 12, 1951.

7 ~ PUBLICATIONS

THIS CHAPTER in turn looks at a couple dozen articles, essays, and books pertaining to Teilhard published between the years of 1968 and 1971 to determine his reception during this time. These publications were written during the earlier years of hope; after 1968, the number of publications decreases significantly.

The broad trends concerning the late 1960s, as delineated by U.S. historian Sydney Ahlstrom, will be of use here. These are: (1) a growing attachment to naturalism or "secularism" that makes people suspicious of any supernatural doctrines or, in the opposite corner, produces a fascination with the most radical brands of magic, superstition, and divine intervention; (2) an awareness of the vast contradictions in American life between profession and performance, the ideal and the actual; and (3) increasing concern about the capacity of political, social, educational, and religious institutions to correct these contradictions.[1]

In part as a result of these trends, for many these were the years in which doubt about the optimistic Teilhardian worldview must be addressed. As we have already seen, he was accused of naïve optimism more than once. However, in the face of mounting naturalism

1. Sydney Ahlstrom, "The Radical Turn in Theology and Ethics: Why It Occurred in the 1960s," *Annals of the American Academy of Political Science*, special issue, *The Sixties: Radical Change in American Religion* 387 (1970).

it became increasingly difficult, despite ongoing fascination with mysticism, for many to understand the Christocentric incarnational vision espoused by Teilhard.

The divide between science and religion, particularly religion as practiced in the mainline churches, appeared wider than ever as this decade drew to a close. Similarly, the gap between Teilhard's brand of theology, which was such an influence upon many of the Vatican II documents, and that of neo-scholastics such as Maritain and those concerned about the implementation of the Council, was again rearing its head. This is reflected in a renewed confusion and debate as to Teilhard's methodology, as well as that concerning the theological and scientific validity of his arguments. The discussions over not only the classification of his work, but the value of it, particularly the spiritual value of it for contemporary society, again became quite heated at times.

For a few the source and value of his work were quite apparent. These scholars and authors asserted that what Teilhard was doing was a *ressourcement* of the Pauline tradition associated with the Cosmic Christ, one updated by modern scientific knowledge concerning paleontology and evolution and transmitted through a mystical lens in a manner that spoke to the needs of a young, contemporary, and secular world. As explained in the introduction to this work, Teilhard's Christology is supremely incarnational; as such, an inherent aspect of this is his emphasis upon the value of the secular, material world. Those who understood Teilhard's Christocentric focus also appeared to realize that to expect to bypass the confusion and suffering encountered along the path to the new forms of life slowly evolving in U.S. society was impossible, for these were obligatory, if difficult, aspects of a lived Paschal mystery. When this inherent component of a spiritual life was understood, whether in the case of an individual person or a society, ambiguity, sorrow, even death could then be tolerated and employed as a springboard for new growth. Difficulty and paradox might be inevitable, yet they were not the final call.

However, all too few who wrote on Teilhard's thought during these years appeared to have this Christological understanding. Instead, most were eager to continue to focus on the use of his theories for secular purposes, particularly the further study of scientific evolution, the future of technology, process theology, psychology, and sociology, or a general global mysticism or humanism. In the end, it becomes clear that it was indeed these latter forms of exploration of Teilhard's thought that predominated during these years and those that immediately followed. Indeed, for almost the entire decade of the 1970s, even as the numbers of publications produced concerning Teilhard's work plummeted in volume, the vast majority investigated just these subject matters.

SIGNIFICANT PUBLICATIONS

Although far from a comprehensive enumeration of all publications of the time, those presented in this chapter were chosen as representative of five specific categories produced during these years. The first category is that of works that examine the Christological basis of Teilhard's work as foundational for a full appreciation of Teilhard's thought. Following these are treatises written by Teilhard and either translated or edited by Father Henri de Lubac.

The chapter then examines several essays from interdisciplinary journals that, even as they stress Teilhard's own synthetic nature, attempt to classify his work. These then lead into a reflection upon essays and books that examine Teilhard's spirituality and its relevance to contemporary society and the church. Finally, this chapter ends with an examination of several books that move even further away from Teilhard's Christology, considering his work instead from what might be considered a generic secular humanist or even materialist viewpoint.

PUBLICATIONS CONCERNING TEILHARD'S CHRISTOLOGICAL VISION

Five significant publications from these years examine Teilhard's Christology. In continuation of a theme prevalent during the years 1965–67, the first publication considered here takes as its starting point the intersection of Teilhard's thought, particularly his Christology, and the "secular city."[2] At least on the surface, Sister Maria Gratia Martin's book would seem to speak to the situation of many Catholic religious of the time. She emphasizes that one of the results of "God is Dead" theology and the new post–Vatican II laity is that the people of the church want to cultivate and live *the real presence* of Christ in the secular city. In her mind, the spirituality of Teilhard speaks to those in the secular city concerning these issues, as it flows from "his vision of Christ everywhere giving a face and a heart to the world." His wisdom may well satisfy "the contemporary Christian's deepest longings to find Christ *where He is.*"[3]

In particular, examining a theme that will prove quite prevalent during this time period, the author contends that Teilhard's spirituality as it is found in *The Divine Milieu* is a mysticism of co-creative union with the Trinity through the Eucharistic Christ. Sister Maria, then, grasps not only the urgent importance of Teilhard's Christology for a true understanding of his work, but also the kenotic and mystical Eucharistic quality of that thought. She argues that the primary role of the Christian is to labor toward further universal progress for the love of Christ, the Christ whose cosmic Body he is building up collaboratively with the Father and Holy Spirit. Additionally, through the acceptance of suffering we are purified by God within, making us a yet "more perfect instrument of cosmic unification." Only a mystical awareness obtained through prayer of Christ's universal presence, however, will allow unification of our personal world with that of all others. Teilhard's very Christian spirituality or mysticism is basically the collaboration with the Trinity in the "progressive realization of Jesus' priestly prayer that all may be one."[4]

2. Maria Gratia Martin, IHM, *The Spirituality of Teilhard de Chardin* (Westminster, Md.: Newman, 1967).

3. Ibid., viii; emphasis is the author's.

4. Ibid., x. His "Christian" spirituality is highlighted in contrast to the Eastern spiritualities much in vogue at the time of publication. Martin also, like many of the other authors later discussed in this chapter, asks whether in the "God is dead" era humanity is outgrowing Christianity. As science advances toward a self-created "terrestrial ultra-humanity," similar to that of Marxism, mankind feels that much more self-sufficient and autonomous. As a result, the need for the "old" Christian god of the "above," associated with despising the world, disappears. The latter implies the type of

Martin suggests that this is the tension as Teilhard sees it at the heart of the contemporary religious crisis. Beyond atheist humanists, it is a tension found among Christians themselves, who often suffer from a "religious schizophrenia." They struggle between their desire to love God above all else—the God of the Above, that is—and their increasing attraction toward the "new type of God ahead," present in the perfection of the world in man.

Martin notes that Vatican II recognized the value of this form of Christianity in the world and calls on all Christians to realize they are to live their Christian vocation in this way. One is to live the gospel in "the sort of mysticism that makes one seek passionately for God in the heart of every substance and every action."[5] Although the publication date of this book preceded the events of 1968–70, the reader of today must wonder if Martin was ever able to see these hopes playing out in the reality of the church and society of the late 1960s. One might argue that of all the authors profiled in this chapter, in many ways she grasps and utilizes Teilhard's Christology most fully. It does not appear, however, that those who grew impatient with the "co-laboring" required to maintain the nonviolence movements were interested in seeking passionately for God or understood the suffering required to "build the earth" in the Teilhardian fashion she suggests is necessary.

Yet another publication that addressed the issues of the "Death of God" theologians is Christopher Mooney's essay "Teilhard on Man's Search for God" in a 1968 issue of *Continuum*. The essay also explores the role of the secular for Teilhard and, like the previous work, concurrently explicates a great deal about Teilhard's own mystical, Christ-centered theology.[6]

---

religion reviled by the atheistic humanist who touts the "economic and social emancipation of man" while believing that religion thwarts liberation by "arousing hope for a deceptive future next life," which then diverts humankind from the construction of the earthly city (46).

5. Teilhard de Chardin to Marguerite M, March 29, 1917, in Martin, *Spirituality of Teilhard de Chardin*, 112.

6. Christopher Mooney, SJ, "Teilhard on Man's Search for God," *Continuum* 5, no. 4 (Winter 1968): 643–54; hereafter referred to as "Search." One might add also that this essay offers further ammunition for Flower Children who are all about "LOVE" as well as an affirmation of the Beatles' hit song "All You Need Is Love."

Mooney notes that in general the consensus of Death of God theology is that contemporary culture is estranged from Christianity, and, concomitantly, today Christianity is not possible without secularity. His thesis in this essay is that Teilhard's primary focus is exactly this; Teilhard strives to overcome the present cultural estrangement of Christianity and the divide between humanity and God, as well as the divide between God and the world.[7] As Mooney points out, the lifelong efforts of Teilhard and many others contributed to the creation of the recent *Gaudium et spes, The Constitution on the Church in the Modern World*, an indicator that the Second Vatican Council itself recognizes the necessity of addressing this concern with estrangement.

Surely no one was more conscious of these "happenings, needs, and desires" of our age than Teilhard, Mooney argues. Nor was anyone more anxious than he to find therein "authentic signs of God's presence and purpose," so that the unbeliever might see how Christian faith "directs the mind to solutions which are fully human."[8] In an effort to overcome this present-day estrangement from God, Teilhard developed a theology as oriented toward the material and temporal as the eternal. Still, Mooney insists, one must realize that for Teilhard the problem of God was foremost a personal one; his personal, mystical experience of the divine was what convinced him he might have a message for contemporary humankind. This message has two prongs: humanity's need for an absolute and humanity's need for Christ. The parallels to these two needs Teilhard had himself experienced in his own commitment to science and to contemporary culture or the material world.

Mooney includes an explanation of Teilhard's Christology in this essay as a means by which to encourage others to recognize that without this foundation, the remainder of Teilhard's thought is almost inexplicable—as the hoped-for ongoing public and academic debate over how to "classify" or make use of this thought indicates. Only when a religious conversion of sorts occurs so that the reflective reader realizes that the "love" about which Teilhard writes is a

7. Mooney, "Search," 643.
8. Ibid., 644.

personal love drawing all of creation, all of humanity, all of matter, in fact, teleologically toward the Omega Point or Cosmic Christ, does the remainder of his thought—evolutionary or spiritual—fall into place.

Mooney—and Sister Martin also, we might argue—realized with Teilhard that unless our society accepts and experiences a personal God who loves us, as shown in the historic incarnated Jesus who was willing to suffer and die for us, all the potential of individuals and the world at large become oriented toward violence and suppression rather than toward love, growth, and unification.[9] This statement alone would seem to explain a great deal as to why Teilhard's optimistic worldview was misunderstood in the decade following these bitter years by those who rejected or did not comprehend the Christocentric nature of Teilhard's mystical thought.

Indeed, Mooney and Teilhard are also very aware that most modern Christians had no interest either in building the earth or seeking out the personal God. What then will happen to succeeding generations? "There is only one way for believers to bring God to the men of our time," Teilhard insisted, "and that is to share their human ideal, and to search at their side for the God whom we already possess but who is present among us yet as if we did not recognize him."[10] The "presence" of God of which he writes is best manifested "in and through the events of man's life" in the secular world and in matter. Only this kind of understanding of God can leap the chasm between the Christian faith and contemporary culture. As Mooney notes, "His Christology was a further effort in this same direction: faith in the Incarnation is precisely a recognition that God has become so immanent in human life that the distinction between sacred and secular must henceforth be considered more rational than real."[11]

9. Ibid., 649.

10. Pierre Teilhard de Chardin, "Note pour servir à évangelisation des temps nouveaux," 1919, in *Écrits du temps de la guerre: 1916–1919*, 367, quoted in Mooney, "Search," 354.

11. Mooney, "Search," 654. We can conclude that for Teilhard to be a Christian is simply to take part daily in God's plan, which is cosmological, secular, and sacred, encompassing all that involves man's work as well as God's. "And thus in the end," states Teilhard, "above the rediscovered greatness of man, above the newly revealed greatness of humanity, not violating but preserving the integrity of science, the face

For Mooney then, as for Teilhard, what is needed is not just some amorphous "love," but an effort to see God and to participate in God's work of building the earth and moving ahead the evolution of the world. The work taking place in the political and social worlds of the United States will have no long-term effects if those involved do not recognize that the work is "God's work" and not their own. The face of God must be found in the secular, an orientation toward God must take place, and the divine love must be nurtured in the everyday lives of all people. This is how the unity and hope sought by civil rights and student and antiwar protestors will be found, but as this chapter has shown, will unfortunately for the most part not be.

Yet another treatise concerned with both Teilhard's Christology and its application to the times of the 1960s was one by A. O. Dyson. Dyson also is convinced Teilhard has a schema that responds well to the angst of a generation sure Christianity is no longer relevant. In particular he counters James Mitchell, who Dyson notes has described Teilhard de Chardin as "a pseudo-religio-scientific fraud" and, in another place, as an "ecclesiastical witchdoctor."[12] Mr. Mitchell asserted in his own essay that "such unlikely fellow-travelers as Teilhard and Billy Graham," whom Mitchell compares to "some old-style Music Hall hypnotist," are in vain attempting to keep Christianity alive for another generation. In this view, Teilhard is seen as fraudulently patching together a Christianity that is a "dying mythology," "no longer able to illuminate the human condition."[13]

---

of God reappears in our modern world"; Teilhard de Chardin, "La Place de l'homme dans l'univers," 1942, in Les Amis de Teilhard, eds. *Les Oeuvres de Teilhard de Chardin*, vol. 3, *La Vision du passé* (Paris: Éditions du Seuil), 324, quoted in "Search," 654.

12. James Mitchell, "The God I Want," *New Blackfriars*, June 1967, quoted in A. O. Dyson, "Christ and Man's Place in Nature: Man and Evolution," *Theology* 72 (1969): 98–102. These descriptors of Teilhard from Mitchell sound like those of Jacques Maritain, in *The Peasant of the Garonne: An Old Layman Questions Himself about the Present Time* (Eugene, Ore.: Wipf and Stock, 2013).

13. Dyson, "Christ and Man's Place in Nature," 98. Dyson acknowledges the validity of Mitchell's complaint that much contemporary theology ignores recent modern achievements concerning humanity and the world and instead continues to sequester itself within the cloister of academia and church. However, Dyson also contends that Teilhard's project has something hopeful to offer in regard to this complaint. If nothing else, one must concede the risk Teilhard takes in candidly facing his own "Kierkegaardian streak" and acknowledging that perhaps human reality really does speak only of meaninglessness and absurdity—an acknowledgment that society increasingly appears

Dyson suggests that Teilhard's underlying primary task is to determine whether the known world of man, society, and the natural world is attuned by nature with the claims Christianity makes for it. Is there really any compatibility between Christianity's assertion of Christ as the center and the goal of all things and the reality of the space-time continuum in which we live? That the compatibility could even be envisaged became a possibility for Teilhard only as he developed his evolutionary hypothesis. This enabled him to posit the theory of a converging evolution passing from multiplicity into a complex unity over an incredible period of deep time; this evolution sheds illumination not only on humanity's past, but also on the present and future as we evolve or are drawn toward Omega. It is Teilhard's conclusion, and that of Dyson, that indeed coherence very much exists between the Christian faith and our lived understanding and observation of human life, society, and nature. This is, actually, the basis of Teilhard's Christology.[14]

For Christians the Cosmic Christ of their faith is the Christ who permits the universe to get on with being and becoming what is proper to it, a way in which the stuff of life—evil, suffering, chance, failure, new life—cannot be avoided and is, in fact, the heart of what we call the "Paschal mystery." We recognize and affirm that Christ is involved at every level of our lives and history; indeed, he is essential to the whole cosmic order. For Teilhard, however, coherence between these principles of the Christian faith and cosmic natural history goes a step forward as it illuminates the present and guides the shape of the future.[15]

To Dyson it seems that without Teilhard's exploration and risk-taking in this area, Mitchell and others may indeed have good reason to ask whether Christianity is not dying. This is particularly true when one observes what was then currently occurring within the

---

willing to make. To challenge this is a massive threat, and for this Dyson points to Teilhard's genuine faith. The willingness of Teilhard to stand in personal continuity with the Christian tradition even as he stands with open eyes before modern reality speaks to Dyson of Teilhard's sincerity and suggests the equal imperative to as willingly examine his proposals.

14. Ibid., 100.

15. Ibid., 101.

churches and the social activism inspired by Christian movements.[16] For this reason, Dyson, in addition to Mooney and Martin, advocates that Teilhard's task should be a matter of ongoing urgency, engaging "a whole new theological generation" that comprehends and practices his Christology.[17] One might argue that it was indeed an unwillingness or inability to practice this form of Christology—whether for lack of interest, understanding, or desire—that not only caused many to permit the social movements of the earlier 1960s to be directed away from a Christian foundation and toward violence and revolution; it also perhaps precluded their understanding that cycles of frustration and disappointment are inherent to the Christian life.

Now that this chapter has examined several publications that emphasize the importance of Teilhard's Christocentric vision, both for an understanding of his thought and as a means by which to live it in 1960s society, this next section will consider a book that speaks of the sources of that Christology. Harry J. Cargas's *The Continuous Flame: Teilhard in the Great Traditions* attempts to connect Teilhard with other great visionaries and, for purposes of this book, specifically to establish links between Teilhard's Christology and that of the Apostle Paul.[18]

According to Cargas, the editor of this collection, "What the essays in this book show, it is hoped, is that indeed Teilhard is an eclectic, but one of the most adventurous and exciting synthesizers in modern history."[19] Cargas argues that Teilhard's work is a *ressourcement* from varied parts of the Christian tradition. He also notes that Teilhard is actually in "a double Christian tradition," one that both

16. When these types of ongoing open reflections upon the nature of humankind through the lens of contemporary knowledge, including scientific knowledge, are sacrificed, particularly to nothing more than what Dyson terms mind-numbing "repetition of New Testament language" or the subjective "feelings which Jesus Christ provokes in us," the temptation is to conclude that no grounds exist at all for Christian belief. If this sacrifice occurs, Dyson is certain that the Christian gospel will indeed be rendered incommunicable to this and future secular ages.

17. Dyson, "Christ and Man's Place in Nature," 102.

18. Harry Cargas, ed., *The Continuous Flame: Teilhard in the Great Traditions* (St. Louis, Mo.: B. Herder, 1969). Contradictory publication dates are given. The dedication to this book is to "Jessie Teilhard Cargas: In Whom the Flame Continually Burns."

19. Ibid., ix.

appreciates and utilizes the great religious and secular movements of the past, as well as one who advances that already established tradition further forward.

Cargas concedes that the late 1960s are a curious time when young people are scoffed at for losing touch with the past, as well as for their apparent lack of a sense of continuity; yet, they seem to love Teilhard. Teilhard, however, is "surely the most aware man as to where he has come from; this is how he knows where he, and we, are going."[20] Obviously, Cargas believes, we have much use for Teilhard today. With that in mind, *Continuous Flame* attempts to show Teilhard in relation to many diverse writers and visionaries, not only St. Paul, but also Jung, Dante, Whitman, and Bonhoeffer. Cargas, therefore, in keeping with the ecumenical spirit of the age, situates Teilhard not only within the Catholic tradition, but beyond this within a broader Christian mysticism. Within the next decade of the publication of the volume, Cargas suggests that scholars will be contextualizing Teilard within a global mystical tradition.

James Adams, OFSF, the author of "St. Paul and Teilhard de Chardin," which is included within *Continous Flame,* contends that Paul and Teilhard have the same end objective in mind—namely, to show how the material world proclaims God's glory. As a result, matter itself is sanctified by its participation in this glorification, a process that continues to occur at this very moment. Concerning how this divinization pertains to the era of the late 1960s, the author notes that "all things," including "tribulations or poverty or imprisonment," are a way to further spiritualize matter and consecrate the world through working together with God. This is why, Adams exhorts, Teilhard insists the duty of every Christian is to be a co-creator, for "true Christian asceticism inevitably flows from the requirement of creation to be essentially painful and mortifying," as "the mystery of the cross is present, operating in all creation, in the whole of creation."[21]

20. Ibid., x.

21. Additionally, as both Paul and Teilhard write, the Christian life may imply an acceptance of the human condition, but this does not happen in a passive fashion, as instead it looks forward to and works toward a goal. That goal is the union of all

The editor hopes therefore that the book portrays Teilhard for this generation and the next "not as a freak who happened at one moment in the twentieth century. He is both a culminating point and a commencing point from which we can branch out in the future with joy, love, and hope."[22] He believes that those who find hope in Teilhard's thought also anticipate that their efforts, even if apparently unsuccessful at that moment, are indeed 'building the earth" and creating results. As Teilhard wrote in *The Divine Milieu,* "Where are we to look for the source of rejuvenation? ... except from the perception of *a more intimate connection* between the victory of Christ and the outcome of the work which our human effort here below is seeking to construct ... the expectation of the kingdom cannot remain alive unless it is incarnate in our body today?"[23]

The last work to be considered here that specifically addresses Teilhard's Christology is another by Christopher Mooney published at the very end of the time period this work discusses. A book review of Teilhard's *Christianity and Evolution,* it argues that not only is this book quite Christological, it also includes an exploration of the topic that will prove paramount in Teilhardian circles in the decade to come—that of evolution.[24]

Mooney begins his review by suggesting that the significance of Teilhard lies in his willingness to continue to ask, throughout a forty-year period, unique questions of theologians. In his previous essay already discussed in this chapter, Mooney pondered Teilhard's relationship to the "Death of God" theologians; here Teilhard is by contrast questioning Roman Catholics, including, perhaps, fellow Jesuits. As were the Death of God theologians, Teilhard was concerned about the irrelevance of much of twentieth-century theology to those

---

creatures in Christ. All sufferings are to be endured through the desire to see God glorified; both successes and failures become efficacious means by which Christians contribute to the "New Creation." See, for example, Col 1:24: "Now I rejoice in my sufferings for your sake, and in my flesh I am filling up what is lacking in the afflictions of Christ on behalf of his body, which is the church."

22. Cargas, *Continuous Flame,* xi.

23. Teilhard de Chardin, *The Divine Milieu: An Essay on the Interior Life* (New York: Harper and Row, 1960), 136.

24. Christopher Mooney, SJ, review of *Christianity and Evolution,* by Pierre Teilhard de Chardin, *America,* December 25, 1971, 563ff.

questions that haunted contemporary society. So, his attempts to work out answers to nineteen of these questions from within a Roman Catholic worldview are found in the essays in this book.[25]

Several of the essays are Christological in character, and within these Teilhard especially attempts to clarify his concept of Christogenesis.[26] In particular, Mooney notes, the essays are significant, as they portray Teilhard as a scientist trying to elucidate and work out religious conjectures. In an age of "Jesus freaks" and mystical experiences, Mooney ends, not surprisingly, by stressing the existential, mystical quality of Teilhard's "highly personal Christian spiritual experience." Once again, Mooney concludes by contending that Teilhard's ultimate goal was to help theologians better "see" the contemporary situation. It therefore appears Mooney's own purpose in writing this book review was to encourage Teilhard's American fans to take seriously his Christocentric worldview and to understand how formational this is for his writings. His concern was that those readers recognize how critical it is that if one is to make use successfully of Teilhard's thought, it must be understood in its synthetic entirety.

TEILHARD AND HENRI DE LUBAC

We now move from discussion of publications of a specifically Christological nature to those produced by Teilhard himself, and notably those that involved Henri de Lubac, SJ, as editor or translator. During the time period from 1968 to 1971, six manuscripts of Teilhard were published in the United States.[27] If nothing else, the

25. For example, eight of these essays deal with original sin, as Teilhard was concerned with safeguarding the cosmic significance of Christ's work of redemption in the face of new theories of evolution and science. Christ's death and resurrection were for Teilhard the signs and guarantee of the ultimate goal of human life, yet the theology behind original sin with which he was familiar seemed to him to ignore completely the cosmic character of redemption.

26. This in turn requires him to consider Christian work in the world, the role of the church, and his attempt to unite creation and salvation as similar aspects of the divine plan.

27. These include *Letters from Hastings: 1908–1912*, ed., with an Introduction by Henri de Lubac, trans. Judith de Stefano (New York: Herder and Herder, 1968); *Writings in Time of War*, New York: Harper and Row, 1968; and *Science and Christ* (New York: Harper and Row, 1969). In 1971, *Human Energy* (New York: Harcourt, Brace,

ongoing publication of various collections of Teilhard's letters and other manuscripts speaks to the societal demand for yet more. At least up to a point, which appears to be in the early 1970s, all things Teilhardian continued to be a lucrative market for publishers.

Due to its special importance as an examination of Teilhard's Christocentric "Dialectic of Spirit," the last of these books was already briefly presented in a book review by Christopher Mooney, and space does not permit a summary of each of the others.

However, regarding the publication of the first, *Letters from Hastings*, the February 1969 issue of the quarterly *New Book Review* does suggest a possible oversaturation of the publication market.[28] In this journal, critic Michael McMahon gave his annual list of 1968's "Ten Best" and "Ten Worst" books in religious publishing. Included in the ten-worst category—along with *Relax and Rejoice for the Hand on the Tiller Is Firm* and *Religion: Out or Way Out?*—is *Letters from Hastings*, a collection of early Teilhard de Chardin correspondence as edited by Henri de Lubac. Although the jacket blurb portrays the volume as "an important chapter in the history of [Teilhard's] spiritual and intellectual development," McMahon instead terms it "a particularly odious sort of exploitation." He first rejoices that Teilhard did not live to see the publication of his private and sensitive early correspondence; he then concludes with a facetious forecast: "Coming next—*The Teilhard Cookbook, Teilhard and Vietnam*, and *Teilhard: My Uncle*." Interestingly enough, Herder and Herder published *Letters from Hastings* as well as *New Book Review*.

Several of Henri de Lubac's manuscripts on Teilhard were discussed in previous chapters; he continued to write more books about his fellow Jesuit and friend Teilhard de Chardin between 1967 and 1971, at least in part at the urging of the Jesuit general. Those briefly discussed here because of their significance are *The Religion of Teilhard de Chardin* and *The Eternal Feminine*.[29]

Jovanovich), *Activation of Energy* (New York: Harcourt, Brace, Jovanovich), and *Christianity and Evolution*, trans, René Hague (New York: Harcourt) were published.

28. Reference to this book review was found in "Integrity of the Week Award," *Christian Century*, April 2, 1969, 437.

29. Henri de Lubac, SJ, *The Religion of Teilhard de Chardin*, trans. René Hague (New York: Desclee, 1967); *Teilhard Explained*, trans. Anthony Buono (New York:

Due to life circumstances, de Lubac likely had the most familiarity with Teilhard's mind and history. He knew Teilhard through both letter and conversation. From the beginning of his efforts concerning Teilhard's work, de Lubac's aim, like those of many of the scholars already discussed, was to show that Teilhard's writings are not as unorthodox as they sometimes seem. Against critics like some of those mentioned in this and previous chapters, de Lubac urges readers to remember that those who have no religious experiences to describe, no new "seeds of thought" to bring before the church and public, know nothing, as he puts it, "of the difficulties, the hesitancies" that are part of the effort to express one's unique ideas or experiences in an adequate manner. In his own mind a significant gap exists between those who are teachers and those who are attempting a lasting contribution to humankind.[30]

In regard to *The Religion of Teilhard de Chardin*, in conjunction with a theme that has occurred consistently through this and prior chapters, de Lubac promotes Teilhard's Christian spirituality as one that engages the secular world. As he notes, many Protestants, perhaps especially, are inclined to think of Roman Catholics in the United States as either overly dogmatic or overly private and moralistic, both attributes that tend to maintain a distance from the world. As presented by de Lubac, however, Teilhard's incarnational spirituality actively engages Christians with their worldly ministry. Further, even the uniquely Roman Catholic elements of Teilhard's spiritual rhetoric are readily adaptable to any Christian lifestyle. De Lubac therefore contends that his is a spirituality well-suited to ecumenical efforts.

It is likely no surprise that de Lubac considers the greatest theological contribution of Teilhard's thought to be his focus on the cosmological reality of Christ. He argues that Teilhard's focus on the Cosmic Christ offers opportunities for an expansion of Christian thought in several directions. First, humanity and its religious activity

Paulist Press, 1968); *The Eternal Feminine: A Study on the Poem by Teilhard de Chardin, Followed by Teilhard and the Problems of Today*, trans. René Hague (New York: Harper and Row, 1971).

30. De Lubac, *The Religion of Teilhard*, 17.

can be understood as a part of the natural, material world, which is its "own thing," not simply something conceived of by humankind. This notion of nature as constituting an important component of human life, rather than simply as being something outside ourselves, will soon strongly influence the ecological movement. Second, technology and the technological sciences can be appreciated in their natural place as something that is now an instrumental factor in evolution. They need not be a threat to humanity's existence; instead, people are to master technology and put it to use.

Finally, Teilhard's emphasis on the Cosmic Christ legitimizes the theme of God's majesty in nature, an essential theme of scripture and one that will again be especially vital to Christian environmentalists. Also it can now be given a central place in theology just as it has had in scripture, particularly Pauline scripture, as noted in the Cargas book.[31]

De Lubac points out the similarities between these components of Teilhard's theological concerns, particularly those around the need to recapture and reexamine scriptural themes, and many raised by other *nouvelle* theologians in France prior to Vatican II. In this way he again situates Teilhard within the same conversations as those, including himself, who had an important influence upon the Council.

The Eternal Feminine consists of two parts: the first is a study by de Lubac of Teilhard's 1918 essay "The Eternal Feminine," and the second is titled, "Teilhard and the Problems of Today." In an age seemingly fascinated by the notion of "love," in a time when feminist consciousness is just beginning to germinate, Teilhard and de Lubac present a work that offers a countercultural reading of both these concepts.

The first part of the book traces the development of the essay from its conception in Teilhard's mind to its birth in the written form now available to us in Teilhard's *Writings in Time of War*.[32] Teil-

31. And of course, the issues surrounding eschatology, particularly eschatological hope, can now be taken more seriously, as was discussed in previous chapters in regard to the ties between the Theology of Hope and Teilhard's own work.

32. Pierre Teilhard de Chardin, *Writings in Time of War* (New York: Harper and

hard knew that his vow of chastity could never be for him a negation or rejection of life. De Lubac argues that he therefore presents the feminine, despite his struggles to define its role, as absolutely necessary for both personal and cosmic maturity. The "essential Feminine"—another name, at least in de Lubac's eyes, for the principle of love—is "the unitary aspect of beings."[33] Teilhard writes, "Driven by the forces of love, the fragments of the world seek each other so that the world may come into being."[34] He even looks forward to a time when feminine love so transforms the earth through personalization that the present sexual triangular relationship of Man-Woman-Child will be sublimated by the relationship of Man-Woman-God. This is certainly a different vision of chastity, and love, from that celebrated by the counterculture and the Summer of Love. It is also one with which we must suppose young lovers of Teilhard of the time struggled mightily.[35]

The second half of the book, first published in Paris in 1968, three years after the end of the Second Vatican Council, is titled, "Teilhard and the Problems of Today." It is, in the spirit of the social scientists who had already done the same, de Lubac's own attempt to use Teilhard's work to give guidance to a post–Vatican II world. In his first essay de Lubac suggests that Teilhard's impact has been great because "readers have found in [him] ... undeterred by disappointments, 'stronger than every obstacle and counterargument'

Row, 1968). What becomes obvious is that Teilhard really was not clear as to where the "feminine" fit into his overarching system. From the first page, however, we see him struggling with a subject about which he was deeply interested: virginity. In April 1916 a notation in his notebook remarks, "Virginity: an undoubted invasion of the cosmos by the Revealed." A few days later, he made the decision to undertake this study "in honour of Our Lady"; *Eternal Feminine*, 9. He was trying to define the cosmic nature of virginity, which eventually he associates not only with the Blessed Virgin, but concurrently with purity, chastity, fruitfulness, love, and ultimately union.

33. De Lubac, *Eternal Feminine*, 86.

34. Teilhard de Chardin, *The Phenomenon of Man*, trans. Bernard Wall, introduction Sir Julian Huxley (New York: Harper, 1959), 264–65, quoted in de Lubac, *Eternal Feminine*, 87.

35. Chapter 2 of the book summarizes Teilhard's "Poem of Love" and discusses its sources and antecedents. As mentioned earlier, Teilhard sees the evolutionary process as bound up with the evolution of love, but it would be just as valid to view the essay as "A Poem of Matter." The similarities between Teilhard's poetic description of Matter and the entity he calls "the Feminine" are striking.

... the same hope and the same eagerness to get to work" as Vatican II urges.[36] It is as a result of Teilhard's willingness to express these hopes and fears, the guidance he offers through them, that de Lubac believes he is so widely read. Still, he admits, Teilhard was at least a generation ahead of most people; he wonders therefore how he will be received in another two decades.[37]

One might note in regard to these comments de Lubac's own concern that as with the documents of Vatican II, Teilhard's thought too was being interpreted along trajectories with which he would not agree. He argues in the second chapter of this section of the work that "small groups of impatient people are going too far ... a number of extremists are trying to use the present transitional period to promote their own views rather than wholeheartedly adhere to what was written ... enthusiasm is taking the form of an extremism."[38]

Finally, in the chapter "Jesus Christ," de Lubac again emphasizes the inspiration Teilhard found in the writings of St. Paul and the resultant importance of Teilhard's Christology at the heart of his thought. He notes Teilhard's comment that "without Jesus Christ, centre of consistence, I crumble away within—everything outside me crumbles away also."[39] With equal force, de Lubac argues, Teilhard emphasized the necessity of the gospel life for humanity's progress, for "without faith, purity and charity, the three fundamental interior attitudes taught by Christ ... neither could the divine milieu be constituted nor could the Kingdom of God flourish. Without them, the progress of earthly society could lead ultimately only to inhuman structures."[40] Still, as de Lubac writes, for Teilhard—as it should be

36. Teilhard de Chardin, "A Note on Progress" (1920): 19. This was a self-published, mimeographed article; quoted in de Lubac, *Eternal Feminine*, 134.

37. De Lubac, *Eternal Feminine*, 145. Reading between the lines here it is easy to get a sense of his anguish at the direction he sees many taking.

38. Ibid. The remaining chapters of this part of the book, titled "A Personal God," "Jesus Christ," "The Church of Christ," and "Tradition and Obedience," explicate Teilhard's popular thought in a fashion proposed to inform Roman Catholics especially as to what de Lubac considers a valid interpretation of the Vatican II changes.

39. Teilhard, personal note at Tientsin, November 27, 1939, quoted in de Lubac, Eternal *Feminine*, 170.

40. Teilhard de Chardin, *Writings in Time of War*, 92–94, quoted in de Lubac, *Eternal Feminine*, 175.

for every Christian—hope must not be abandoned. Even if an occasion exists for despair, pessimism is not the final word. It must be remembered that "times of crisis will always be ... pre-eminently times for hope."[41] In this period during these last years of the sixties there would seem to be no doubt that Teilhard would have suggested to those students and activists who were in despair that "the star for which the world is waiting, without yet being able to give it a name ... is necessarily Christ Himself, in whom we hope.... We must try everything for Christ, we must hope everything for Christ."[42]

WORKS IN INTERDISCIPLINARY JOURNALS

The next section of this chapter is a discussion of four essays on Teilhard published in journals specifically established in the 1960s to explore interdisciplinary topics, particularly those of the humanities and science. These essays all discuss the various ways in which scholars were "reading" or interpreting Teilhard during these years, and particularly whether it is possible to successfully "do" both science and theology as Teilhard has. If so, just what type of science and theology is he actually doing, and is it valid?

An examination of these essays is indeed important simply to reaffirm that as synthesizer of faith and science Teilhard's work was notable, particular at this point in time. Beyond this, however, consider again Ahlstrom's comments at the beginning of the chapter regarding this age of increasing secularism and suspicion about organized religion as well as the value of science. In light of that, these essays point to at least a few well-respected scientists or intellectuals willing to admit to the ongoing importance of both a life of faith and the necessity of concomitantly further developing scientific knowledge. Or, as Teilhard wrote, "Humanity is no longer imaginable without science. But no more is science possible without some religion to animate it. Christianity is an exemplary form of the religion of science."[43] Note, however, that it is only the last of these works that

41. De Lubac, *Eternal Feminine*, 145.
42. Teilhard de Chardin, *Divine Milieu*, 137.
43. Teilhard de Chardin, *Human Energy*, 180.

significantly references the importance of Christ for Teilhard or the implications of his Christology.

The first of these essays is George Riggan's "Testing the Teilhardian Foundations," which examined at length the scientific basis of Teilhard's claims, and which will also reaffirm several conclusions already obtained within previous chapters of this work.[44] Riggan ultimately decides that Teilhard's synthesis "is embarrassed" because he "deceives himself as to what constitutes scientific evidence."[45] Although Riggan reassures the reader that the support of religious faith by scientific evidence is fine, in his view Teilhard pushes his definition of science past the limits.

In Riggan's eyes, Teilhard insists upon an intimate relationship between Christian faith and science even as he appears to regard his own work as the initiating moment of a revolution in the natural sciences; he also rests his case upon his theory that evolution is primarily a spiritual process. Riggan's response to this is "Whatever their status in Catholic dogma, extrapolations such as these have scientific standing only in science fiction."[46]

Still, Riggan agrees, the significance of Teilhard's work cannot be measured only by its scientific inadequacies. He elucidates four points regarding this that are of particular importance for this work

44. George A. Riggan, "Testing the Teilhardian Foundations," *Zygon: Journal of Religion and Science* 3, no. 3 (September 1968): 259–313. *Zygon* was introduced in chapter 5 of this work. The journal was started at Meadville Theological School of Lombard College in 1965 following any number of years of increasing collaboration at the school between theologians and scientists, and in particular as the result of a conference titled, "A Reconsideration of the Relation of Theology to the Sciences" that same year, which was in large part devoted to a trajectory of Teilhardian thought. The goals of *Zygon* state that "the contemporary sciences provide a rich lode of reliable knowledge about man's nature, destiny, and cosmic setting. Theologies which take this knowledge seriously might vitalize their religions and find themselves moving toward greater consensus. The function of the Committee on Theology and the Sciences which directs this journal is to assess the religious relevance of this increasingly interlinked network; from "Theological Resources from the Sciences," *Zygon* 1, no. 1 (January 1965): 11. The same issue of *Zygon* includes, compiled by Riggan, "A Selected Bibliography of the Works of Teilhard de Chardin" (314–22), in which he includes in alphabetical order those essays of Teilhard's from the years 1913 to 1955 that attempt some synthesis of the scientific and spiritual.

45. Riggan, "Testing the Teilhardian Foundations," 303.

46. Ibid.

and that reaffirm conclusions made earlier concerning the reception of Teilhard during this decade. In the first place, Riggan writes, the Vatican ban against publication of Teilhard's works most likely magnified their influence in Catholic circles both during his own lifetime, as he proceeded to circulate them privately despite the ban, and especially when published by Jeanne Mortier and others after his death. Second, his "proposal to translate the Gospel in evolutionary terms" hastened a discussion that assisted in preparing the way for the Second Vatican Council and the eventual movement of Catholic theology into the twentieth century.

Third, Riggan admits, Teilhard's synthesis is not wholly without scientific merit.[47] Indeed, Riggan perceives that, beyond his poetry, mysticism, and neologisms, Teilhard remains a consistent evolutionist, always viewing man as a participant in the process and subject to its laws, including those of natural selection and mutation. He incorporates a necessary holistic, synthetic viewpoint into what could otherwise become a very narrow and deterministic science. In Riggan's eyes, however, the most important significance of the Teilhardian synthesis is Teilhard's efforts toward establishing the scientific foundations for a naturalistic theology based on a directional evolutionary trajectory.[48]

In conclusion, Riggan asks what the theological consequences might be of "retranslating Christian theism from a biblical into such a contemporary scientific world view." The answer to him appears to be the role God already plays, redefined in terms of mutations and

47. The harsh reviews Teilhard's thought received from some such as Medawar and Simpson are at least partially balanced in Riggan's mind by the restrained approval of other outstanding scientists, among them Dobzhansky, Huxley, and Needham, who commonly stress that his work should be read as that of a poet and mystic as well as a scientist. As Ian Barbour's "Five Ways to Read Teilhard" (*Soundings: An Interdisciplinary Journal* 51, no. 2 [Summer 1968]) will elucidate, we could also add Barbour to this list.

48. Riggan, "Testing the Teilhardian Foundations, " 305. Riggan believes Teilhard quite thoroughly compromises his repeatedly announced intention to remain within a scientific frame of reference. He subsequently then evades the very findings implicit in a satisfactory scientific approach to his proposals. Despite this (or perhaps because of it), Riggan finds that the guidelines he suggests for a natural theology have great merit.

selection in both biological and cultural systems.[49] Even so, Riggan believes the sciences need to be part of that investigation if we do not wish to subject ourselves to further technological and cultural abuses that might "hasten the extinction of all life upon the earth."[50] He finds then that the interest in Teilhard's efforts is timely and imperative and, it is hoped, will continue far into the future.

Ian Barbour, son of George Barbour, good friend of Teilhard himself, was introduced in chapter 4 of this book. At about the same time the previous essay was being published, he wrote an essay titled, "Five Ways to Read Teilhard," for *Soundings*. Like several others in this chapter, this is an effort to explain, for those on both sides of the "divide," just what it was that Teilhard was attempting.[51] Barbour was concerned that Teilhard's work has "evoked an extraordinary diversity of appraisals" since *The Phenomenon* was first published in the United States in 1959. As did his father, George, Ian Barbour felt that most of the controversy and contradictions could be "traced to the unexamined assumptions" of those reviewing Teilhard's thought. These primarily dealt with the issue of what criteria should be used to evaluate his ideas; or, considered in another fashion, on what basis and with what categories his writings are to be judged.

This particular essay is included here in the hope that it will reaffirm how Teilhard's work was classified during this decade. Barbour successively considers Teilhard's work within the five categories of: (1) evolutionary science; (2) poetry and mystical theology; (3) natural theology; (4) Christian theology; and (5) process philosophy. Note that indeed these five categories are those by which Teilhard's thought has been categorized to this point within these chapters.

(1) Considering Teilhard as evolutionary scientist, Barbour concedes that Teilhard's technical papers, some of which are collected

49. What this view of God might possibly mean for Christianity and ethical values must still be explored. This exploration by necessity must take place beyond the sciences, Riggan asserts.

50. Riggan, "Testing the Teilhardian Foundations," 306.

51. Ian G. Barbour, "Five Ways of Reading Teilhard," 115–45. Note that it is both appropriate and significant that an essay on Teilhard should be published in an interdisciplinary journal attempting to bridge the divide between science and the humanities.

in *The Appearance of Man*, are sound contributions to science.[52] Still, Teilhard's strong concern for "the totality of the phenomenon of man" moves him far beyond the specialized sciences; he tries to reconcile quite diverse types of data within his "comprehensive framework."[53]

Also problematic is Teilhard's metaphorical use of scientific terms, such as his overuse of superlatives and neologisms. It is apparent his sources lay outside science, and as others cited within this work have suggested, these should "have been more explicitly indicated."[54]

(2) Teilhard as poet and mystic: Barbour admits that much of *The Phenomenon* is not strictly scientific by even the broadest definition, so some interpreters have gone to the opposite corner, considering it a poetic epic inspired by evolutionary science.[55] *The Phenomenon* could then be read as a "kind of religious meditation on evolution."

(3) Teilhard as natural theologian: Barbour also suggests that *The Phenomenon of Man* can be read as a reformulated argument of natural theology in which the directionality of evolution is taken as evidence for the existence of God.[56] Barbour points out that de Lubac, for example, in *Teilhard de Chardin: The Man and his Meaning*, feels that it is unfair to criticize Teilhard for not stressing God's transcendence or the scholastic separation of nature and grace,[57] as these would have not made sense in an "apologetic aimed at the agnostic

52. Barbour, "Five Ways of Reading Teilhard," 118. Barbour agrees that as might be expected by the "enthusiastic endorsement from many prominent biologists" his work has received, nothing that contradicts established scientific understanding can be found here.

53. Where, however, Barbour asks, is the "absolute line" between fact and interpretation? One cannot deny, however, that "creative imagination" is necessary in the synthesis Teilhard was attempting; ibid.

54. Ibid., 121.

55. Ibid.

56. Ibid., 124.

57. De Lubac, *Teilhard de Chardin: The Man and his Meaning* (New York: New American Library, 1965). The second half of the book (133ff.) defends Teilhard's essay "Comment je crois" against its critics—largely on the grounds that it is a form of "natural theology." Note that although Barbour speaks of Teilhard's eschatological hope in this section, no direct reference is made to his Christology.

and based only on what the latter could accept."[58] In particular his vision of hope is significant, especially in a day when "most authors instead write of despair, meaninglessness, and estrangement from nature." In Teilhard lies a scientist who sees in the evolution of the world a reason for "faith in progress, cosmic optimism, and a sense of kinship with nature."[59]

(4) Instead of reading *The Phenomenon* as a natural theology—an argument from nature to God—one could read it as Teilhard's attempt to observe nature from a theological perspective.[60] In this the religious ideas that are his main source lie outside science; the starting point would be the biblical revelation and the Christian heritage in which Teilhard's thought was profoundly molded.

On this reading, Teilhard's arguments concerning the teleology of history and personal nature of evolution come from his religious beliefs, and his optimism for the future is primarily an expression of Christian eschatological hope rather than any evolutionary inference.[61] Through this lens Barbour argues that much of Teilhard's writing is easily considered as the articulation of traditional Christian doctrine within an evolutionary universe. *The Phenomenon* therefore contains variations on the doctrines of creation, providence, and eschatology.[62] His thought is implicitly incarnational and sacramental; divine involvement in the history of the world through the Christ-event shows the value God places on the world and the idea that Christians should likewise be involved in the world.[63]

58. Barbour, "Five Ways of Reading Teilhard," 125.

59. As we have already noted at numerous points, this is of course one of the primary motivators for his positive reception during this era, although many who point to this aspect of his thought do not connect it to his Christological faith.

60. Barbour, "Five Ways of Reading Teilhard," 129.

61. Ibid.

62. Additionally, Teilhard's "theology of nature" could also be understood as an expression of his theology of the secular, including his affirmation of the creative potentialities of the world and his rejection of the dualistic tendency to view matter as evil.

63. Barbour, "Five Ways of Reading Teilhard," 131. Here Barbour comes closest to acknowledging Teilhard's Christocentric view, although he does not fully develop this. But, he also reiterates that if Teilhard is to be considered a Christian theologian, then of course this makes his work more vulnerable to theological criticism. As a result, Teilhard's defenders are left attempting to show that he is orthodox, or at least

(5) Barbour would argue that Teilhard is actually something of a process philosopher. Process categories play an important role in Teilhard's theological writings in that he reinterprets the nature of man and the meaning of creation, redemption, and eschatology in an evolving universe.[64]

Barbour agrees that most of Teilhard's work, including *The Phenomenon,* is multifaceted and not easily "pigeon-holed" into any particular discipline. Moreover, Teilhard barely acknowledges any specific methodology, and most of his key terms are ambiguous. For these reasons, Barbour notes, Teilhard's thought is "peculiarly vulnerable to one-sided interpretations by both critics and supporters. In any book—but especially in one that crosses lines between fields—the reader tends to see what he is looking for and to use what he finds for his own purposes."[65] This is certainly occurring in this period with Teilhard's publications.

Teilhard's unity, Barbour reiterates, can be found at several levels; what is foundational, however, is his personal, passionate, existential, mystical experience. Here is found the "intense conviction of cosmic unity and a powerful imaginative expression" of God's presence that

really not very unorthodox. Consider that although he stresses God's immanence, the allegation that he is a pantheist Barbour contends is surely unfair, since he repeatedly stresses God's transcendence and the individuality of each person over against God. Critics operating out of the Scholastic tradition must also recognize that for him there is no absolute dichotomy between "natural" and "supernatural" events. Barbour asserts that Teilhard's biblical assumptions cannot be denied, although he does not indicate what these are. However, his work is not just about the *ressourcement* of a neglected historic tradition; once again Barbour does not name this tradition. Still, he says, Teilhard's indebtedness to both religious and scientific sources needs to be kept in tension and the interaction between scientific and religious concepts acknowledged. Theology is not itself revealed, Barbour reminds the reader; it always involves an interpretation of the (usually) historical events in which God is understood to have acted. Teilhard then is definitely something more than a classical systematic Christian theologian. Barbour notes that Teilhard's appreciation of the value of secularity is similar to that of Dietrich Bonhoeffer, Harvey Cox, and other recent exponents of "worldly Christianity" as already noted in the previous chapter.

64. Ibid., 115. Barbour writes that Teilhard's evolutionary outlook leads him to emphasize such genuinely biblical themes as continuing creation, the significance of time and history, an affirmation of "secular" life, the unity of man as a total being, the reality of a living God involved in the world, and the cosmic significance of Christ, all concepts with which process philosophy deals regularly.

65. Ibid., 137.

underlies the rest of the work.[66] This experience, Barbour believes, is key to understanding that work and cannot be discounted. Note here that again in this series of essays, rather than an explicit acknowledgment of Teilhard's Christ-centered worldview, we see a nod toward some ambiguous cosmic mysticism.

According to Barbour, therefore, a process metaphysics that combines the fourth and fifth of his own classifications, that of Christian theology and process philosophy, consistently runs through all of Teilhard's works.[67] He argues that Teilhard has given us a genuine synthesis of scientific and religious insights rather than a natural theology derived from science alone or a Christian theology derived from revelation alone. Barbour's conclusion is that "in a day of increasing specialization and fragmentation, [Teilhard's] concern for the totality of man and his vision of a unified world may themselves be his most enduring contribution."[68]

In 1968 Ian Barbour was also found on the editorial advisory board of *Zygon: Journal of Religion and Science*, for which Ralph Wendell Berhoe was the editor.[69] The December 1968 issue of *Zygon* was completely dedicated to various interpretations of Teilhard and his work in light of both science and religion. The next two essays are both found in this issue. Additionally, Berhoe's editorial concerning this issue observed that the journal's purpose of integrating religious

66. It is interesting that Barbour plays the mystic note, as do several of these writers; in an age where mysticism has become much more "socially acceptable," to mark Teilhard as one is to almost immediately draw the attention of the reading public to his work. Also, Barbour comments that many have contrasted Teilhard's various works, considering *The Phenomenon* an example of natural theology aimed at the unbeliever and *The Divine Milieu* as Christian spiritual theological work intended for the believer. Although the differences exist, he argues, still he finds more unity among them than many acknowledge. He instead sees that this separation of audiences into "believers" and "unbelievers" is not simple, as most people are a mix of faith and doubt, belief and its opposite. Then, too, we know that Teilhard was also concerned with reconciling the scientific and the religious in his own life and thought. Teilhard and dualistic thought do not deal well together; ibid., 148.

67. Ibid., 138.

68. Ibid., 143.

69. Ralph Wendell Berhoe, ed., Editorial, *Zygon: A Journal of Religion and Science* 3, no. 4 (December 1968): 366. Berhoe was the director of the Center for Advanced Study in Theology and the Sciences, Meadville Theological School, Lombard College, Chicago.

"notions of what is meaningful and sacred" about humanity's identity with scientific notions about the world was not solely dependent upon Teilhard's synthesis. However, an evaluation of Teilhard was certainly "both a useful guide and a caution."

He continues to note that one scientific criticism of Teilhard was that his "theology" was not really scientific enough to make it credible. In this particular issue, the included transcript of a symposium on "Do Life Processes Transcend Physics and Chemistry?" raised a reverse criticism of *Zygon*'s purposes. Within the symposium it was suggested that science may be implicitly insufficient for handling theological questions. This suggestion was raised not by theologians, but scientists. What Berhoe fears is that if physics is unable to explain chemistry, nor chemistry biology, then perhaps the distinctive barriers between disciplines are so high that what those on the board of the journal hope is without substance. In particular this implicates their belief that the sciences can be of possible assistance to even more distant disciplines—such as ethics or theology. If this is the case, then what does one do with someone like Teilhard? If nothing else, Berhoe concludes, the experience has taught the board members how difficult Teilhard's efforts at integrating the two sciences in a similar fashion were, as well as why his work has received such criticism.

Another of the essays to be discussed from this issue of *Zygon*, and the last in this series, is Alfred Stiernotte's "An Interpretation of Teilhard."[70] In this very thorough and lengthy essay Stiernotte, a professor of philosophy, summarizes the more important works of Teilhard as well as some of the commentaries, admirers, and critics in recent French and English literature.[71] Finally he examines scientific evaluations and criticisms. He too offers his own interpretation

70. Alfred Stiernotte, "An Interpretation of Teilhard: As Reflected in Recent Literature," *Zygon* 3, no. 4 (December 1968): 377–425. Stiernotte, a professor of philosophy, begins his essay by observing that Teilhard is enjoying a popularity seldom given a scientific scholar, particularly one who considers the implications of science as religion (377).

71. Stiernotte addresses basic studies, fundamental aspects, and controversial points, first from Roman Catholic sources but then from Protestant sources as well; "Interpretation of Teilhard."

of the Teilhardian system in an attempt to explain the reasons it has appealed to so many of differing philosophical and religious orientations.[72] In this essay we see again an acknowledgment of the incredible importance of a particular Christology for living Teilhard's thought, as well as the difficulties some had in accepting Teilhard's vision of the evolutive, Cosmic Christ.

In stressing Teilhard's importance and influence, Stiernotte suggests that Teilhard is difficult to understand for many because "one of the most significant academic shortcomings of our time is the trained mind of the specialist who does indeed know his own research but has not learned to leap over walls separating his from other specialties with the same agility as did Teilhard."[73] Stiernotte asserts in accord with Barbour's interpretation that Teilhard's system is not to be understood merely as a scientific, intellectual, or philosophical worldview; he too emphasizes Teilhard's mysticism, but implies it is a new type of mysticism, a mysticism of process rather than

72. Stiernotte acknowledges that the friendship and admiration Teilhard found in the likes of Julian Huxley and Theodosius Dobazhansky pay tribute to his mind and dedication. Even Mircea Eliade noted his significance: "At least one hundred volumes and many thousands of articles have been published all over the world in less than ten years, discussing—in most cases sympathetically—Teilhard de Chardin's ideas. If we take into consideration the fact that not even the most popular philosopher of this generation, J. P. Sartre, attained such a massive response after twenty-five years of activity, we must acknowledge the *cultural* significance of Teilhard's success"; Eliade, "Cultural Fashions and the History of Religions," in *The History of Religions: Essays in Divinity*, ed. Joseph M. Kitagawa, Mircea Eliade, and Charles H. Long (Chicago and London: University of Chicago Press, 1967), 1:32, quoted in Stiernotte, "An Interpretation of Teilhard," 377.

73. Stiernotte, "Interpretation of Teilhard," 380. One of those who admired Teilhard, according to Stiernotte, is Paul Tillich. Tillich wrote, "I happened to read Pierre Teilhard de Chardin's book, *The Phenomenon of Man*. It encouraged me greatly to know that an acknowledged scientist had developed ideas about the dimensions and processes of life so similar to my own. Although I cannot share his rather optimistic vision of the future, I am convinced by his description of the evolutionary processes in nature"; Tillich, *Systematic Theology* (Chicago: University of Chicago Press, 1963), 3:5. In fact, Stiernotte notes that volume 3 of Tillich's *Systematic Theology* contains "thirty-five pages which are strictly in accord with the general evolutionary view of reality"; Stiernotte, "Interpretation of Teilhard," 378. Additionally, Stiernotte comments that the number of societies dedicated to the study of Teilhard continues to increase, including among Marxist scholars such as Roger Garaudy. See, for example, Garaudy, *From Anathema to Dialogue* (New York: Herder and Herder, 1966), 48–54, for references to Teilhard.

that of a static vision, one of a communion with the universe, including the inorganic, the organic, humanity, and Christ. Christ here is "nothing less than the pervasiveness of altruistic love in self-sacrifice as fully as it is possible to reveal love in a man of our species living under existential conditions but maintaining unbroken his sense of communion with God as love."[74]

What has been the response of the Catholic world to this cosmic understanding? On the part of great theologians and philosophers, specifically those such as Maritain and Gilson, polished Thomists both, Stiernotte finds the reaction has been one of both mild admiration and great puzzlement at Teilhard's audacity of mingling the scientific, philosophical, and theological.[75]

Stiernotte suggests that the summary of *The Phenomenon of Man* found in *Masterpieces of Catholic Literature* explicates Teilhard's accomplishment well: "Perhaps the real "scandal" of Teilhard and *The Phenomenon of Man* lies in his attempt to achieve, in an evolutionary account, a solidly knit synthesis of the biological and spiritual worlds, two worlds which, despite the teachings of Christ, Paul, and many others in the Christian tradition, have continued to be regarded by Platonic-Cartesian dualism as isolated from each other."[76] Teilhard,

74. Stiernotte, "Interpretation of Teilhard," 388.

75. Ibid., 389. Stiernotte's thought is that Maritain especially appears to favor a philosophy of being over that of the philosophy of becoming that is implicit in a process theology such as Teilhard's. See, for example, James Collins, in "Maritain Asks Some Questions": "As for Teilhard, he had a poetic intuition of the sacred worth of created nature. But the Teilhardians substitute evolutionary becoming for being and subordinate all metaphysical and religious questions to the panchristizing and pancosmicizing process"; Collins, "Maritain Asks Some Questions," *America*, January 13, 1968, 32, quoted in Stiernotte, "Interpretation of Teilhard," 389.

76. Frank M. Magill, ed., *Masterpieces of Catholic Literature* (New York: Harper and Row, 1965), 1017–21, quoted in Stiernotte, "Interpretation of Teilhard," 391. In a similar fashion, Petro Bilaniuk of St. Michael's in Toronto is quoted in this essay as commenting that the opposition of many to Teilhard is a result of an underlying fear of violating the divine transcendence by exaggerating the divine immanence in the world: "They think that by minimizing immanence they will preserve transcendence. However, is it not possible to say that immanence and transcendence complement each other on the part of the absolutely simple pure act of the subsisting existence itself, the ground of being, that is God?"; Bilaniuk, "The Christology of Teilhard de Chardin," quoted in Robert J. O'Connell, SJ, ed., *Proceedings of the Teilhard Conference 1964* (New York: Human Energetics Institute, Fordham University, 1965), 113–15;

Stiernotte concedes, is definitely not a dualist, and this in itself—for both academy and church—is scandalous![77]

Catholic opposition to Teilhard, according to Stiernotte, has primarily centered on the criticism of Philippe de la Trinité. The heart of his disagreement with Teilhard, ironically for this book, lies in Teilhard's cosmic Christology: "No, the Teilhardian cosmo-anthropo-christogenesis does not develop Catholic dogma in a homogeneous and legitimate way. It perverts it, it warps it."[78] To such an accusation, de Lubac replies, "One thing at any rate is clear, that he [Philippe de la Trinité] denies to the glorified humanity of Christ the cosmic role which a number of commentators ... saw, as did Teilhard, in St. Paul's statement: a role which some first-rate theologians of today still attribute to him."[79] As Stiernotte neatly concludes in this essay, these arguments point out that an understanding of a cosmic Christology associated with divine immanence, as contrasted to a Christology of divine irruption associated with divine transcendence, seems to be the dividing line between those who favor Teilhard and those who do not.[80] Stiernotte suggests, as Teilhard had decades earlier, that they are perhaps not quite "ripe yet!"

---

note in Stiernotte, "Interpretation of Teilhard," 394. Stiernotte considers the whole volume (discussed in chapter 3 of this work) extremely informative.

77. In regard to this argument Stiernotte also suggests that the reader should especially note de Lubac's vindication of Teilhard's synthetic vision by reference to Cardinal Newman's *Idea of a University*; this discusses the freedom of inquiry into many diverse fields that is the raison d'être of a university; de Lubac, *Teilhard de Chardin: The Man and His Meaning*, 109–10, quoted in Stiernotte, "Interpretation of Teilhard," 395. He is also struck that de Lubac contends that Teilhard's approach is more existential than is usually assumed, involving his personal witness to his all-encompassing faith in the cosmic Christ; de Lubac, *Teilhard de Chardin: The Man and His Meaning*, 143, quoted in Stiernotte, "Interpretation of Teilhard," 395.

78. Philippe de la Trinité, *Rome et Teilhard de Chardin* (Paris: Librairie Arthème Fayard, 1964), 125–26; quoted in Stiernotte, "Interpretation of Teilhard," 395. The translation is Stiernotte's; the original French is "Non, la cosmo-anthropo-christogénèse teilhardienne ne développe pas le dogme catholique de manière homogène ni légitime, elle le fausse, elle le gauchit. Les eaux vives ne gardent plus leur pureté."

79. De Lubac, *Teilhard de Chardin: The Man and His Meaning*, 53, quoted in Stiernotte, "Interpretation of Teilhard," 396. Stiernotte includes among those who recognized this "Père Ferdinand Prat, Père Joseph Huby, and Père Benoit." "St. Paul's statement," to which de Lubac refers, is the Pauline basis for the cosmic Christ found in Colossians 1:16: "For by him were all things created, that are in heaven, and that are in earth, visible and invisible.... All things were created by him and for him."

80. Stiernotte, "Interpretation of Teilhard," 396.

In conclusion, Stiernotte nods toward a book review by Peter C. Hodgson concerning Teilhard with which he agrees.[81] The two concur that the thought of Teilhard is likely to grow in the next decade for the following reasons, none of which will be surprising to readers of this work: (1) recent developments in Catholic theology, including many of the documents of Vatican II, which cannot be understood without reference to Teilhard; (2) the recognition by Protestants that eschatology, which is a leitmotif in influential present-day Protestant circles, is also at the center of Teilhard's hope-filled thought; (3) the contribution of Teilhard "to the encounter between theology and natural science, the possibilities of which have by no means been exhausted."[82]

PUBLICATIONS CONCERNING THE UTILIZATION OF TEILHARD'S SPIRITUALITY

The next four publications discussed in this chapter consider from different perspectives what is of value for the spiritual growth of the ordinary person in what Teilhard has written, particularly in an age of upheaval. The first two again address the question of the value of the secular, particularly that of daily effort, as elucidated by Teilhard. The subsequent essay by Sheets queries how Teilhard's thought might contribute to understanding the evolutionary development of Roman Catholic doctrine in the era of Vatican II. Finally, Donald Gray considers the ancient question of mystical union from within the lens of Teilhard's spirituality.

As explained in the introduction to this book, the emphasis of Teilhard upon the secular is a result of his incarnational worldview; the reader should note, however, that in making use of Teilhard's

81. Peter Hodgson, "Religion in Life" (Review) (Autumn 1966): 617–21; quoted in Stiernotte, "Interpretation of Teilhard," 405. Hodgson's review concerned three books about Teilhard already mentioned in this work: Michael H. Murray, *The Thought of Teilhard de Chardin: An Introduction* (New York: Seabury, 1966); Robert J. O'Connell, ed., *Proceedings of the Teilhard Conference, 1964* (New York: Human Energetics Institute, Fordham University, 1965); and Christopher Mooney, SJ, *Teilhard de Chardin and the Mystery of Christ* (New York: Harper and Row, 1967).

82. Hodgson, "Religion in Life," 621, quoted in Stiernotte, "Interpretation of Teilhard," 405.

thought in this direction these four scholars do not explicitly acknowledge this underlying foundation in their essays.

The interest in Teilhard by at least some portion of the "whole new theological generation" referenced earlier, particularly in regard to the value of the secular or work in the world, is partially illuminated in Robert Francoeur's book review of Teilhard's *Writings in Time of War*.[83] As Francoeur writes, "The idealistic college grad of today does not find much challenge in making a prettier 'Princess' telephone or a more complex satellite." So, despite better salaries and attractive working conditions, people of a certain generation are "opting out" of the traditional workforce. To counteract this, Francoeur suggests that companies in the late 1960s were increasingly emphasizing the global, one might even say "cosmic," nature of the work in order to appeal to their higher nature.

Francoeur observes that a recent conversation with a friend along these lines brought home to him the appeal of Teilhard for many. "The 'Teilhardian fad' has given way to a more substantial interest simply because Teilhard has struck at the very heart of the crisis of mankind today in a prophetic language that is understandable to today's youth—a youthful spirit, by the way, that has little to do with chronological age." What is the crisis? It can be elucidated in the question as to what, actually, is the purpose of life. Do the efforts of daily work matter? Are they and the suffering of everyday, secular life actually worth something?

Francoeur can only hope that at least a few of these young people discovered in *The Divine Milieu* answers to these questions and the realization along with Teilhard that "creation is not finished. It continues still more magnificently ... we serve to complete it, even by the humblest work of our hands. That is, ultimately, the meaning and value of our acts."[84]

On a very different note is an essay by Sister Viterbo McCarthy,

83. Robert Francoeur, "What Teilhard Is Saying," review of *Writings in Time of War*, by Pierre Teilhard de Chardin, *National Catholic Reporter*, 1968, 11. No additional publication data is available.

84. Teilhard de Chardin, *Divine Milieu*, 62.

CSJ, which appeared in the *Journal of Religion and Science.*[85] Although it was not the original intent, this essay appears to attempt to address those issues raised by the young people mentioned in Francoeur's book review.

As had other social scientists, McCarthy was interested in exploring Teilhard's work for wisdom appropriate to recent advances in the behavioral sciences. She comments that Teilhard's synthetic perspective is especially congenial for psychology, a synthetic discipline itself, where the natural and biological sciences, social sciences, and humanities meet.[86] She believes that Teilhard's thought is interesting for psychologists, as it offers a deeper understanding of the contemporary religious dimension inherent in the daily life of lay people. An essay highlighting this would seem to be especially appropriate during these post–Vatican II years, when a new emphasis on universal holiness had recently been introduced; in addition, McCarthy comments that the quest for holiness is especially urgent during the current time of social upheaval.[87]

In regard to the relational life, McCarthy comments that not only were deep friendships characteristic of and necessary to Teilhard's life, so too was his understanding that love of others is essential even though it exposes us to hurt. Despite the probability of suffering, however, Teilhard repeatedly suggests that human love will evolve into yet nobler expressions on the cosmic dimension.[88]

85. Viterbo McCarthy, CSJ, "Maturity: Pierre Teilhard de Chardin and Gordon W. Allport," *Journal of Religion and Health* 7, no. 2 (April 1968): 141–50.

86. McCarthy, "Maturity," 142.

87. What are Teilhard's contributions to this conversation? The Jesuit psychologist W. W. Meissner wrote, almost in answer to Francoeur's earlier comments, that "no one in contemporary thought has better grasped and expressed the realities of the Christian life in the world than Pierre Teilhard de Chardin." In particular, Meissner refers to Teilhard's focus upon detachment from egoism and subsequent attachment instead to all that is good, progressive, and unifying when accomplished through daily work, "provided a man gives himself to it faithfully and without a rebellion"; Meissner, *Foundations for a Psychology of Grace* (Glen Rock, N.J.: Paulist Press, 1966), 5 and 222, quoted in McCarthy, "Maturity," 142.

88. McCarthy comments here, "As these new forms of relationship evolve, they will demand enlarged hearts to match the evolving noosphere. Love will increasingly demand more of humanity. As the human personality grows, a synthesis of the masculine and feminine will also occur, and in each person this will occur in a unique fashion as their life progresses. However, eventually both components must be united

McCarthy observes that in Teilhard's own life this "high degree of insight" was accomplished through "an extraordinary and unique integration of the data of science, philosophy and theology." The result was the ever-deepening conviction that the best of everyday human effort and achievement would persist, as "a harmony, a particular expression of love, the enchanting complexity of a smile or a look ... for the Incarnate God did not come to diminish the magnificent responsibility and splendid ambition that is ours of becoming our own self."[89] Note, however, that McCarthy did not attempt to explicate what this "unique integration" in Teilhard's life might look like or explicitly mention the Christocentric nature of that integration. Nor does she acknowledge that Teilhard might suggest this was the means by which the Paschal mystery was playing itself out in the contemporary society of the moment. Still, McCarthy urges that surely reflection upon Teilhard's wisdom can only continue to aid in "building the earth," even in the midst of the challenging era that was then occurring. As chapter 6 suggested, however, those seriously willing to stop and consider the application of this wisdom to the "signs of the times" and those who were able to comprehend the origin of Teilhard's vision appeared to be all too few and far between during these years.

A very different, very Catholic essay was that which came from John Sheets of Marquette.[90] It is included here primarily because of its uniqueness, both due to the author's attempts to make use of Teilhard's Christology in the fashion he does and because that use is so appropriate for this particular era in light of Vatican II.

Sheets's primary question is whether it is possible to provide an answer to the problem of development of Catholic dogma through the lens of Teilhard's evolutionary principles.[91] Sheets would ar-

in love, whether this is achieved in marriage, in friendship, or within the family itself"; McCarthy, "Maturity," 144.

89. Teilhard de Chardin, *Divine Milieu*, 33, quoted in McCarthy, "Maturity," 147.

90. John Sheets, SJ, "Teilhard and Development of Dogma," *Theological Studies* 30, no. 3 (Summer 1969): 445–62. The substance of this essay formed the contents of a paper delivered at a symposium on Teilhard held at Marquette University on the weekend of November 1, 1968.

91. Note that Teilhard himself never proffered any theory of development based on these principles. Sheets believes that we should be able, however, to validly apply

gue that the whole process of development can be explicated as an expansion of the power "to see." Through the lens of Teilhard's Christology constantly more opportunity exists to see revealed truth, where the "act of seeing and the truth which is seen unite and reinforce each other in constantly complexifying new synthesis."[92]

As has been shown, Teilhard was very concerned with the prevailing pessimism, despair, and aimlessness of the modern world. His goal was to give humanity a guarantee beyond final death. In his theory that "everything which rises must converge," he found a corroboration of the gospel message of hope. But Christian hope for the church must be primarily focused on the assurance of Christ to the church that death will not prevail. In Teilhard's case he emphasizes that promise is cosmic in nature for the "church," for it offers hope for the entire world, not simply a small portion of it. For this reason, Sheets contends, the church and particularly its teaching role must be seen as part of the gift of Christ to all humankind; similarly, the church itself must recognize its global and cosmic role and act upon this accordingly. These are principles that will not be foreign to those who closely read *Gaudium et spes.* They are, one might argue, a corroboration of the statements of many that Teilhard's thought was quite influential in the writing of this document. At the time of this essay, however, the church found itself greatly struggling with the means by which to actualize this document, perhaps particularly

---

them to Christianity, and in particular to the phenomenon that we call the "development of dogma."

92. Sheets, "Teilhard and Development of Dogma," 459. Another fundamental principle in Teilhard is the idea of seeing, and as has already been stated, he sums up the purpose of his work in terms of the meaning of seeing. For Sheets, so it goes with the church, also. The church is necessary, Sheets writes, for it is the church that is to see where Christ leads, and to teach with a God-given authority what is to be believed. In the church Teilhard sees the phylum that "incorporates the suranimating principles of the risen Christ and transmits the life of Christ to the world" (462). The ultimate meaning of the church is to *see,* to see with the same power that belonged to Christ, and to unfold Christ to the world; the church therefore is "to transmit Christ both as Seer and as seen." If it does not progress in its ability to see, acknowledging there is increasingly more to see, it will succumb to the law of entropy. The object of faith must be made more explicit and unfolded; this unfolding is that of a person, Christ, who suranimates the church with and through his life. The unfolding of Christ correlates with a development of the power to see the mystery of Christ in a clearer fashion; ibid. 455–57.

in the United States, where the still-existing if struggling Americanist minority would likely take it along a particular trajectory.

The last publication concerning Teilhard's spirituality to be discussed in this section is one that considered his concepts of mystical union. *The One and the Many*, by Donald Gray, purports to have its genesis in an original and unusual reading of Teilhard. The author attempts to investigate systematically the whole question of unity, or creative union, that he would claim predominates in Teilhard's thought and spirituality. As the concept of union is central to most mystical theologies, his reading is quite appropriate for and also reflects what was, as we have discussed, one of the primary spiritual concerns of the time.

By studying Teilhard's early writings from 1916 to 1927 or so, Gray draws into focus Teilhard's own attempt to work out the metaphysical understructure of his thought on this subject during these years, which Gray contends were crucial to his later work. In this, Gray claims that Teilhard's central concern is the problem of the one and the many.

This problem may be classical in nature, but by viewing it through the lens of evolution, Teilhard brings a fresh perspective. He sees evolution as a movement from the many to the one, through convergence by way of creative union, yet in such a way that through the energy of love inherent in that union, many become one without simultaneously losing their identity.

The process of convergent unification leads to the emergence of new possibilities; hence, through the gradual process of unification, the world is continually being created and re-created. In this emphasis upon creative unity as a solution to the classical problem of the one and the many, Gray argues that Teilhard finds a way of unifying science, philosophy, and religion while retaining the unique distinctiveness of each. Additionally, as those whose study includes the great mystics would argue, it is this that is at the heart of Teilhard's mystical spirituality. As with the previous text, however, one must ask if Gray considered how this process was transpiring within U.S. society during these years, particularly when it appeared that dispersion, rather than convergence, was the primary form of movement.

Additionally, note that Gray's argument, although it acknowledges Teilhard's trinitarianism, does not make much mention of his very personal Christocentric spirituality. Gray's focus is far more upon a generic, cosmic mysticism.

PUBLICATIONS OF A SECULAR NATURE

The next three books, and the last discussed in this chapter, are each unique in their focus for this time period. The fact of their publication in itself shows both the desire of those who appreciated Teilhard to share his thought more widely and his ongoing appeal for a diverse variety of people. Each attempts to place Teilhard within particular contexts for specific audiences, whether these are Christian humanists, those comfortable with the new technologies of the era, or the educated, intellectual youth of the time. It would seem that these groups combined would constitute a very large percentage of those who are reading Teilhard's works. With these as the intended audience, however, it is not surprising that none of these publications are in any manner concerned with Teilhard's Christology or incarnational spirituality. Nor should we be startled that so few of those who read Teilhard, particularly through these sorts of publications, recognized the importance of this Christocentrism for him.

First, the Lutheran theologian Philip Hefner offers his book *The Promise of Teilhard* specifically in hopes that it will shift the focus of many from Teilhard's theology to his efforts as a "Christian Humanist."[93] As Martin Marty suggests in the foreword, Hefner offers his distinctive focus by locating Teilhard "as the newest-fangled representative of an old-fashioned category, that of the Christian humanist."[94] Hefner believes that Christians must come to terms with scientific humanism, and Christian theology must become comfortable with the "possibilities offered by evolutionary and developmental processes."

This work paints Teilhard not chiefly as a Christian "theologian," but as one simply attempting to discern meaning in the age in which

93. Philip Hefner, *The Promise of Teilhard: The Meaning of the Twentieth Century in Christian Perspective* (Philadelphia and New York: J. B. Lippincott, 1970).

94. Martin Marty, quoted in Hefner, *Promise of Teilhard*, 5.

he lived and worked.[95] With this in mind, then, Hefner's book offers a portrait of Teilhard as first a human, one who was "fully man," open to a wide range of experiences, and one whose work reflects that range of experiences. Additionally, Teilhard was able to unify those experiences into his personality and religious life: he was, as Hefner names it, "the antithesis of the compartmentalized man."[96]

This integration is why, however, the genre of his work, and consequently its significance, are so difficult to classify. Hefner's argument is that someone who was less concerned with bringing to bear that integrity and the full ramification of his life experiences upon his theories, perhaps one more concerned with intellectual and ecclesial specialization, would be much easier to understand, classify, and critique. At the same time, however, this broad acceptance of so many facets of life enables his work to find a home in the lives of disparate groups of people—those in the academy, housewives, young Jesus freaks and hippies, politicians, Bell Telephone scientists, and Montessori teachers—as the vast array of publications in these last two chapters show.[97] As a result of this way of being and living, he is a role model for the contemporary people of the present time.

Taking all this into consideration, Hefner contends that Teilhard is "best understood as a man who built a number of comprehensive theories for the purpose of clarifying the meaning of the contemporary history he was living through."[98] He was, in other words, "an interpreter of current events on a grand scale."

95. Hefner explains that although Teilhard might be considered to "do" theology, and his first works tended to be critiqued by his compatriots who were overwhelmingly professional theologians, we cannot ignore the fact that immense numbers of people today outside the realm of professional theology appreciate and are attempting to live what he teaches. One could include here the audiences for many of the books discussed in this chapter.

96. Hefner, *Promise of Teilhard,* 16. By 2005, rather than humanism, Hefner was emphasizing instead the poetic Eucharistic image of Teilhard's thought. As Hefner then wrote, Teilhard's evolution is all about Christ and the emergence of Christ in the universe; faith itself concerns a focus on unification with Christ. This implies grasping "every opportunity of growing greater and in accepting every summons to die." In this, growth and death are mystically conjoined; they are then "our access to unification with Christ and God"; from Hefner, "Teilhard de Chardin and His Relevance for Today," *Woodstock Report* 82 (June 2005).

97. Hefner, *Promise of Teilhard,* 26.

98. Ibid., 28.

The last two books discussed in this chapter are lighthearted and obviously aimed at a young, modern audience. Both present at least the basic rubrics, if not the underlying Christological themes, of Teilhard's thought as found in *The Phenomenon*. *Survival*, the first, is a most unusual book, one developed by the Phenomenon of Man Project out of San Francisco and published as a spiral-bound paperback in 1970.[99] The book is titled "Survival" because, as the authors state, the final segment of *The Phenomenon of Man* concerns the future of life, or "survival," as Teilhard calls it.

Paralleling *The Phenomenon* itself, the remainder of *Survival* is divided into four primary chapters of "PreLife," "Life," "Thought," and "Survival."[100] This part of the study guide "builds" toward and ends with the words "God-Omega!" An epilogue follows on the "Christian Phenomenon," itself consisting of eighty-eight illustrated study points. Point number 27, for example, comments that "people often think they are honoring Christianity when they reduce it to a gentle humanitarianism," only to be followed by "those who fail to see in Christianity the most cosmic of hopes completely fail to comprehend its 'mysteries.'" The authors include a series of three explanations as to why Christianity is crucial, as well as an extended treatise on the value of Christian love, concluding with the note that "at the present moment Christianity is the only current of thought which is sufficiently audacious and sufficiently progressive to lay hold of the world . . . in an embrace where faith and hope reach their fulfillment in love."[101]

Despite this, an editorial comment at the end of this epilogue points out that, although Teilhard was a devout Christian, he recognized the value of the other major world religions. "Hence," the

99. Phenomenon of Man Project (POM), *Survival: A Study Guide for Teilhard's "The Phenomenon"* (San Francisco: The Project, 1970). The previous chapter mentioned a joint project of the ATA with the POM Project to develop a slide show that explained Teilhard's thought. I was unable to determine whether this book is actually the published slide show, although it is likely this is the case.

100. It begins (with no preface or introduction) with an alphabetic glossary of Teilhardian terms that might be of use for the perusal of Teilhard's work, and the chapters are themselves divided into a total of some 510 study points, each illustrated with an appropriate line drawing or diagram.

101. Ibid., 137.

authors write, "it is perfectly proper for someone not in the Christian tradition to interpret Teilhard's remarks on the relationship between the Omega Point and Christ in light of his own religious tradition," a statement that certainly reflects the then strong emphasis upon ecumenical effort.[102] The focus of the book, one can therefore conclude, is neither the academic nor the devout Christian, nor one specifically interested in Teilhard's Christology, but most likely the somewhat educated young person who wishes to understand, without too much effort, just what the fuss is concerning this man Teilhard. Although an entire chapter is included that explores the Christian basis of Teilhard's theories, the book does so superficially and at a distance.

A more unique book and the last one discussed here is *The Vision of Teilhard Programmed for VIPs*, by Thomas Alexander.[103] The overleaf explains that this is "my thoughts about the thoughts of Pierre Teilhard de Chardin with the fixed idea to 'program' them for V.I.P.'s and all others, who don't have much time available to bother with things like these." This explanation is signed by the author, noted as "The Programmer." Like the previous publication, this obviously is a book aimed at a particular portion of a most-likely younger population, one aware of and comfortable with the new data-processing technologies just becoming available within universities if not yet to the general public. It appears that the author's focus on Teilhard's work is primarily through the lens of evolution and generic "feel good" spirituality, one meant to appeal specifically to this audience.

Alexander's goal is to "program" Teilhard's work for those who do not understand it. He wishes to present his "philosophy" in such a short and easy form that the ordinary human brain can under-

102. Ibid. The entire author's note states, "Teilhard lived most of his life in close association with Buddhists, Mohammedhans, Confucianists, and agnostics. While he was always a devout Christian, he still realized the truth that these various traditions contained. Hence, it is perfectly proper for someone not in the Christian tradition to interpret Teilhard's remarks on the relationship between the Omega Point and Christ in terms of his own religious tradition. If Teilhard's analysis of cosmic evolution remains faithful to phenomena as they are in truth, then his synthesis should be open enough to incorporate and embrace truth wherever it may be found."

103. Thomas Alexander, *The Vision of Teilhard de Chardin Programmed for V.I.P.'s* (New York: Vantage, 1969).

stand it in a fairly short time ... in "that amount of time which busy people are willing to spend reading on trains, at the seashore or between other 'important things."[104] This is important to do, as Teilhard definitely has "something to say, something for which most of us are searching, something to believe, to 'hang on to' in this new, seemingly quite messy world of ours."

Alexander calls Teilhard's philosophy "The Beatification of Evolution," one that sanctifies everyday life, making it "not only logical but in a way beautiful and holy." This, he argues, is exactly what the people of the time need and want. As is hopefully already quite apparent, the tone and focus of the book are quite different from any of those already discussed in this chapter. In addition to "programs" in Fortran situated throughout, the author has included numerous drawings and diagrams to visually explain Teilhard's thought to a particular segment.

The book itself ends with the quote, "So, my dear sick pessimists, you are wrong once more. This phenomenon on planet Earth is going to make it. According to Pierre Teilhard de Chardin all that one has to do is to be willing to take off the blindfold and *see.*"[105] Nowhere, however, does Alexander suggest that Teilhard's *seeing* may consist of anything of a Christian or even religious nature.[106]

104. Ibid., 15. The introduction, which unquestionably sets the tone for what follows, begins with the sentence "It was a cold night in November of 1964, and I was out on a "first date" with a nice cute blonde." This prologue continues with Alexander's story of how that evening he attempted to explain to the blonde that his search for existential "TRUTH" had led him in various directions, yet none seemed to suffice. After a time of listening to all this, eventually she asked if the author had ever read the works of Teilhard, "for she thought he may have the answer to some of my questions." Although he did not at the time take her seriously, the next time he was browsing in a bookstore, he picked up a copy of *The Future of Man* and ended up missing his train.

105. Ibid., 78.

106. As a further example of how removed this tome is from Teilhard's Christological foundations, Alexander ends his book with an epilogue of "my own short answers to 3 basic questions." These include an explanation of what "Teilhardism" is, whether "Teilhardism" is a religious idea, and the next step for readers who are now able to "see on a Universal level" and who wish further ideas as to how to live a mystical life in a secular world. So, is "Teilhardism" a religious idea? To this the author replies, "This is a question of language–terminology.... When someone says 'Christ,' 'Buddha' or 'The Scientific Evolution of Man' these things mean different concepts to each individual." Similarly, the inquiry of how to live a mystical life receives the

Without a doubt, this was a book written in a very particular time, for a very specific culture. That it *was* written and published, however, exemplifies the fact that at least some portion of the population attempting to make sense of Teilhard's thought was quite comfortable with it being stripped of any vestige of his Christology.

FINAL THOUGHTS

As has been detailed in the last two chapters, 1968–71 were irretrievably difficult years for the United States. North American society was increasingly polarized by war, assassinations, riots, and overall violence. Rather than evolving unity, the norm seemed instead to be disintegration.

For many these were concurrently the years in which doubt about the optimistic Teilhardian worldview increased exponentially. Teilhard himself was quite adamant in stating that one must choose either absolute optimism or absolute pessimism, as he saw no valid middle ground, for "only, in support of hope, are there rational invitations to an act of faith."[107] Later in his life Teilhard said that he limited himself to bringing out the positive and did not find it necessary to provide the negative, protesting in a typically intuitive fashion that "surely [such things] were obvious enough. I have assumed that what I have omitted could nevertheless be seen."[108]

This chapter examined two dozen essays and books about Teilhard published during this time by various scholars, some of whom did understand this of Teilhard. The few who did knew that Teilhard's hope was not predicated upon naïve optimism or the anticipated final results of scientific evolution and human progress, but rather on both his relationship with a God who is Love, as well as his incarnational worldview. These scholars and authors asserted that what Teilhard was doing was a *ressourcement* of the Pauline tradition associated with the Cosmic Christ, one updated by modern scientific

response, "All the rest has to do is to try to get motivated for life to a degree to avoid an obvious suicide."

107. Teilhard de Chardin, *Phenomenon of Man*, 233.

108. Teilhard de Chardin, *Divine Milieu*, 311.

knowledge concerning paleontology and evolution and transmitted through a mystical lens in a manner that spoke to the needs of a young, contemporary, and secular world. Eschatology and evolution in this model were understood as Christocentric, oriented toward the Omega Point of love. Therefore, those who knew to see this, those who were in Teilhard's own words "ripe," could not help but have hope, even through the darkest days of the late 1960s. Those who grasped Teilhard's Christocentric focus also appeared to realize that to expect to bypass the confusion and suffering encountered along the path to the new forms of life slowly evolving in U.S. society was impossible, for these were obligatory if difficult aspects of a lived Paschal mystery. When this inherent component of a spiritual life was understood, either in the case of an individual person or a society, then ambiguity, sorrow, and even death could be tolerated and employed as a springboard for new growth. Difficulty and paradox might be inevitable, yet they were not the final word.

Still, not too many seemed to comprehend this essential component of Teilhard's thought. Indeed, that some of these publications exist is a commentary on the hypothesis that few who wrote on Teilhard's thought during these years had a Christological understanding of his work. Instead, most were eager to continue to focus on a reductionist use of his theories for secular purposes, particularly the further study of scientific evolution or the future of technology; others made use of his thought for process theology, psychology, and sociology, or as a schema to investigate a general global mysticism or humanism. In the end, it appears that these latter forms of exploration of Teilhard's thought predominated during the decade that immediately followed.[109]

109. See, for example, *ATA*, 42: "It was agreed that the first wave of enthusiasm of the early 1960s had run its course, but that Teilhard's dynamic influence was still germinating within the minds of both religious and non-religious persons and that it had a role to play not only in shaping the basis of individual beliefs but also in the general intellectual and religious reappraisal of the total world view."

CONCLUSION

CONCLUSION

THIS BOOK has discussed how it was that Pierre Teilhard de Chardin, visionary priest, paleontologist, and writer, significantly impacted the United States between the years of 1959 and 1972. The focus has been on the U.S. reception of Teilhard's work during these years. This period, also the decade of the counterculture, the Second Vatican Council, and the dissolution of the immigrant subculture of the church in the United States, were the years in which the first American scholars responded to his theology and so set the foundation for later interpretations.

The primary argument of this work was that the manner in which this reception occurred, including the intensity of this phenomenon, happened as it did at this particular point in the history of both the United States and the Catholic Church for several reasons. These include the confluence of the then-developing social and political milieu, the opening of the global Roman Catholic Church to the world through Vatican II, and unique developments within U.S. Christian theology. Additionally, as these social and historical events unfolded within U.S. culture during these dozen years, the manner in which Teilhard was read as well as the aspects of his thought that were especially deemed of value changed.

At various times Teilhard's work became a carrier for an almost Americanist emphasis upon progress, energy, and hope; at other times, his teleological understanding of the value of suffering and exile moved to center stage. Teilhard wrote concerning humanity's desire for the divine and strove to place that desire for unity within the context of both religion and science. In the end, it was his attempt to bridge the divide between the secular and the sacred and to place this within his unique Christological vision, a vision that in itself positioned Paul's Cosmic Christ within the context of evolutionary theory, that remains of value today. It is this attempt that has had, and that continues to have, impact today, especially upon U.S. Catholic theology. In regard to the reception of Teilhard at the conclusion of the time period discussed within this work, an editorial in *America* in 1975 on the twentieth anniversary of Teilhard's death noted:

> Teilhard dealt in millennia; two decades therefore seems a pitifully short time in which to judge the success of so sweeping a venture. Indeed, his falling stock in the popular marketplace of ideas over the past 10 years tells us as much about ourselves as about him. Our buoyant optimism ran aground in the sands of a war we could not win abroad and of a peace we could not keep at home. Military debacles, political assassinations, race riots, government scandals, double-digit inflation and unemployment—such have been the dolorous milestones on the journey we began so bravely with Teilhard 15 years ago. We can be excused for feeling that Point Omega looks much further away now than it did then. But a sustaining vision is still necessary.[1]

Two years later Father Henri de Lubac wrote "a little book" on Teilhard in which his essential goal was to show the dissimilarity of what he calls a certain "Teilhardism" to Teilhard's actual thought. Even many of the serious authors, de Lubac believed, did not seem to grasp Teilhard's underlying synthetic Christocentric character. This foundational Christology he believed is the reason "Teilhard found scarcely any hearing anymore."[2] Instead, de Lubac argued, a

1. "The Teilhard Phenomenon after 20 years," Editorial, *America,* April 12, 1975, 2.

2. Henri de Lubac, *At the Service of the Church: Henri de Lubac Reflects on the Circumstances that Occasioned His Writings,* trans. Anne Elizabeth Englund (San Francisco: Ignatius Press, 1998), 153. *Teilhard Posthume: Réflexions et Souvenirs* was published by Fayard in 1977 in Paris.

"pan-critical, pulverizing mentality" reigned, "crushing" everything else potentially possible.[3]

A while after this de Lubac also wrote that having published so many works on Teilhard explicating his work, not to mention his participation in conferences and dissertations directed on the same subject, he felt he had well contributed to the recognition that Teilhard was "a true religious and a faithful Catholic." Perhaps as a result of this, however, de Lubac lamented, people have lost interest in Teilhard. He was no longer either "a scandal or one who could easily be derided for heretical notions." Additionally, Teilhard's characteristics and thought, de Lubac noted, are quite contrary to the "critical, analytical, pulverizing mentality," the "anti-intellectualism," and excessive individualism so rampant everywhere. His thought was at its heart absolutely counter to the "anti-establishmentarianism" prevalent from the late 1960s forward. Teilhard was, instead, "hyper-Catholic." Very few, he believed, have perceived the historical importance of Teilhard's effort to create a "spiritual interpretation of universal evolution that featured the 'transcendence of man, the value of the personal being, freedom, openness to God, and most importantly, consummation in Christ.'"[4]

From the very halls that twenty years earlier had lambasted him came the glimmerings of understanding at the centennial of Teilhard's birth. Consider this quote from the front-page article by Cardinal Agostino Casaroli in *l'Osservatore Romano*:

> What our contemporaries will undoubtedly remember, beyond the difficulties of conception and deficiencies of expression in this audacious attempt to reach a synthesis, is the testimony of the coherent life of a man possessed by Christ in the depths of his soul. He was concerned with honoring both faith and reason, and anticipated the response to John Paul II's appeal: "Be not afraid, open, open wide to Christ the doors of the immense domains of culture, civilization, and progress."[5]

3. De Lubac notes that the quoted phrases are from von Balthasar, and it appears that both here refer to the critical theory of the Frankfurt School.

4. De Lubac, *At the Service of the Church,* 110. De Lubac also notes that it was already at that time necessary, in order to truly understand Teilhard's purpose, to historically contextualize the religious France of around 1900 and the "positivist, antireligious mentality" that then dominated.

5. "Cardinal Casaroli praises Teilhard de Chardin on behalf of John Paul II."

Numerous years later, in 2007, Cardinal Christoph Schoenborn of Austria wrote that "hardly anyone else has tried to bring together the knowledge of Christ and the idea of evolution [as Teilhard] has done ... the fascination which Teilhard exercised for an entire generation stemmed from his radical method of looking at science and Christian faith together."[6]

Finally, Pope Benedict XVI noted in a homily that an understanding of the sacred teleology of secular matter as it participates in evolution toward the Cosmic Christ could be at least in part attributed to Teilhard: "This is also the great vision of Teilhard de Chardin: in the end we shall achieve a true cosmic liturgy, where the cosmos becomes a living host."[7]

During the years discussed in this work, it was those who grasped Teilhard's attempts through his integrated Christological vision, to bridge the gap between nature and grace and religion and science, as well as those who appreciated his embrace of the everyday material world, who were best able to carry his thought beyond the difficult days at the end of this time period. Although the number of publications concerning Teilhard may have decreased, his thought certainly did not consequently die.

Instead there would continue to be those who saw the possibilities of his work not only for the emerging laity of the church living and struggling in the world, but also in those political organizations, such as the United Nations, that were attempting to achieve

---

This was written by Cardinal Casaroli at the request of Pope John Paul II on June 10, 1981; accessed November 9, 2013, at https://www.traditioninaction.org/ProgressivistDoc/A_020_CasaroliTeilhard.htm.

6. The entire quote is: "Hardly anyone else has tried to bring together the knowledge of Christ and the idea of evolution as the scientist (paleontologist) and theologian Fr. Pierre Teilhard de Chardin, S.J. has done.... His fascinating vision ... has represented a great hope, the hope that faith in Christ and a scientific approach to the world can be brought together.... These brief references to Teilhard cannot do justice to his efforts. The fascination which Teilhard de Chardin exercised for an entire generation stemmed from his radical manner of looking at science and Christian faith together"; Cardinal Christoph Schoenborn, *Creation, Evolution, and a Rational Faith* (San Francisco: Ignatius Press, 2007), 141.

7. Pope Benedict XVI, *Homily for Vespers at the Cathedral of Aosta*, July 24, 2009, http://www.vatican.va/holy_father/benedict_xvi/homilies/2009/documents/hf_ben-xvi_hom_20090724_vespri-aosta_en.html.

the unity that Teilhard thought inevitable.[8] If, at least temporarily, Teilhard's spirituality was deemed inadequate, too optimistic, or too Christocentric for the general population, in other ways his influence lived on.

One area in which it survived is the popular culture that, already starting in the late 1960s, developed around it. As was noted earlier, even then, in the wide variety of topics and approaches found in Teilhard conferences, anthologies, and articles, one notices the diverse application of his thought. It is therefore, perhaps, no surprise that those in the performing and visual arts saw possibilities as well. As Ewert Cousins remarked several years later, "The thought of Teilhard has become a major force in the intellectual world. It has attracted the attention of a wide spectrum of professional groups: scientists and theologians, psychiatrists and city planners, litterateurs and technologists."[9] Several examples of those who carried Teilhard's evolutionary Christological thought into popular culture and the arts would include the composer Edmund Rubbra, the architect Paolo Soleri, who was the creator of Arcosanti, and the sculptor Henry Setter, who created the "Omega Point" sculpture at the University of Dayton.[10]

8. On September 20–21, 1983, an international colloquium in honor of Teilhard was held at the United Nations headquarters in New York in conjunction with the opening of the 38th General Assembly. The findings were published in 1985 to celebrate forty years of the UN and the International Year of Peace; Leo Zonneveld, ed., *Humanity's Quest for Unity: A United Nations Teilhard Colloquium* (The Hague: Marananda, 1985). During the first plenary session of this colloquium, the first International Teilhard Award was presented to Robert Muller, who worked with the United Nations for over forty years and was secretary of the Economic and Social Council. His "Five Teilhardian Enlightenments" was a reflection on the United Nations within biological evolution, based upon his most basic conviction that life is divine. One of the enlightenments speaks of spirituality as "the ultimate key to our earthly fate in time and in space"; Robert Muller, *New Genesis* (New York: Doubleday, 1984), 159–68. Muller was first exposed to Teilhard's thought through Emmanuel de Breauvery, who worked for the Natural Resources Division of the United Nations and who lived with Teilhard in New York; Robert Muller, *And Most of All They Taught Me Happiness* (New York: Doubleday, 1978), 113–17.

9. T. Ewert Cousins, quoted in Alice Valle Knight, *The Meaning of Teilhard de Chardin: A Primer* (Old Greenwich, Conn.: Devin-Adair, 1974), xi.

10. Edmund Rubbra was an English composer whose work was extensively performed in the United States. It is especially his "Hommage à Teilhard de Chardin," *Eighth Symphony Opus 132*, written in the late 1960s and first performed in 1971, that

Another direction in which Teilhard's thought would be used beginning in the 1970s was in ecospirituality and the environmental movement. People like Thomas Berry employed Teilhard's work to speak about the story of the universe and "deep ecology."[11] Berry would ultimately write the first of the American Teilhard Association's edited *Teilhard Studies* volumes in 1978 with his "New Story." This work was followed by several other Teilhardian volumes over the years.[12] Berry's story of evolution, however, is purposefully not as exclusively Christocentric as is Teilhard's, as Berry's intent was to instead appeal not only to the Christian community, but beyond it.

---

is the focus here. The symphony very much reflects Rubbra's Roman Catholicism and is "in the deepest sense, a spiritual journey." Rubbra noted that "it was not part of my intention, even if possible, to translate these [Teilhard's] ideas into music, but they meet, I hope, in a like optimism"; quoted in liner notes from Robert Saxton, *Rubbra: Symphony No. 5, Symphony No. 8, Ode to the Queen*, Chandos, 1999. Paolo Soleri was an architect who was influenced by Teilhard in the development of his science of arcology, the fusion of architecture and ecology. His essay, "Myriad Specks/Teasing Grace," continues his reflections on urbanization in a Teilhardian spirit deprived of one ingredient of Teilhard's foundation—God: "My revisionism deals with a Teilhardian model that has been 'robbed' of God"; Soleri, "Myriad Specks, Teasing Grace," in *The Spirit of the Earth: A Teilhard Centennial*, ed. Jerome Perlinski (New York: Seabury, 1981), 132. He is especially known for Arcosanti, a planned community being built by students and volunteers in the Arizona desert some seventy miles from Phoenix. Even before beginning his sculpture, Setter had been greatly inspired for many years by the work of Teilhard. When in the late 1960s the directors of the Marianist University of Dayton began looking for a sculpture that would represent both its commitment to the future as a place of higher learning and its Catholic identity, they turned to the work of Teilhard and Setter. Setter created several other Teilhardian-inspired works of art during his lifetime.

11. Thomas Berry, CP (1914–2009) was a Passionist priest, cultural historian, and ecotheologian (although he preferred to call himself a cosmologist and geologian—or "Earth scholar"). Berry was president of the ATA from 1975 to 1987. Among his publications were "Teilhard in the Ecological Age," *Teilhard Studies*, no. 7 (Woodbridge, Conn.: American Teilhard Association and Anima Press, 1982); "Technology and the Healing of the Earth," *Teilhard Studies*, no. 14 (Woodbridge, Conn.: American Teilhard Association/Anima Press, 1985); *Dream of the Earth* (San Francisco: Sierra Club, 1988); *The Great Work: Our Way into the Future* (New York: Harmony Bell Tower, 2000); *The Sacred Universe: Earth Spirituality and Religion in the 21st Century*, ed., foreword Mary Evelyn Tucker (New York: Columbia University Press, 2009); and *The Christian Future and the Fate of Earth*, ed. Mary Evelyn Tucker and John Grim (Maryknoll, N.Y.: Orbis, 2009); as well as Berry and Thomas Clark, *Befriending the Earth: A Theology of Reconciliation between Humans and the Earth* (Mystic, Conn.: Twenty-Third Publications, 1991); and Berry and Brian Swimme, *The Universe Story* (San Francisco: HarperSanFrancisco, 1994). The *Teilhard Studies* series have since been continuously published semi-annually by the ATA.

12. "New Story" was published nearly a decade later by *CrossCurrents*. It was also included in the *Dream of the Earth* in 1988.

Teilhard's thought would also be appropriated by those in political circles. As one example, during the 1972 U.S. presidential election, Sargent Shriver was George McGovern's running mate as the Democratic Party's nominee for U.S. vice president, replacing Thomas Eagleton, who had resigned from the ticket. In contrast to his in-laws, Shriver's Catholicism appeared to be one of deep discipleship, and he treasured Teilhard's thought until his death.[13] In his first speech as candidate for vice president in 1972, Sargent Shriver closed his remarks in the most memorable of ways, electrifying the reporters present, by quoting Teilhard: "Someday, after mastering the winds, the waves, the tides, and gravity, we shall harness for God all the energies of love, and then, for a second time in the history of the world, man will have discovered fire."[14] Shriver continued to read and use Teilhard's concepts and to be involved in the leadership of global organizations throughout the remainder of his life.

With the dawning of the 1970s, some previously under the Teilhardian influence were undoubtedly stymied or dismayed by what they saw as the havoc of the last few years. This was likely particularly true of those who had not "caught" his particular brand of persevering faith. Still, Teilhard's thought had already so become part of the

13. As one former employee wrote, "During the Kennedy years and after, Shriver was hiring so many former nuns, priests and brothers that OEO [Office of Economic Opportunity] might well have been the Office of Ecclesiastical Outcasts. Sarge's Catholicism ranged from ordinary pieties—a rosary always in his pocket—to mindfulness of the church's teachings on social justice and nonviolence"; from Colman McCarthy, "Sargent Shriver: A Life of Grace," January 19, 2011, accessed December 3, 2013, http://www.washingtonpost.com/wp-dyn/content/article/2011/01/18/AR2011011804789.html. Michael Novak also wrote that Shriver always hired people to whom he could talk about Teilhard de Chardin, Dorothy Day, G. K. Chesterton, or the Worker Priests of France. He "loved the vein of Catholic thought that wanted to 'reconstruct the social order,' 'put the yeast of the gospel in the world.'" Novak saw Shriver as a Catholic who thought of his faith "as a culture-changing force, a shaper of civilizations, an inspirer of great works, a builder of great institutions that bring help of all kinds to the needy in all dimensions of need," and who took great joy in learning from others, like Teilhard, who thought the same way; Novak, "The Last Liberal," at AEI: American Enterprise Institute, May 24, 2004, http://www.aei.org/article/politics-and-public-opinion/elections/the-last-liberal/. This is a review of *Sarge: The Life and Times of Sargent Shriver.*

14. Teilhard, "The Evolution of Chastity," in *Toward the Future,* trans. René Hague (London: William Collins Sons and Harcourt, 1975), 86–87. This was written in Peking in 1934.

foundation of modern Catholic religious thought and U.S. culture as a whole that it could neither be ignored nor wholesale rejected without tumbling the entire edifice of American modernity. Instead, it would go underground for much of this next decade. It would emerge at various times in the work of politicians, artists, writers, theologians, and social theorists, but too often remained unnamed, as if in fear that to claim a Teilhardian influence was to immediately elicit categorical rejection.

Resurrection of Teilhard's thought, however, would occur repeatedly and cyclically during the next four decades as those optimistic about the future of the world were willing to take it up and reconsider it. As Teilhard himself wrote during a very dark period when the Japanese occupied China in World War II:

> Everything strengthens my conviction that the future can be forced and led only by a group of men united by a common faith in the spiritual future of the earth. "Get behind me," I would make bold to say, "all Godless pessimists and all Christian pessimists. We must take up again, on a sounder scientific basis and as a more exact philosophical concept, the idea (or, if you prefer it, the "myth") of progress. This is the essential setting in which I see the simultaneous rebirth of humanism and Christianity.[15]

As this work has shown, however, Teilhard's optimism and belief in progress were not rooted solely in the belief that humanitarian activism in the world, even communal activism, was sufficient. Teilhard's optimism was instead a hopeful understanding that despite the daily diminishments we suffer, all of humanity, all the matter of the world, all the effort expended on a daily basis, and all our own suffering are redeemed through the power of the Paschal mystery and especially the Resurrection of Christ. This is why, above all else, we are to love Christ with all our strength, even as we love the matter of the universe and the stuff of everyday life.[16]

15. Teilhard, *Letters to a Traveler* (New York: Harper, 1962), 277; from Peking, January 12, 1941.

16. See especially Teilhard, letter to Marguerite Teilhard-Chambon, March 15, 1916: "I want to love Christ with all my strength in the very act of loving the universe. Can this be absurdity, blasphemy?"

APPENDIX ~ TEILHARD PUBLICATIONS WORLDWIDE PER YEAR, 1956–1971

Table A-1. Teilhard Publications, 1956–71

Year	*Number of Books*	*Year*	*Number of Books*
1956	18	1965	250
1957	25	1966	145
1958	63	1967	399
1959	47	1968	202
1960	77	1969	150
1961	50	1970	136
1962	108	1971	109
1963	153	1972	94
1964	265		

Source: Data from Alessandro Dall'Olio, SJ, "Teilhard de Chardin: Thinker Wedded to Wisdom," in *The Jesuits 1972–1977*, 82.

This count is from the annual bibliography of publications from the Society of Jesus, in this case with reference to Teilhard de Chardin. These statistics do not include editions or translations of Teilhard's own writings or articles and essays in periodicals.

BIBLIOGRAPHY

ARCHIVAL SOURCES

The Barbour Collection, Woodstock Library, Georgetown University.

Robert Francoeur papers, Lauinger Library Archives, Georgetown University.

Marie Therese Dubalen–Nancy Corson Carter Collection, Lauinger Library Archives, Georgetown University.

BOOKS, ARTICLES, AND ESSAYS

Abbott, W. M., SJ, ed. *The Documents of Vatican II.* New York: American Press, 1966, including the six documents mentioned in this text:

Dogmatic Constitution on the Church (*Lumen gentium,* 1964), 14–101.

Declaration on Christian Education (*Gravissimum educationis,* 1965), 637–51.

Declaration on Religious Freedom (*Dignitatis humanae,* 1965), 675–96.

Decree on the Apostolate of the Laity (*Apostolicam actuositatem,* 1965), 489–521.

Decree on the Church's Missionary Activity (*Ad gentes,* 1965), 584–630.

Pastoral Constitution on the Church in the Modern World (*Gaudium et Spes,* 1965), 199–308.

Aczel, Amir. *The Jesuit and the Skull: Teilhard de Chardin, Evolution, and the Search for Peking Man.* New York: Riverhead, 2007.

Ahlstrom, Sydney. "The Radical Turn in Theology and Ethics: Why It Occurred in the 1960s." *Annals of the American Academy of Political and Social Science.* Special issue, *The Sixties: Radical Change in American Religion* 387 (January 1970): 1–13.

Alexander, Thomas. *The Vision of Teilhard de Chardin Programmed for V.I.P.'s.* New York: Vantage, 1969.

Alioto, Joseph, Geraldine Browning, and Seymour Farber, eds. *Teilhard de Chardin: In Quest of the Perfection of Man.* Madison, N.J.: Fairleigh Dickinson University Press, 1973.

Aller, Catherine. *The Challenge of Pierre Teilhard de Chardin.* New York: Exposition, 1964.

Allit, Patrick. *Religion in America since 1945: A History.* New York: Columbia University Press, 2003.

The Americanist Controversy: Recent Historical and Theological Perspectives, special issue, *U.S. Catholic Historian* 11, no. 3 (Summer 1993).

American Teilhard Association (ATA). Accessed January 12, 2011. http://teilharddechardin.org/biography.html.

"And the Angel Said unto Them, Fear Not. . . ." *Newsweek,* December 23, 1957, 52–53.

Anderson, Terry H. *The Movement and the Sixties: Protest from Greensboro to Wounded Knee.* New York: Oxford University Press, 1995.

Appleby, Scott. "The Neo-Americanist Center and the Limits of Conservative Dissent." *Americanism and Americanization: Essays in Honor of Philip Gleason,* special issue, *U.S. Catholic Historian* 17, no. 1 (Winter 1999): 13–27.

Baltazar, Eulalio. *Teilhard and the Supernatural.* Baltimore: Helicon, 1966.

———. *God within Process.* New York: Newman Press, 1970.

Barbour, George B. "Memorial to Pierre Teilhard de Chardin." *Proceedings Volume of the Geological Society of America: Annual Report for 1955* (July 1956).

———. *In the Field with Teilhard de Chardin.* New York: Herder and Herder, 1965.

Barbour, Ian G. "The Significance of Teilhard." *Christian Century,* August 30, 1967, 1098–1101.

———. "Five Ways of Reading Teilhard." *Soundings: An Interdisciplinary Journal* 51, no. 2 (Summer 1968):115–45

———. "Teilhard's Process Metaphysics." *Journal of Religion* 49 (1969): 136–59.

Barringer, Mark. "Warning on Teilhard." *Catholic Messenger,* Davenport, Iowa, July 26, 1962.

———. "The Anti-War Movement in the United States." In *The Oxford Companion to American Military History.* New York: Oxford University Press, 1999. See online at *Modern American Poetry.* Accessed July 11, 2013. http://www.english.illinois.edu/maps/vietnam/antiwar.html.

Baum, Gregory, OSA, ed. *The Twentieth Century: A Theological Overview.* Maryknoll, N.Y.: Orbis, 1999.

Bell, Daniel. "Religion in the Sixties." *Social Research* 38 (Autumn 1971): 447–97.

Benedict XVI. *Homily for Vespers at the Cathedral of Aosta* (July 24, 2009). Accessed July 11, 2013. http://www.vatican.va/holy_father/benedict_xvi/homilies/2009/documents/hf_ben-xvi_hom_20090724_vespri-aosta_en.html.

Bergson, Louis. *L'Evolution créatrice.* Paris: F. Alcan, 1907.

———. *Creative Evolution.* Translated by Arthur Mitchell. Lanham, Md.: University Press of America, 1911.

Berhoe, Ralph Wendell, ed. *Zygon: A Journal of Religion and Science* 3, no. 4 (December 1968).

Berry, Thomas. "Teilhard in the Ecological Age." *Teilhard Studies*, no. 7 (Woodbridge, Conn.: American Teilhard Association/Anima Press, 1982).

———. "Technology and the Healing of the Earth." *Teilhard Studies*, no. 14 (Woodbridge, Conn.: American Teilhard Association/Anima Press, 1985).

———. *Dream of the Earth.* San Francisco: Sierra Club, 1988.

———. *The Great Work: Our Way into the Future.* New York: Harmony Bell Tower, 2000.

———. *The Christian Future and the Fate of Earth.* Edited by Mary Evelyn Tucker and John Grim. Maryknoll, N.Y.: Orbis, 2009.

———. *The Sacred Universe: Earth Spirituality and Religion in the 21st Century.* Edited, with a foreword by Mary Evelyn Tucker. New York: Columbia University Press, 2009.

Berry, Thomas, and Thomas Clark. *Befriending the Earth: A Theology of Reconciliation between Humans and the Earth.* Mystic, Conn.: Twenty-Third Publications, 1991.

Berry, Thomas, and Brian Swimme. *The Universe Story.* San Francisco: HarperSanFrancisco, 1994.

Berton, Pierre. *The Comfortable Pew: A Critical Look at Christianity and the Religious Establishment in the New Age.* Philadelphia: Lippincott, 1965.

Bilaniuk, Petro. "The Christology of Teilhard de Chardin." In *Proceedings of the Teilhard Conference 1964*, edited by Robert J. O'Connell, SJ, 113–15. New York: Human Energetics Institute at Fordham University, 1965.

Bonato, Sergio. *La presenza del pensiero di Teilhard de Chardin nei lavori del Concilio Vaticano II.* Unpublished thesis. University of Genoa, 1967.

Bonhoeffer, Dietrich. *Letters and Papers from Prison.* New York: SCM, 1953.

Bravo, Francisco. *Christ in the Thought of Teilhard de Chardin.* Notre Dame, Ind.: University of Notre Dame Press, 1967.

Bricourt, J. "Américanisme." *Revue du Clergé Français* 15 (June–August, 1898): 416–35.

Brown, Mary J. "An 'Inevitable' Campus Controversy: The 'Heresy Affair' at the University of Dayton, 1960–1967." *American Catholic Studies: Journal of the American Catholic Historical Society* 113 (Spring–Summer 2002): 79–95.

Bruns, J. Edgar. "God Up Above, or Up Ahead?" *Catholic World* 191, no. 1141 (April 1960): 23–30.

Buckley, Tom. "The Battle of Chicago: From the Yippies' Side." *New York Times Magazine*, September 15, 1968, 28.

Burns, Stewart. *To the Mountaintop*. New York: HarperCollins, 2004.

Callahan, Daniel. "America's Catholic Bishops," *Atlantic Monthly*, April 17, 1967. Accessed August 8, 2013, http://www.theatlantic.com/magazine/archive/1967/04/america-s-catholic-bishops/308898/.

———, ed. *The Secular City Debate*. New York: McMillan, 1967.

Campion, Donald R., SJ. "The Phenomenon of Teilhard." *America*, April 10, 1965, 480–81.

Caprile, Giovanni, SJ. *Il Concilio Vaticano II: Cronache del Concilio vatincano II*. Vols. 4 and 5. Rome: La Civiltà cattolica, 1966.

Carey, Patrick. *Catholics in America: A History*. Westport, Conn.: Praeger, 2004.

Cargas, Harry, ed. *The Continuous Flame: Teilhard in the Great Traditions*. St. Louis, Mo.: B. Herder, 1969.

Casaroli, Cardinal Agostino. "Cardinal Casaroli praises Teilhard de Chardin on behalf of John Paul II." Accessed November 9, 2013. https://www.traditioninaction.org/ProgressivistDoc/A_020_CasaroliTeilhard.htm.

Chauchard, Paul. *Teilhard de Chardin: Un modèle et un guide pour notre temps*. Paris: Éditions du Levain, 1963.

———. *Teilhard de Chardin on Love and Suffering*. Translated by Marie Chène. Glenn Rock, N.J.: Paulist Press, 1966.

Cherry, Conrad, ed. *God's New Israel: Religious Interpretations of American Destiny*. 2nd ed. Chapel Hill: University of North Carolina Press, 1998.

Chinnici, Joseph P., OFM, ed. *Devotion to the Holy Spirit in American Catholicism*. Mahwah, N.J.: Paulist Press, 1985.

———. *Living Stones: The History and Structure of Catholic Spiritual Life in the United States*. New York: Macmillan, 1989.

Clarke, Thurston. "The Last Good Campaign." *Vanity Fair*, June, 2008, 173.

Collier, Peter, and David Horowitz. *The Kennedys: An American Drama*. New York: Summit, 1984.

Collignon, Joseph. "The Christian's Dilemma." *Saturday Review*, June 27, 1964, 14–16.

———. "The Phenomenon of Teilhard: In Man's Past This Priest-Paleontologist Found Truths Which Show a Direction for Man's Future." *Christian Century*, November 1965, 426–28.

Collins, James. "Maritain Asks Some Questions." *America*, January 13, 1968, 32.

Compe, Máire, ed. *Optimism or Pessimism in our Brave New World: Teilhardian Perspectives*. Special issue of *PRJ* 2 (1967).

Corbishley, Thomas. *The Spirituality of Teilhard de Chardin*. New York: Paulist Press, 1971.

Corté, Nicholas. *Pierre Teilhard de Chardin: His Life and Spirit*. New York: Macmillan, 1960.

Cousins, Ewert H., ed. *Process Theology: Basic Writings.* New York: Newman Press, 1971.

———. *Hope and the Future of Man.* Philadelphia: Fortress, 1972.

Cox, Harvey. *The Secular City.* New York: Macmillan, 1965.

Coyne, John. "The Famous Peace Corps Book Locker, Part I." May 13, 2009. Accessed December 7, 2013. http://peacecorpsworldwide.org/babbles/2009/05/13/the-fabulous-peace-corps-book-locker-part-i/.

Crespy, Georges. *La Pensée Théologique de Teilhard de Chardin.* Paris: Éditions Universitaires, 1961.

———. *De la Science à la Théologie: Essai sur Teilhard de Chardin.* Neuchâtel: Delachaux et Niestlé , 1965.

———. *From Science to Theology: An Essay on Teilhard de Chardin.* Nashville, Tenn.: Abingdon, 1968.

Cronkite, Walter, with Brian VanDeMark. *In Retrospect: The Tragedy and Lessons of Vietnam.* New York: Times Books, 1995.

Cuėnot, Claude. *Teilhard de Chardin: A Biographical Study.* Edited by Renė Hague. Translated by Vince Colimar. Baltimore: Helicon, 1965.

Cunningham, Philip J., CSP. "Teilhard de Chardin and the Noosphere." *CMC* (Computer Mediated Communication) *Magazine,* March 1997.

Daecke, Siguard Martin. *Teilhard de Chardin und die evangelische: Theologie Die Weltlichkeit Gottes und die Weltlichkeit der Welt.* Göttingen: Ort Verlag, 1967.

Dall'Olio, Allesandro, S.J. "Teilhard de Chardin: Thinker Wedded to Wisdom," in *The Jesuits 1972–1977.*

Delaney, John J., ed. *Saints Are Now: Eight Portraits of Modern Sanctity.* Garden City, N.Y.: Doubleday, 1981.

De la Trinité, Philippe. *Rome et Teilhard de Chardin.* Paris: Librairie Arthème Fayard, 1964.

De Lubac, Henri, SJ. *La Pensée Religieuse du Pere Teilhard de Chardin.* Paris: Aubier, 1962.

———. *Blondel et Teilhard de Chardin: Correspondance.* Paris: Beauchesne, 1965.

———. *Écrits du temps de la guerre 1916–1919.* Introduction by Bruno de Solages and Henri de Lubac. Paris: B. Grasset, 1965.

———. *The Faith of Teilhard de Chardin.* London: Burns and Oates, 1965.

———. *Teilhard de Chardin: The Man and His Meaning.* New York: New American Library, 1965.

———. *Teilhard: Missionaire et apologist.* Toulouse: Prière et Vie, 1966.

———. *La Priere du Pere Teilhard de Chardin.* Paris: A. Fayard, 1967. Originally published in 1964.

———. *Pierre Teilhard de Chardin–Maurice Blondel Correspondence.* Translated by William Whitman. New York: Herder and Herder, 1967.

———. *The Religion of Teilhard de Chardin.* Translated by René Hague. New York: Desclee, 1967.

———. *Teilhard Explained.* Translated by Anthony Buono. New York: Paulist Press, 1968.

———. *The Eternal Feminine: A Study on the Poem by Teilhard de Chardin, Followed by Teilhard and the Problems of Today.* New York: Harper and Row, 1971.

———. *Lettres intimes à Auguste Valensin, Bruno de Solages, Henri de Lubac, 1919–1955.* Paris: A. Montaigne, 1973.

———. *Teilhard Posthume: Réflexions et Souvenirs.* Paris: Fayard, 1977.

———. *Theology in History.* Foreword by Michael Sales, SJ. Translated by Anne Englund Nash. San Francisco: Ignatius Press, 1996.

———. *At the Service of the Church: Henri de Lubac Reflects on the Circumstances That Occasioned His Writings.* Translated by Anne Elizabeth Englund. San Francisco: Ignatius Press, 1998.

———. *Athéisme et sense de l'homme: Une double requête de "Gaudium et spes."* Paris: Éditions du Cerf, 1968. Translated by D. C. Schindler as "The Total Meaning of God and the World." *Communio* 35 (Winter 2008): 613–41.

De Solages, Bruno. "Christianity and Evolution: An Introduction to the Thought of Père Teilhard." *CrossCurrents,* no. 4 (Summer 1951): 26–37.

Dobzhansky, Theodosius. "An Essay on Religion, Death, and Evolutionary Adaptation." *Zygon: Journal of Religion and Science* 1, no. 4 (1966).

Dolan, Jay. *The American Catholic Experience: A History from Colonial Times to the Present.* Notre Dame, Ind.: University of Notre Dame Press, 1992.

Donovan, Leo, SJ. "Was Vatican II Evolutionary? A Note on Conciliar Language." *Theological Studies* 36 (1975): 493–502.

Duffy, Kathleen, SSJ. *Rediscovering Teilhard's Fire.* Philadelphia: St. Joseph's University Press, 2010.

Dugan, George. "Theologians Find That Hope Survives." *New York Times,* October 11, 1971, 20. Accessed from ProQuest Historical Newspapers: *The New York Times* (1851–2009) with Index (1851–1993).

Dyson, A. O. "Christ and Man's Place in Nature: Man and Evolution." *Theology* 72 (1969): 98–102.

Echols, Alice. *Shaky Ground: The 60s and Its Aftershocks.* New York: Columbia University Press, 2002.

Eliade, Mircea. "Cultural Fashions and the History of Religions." In *Essays in Divinity,* vol. 1, *The History of Religions: Essays on the Problem of Understanding,* edited by Joseph M. Kitagawa, Mircea Eliade, and Charles H. Long, 21–38. Chicago and London: University of Chicago Press, 1967.

———. *No Souvenirs: Journal, 1957–1969.* Translated by Fred H. Johnson Jr. New York: Harper and Row, 1982.

Ellis, John Tracy. "American Catholics and the Intellectual Life." *Thought* 30, no. 116 (Spring 1955): 388.

Ellwood, Robert. *The Sixties Spiritual Awakening: American Religion Moving from Modern to Postmodern.* New Brunswick, N.J.: Rutgers University Press, 1994.

———. *The 50s Spiritual Marketplace: American Religion in a Decade of Conflict.* New Brunswick, N.J.: Rutgers University Press, 1997.

Evans, John Whitney. "Dilemmas and Limitations." *Commonweal* 72, no. 19 (1960): 439–41.

Evans, M. Stanton. *Revolt on the Campus.* Chicago: Henry Regnery, 1961.

"Evolution, Science and Religion." *Jubilee* (May 1960): 48–51.

Ewing, J. Franklin, SJ. "Notes: The Human Phenomenon." *Theological Studies* 22, no. 1 (March 1961): 86–102.

———. Book review. *American Anthropologist.* 64, no. 5 (October 1962): 1132. Accessed October 5, 2018. https://anthrosource.onlinelibrary.wiley.com/doi/abs/10.1525/aa.1962.64.5.02a00580.

Faricy, Robert L., SJ. *Teilhard de Chardin's Theology of the Christian in the World.* New York: Sheed and Ward, 1967.

Farina, John, ed. *Hecker Studies: Essays on the Thought of Isaac Hecker.* New York: Paulist Press, 1983.

Fehlner, Peter, OFM Conv. Review of *The Cosmic Christ: From Paul to Teilhard,* by George A. Maloney. *Theological Studies,* March 1, 1969, 127–29.

Fiske, Edward B. "Yellow Submarine Is Symbol of Youth Churches." *New York Times,* April 20, 1970, 23.

"Flannery O'Connor (1925–1964)." Accessed June 4, 2013. http://www.georgiaencyclopedia.org/nge/Article.jsp?id=h-498.

Flowers, Ronald B. *Religion in Strange Times: The 1960s and 1970s.* Macon, Ga.: Mercer University Press, 1984.

Forbes, Bruce David, and Jeffrey H. Mahan. *Religion and Popular Culture in America.* San Diego: University of California Press, 2000.

Francoeur, Robert T. "A Call to Greatness." *Commonweal,* 1960, 441–43.

———. "For Teilhard, No Flight from Time." *Catholic World* (September 1961): 367–73.

———. ed. *The World of Teilhard.* Baltimore: Helicon, 1961.

———. "The Cosmic Christianity of Teilhard." *Sign,* February 1967, 7.

———. "What Teilhard Is Saying." Review of *Writings in Time of War,* by Pierre Teilhard de Chardin. *National Catholic Reporter,* 1968, 11.

Galbraith, John Kenneth. *The Affluent Society.* Boston: Houghton Mifflin, 1958.

Garaudy, Roger. *From Anathema to Dialogue.* New York: Herder and Herder, 1966.

Gelernter, David. "Americanism—and Its Enemies." *Commentary,* January 2005, 41–48.

Giovannetti, Albert. *A Portrait of His Holiness: John XXIII.* Translated by John Chapin. Westminster, Md.: Newman Press, 1959. Accessed April 11, 2013. http://archive.org/stream/wehaveapopeaporto13181mbp/wehaveapopeaporto13181mbp_djvu.txt.

Gilligan, Bernard B. Review of *The Phenomenon of Man,* by Pierre Teilhard de Chardin. *New Scholasticism* 34 (1960): 515.

Gitlin, Todd. *The Sixties: Years of Hope, Days of Rage.* New York: Bantam, 1993.

Gleason, Philip. "A Browser's Guide to American Catholicism, 1950–1980." *Theology Today* 38 (October 1981): 375.

———. "The New Americanism in Catholic Historiography." *The Americanist Controversy: Recent Historical and Theological Perspectives.* Special issue, *U.S. Catholic Historian* 11, no. 3 (Summer 1993):1–18.

Gould, Stephen Jay. "Piltdown Revisited." *Natural History,* March 1979, 86.

———. "The Piltdown Conspiracy." *Natural History,* August 1980, 8–28.

Gray, Donald. "The Phenomenon of Teilhard." *Theological Studies* 36, no. 1 (March 1975): 19–51.

Greeley, Andrew. *The Catholic Experience: A Sociologist's Interpretation of the History of American Catholicism.* New York: Doubleday, 1967.

Green, Jonathon. *All Dressed Up: The Sixties and the Counter Culture.* London: Pimlico, 1998.

Grummett, David. "Eucharist, Matter and the Supernatural: Why de Lubac Needs Teilhard." *International Journal of Systematic Theology* 10, no. 2 (April 2008): 165–78.

Halle, Louis. "Ariadne's Thread." *New Republic,* December 22, 1962.

Harvey, Paul, and Philip Goff, eds. *The Columbia Documentary History of Religion in America Since 1945.* New York: Columbia University Press, 2007, 94–95.

Haugen, David M., and Matthew J. Box, eds. *Examining Pop Culture: The 1960s.* Detroit: Greenhaven, 2005.

Haught, John F. "More Being: The Emergence of Teilhard de Chardin." *Commonweal,* June 5, 2009, 17–19. Reprinted in *Reclaiming Catholicism: Treasures Old and New,* edited by Michael Daley and Thomas Groome, 93–98. Maryknoll, N.Y.: Orbis, 2010.

———. "Teilhard and the Question of Life's Suffering." In *Rediscovering Teilhard's Fire,* edited by Kathleen Duffy, SSJ, 53–68. Philadelphia: St. Joseph's University Press, 2010.

Hefner, Philip. *The Promise of Teilhard: The Meaning of the Twentieth Century in Christian Perspective.* Philadelphia and New York: J. B. Lippincott, 1970.

Hegarty, Charles. "Boenhoeffer and Teilhard on Worldly Christianity." *Science et Esprit* 21 (1965): 35–70.

———. "Boenhoffer and Teilhard: Christian Prophets of Secular Sanctity." *Catholic World* 207 (1968–69): 31–34.

Hodgson, Peter. Book review. "Religion in Life." (Autumn 1966).

Houston, Jean. "A Chance Encounter with Pierre Teilhard de Chardin." *EnlightenNext Magazine.* Accessed August 16, 2013. http://magazine.enlightennext.org/2010/11/03/a-chance-encounter-with-pierre-teilhard-de-chardin-think-about-this/.

———. "Jean Houston." Accessed August 16, 2013. http:www.jeanhouston.org and http://www.jeanhouston.com/blog/?p=42#more-42.

Huebsch, Bill. *Vatican II in Plain English: The Council.* Allen, Tex.: Thomas More, 1997.

Human Energetics Research Institute. *1964 Fordham Conference Proceedings.* Bronx, N.Y.: Fordham University Press, 1964.

Huxley, Julian. "Message." *Europe* 43 (1965): 12–14.

"Integrity of the Week Award." *Christian Century* 86, no. 14 (April 2, 1969): 437.

"Is 'God Is Dead' Dead?" *Time,* May 2, 1969, 46.

Jacob, Philip E. *Changing Values in College.* New York: Harper and Brothers, 1957.

Jenkins, Philip. *Decades of Nightmares: The End of the Sixties and the Making of Eighties America.* New York: Oxford University Press, 2006.

John XXIII. Announcement of an Ecumenical Council of January 25, 1959. Accessed February, 22, 2014. http://www.vatican2voice.org/91docs/announcement.htm.

———. *Mater et magistra.* May 15, 1961.

———. "Opening Speech of the Second Vatican Council." October 11, 1962. Accessed April 2, 2013. http://conciliaria.com/2011/12/john-xxiii-convokes-council/.

———. *Pacem in terris* (Peace on Earth). *On Establishing Universal Peace in Truth, Justice, Charity and Liberty.* April 1963.

Johnson, Lyndon Baines. "On the Assassination of Dr. Martin Luther King." Presidential Address, April 4, 1968. Accessed April 3, 2013. http://www.pbs.org/wgbh/americanexperience/features/primary-resources/lbj-assassination/.

Jones, D. L. "Teilhard and Blondel." *La Nouvelle Théologie Blog.* August 18, 2005. Accessed September 3, 2011. http://ressourcement.blogspot.com/2005/08/teilhard-blondel.html.

Kahane, Ernest, and Roger Garaudy. *Teilhard de Chardin.* Budapest: Kossuth Könyvkiadó, 1967.

Keniston, Kenneth. *Young Radicals: Notes on Committed Youth.* New York: Harcourt Brace, 1966.

Kennedy, John F. "Houston Ministerial Association Address." September 1960. In *Public Voices: Catholics in the American Context,* edited by Elizabeth McKeowan and Steven M. Avella, 361–64. Maryknoll, N.Y.: Orbis, 1999.

———. "President John F. Kennedy's Inaugural Address." Accessed February 23, 2013. https://archive.org/details/JFK_Inaugural_Address_19610120.

Kennedy, Robert F. "Remarks on the Assassination of Martin Luther King, Jr." April 4, 1968. Accessed April 4, 2013. http://rapgenius.com/Robert-f-kennedy-remarks-on-the-assassination-of-martin-luther-king-jr-lyrics#note-1420015.

Kenney, W. Henry, SJ. *A Path through Teilhard's Phenomenon.* Dayton, Ohio.: Pflaum, 1970.

Kent, Stephen A. *From Slogans to Mantras: Social Protest and Religious Conversion in the Late Vietnam War Era.* Syracuse, N.Y.: Syracuse University Press, 2001.

Kessler, Marvin, SJ, ed. *Dimensions of the Future: The Spirituality of Teilhard de Chardin.* Washington, D.C.: Corpus, 1968.

King, Martin Luther, Jr. "Beyond Vietnam: A Time to Break Silence." April 4, 1967. Accessed July 17, 2013, http://www.hartford-hwp.com/archives/45a/058.html.

———. "I've Been to the Mountaintop." April 3, 1968. Accessed April 3, 2013. http://www.americanrhetoric.com/speeches/mlkivebeentothemountaintop.htm.

King, Thomas A., SJ. *Teilhard de Chardin: The Way of the Christian Mystics.* Vol. 6. Wilmington, Del.: Michael Glazier, 1988.

———. "A Holy Man and Lover of the World." *America,* March 28, 2005, 7–10.

King, Ursula. *Spirit of Fire: The Life and Vision of Teilhard de Chardin.* Maryknoll, N.Y.: Orbis, 1996.

Klein, Félix. *Americanism: A Phantom Heresy.* Cranford, N.J.: Aquin, 1951.

Knight, Alice Valle. *The Meaning of Teilhard de Chardin: A Primer.* Old Greenwich, Conn.: Devin-Adair, 1974.

Kobler, John. "The Priest Who Haunts the Catholic World." *Saturday Evening Post,* October 12, 1963, 42–51.

Komonchak, Joseph. "Theology and Culture at Mid-Century." *Theological Studies* 51 (1990): 579–600.

———. "Recapturing the Great Tradition: In Memoriam, Henri de Lubac." *Commonweal,* January 31, 1992, 14–17.

Kurlansky, Mark. *1968: The Year that Rocked the World.* New York: Random House, 2004.

Lane, David. *The Phenomenon of Teilhard.* Macon, Ga.: Mercer University Press, 1996.

Laurence, William. "China Cave a Lead to 'Missing Link.'" *New York Times,* March 20, 1937, 9.

Leahy, William, SJ. "Catholics and Educational Expansion after 1945." In *Contemporary Higher Education: Catholic Education at the Turn of a New Century,* edited by Joseph M. O'Keefe, 47–78. New York: Garland, 1997.

Les Amis de Teilhard, eds. *Les Oeuvres de Teilhard de Chardin.* Paris: Ėditions du Seuil, 1955–76, including: vol. 1, *Le Phénomène Humain* (1955); vol. 2, *L'Apparition de l'Hommme* (1956); vol. 3, *La Vision du Passé* (1957); vol. 4, *Le Milieu divin* (1957); vol. 5, *'Avenir de l'Homme* (1959); vol. 6, *L'Ėnergie Humaine* (1962); vol. 7, *L'Activation de l'Ėnergie* (1963); vol. 8, *La Place de l'Homme dans la Nature* (1963); vol. 9, *Science et Christ* (1965); vol. 10, *Comment Je Crois* (1969); vol. 11, *La Direction de l'Avenir* (1973); vol. 12, *Ėcrits du Temps de la Guerre*, 1916–1919 ([Paris: Grasset,] 1965); and vol. 13, *La Coeur de la Matiere* (1976).

Lonergan, Bernard. "The Transition from a Classicist World-View to Historical Mindedness." In *A Second Collection*, edited by W. F. J. Ryan, SJ, and B. J. Tyrell, SJ, 1–9. Philadelphia: Westminster Press, 1974.

Lukas, Mary. "Teilhard de Chardin: A Cathedral for the Wasteland." *Show: A Magazine of the Arts*, December 1963, 100–11, 162–63.

———. "Teilhard and the Piltdown 'Hoax.'" *America*, May 1981, 424–27.

Lukas, Mary, and Ellen Lukas. *Teilhard: A Biography*. New York: McGraw-Hill, 1977.

Lyotard, Jean-Francois. *The Postmodern Condition: A Report on Knowledge*. Translated by Geoff Bennington and Brian Massumi. Minneapolis: University of Minnesota Press, 1984.

Lytle, Mark. *America's Uncivil Wars: The Sixties Era from Elvis to the Fall of Richard Nixon*. New York: Oxford University Press, 2006.

Magill, Frank M., ed. *Masterpieces of Catholic Literature*. New York: Harper and Row, 1965.

Maloney, George. *The Cosmic Christ: From Paul to Teilhard*. Baltimore: Sheed and Ward, 1968.

"Man's Moon." *Living Church*, October 20, 1957, 14.

Maritain, Jacques. *The Peasant of the Garonne: An Old Layman Questions Himself about the Present Time*. Eugene, Ore.: Wipf and Stock, 2013.

Martin, Maria Gratia, IHM. *The Spirituality of Teilhard de Chardin*. Westminster, Md.: Newman, 1967.

Marwick, Arthur. *The Sixties*. Oxford: Oxford University Press, 1998.

Massa, Mark. *Catholics and American Culture: Fulton Sheen, Dorothy Day, and the Notre Dame Football Team*. New York: Crossroad, 1999.

———. *The American Catholic Revolution: How the Sixties Changed the Church Forever*. New York: Oxford University Press, 2010.

McAvoy, Thomas. *The Great Crisis in American Catholic History, 1895–1900*. Chicago: Henry Regnery, 1957.

McCann, Dennis. *New Experiment in Democracy*. Kansas City: Sheed and Ward, 1987.

McCarthy, Colman. "Sargent Shriver: A Life of Grace." January 19, 2011. Accessed December 9, 2013. http://www.washingtonpost.com/wp-dyn/content/article/2011/01/18/AR2011011804789.html.

McCarthy, Viterbo, CSJ. "Maturity: Pierre Teilhard de Chardin and Gordon W. Allport." *Journal of Religion and Health* 7, no. 2 (April 1968):141–50.

McCartin, James P. *Prayers of the Faithful: The Shifting Spiritual Life of American Catholics*. Cambridge, Mass: Harvard University Press, 2010.

McCulloch, Winifred. *A Short History of the American Teilhard Association*. Chambersburg, Pa.: American Teilhard Association for the Future of Man, 1979.

McElwain, Hugh T. *Introduction to Teilhard de Chardin.* Chicago: Argus Communications, 1967.

———. "Teilhard and John Stewart: A Metaphysics of the Future." In *Rediscovering Teilhard's Fire,* edited by Kathleen Duffy, SSJ, 147–62. Philadelphia: St. Joseph University Press, 2010.

McLeod, Hugh. *The Religious Crisis of the 1960s.* Oxford: Oxford University Press, 2007.

McLuhan, Marshall. *The Mechanical Bride.* London: Routledge, 1967.

Meade, Dave. "Evolution: A Scientific New Gospel." *Chicago Daily News,* January 9, 1965, 19.

Meissner, W. W., SJ. *Foundations for a Psychology of Grace.* Glen Rock, N.J.: Paulist Press, 1966.

Merton, Thomas. *Love and Living.* Edited by Naomi Burton Stone and Patrick Hart. New York: Farrar, Straus and Giroux, 1979.

———. *The Road to Joy: Letters to New and Old Friends.* Edited by Robert E. Daggy. New York: Farrar, Straus and Giroux, 1989.

Miles, Barry. *Hippie.* New York: Sterling, 2004.

Miller, Timothy. *The Hippies and American Values: The Utopian Ethics of the Counterculture 1965–1970.* Knoxville: University of Tennessee Press, 2011.

Mills, C. Wright. *White Collar: The American Middle Classes.* New York: Oxford University Press, 1962.

Mitchell, James. "The God I Want." *New Blackfriars,* June 1967.

Moltmann, Jürgen. *Theology of Hope.* Philadelphia: Fortress, 1993.

Mooney, Christopher, SJ. "Blondel and Teilhard de Chardin." *Thought: Fordham University Quarterly* 37 (December 1962): 543–62.

———. "Anxiety and Faith in Teilhard de Chardin." *Thought: Fordham University Quarterly* 39 (December 1964): 510–30.

———. "The Body of Christ in the Writings of Teilhard de Chardin." *Theological Studies* 25, no. 4 (December 1964): 576–610.

———. "Teilhard de Chardin and the Christological Problem." *Harvard Theological Review* 58, no. 1 (January 1965): 91–126.

———. Review of *The Making of a Mind,* by Pierre Teilhard de Chardin. *America,* October 23, 1965, 475.

———. "A Fresh Look at Man." *Saturday Review,* February 26, 1966, 21–25.

———. "Teilhard de Chardin and Christian Spirituality." *Thought: Fordham University Quarterly* 42 (Fall 1967):383–402.

———. *Teilhard de Chardin and the Mystery of Christ.* New York: Harper and Row, 1967.

———. "Teilhard on Man's Search for God." *Continuum* 5, no. 4 (Winter 1968): 643–54.

———. Review of *Christianity and Evolution,* by Pierre Teilhard de Chardin. *America,* December 25, 1971, 563–65.

Mortier, Jeanne, with Marie-Louise Aboux. *Teilhard de Chardin Album.* New York: Harper and Row, 1966.

Muller, Robert. *And Most of All They Taught Me Happiness.* New York: Doubleday, 1978.

———. *New Genesis.* New York: Doubleday, 1984.

Murphy, John M. "'A Time of Shame and Sorrow': Robert F. Kennedy and the American Jeremiad." *Quarterly Journal of Speech* 76 (1990): 401–14.

Murray, Michael H. *The Thought of Teilhard de Chardin: An Introduction.* New York: Seabury, 1966.

"The New Ministry: Bringing God back to Life." *Time,* December 26, 1969, 48–57.

"New Political Labels Confuse." *Kittanning Simpson Leader Times,* March 2, 1970. Accessed October 4, 2013. http://newspaperarchive.com/kittanning-simpson-leader-times/1970-03-02/page-4.

Niebuhr, H. Richard. *Radical Monotheism and Western Culture.* Louisville: Westminster John Knox Press, 1960.

"The Noosphere around Us." *Newsweek,* August 31, 1964, 70–71.

Novak, Michael. "The Last Liberal." May 24, 2004. Accessed August 3, 2013. http://www.aei.org/article/politics-and-public-opinion/elections/the-last-liberal/.

———. "Harvey Cox's Secular City." *First Things,* March 5, 2007. Accessed June 4, 2012. https://www.firstthings.com/web-exclusives/2007/03/harvey-coxs-secular-city.

O'Brien, David J. "The American Laity: Memory, Meaning and Mission." *America,* March 7, 1987, 189–93.

———. *Public Catholicism.* Maryknoll, N.Y.: Orbis, 1996.

O'Connell, Robert J., SJ, ed. *Proceedings of the Teilhard Conference 1964.* New York: Human Energetics Institute, Fordham University, 1965.

O'Connor, Flannery. *Everything That Rises Must Converge.* New York: Farrar, Straus and Giroux, 1965.

———. *Flannery O'Connor: Mystery and Manners.* Edited by Robert Fitzgerald and Sally Fitzgerald. New York: Farrar, Straus and Giroux, 1969.

———. *Habit of Being.* Edited by Regina O'Connor. New York: Farrar, Straus and Giroux, 1979.

Oden, Thomas. "Contemporary Theology and Psychotherapy." *Philadelphia* (1967): 51–52.

O'Malley, John. "The Style of Vatican II." *America,* February 24, 2003, 6.

———. "Vatican II: Did Anything Happen?" *Theological Studies* 67 (2006): 3–33.

———. *What Happened at Vatican II.* Cambridge, Mass.: Harvard University Press, 2010.

O'Neill, William L. *Coming Apart: An Informal History of the United States in the 1960s.* Chicago: Quadrangle, 1971.

"Passionate Indifference." *Time,* February 10, 1961. Accessed July 11, 2012. http://www.time.com/time/magazine/article/0,9171,872124,00.html#ixzz1QKfKPjDF.

Paul VI. Speech to Employers and Workers of a Pharmacy Company (February 24, 1966). In *Insegnamenti di Paolo VI,* 992–993. Vatican: Poliglotta Vaticana, 1966. Accessed March 25, 2013. http://www.traditioninaction.org/ProgressivistDoc/A_035_Paul6Teilhard.htm.

"Pierre Teilhard de Chardin." Obituary. *Time,* April 25, 1955, 104.

Phenomenon of Man Project (POM). *Survival: A Study Guide for Teilhard's The Phenomenon.* San Francisco: The Project, 1970.

Pius X Society. "They Think They've Won." Accessed July 5, 2013. http://www.sspxasia.com/Documents/SiSiNoNo/1994_April/They_Think_Theyve_Won_PartV.htm.

Porterfield, Amanda. *The Transformation of American Religion: The Story of a Late-Twentieth-Century Awakening.* Oxford: Oxford University Press, 2001.

Portier, William L. "Here Come the Evangelical Catholics." *Communio* 31, no.1 (Spring 2004): 35–66.

———. "What Kind of a World of Grace." *Communio* 39, no. 1–2 (Spring–Summer 2012): 136–51.

"Portrait." *Newsweek,* March 27, 1939, 31.

Poulain, Dorothy. "Evening Star." *Ave Maria,* January 31, 1953, 135–41.

———. "Christ and the Universe." *Commonweal,* January 30, 1959, 460–64.

Ratzinger, Joseph Cardinal. "*Gaudium et spes* Took Its Notion of Christianity from Teilhard de Chardin." In *Les Principes de la Theologie Catholique: Esquisse et Materiaux,* 374–75. Paris: Tequi, 1982. Accessed May 5, 2012. http://www.traditioninaction.org/ProgressivistDoc/A_034_RatzTeilhard.htm.

Raven, Charles. *Teilhard de Chardin: Scientist and Seer.* Oxford: Blackwell, 1968.

Reher, Margaret. "Phantom Heresy: A Twice-Told Tale." *The Americanist Controversy: Recent Historical and Theological Perspectives.* Special issue of *U.S. Catholic Historian* 11, no. 3 (Summer 1993): 93–105.

"Religion: Toward Omega." *Time,* December 14, 1959. Accessed June 22, 2011, http://www.time.com/time/magazine/article/0,9171,894362,00.html#ixzz1QKk1rHWJ.

Rice, David. *Shattered Vows: Exodus from the Priesthood.* London: Fleming Revell, 1992.

Riesman, David, Nathan Glazer, and Reuel Denney. *The Lonely Crowd: A Study of the Changing American Character.* New Haven, Conn.: Yale University Press, 1950.

Riggan, George A. "A Selected Bibliography of the Works of Teilhard de Chardin." *Zygon* 3, no. 3 (September 1968): 314–22.

———. "Testing the Teilhardian Foundations." *Zygon: Journal of Religion and Science* 3, no. 3 (September 1968): 259–313.

Robinson, John A. T. *Honest to God.* Louisville: Westminster John Knox Press, 1963.

Roof, Wade Clark. *A Generation of Seekers: The Spiritual Journeys of the Baby Boom Generation.* San Francisco: Harper San Francisco, 1993.

———. *Spiritual Marketplace: Baby Boomers and the Remaking of American Religion.* Princeton, N.J.: Princeton University Press, 1999.

Rorabaugh, W. J. *Berkeley at War.* New York: Oxford University Press, 1990.

Roszak, Theodore. *The Making of a Counterculture: Reflections on a Technocratic Society and Its Youthful Opposition.* New York: Doubleday, 1969.

Roth, Robert J. "The Importance of Matter." *America,* December 21, 1963, 792–94.

Rubbra, Edmund. "Hommage à Teilhard de Chardin." *Rubbra: Symphony No. 5, Symphony No. 8, Ode to the Queen.* Conducted by Robert Saxton. Chandos, 1999.

Russo, Francois, SJ. "The Phenomenon of Man." *America,* April 30, 1960, 185–89.

Sacred Congregation of the Holy Office. "Warning Considering the Writings of Father Teilhard de Chardin." June 30, 1962.

Schedler, Norbert O., ed. *Philosophy of Religion: Contemporary Perspectives.* New York: Macmillan, 1973.

Schell, Jonathan. *The Village of Ben Suc.* New York: Alfred Knopf, 1967.

Schlesinger, Arthur M. *Robert Kennedy and His Times.* New York: Ballantine, 1996.

Schloesser, Stephen. *Jazz Age Catholicism: Mystic Modernism in Post-War Paris 1919–1933.* Toronto: University of Toronto Press, 2005.

Schoenborn, Cardinal Christoph. *Creation, Evolution, and a Rational Faith.* San Francisco: Ignatius Press, 2007.

Shafer, I. H. "From Noosophere to Theosphere: Cyclotrons, Cyberspace and Teilhard's Vision of Cosmic Love." *Zygon: Journal of Religion and Science* 37 (December 2002): 825–52.

Shaw, Russell. "Americanism: Then and Now." Accessed June 22, 2012. http://www.ewtn.com/library/ISSUES/AMERICAN.TXT.

Sheed, Wilfrid. "Pere Teilhard's View of Evolution." *Jubilee* 7, no. 8 (1959): 42–49.

Sheets, John, SJ. "Teilhard and Development of Dogma." *Theological Studies* 30, no. 3 (Summer 1969): 445–62.

Silk, Mark. *Spiritual Politics: Religion and America since World War II.* New York: Simon and Schuster, 1988.

Soleri, Paolo. "Myriad Specks, Teasing Grace." In *The Spirit of the Earth: A Teilhard Centennial,* edited by Jerome Perlinski. New York: Seabury Press, 1981.

Speaight, Robert. *The Life of Teilhard de Chardin.* New York: Harper and Row, 1967.

Speaight, Robert, Robert Wilshire, and Julian Victor Langmead Casserley. *Teilhard de Chardin: Re-mythologization.* Chicago: Argus, 1970.

"The Spirit Is at Work." *Life,* March 31, 1961, 30.

Spülbeck, Otto. "Fortschrittsglaube und Evolution." In *Der Fortschrittsglaube: Sinn und Gefahren,* edited by Ulrich Schöndorfer, 85–107. Graz: Verlag Styria, 1965.

———. "Teilhard de Chardin und die Pastoralkonstitution." In *Die Autorität der Freiheit,* edited by Johann Christoph Hampe, 3:86–97 (Munich: Kosel, 1967).

"Sputnik's Wake." *America,* October 26, 1957, 94.

Stiernotte, Alfred. "An Interpretation of Teilhard: As Reflected in Recent Literature." *Zygon* 3, no. 4 (December 1968): 377–425.

Stossel, Scott. *Sarge: The Life and Times of Sargent Shriver.* New York: Other Press, 2011.

"Teilhard de Chardin." *Record,* February 1966, 1, 5–6.

Teilhard de Chardin, Pierre. *La Vision du passé,* Paris: Éditions du Seuil, 1957.

———. *Building the Earth.* Paris: Éditions du Seuil, 1958.

———. *The Phenomenon of Man.* Translated by Bernard Wall. Introduction by Sir Julian Huxley. New York: Harper, 1959.

———. *The Divine Milieu: An Essay on the Interior Life.* New York: Harper and Row, 1960.

———. *Genèse d'une pensée: Lettres 1914–1919.* Paris: Grasset, 1961.

———. *Hymn of the Universe.* New York: Harper and Row, 1961.

———. *Letters from a Traveler.* New York: Harper, 1962.

———. *L'Énergie humaine.* Paris: Èditions du Seuill, 1962.

———. *Lettres d'Égypte 1905–1908.* Edited by Henri de Lubac. Paris: Aubier Éditions Montaigne, 1963.

———. *The Future of Man.* New York: Harper and Row, 1964.

———. *The Appearance of Man.* New York: Harper and Row, 1965.

———. *Hymn of the Universe.* New York: Harper and Row, 1965.

———. *Lettres d'Hastings et de Paris 1908–1914. Edited by Henri de Lubac.* Paris: Aubier-Monataigne, 1965.

———. *Letters from Egypt 1905–1908.* Edited, with an Introduction by Henri de Lubac. Translated by Mary Ilford. New York: Herder and Herder, 1965.

———. *Science et Christ.* Paris: *Èditions du Seuil,* 1965.

———. *Érits du temps de la guerre.* Paris: Grasset, 1965.

———. *The Making of a Mind: Letters of a Soldier-Priest 1914–1919.* New York: Harper and Row, 1965.

———. *Writings in Time of War.* New York: Harper and Row, 1968.

———. *Science and Christ.* New York: Harper and Row, 1969.

———. *Letters from Hastings: 1908–1912.* Edited, with an Introduction by Henri de Lubac. Translated by Judith de Stefano. New York: Herder and Herder, 1968.

———. *Christianisme et Evolution.* Paris: Ėditions du Seuil, 1969.

———. *Comment Je Crois.* Paris: Ėditions du Seuil, 1969.

———. *Let Me Explain.* New York: HarperCollins, 1970.

———. *Human Energy.* New York: Harcourt Brace Jovanovich, 1971.

———. *Activation of Energy.* New York: Harcourt, Brace, Jovanovich, 1971.

———. *Christianity and Evolution.* Translated by René Hague. New York: Harcourt, 1971.

———. *Toward the Future.* Translated by René Hague. London: William Collins Sons and Harcourt, 1975.

———. *The Heart of Matter.* New York: Harcourt, Brace Jovanovich, 1979.

———. *The Human Phenomenon.* Translated by Sarah Appleton-Weber. With a Foreword by Brian Swimme. Brighton and Portland: Sussex, 1999.

"Teilhard de Chardin and His Relevance for Today." *Woodstock Report* 82 (June 2005). Accessed December, 2009. http://woodstock.georgetown.edu/publications/report/r-fea82a.htm.

"Teilhard de Chardin and Vatican II—and the Monitum." British Teilhard Association Newsletter, February 2007.

"The Teilhard Phenomenon after 20 Years." *America*, April 12, 1975, 2.

"Theological Resources from the Sciences." *Zygon* 1, no. 1 (January 1965): 11.

"Theology: Life in a Defatalized World." *Time Magazine*, April 2, 1965. Accessed May, 2013, http://www.time.com/time/magazine/article/0,9171,941039,00.html#ixzz2Br7yBowP.

Thompkins, Charles. "Fads upon Fads." *Continuum* 3, no. 3 (Autumn 1965): 396–98.

"Thoughts on Teilhard." *Claremont Collegian*, November 30, 1966.

Tillich, Paul. *Systematic Theology.* Vol. 3. Chicago: University of Chicago Press, 1963.

Toulmin, Stephen. "On Teilhard de Chardin." *Commentary* 39 (March 1965): 50–55.

Tresmontant, Claude. *Introduction a la pensée de Pierre Teilhard de Chardin.* Paris: Editions du Seuil, 1956.

———. *Pierre Teilhard de Chardin: His Thought.* Translated by Salvator Attanasio, with a preface by Gustave Weigel. Baltimore: Helicon, 1959.

Vahanian, Gabriel. *The Death of God: The Culture of our Post-Christian Era.* New York: George Braziller, 1961.

Viorst, Milton. *Fire in the Streets: America in the 1960s.* New York: Simon and Schuster, 1979.

Vollert, Cyril, SJ. "Toward Omega: The Vision of Man." *Theology Digest* 8, no. 3 (1960): 133–36.

———. "Teilhard in the Light of Vatican II." In *Dimensions of the Future*, edited by Marvin Kessler, SJ, and Bernard Brown, SJ, 147–68. Washington, D.C., and Cleveland: Corpus, 1968.

Von Hildebrand, Dietrich. *Trojan Horse in the City of God: The Catholic Crisis Explained.* Chicago: Franciscan Herald Press, 1967.

Vorgrimler, Herbert, ed. *Commentary on the Documents of Vatican II.* Vol. 5. New York: Burns and Oats, 1967.

Watkins, Steven. *Flannery O'Connor and Teilhard de Chardin: A Journey Together Towards Hope and Understanding about Life.* New York: Peter Lang, 2009.

White, Theodore. *The Making of the President, 1968.* New York: Athenaeum, 1969.

Whyte, William H. *The Organization Man.* New York: Simon and Schuster, 1956.

Williams, Daniel Day. "Hope and the Future of Man: A Reflection." In *Hope and the Future of Man,* 83–88. Philadelphia: Fortress, 1972.

Wills, Garry. *Bare Ruined Choirs: Doubt, Prophecy and Radical Religion.* Garden City, N.Y.: Doubleday, 1972.

Wind, James P., and James W. Lewis, eds. *American Congregations.* Vol 2, *New Perspectives in the Study of Congregations.* Chicago: University of Chicago Press, 1994.

Winter, Gibson. *The Suburban Captivity of the Churches.* New York: Doubleday, 1961.

Wright, Amy Nathan. *Civil Rights "Unfinished Business": Poverty, Race, and the 1968 Poor People's Campaign.* Ph.D. diss., University of Texas at Austin, 2007.

Wuthnow, Robert. *Experimentation in American Religion: The New Mysticisms and Their Implications for the Churches.* Los Angeles: University of California Press, 1979.

———. *After Heaven: Spirituality in America since the 1950s.* San Diego: University of California Press, 1998.

Zaehner, R. C. *Matter and Spirit: Their Convergence in Eastern Religions; Marx and Teilhard de Chardin.* Edited by Ruth Nanda Anshen. Religious Perspectives. New York: Harper and Row, 1963.

Zonneveld, Leo, ed. *Humanity's Quest for Unity: A United Nations Teilhard Colloquium.* The Hague: Marananda, 1985.

INDEX

aggiornamento, 109, 148, 179
Alexander, Thomas, 285
Aller, Catherine, 125–29, 185
Americanism, 2, 25, 32, 86, 97, 98, 100–108, 110n40, 114, 120, 133, 227, 281, 291
American Teilhard Association, 5, 24, 30, 122, 123, 162, 235, 236, 237, 240, 296, 302, 303, 311, 312
American Teilhard organizations, 65, 85–87, 89, 117, 121–24, 126n81
Amis. *See* Les Amis de Teilhard
antiwar, 26, 99, 146n28, 149, 152–58, 165, 215–19, 227–29, 253
Aquinas, 20, 70, 73, 76, 90, 93, 116, 124, 141, 178, 188
arcology, 296
Arcosanti, 295–96
arts, 295

Baltasar, Eulalio, 197–98
Barbour, Georges, 54, 73, 75, 81, 87, 89, 91–93, 115, 121–22, 125–26, 158, 162, 164, 177–78, 237
Barbour, Ian, 191–92, 198, 266–73
Baum, Gregory, 90–91, 109
Beatles, 112, 158–59, 166, 229–30, 250
Benedict XVI, Pope, 294. *See also* Ratzinger, Joseph
Bergson, Henri, 5–6, 69
Berhoe, Ralph Wendell, 271
Berkeley. *See* University of California at Berkeley
Berrigan, Daniel and Philip, 227–28
Bilaniuk, Petro, 123–24, 274
Black Panthers, 112, 219
Blondel, Maurice, 4, 80
body of Christ, 166, 195, 210. *See also* mystical body of Christ
Bonhoeffer, Dietrich, 169, 173–74, 176, 233, 256, 270
Bravo, Francisco, 195–96
Breuil, Henri, 16
Bruns, Edgar, 53–54, 67, 89–90, 94
Bruteau, Beatrice, 115, 122, 164
building the earth, 144–46, 151, 175, 231, 236, 239, 252–53, 257, 279

Cargas, Harry J., 255–57, 261
Casaroli, Agostino, Cardinal, 293–94
Catholic Church and change, 24–25, 35–37, 40–43, 61–62, 67–68, 81n67, 77–79, 93n101, 94, 99–105, 109–11, 132, 139, 160–61, 171–75, 223–28, 251, 253–54, 257, 276, 279–80, 291. *See also* historical consciousness
Catholic Left, 227
Catholic subculture, 104, 114, 120, 226
Catholic World, 66–67, 77, 83–84, 90, 115–16, 175

Chauchard, Paul, 47, 148, 191
Christian Century, 188, 192, 259
Christocentrism, 6, 15, 19, 21–23, 64, 74, 106, 124, 133, 167, 169, 182, 247, 255, 258–59, 269, 279, 282, 288, 292, 295–96
Christology, 2, 6, 18–25, 48, 54, 56, 66, 71, 82, 95, 96, 98, 113, 123, 143, 158, 174, 176, 180, 183–84, 187, 194–99, 237–38, 239n107, 245–58, 260–63, 265, 268–69, 273–75, 279–80, 284–88, 292–95, 298
civil rights, 34, 53, 98, 100, 106, 112–13, 132, 138, 146, 150–52, 155–59, 165, 168, 172, 198, 206–10, 217, 227, 253
Clarke College, Iowa, 115
Cobb, John, 192, 241–42
Cold War, 32, 34–35, 39–40, 55, 98, 107, 155, 212
Commonweal, 46–47, 66–69, 84, 171
Communion of Saints, 23, 119. *See also* mystical body of Christ
confluence of science and religion, 19–23, 47, 117–18, 145, 147–48, 160, 175, 185, 187, 232, 247, 254, 264–68, 271, 274, 276, 293–94
consensus, 31–37, 40–43, 55, 169, 205, 212, 225, 251; shifts in, 32–36, 107–8, 132, 149–61, 205, 208–9, 218–21
Corté, Nicholas, 51, 79
Cosmic Christ, 19, 20, 22,167, 175, 183, 198, 237–38, 252, 254, 260–61, 273, 275, 287, 292, 294
cosmology, 19, 21, 22, 62, 67, 68, 74, 174. *See also* Teilhard
counterculture, 1, 25–26, 99, 113, 138, 149, 254, 158–61, 165–66, 168, 189, 198, 203, 216–23, 228–30, 232, 261–62, 291. *See also* Catholic Left; hippies; MOBE; SDS; yippies
Cousins, Ewert, 65, 122, 164, 198, 238, 239–41, 295
Cox, Harvey, 168–74, 270
Creative Evolution, 5–6, 69
Crespy, Georges, 84, 176, 183
CrossCurrents, 31, 44, 92, 296
Cuénot, Claude, 3, 5, 51, 75–76, 89, 181–82, 184

Dansereau, Pierre, 115, 162, 164
Darwin, Charles, 48, 67, 69, 76–77, 189
death of God, 168–99, 232–33, 249–51, 257
De Lubac, Henri, 3, 4, 16, 18, 47–48, 62, 80–89, 93, 101, 137, 140–41, 158, 183–84, 197, 248, 260–63, 268, 275, 292–93; difficulties due to involvement with Teilhard, 80–82, 93n101; publications concerning Teilhard, 80–83, 85, 93, 266
De Solages, Bruno, 16, 31, 44, 80, 82
De Terra, Rhoda, 17
Divine Milieu, The, 11, 19, 22–23, 30, 47, 52, 62–64, 74–75, 110, 129–30, 132, 145, 161, 184, 188, 196, 204, 212, 223, 249, 257, 264, 277, 279, 287. *See also Le Milieu Divin*
Divinitas (journal), 48, 89
Dobzhansky, Theodosius, 115, 121, 164, 187, 238, 240, 242, 266
Donceel, J., 65, 164
Dyson, A. O., 253–55

Earlham College, 121
Earth Day, 221
ecumenism, 48, 66–67, 70, 74, 83n71, 84, 125–28, 151, 161, 228–32, 256, 260, 273, 276, 282, 285–86, 296
Eiseley, Loren, 115, 164
Eliade, Mircea, 83, 273
environmental studies, 296
eschatology, 23, 234, 240–43, 261, 268–69
Eternal Feminine, The, 13, 82, 259–64
Everything That Rises, 130–31
Evans, John Whitney, 68
evolution, 4–16, 20, 30–31, 44, 48–50, 54–56, 65–73, 83, 97,113, 124–25, 130–31, 139–43, 147–51, 174–75, 186–89, 196–97, 235–37, 253–58, 262, 265–69, 281–88, 293–96
"Evolution, Science and Religion" (TV show), 65–66
Ewing, J. Franklin, 52, 65–66, 72–73, 88, 90, 92, 123

Fairleigh Dickinson University, 44, 164, 236, 240
Faricy, Robert J., SJ, 196–97
Fordham University, 61, 65, 72, 85,

114–16, 121–22, 124–25, 128, 164, 170, 236, 240
Francoeur, Robert, 24, 44–46, 50–54, 57, 61, 65–72, 75, 77–80, 83–95, 99, 101, 110, 114–17, 121, 125–29, 158, 162, 164, 194, 236, 238–240, 277–78; difficulties due to involvement with Teilhard, 77, 84, 89, 91, 94, 115
Free Speech Movement, 155, 217

G.I. Bill, 33, 38
Gaudium et spes, 25, 140–43, 145–48, 251, 280
Gilligan, Bernard, 71–72
"God is Dead" theology, 223. *See also* death of God
Gould, Stephen J., 19, 117
Gray, Donald, 174–75, 241, 243, 276, 281
Greek fathers, 19, 20, 54
Gregory of Nyssa, 54, 67

Hayden, Tom, 155
Hecker, Isaac, 101–4, 110
Hefner, Philip, 240–42, 282–83
Helicon Press, 46, 51–52, 76, 87
hippies, 154, 158–60, 216–17, 220, 222, 283
historical consciousness, 2, 30, 34, 42, 77, 79n61, 98, 143, 145, 165, 181, 256
hope, 172–75, 190–93, 203–4, 212, 233–35, 240–45, 250–53, 257, 264, 276, 280, 284, 286–88, 298
Houston, Jean, 164, 239
Human Energetics Institute, 114, 122, 274, 276, 303, 313
Human Energetics Research Institute, 114, 122, 125, 170, 274, 276
Human Phenomenon, The, 15, 68–74, 72, 129, 181. See also *Le Phénomène Humain*; *Phenomenon of Man*
Humanae vitae, 225–26
humanism, 123, 147, 169, 175, 187, 209, 248, 250, 282; Teilhard as humanist, 169, 187
Humphrey, Hubert, 219–20
Huxley, Aldous, 190n51
Huxley, Julius, 31, 48–49, 71n35, 148, 190, 266n47, 273n72
Hymn of the Universe, 146, 165, 184, 197, 233
incarnation, 20–22, 64, 83, 194, 203, 232–33, 252
Index of Forbidden Works, 6, 81, 88, 90–91, 129
influence of Teilhard on non-Christians, 70, 72, 74, 148, 176–77, 182, 251–53, 271n66, 296
influence of Teilhard on politics, 210, 214, 227, 232, 253, 294, 297
influence of Teilhard on Second Vatican Council, 4, 61, 110–11, 138–49, 247, 261, 263, 266, 276. *See also* Second Vatican Council
In the Field with Teilhard de Chardin, 54, 91, 121, 177

Jesus movement, 230
John, St., 19, 237
John XXIII, Pope, 32, 42–43, 55, 61, 81, 93, 99–100, 105–6, 109–11, 138, 140, 185, 223, 225–26
John Paul II, Pope, 225, 293–94
Johnson, Lyndon B., 153–58, 206–9, 212–15
Jubilee (magazine), 49, 56, 65, 95, 307

Kahane, Ernest, 183, 191
Kennedy, John F., 25, 32, 40, 98, 100, 104–8, 111n40, 128, 153–54, 171–73, 185, 223
Kennedy, Robert F., 25, 112, 157, 206–12, 214
King, Martin Luther, Jr., 3, 13, 25, 106, 109, 112–13, 150, 153, 156–57, 165–67, 206–10, 213, 219, 228
Knights of Columbus, 65, 72

LaFarge, John, SJ, 52–54
Le Milieu Divin, 11, 30, 50–51, 80. *See also Divine Milieu*
Le Phénomène Humain, 12, 14. *See also Human Phenomenon*; *Phenomenon of Man*
Leo XIII, Pope, 6, 37, 103–04
Les Amis de Teilhard, 30, 46, 50, 81, 83, 126, 180, 238, 253
Licent, Émile, 9, 11
Life (magazine), 32n5, 76
L'Osservatore Romano, 81, 88, 293
Luce, Henry, 32, 123

Lukas, Ellen, 117
Lukas, Mary, 7, 117–18, 121n72

March on Selma (*1965*), 150–53
marches on Washington: *1963*, 112; *1968*, 208
Maria Gratia Martin, 249
Marks, Louis, 65, 116, 122, 164
Mass on the World, 9, 197
materialism, 55, 105n24, 248
McCarthy, Eugene, 157, 219, 224
McCarthy, Viterbo, 277
McGovern, George, 157, 220, 297
McLuhan, Marshall, 173n10
McNamara, Robert S., 108, 156–57, 185, 209, 214
Merton, Thomas, 35, 62–65, 96, 99
Mississippi Summer (*1964*), 151
MOBE (National Mobilization to End the War in Vietnam), 215, 219
modernism, 6, 8, 21, 42, 103, 105–6
modernity, 2, 29, 31, 41–42, 56, 104–5, 110, 112, 120, 298
Moltmann, Jürgen, 233–34, 240, 243
monitum, 77, 81–82, 84–85, 88–97, 116, 123, 139, 184, 188, 266
Mooney, Christopher, 181, 186–87, 191, 193–95, 197, 240–41, 250–53, 255, 257–59, 276
Mortier, Jeanne, 17–18, 30, 50, 83–86, 88–89, 115, 121, 180, 196, 266
Muller, Robert, 295
Murray, Michael H., 104, 164, 194, 197, 237
mystical body of Christ, 23, 45, 119, 195. *See also* body of Christ
mysticism, 2, 5, 9, 11, 19, 56, 70, 73, 76, 118–19, 161, 177, 187, 229, 249, 251

natural theology, 189, 192, 266, 269, 271
natural-supernatural divide, 3, 5, 20–21, 71, 96, 118n55, 140, 169, 194, 232, 252, 270n63
neo-Scholastic, 109, 110, 116, 247
New Age, 170, 229
New Left, 155, 213, 218
Newsweek, 12, 39, 124
New York Times, 12, 207, 241
Nixon, Richard M., 107, 150, 157, 160, 205, 215, 220
nonviolence, 112, 150–51, 205–9, 213, 216, 219, 230, 250, 297
noosphere, 10, 14, 173, 278
Novak, Michael, 75, 104, 171, 297n13

O'Connor, Flannery, 129–32
Omega Point, 6, 14–15, 25, 48–49, 54, 66, 70, 72, 111, 141, 147, 152, 158, 164, 166, 185, 188, 195, 197, 218, 228, 237, 252, 254, 284–85, 288, 292, 295
Ong, Walter, 45–46, 52, 54, 86–87, 87, 89, 173
optimism, 11, 48, 95, 98, 118n62, 119, 131, 140n9, 142, 144, 152, 167–68, 175, 190–93, 198–99, 203–4, 233–35, 243–46, 252, 269, 286–87, 298
Ottaviani, Alfred, Cardinal, 81, 84, 93

Pace College, N.Y., 115, 121
Paschal mystery, 113, 119, 175, 193, 198, 219, 247, 254, 279, 288, 298
Paul, St., 19, 21, 70, 99, 183, 237, 256, 263, 275
Paul VI, Pope, 93, 110, 138–39, 141, 144, 226
Peking Man, 12, 17–18
phenomenology, 53, 68–70
Phenomenon of Man, The, 13–17, 20, 30–31, 48–51, 55, 62–63, 68–72, 75–78, 92, 115, 117, 119, 123, 129–30, 147–48, 164, 189–90, 192, 214, 219, 229, 232, 234, 236, 238, 245, 262, 267–69, 271, 273–74, 284, 287. *See also Human Phenomenon*; *Le Phénomène Humain*; POM Project
Philippe de la Trinité, 81, 183, 275
Pius VI, Pope, 225–26
Pius X, Pope, 6, 8, 37, 142
Pius XII, Pope, 42, 49
POM (Phenomenon of Man) Project, 163n75, 236, 237, 284
Poor People's Campaign (*1967*), 206, 208
Poulain, Dorothy, 46–47, 80, 83–86, 94–95, 101–102, 114
process theology, 198, 232, 238, 240, 248, 267, 270–73, 274n75, 280, 288n117
progress, 78, 97, 107–8, 112, 149–51, 158, 168, 203–4, 216, 239n107, 278n87, 287, 298

publication data, 75–76, 78, 116, 117n60, 179, 184, 259, 273n72

Rabut, Oliver, 51, 129
radical theology, 137, 168–70, 174, 198, 223
Ratzinger, Joseph, 141, 143. *See also* Benedict XVI
Raven, Nicholas, 92, 129
Realm of the Divine, The, 50, 75
religious trends, shifts in, 48, 222–35. *See also* Catholic Church and change; Second Vatican Council
ressourcement, 139, 247, 255, 270, 287
Riggan, George, 265–67
riots, 112, 152, 169, 203, 287, 292
Riverside Church, New York, 156–57, 241
Rubbra, Edmund, 295
Russo, François, 47, 68

San Francisco, 80, 141, 158, 161, 217, 228, 230, 239, 284, 292, 294, 296
Saturday Evening Post, 115
Saturday Review, 186, 188
Savio, Mario, 155, 217
Schoenborn, Christoph, Cardinal, 294
Scholasticism, 37, 67, 71, 103, 116, 270. *See also* neo-Scholasticism
science, 2, 4–5, 8–9, 11, 16, 24– 25, 29–30, 32, 40–42, 49–50, 53–56, 63, 65–71, 76, 78, 83– 84, 95, 97, 102, 106, 109–10, 116–20, 123–24, 127–28, 130, 132–33, 139, 141, 145, 147–48, 160, 163, 174, 178, 185, 187, 189–92, 194, 196, 204, 222–23, 232, 237, 244, 247, 249, 251–52, 258, 264–69, 271–72, 276, 279, 281, 292, 294, 296. *See also* confluence of science and religion; Teilhard
SDS (Students for a Democratic Society), 155–56
Seabury-Western Theological Seminary, 164, 236–37
Second Vatican Council, 1, 4, 24–26, 43, 61, 79, 87, 99–100, 104, 106, 109, 111, 116, 133, 138–51, 168–70, 179–80, 185, 196, 203, 224–27, 247, 249–51, 261–63, 276–79, 291
secular, 2, 48, 71, 96–97, 109, 113, 116, 132, 169–70, 173–75, 185, 194, 196, 247–53, 260, 269n62, 270n63, 276, 286, 292, 294
Secular City, 105, 168–74, 196
secularism, 36, 39, 140, 194, 197, 203, 233–34, 246, 264
Setter, Henry, 295
Sheed,Wilfred, 49–51, 56
Sheets, John, 276, 279–80
Show (magazine), 117, 188
Shriver, Robert Sargent, 108, 206, 209–10, 214, 220, 297
Soleri, Paolo, 295–96
Speaight, Robert, 5, 141, 181–82, 236
Stiernotte, Alfred, 238, 272–76
submarine churches, 229
Suhard, Emmanuel, Cardinal, 71n31
Swan, Lucille, 13

teach-ins, 156, 218, 221
Teilhard: biography, 3–17, 42, 180–82; Christocentric focus, 66, 82–83, 152, 161, 164, 167, 169, 183–84, 187, 191, 193–94, 196–99, 231, 257, 250, 252, 254–58, 274, 283–84, 288, 293, 298; cosmology, 19–23, 174, 183, 186, 258, 260–61, 274; criticism of his work, 77–79, 83–84, 90, 182–83, 204, 260, 265; influences upon, 4–6, 165–66, 183, 192–95, 236–37, 255, 247, 269, 281, 293; Jesuits and, 3–4, 7–8, 11, 80–81, 92, 123, 259; publication of writings, 7, 11, 15, 30, 259, 266; relationships with women, 7, 9, 13; science and, 2, 5, 8–9, 11, 16, 24–25, 29–30, 49–50, 53–54, 56, 63, 65–66, 68, 70–71, 76, 83, 95, 97, 110, 118, 130, 132, 139, 141, 148, 163, 174, 187, 189, 191–92, 194, 204, 222–23, 243, 251, 252n11, 258, 264–65, 268–69, 271, 279, 281, 292, 294; on the secular, 2, 48, 71, 96–97, 116, 132, 169–70, 173–75, 185, 194, 196, 247–53, 260, 269n62, 270n63, 276, 286, 292, 294; suffering and, 2, 18, 47, 73, 92, 95, 113, 130–31, 140n9, 169, 171n6, 185, 190–93, 216, 219, 243–47, 249–50, 254, 256, 277–78, 292, 298; value of everyday life, 120, 132–33, 165, 187–88, 216, 247, 252, 256, 269, 270n64, 277–78, 286, 294, 298;

Teilhard (*cont.*)
value of work, 64, 145, 196–97, 216, 247, 260; on war, 6–8, 10, 16, 95, 111n40, 158, 166, 192, 216; writings as philosophy, 74, 188–89, 192, 197–98, 267, 270, 285n102; writings as poetry, 68–69, 76, 130n95, 187, 192, 266n47, 267–68, 283n96; writings as science, 69, 72, 178, 185, 188n47, 192, 264–65, 267–68. *See also* influence of Teilhard on *various topics*
Teilhard-Chambon, Marguerite, 7, 19, 47, 193, 298
Teilhard Circle, 65
Teilhardian seeing, 11, 47, 79, 127, 130, 175, 231, 258, 280
Teilhardian synthesis, 3–5, 10, 14, 20, 48–50, 52–53, 56, 62–63, 66–70, 76, 78, 103, 110–11, 131, 141n9, 145, 163, 177, 185–87, 191–92, 194, 255–58, 264, 266, 271, 274, 279, 281, 283n96, 293–94
Teilhardian teleology, 8, 14, 66, 187–88, 212, 242–44, 250, 252–54, 256, 265–69, 292, 294
Teilhardian vision, 70, 148, 152, 279, 294
teleology, 2, 6, 14–15, 19, 29, 55, 102n14, 189, 192, 195, 197, 235, 292–94
television programs, 65–66, 75, 236–37
Theological Studies, 72, 139, 174–75, 194, 237, 279
Theology Digest, 66, 72
Theology of Hope, 223, 232–34, 240, 244, 261
Time Magazine, 17, 32, 48–49, 66, 74, 173n8, 233
Tresmontant, Claude, 44, 45, 52, 197
unity, 15, 67, 70–71, 146–47, 152, 158–89, 162, 165–66, 186, 192, 209–10, 218–19, 222, 231, 242–44, 249, 252, 262, 270, 281
University of California at Berkeley, 155–56, 217, 230

Vagnozzi, Cardinal Egidio, 77, 94, 117
validity of works on Teilhard, 81–82, 91–93, 122, 179, 191, 196–97, 203, 229, 247, 259, 263–65, 267–68, 270, 288, 291–92
Van Dusen, Hugh, 50–52, 75–76, 177
Vatican II. *See* Second Vatican Council
Vietnam War, 106, 149, 152–54, 156–57, 159, 169, 206–8, 212–18, 227, 259
Vollert, Cyril, 72, 144–49, 151
Von Hildebrand, Dietrich, 116

Walsh, John, 15, 54, 65–66, 115, 121–23, 162
war, 6–8, 16, 34, 38, 95, 111, 153–54, 156–59, 166, 190, 192–93, 203, 205–8, 211–18, 220, 227–29, 287, 292
War on Poverty, 158, 206–7
Weigel, Gustave, 46, 54, 65, 77, 104
Wolsky, Alexander, 114, 164
World of Teilhard, The, 52, 65, 77, 84, 87, 117
Writings in Time of War, 7, 21–22, 258n75, 261, 263, 277

Yellow Expedition, 12
yippies, 219–20

Zygon (journal), 14, 187, 265, 271–72

America's Teilhard: Christ and Hope in the 1960s was designed in New Baskerville with Big Caslon display type and composed by Kachergis Book Design of Pittsboro, North Carolina. It was printed on 60-pound House Natural Smooth and bound by Sheridan Books of Chelsea, Michigan.